MW00610980

THE INDIVIDUALISTS

The Individualists

RADICALS, REACTIONARIES,
AND THE STRUGGLE FOR THE
SOUL OF LIBERTARIANISM

◆

*Matt Zwolinski and
John Tomasi*

PRINCETON UNIVERSITY PRESS
PRINCETON & OXFORD

Published by Princeton University Press
41 William Street, Princeton, New Jersey 08540
99 Banbury Road, Oxford OX2 6JX

press.princeton.edu

All Rights Reserved

Library of Congress Cataloging-in-Publication Data

Names: Zwolinski, Matt, author. | Tomasi, John, author.
Title: The individualists : radicals, reactionaries, and the struggle for the soul of
    libertarianism / Matt Zwolinski and John Tomasi.
Description: Princeton, New Jersey ; Oxford : Princeton University Press, [2023] |
    Includes bibliographical references and index.
Identifiers: LCCN 2022020457 (print) | LCCN 2022020458 (ebook) |
    ISBN 9780691155548 (Hardback) | ISBN 9780691241043 (eBook)
Subjects: LCSH: Libertarianism. | BISAC: POLITICAL SCIENCE /
    Political Ideologies / Libertarianism | PHILOSOPHY / Political
Classification: LCC JC585 .Z88 2023 (print) | LCC JC585 (ebook) |
    DDC 320.51/2—dc23/eng/20221007
LC record available at https://lccn.loc.gov/2022020457
LC ebook record available at https://lccn.loc.gov/2022020458

British Library Cataloging-in-Publication Data is available

Editorial: Rob Tempio and Chloe Coy
Production Editorial: Theresa Liu
Jacket/Cover Design: Karl Spurzem
Production: Erin Suydam
Publicity: James Schneider and Carmen Jimenez

This book has been composed in Miller (Classic)

Printed on acid-free paper. ∞

Printed in the United States of America

10 9 8 7 6 5 4 3 2 1

Matt Zwolinski

With gratitude to Jen,
Xander, Jack, Zoe, Alexa,
Wilson, Oso, and Tessa,
for a home overflowing with love

John Tomasi

For Amy, Peter, and Lydia

CONTENTS

ACKNOWLEDGMENTS

THIS BOOK has been long in gestation, and we have accumulated many debts. We presented early versions of this manuscript at workshops at the Center for the Philosophy of Freedom at the University of Arizona and the Political Theory Project at Brown University, as well as a memorable gathering of "bleeding heart libertarians" in La Jolla, California.

For hosting or participating in these workshops, or for otherwise helping us with this book, we are grateful to David Schmidtz, George Smith, Ross Levatter, Kevin Vallier, Mark LeBar, Charles Johnson, Roderick Long, Dan Russell, Danny Shahar, Sameer Bajaj, Taylor Davidson, Chris Nelson, Guido Pincione, Jacob Barrett, Fabian Wendt, John Thrasher, Greg Robson, Brian Kogelmann, Steve Wall, Don Fallis, Kathy Mathiesen, Carmel Pavel, Chad Van Schoelandt, Tristan Rogers, Matt Mortellaro, Steve Haessler, Brian Doherty, Jason Brennan, Karl Widerquist, Gary Chartier, Virginia Postrel, Mathias Risse, Lynne Kiesling, David Hart, Steve Horwitz, Alexandre Padilla, Steve Davies, Wendy McElroy, David Hart, Roderick Long, David Levy, Tom Palmer, Nick Geiser, Tom Mulligan, Dan D'Amico, Jeremy Shearmur, Bas van der Vossen, Daniel Layman, and Samuel Fleischacker. Anthony Gregory provided many valuable suggestions on a late version of the manuscript. Many undergraduates at Brown University helped with these ideas. We are grateful to research assistance from Hank Hultman, Ryan Frant, and especially Henry Bartis. For stylistic suggestions throughout the entire manuscript, we thank Jason Swadley. Whatever poorly written sentences remain in the manuscript are entirely our own.

Jacob Levy and Andy Koppleman provided thoughtful and generous readers reports for Princeton University Press. At a key moment, our editor Rob Tempio told us that ours was *not* the slowest book project he'd ever worked on. We thank Rob for proposing this project, for standing by it, and for giving it time to grow into a more ambitious book than he or we had originally foreseen.

We wrote this book together, not merely as coauthors but as thought-partners. Still, for reasons that may be obvious, we wish to encourage the occasional practice of coauthors listing names in reverse alphabetical order. Thus, we choose to list our names in this order: Zwolinski and Tomasi.

THE INDIVIDUALISTS

Introduction

THIS BOOK is a history of libertarian thought. But what is libertarianism? It depends on whom you ask.

If you were to ask an academic philosopher to list some well-known libertarians, they would probably begin (and possibly end) with Robert Nozick. Nozick published *Anarchy, State, and Utopia* in 1974, and that book has represented libertarianism in undergraduate philosophy courses ever since.

If you were to ask an economist, the answer might be Milton Friedman. Winner of the Nobel Prize in Economics in 1976, Friedman wrote libertarian classics such as *Capitalism and Freedom* (1962) and *Free to Choose* (1980).

If you asked a (philosophically precocious) high school student, you might get a different answer: Ayn Rand. Rand's *The Fountainhead* (1943) and *Atlas Shrugged* (1957) have sold tens of millions of copies and continue to serve as a gateway to libertarianism for many.

A different name you might encounter, especially from political activists outside the academy, is Murray Rothbard. Author of *For a New Liberty* (1973), Rothbard was such a tireless promoter of libertarian ideas that he was known by many as "Mr. Libertarian."

Now imagine that we brought together our philosopher, economist, high school student, and general reader to ask them a related question: *What do libertarians believe?*

Our group would probably start with basics, like: "Libertarians don't like government." And: "They're obsessed with private property." And: "Libertarians love capitalism and hate socialism." If we invited group members to elaborate, and share more detailed impressions, they might add: "They seem to care more about logic than about people." And: "They think every social problem can be solved by markets."

Warming to the topic, group members might volunteer: "They support corporations against workers." And: "Libertarians are against social justice." And: "They are racially insensitive and may even be racists." Getting closer to the nub now, group members might continue: "Libertarians claim to combine the best ideas from the left and the right, but when it comes down to it, they most always side with the right." And: "Basically, libertarians are Social Darwinists."

This book tells the story behind those responses: it is an intellectual history of libertarianism. Like every intellectual history, ours is written from a particular moment in time, and is addressed to a particular set of priors in the minds of readers of our era. This was the great challenge in writing this book. For we are in a period—or, perhaps, are only just beginning to emerge from a period—in which the mental model that readers bring to our topic is to an unusual degree already fixed.

Today, a small and relatively homogeneous group of figures, all writing in the same country and against the same historical background, effectively *defines* libertarianism for most readers. To the list of late twentieth-century figures just mentioned—Nozick, Friedman, Rand, Rothbard—we might add a few others such as Ludwig von Mises, F. A. Hayek, and Rose Wilder Lane. But this canon remains compact. The prominence of this particular group of libertarians, writing in same country during the same era, threatens to set the parameters within which any intellectual history of libertarianism must be told.

This book argues that libertarianism has a longer, wider, and more diverse history than is commonly believed. As our opening list of names suggests, most contemporary readers will think of libertarianism as a quintessentially American doctrine that emerged in the twentieth century. In fact, libertarianism was born in the nineteenth century, not the twentieth, and was first developed in Britain and France, only later making its way to the United States.

From the start, libertarians were known for advocating ideas such as private property, free markets, and individualism. Of course, many earlier classical liberals such as John Locke, Adam Smith, and David Hume had endorsed similar ideas. But what sets libertarians apart is the *absolutism* and *systematicity* with which they affirm the more gentle and compromising ideas of the classical liberals. For libertarians, a market economy is not merely a useful form of social organization: it is a moral imperative based on a unified philosophy of individual freedom. Property rights are not merely *among* the basic rights and liberties of free citizens: they are moral absolutes, and may in fact be the only kind of right that exists. In the same way, an uncompromising emphasis on the individual was often seen as a defining element of libertarianism, so much so that one of the earliest libertarian movements in Britain was known simply as "Individualism," while the first libertarians in the United States were referred to as "individualist anarchists."

As a historical matter, libertarianism's radicalism was born out of a desire to preserve existing freedoms against a perceived existential threat. In nineteenth-century France and Britain, libertarianism developed largely in response to the threat of socialism. Faced with the danger of socialist revolutions in the middle of the century, and more gradualist state socialist movements toward century's end, libertarians radicalized the classical liberal principles of property and free trade into nearly absolute imperatives. Not one inch of ground could be ceded to those calling for greater state involvement in the economy, lest society find itself slipping down the road to socialism and collective serfdom.

By contrast, the birth of libertarian thinking in nineteenth-century America was relatively free of that socialist shadow. In the New World, socialist movements were mostly utopian and anarchistic, rather than revolutionary and statist. Partially as a result, the first generation of American libertarians could not merely coexist with socialist thinkers—many early American libertarians enthusiastically *identified* as socialists. For the first American libertarians, the greatest enemy to liberty was not socialism but *slavery*. Libertarian thinking in America first emerged not so much as a reaction against socialism but from a passionate commitment to abolitionism. Building on their analysis of the injustice of slavery, they focused on the property claims of individual workers and insisted that each person had a natural right to the full fruits of their labor: thus condemning not merely slavery but taxation, exploitation, and perhaps even capitalism itself. For many in this first generation of American libertarians, the fight against slavery and the fight for the rights of the laboring classes went hand in hand.

On each continent, then, libertarianism's radicalism emerged and took shape as a reaction against a different set of threats to freedom. In Europe, along with progressive positions such as opposition to colonialism, this defense meant preserving existing liberties against new challenges. In America, it meant tearing down an existing institution to establish freedom anew. But, in both cases, libertarian principles were *dispositionally* ill-suited to serve as mere defenses of the status quo. Taken to their logical conclusion, libertarian principles entail that most existing political and economic institutions are deeply unjust. Libertarianism thus counsels not gradualist reform but a sweeping revolution. The system of welfare—whether social or corporate—is to be abolished. Unjustly acquired property is to be returned to its rightful owner. Restrictions on freedoms of movement and labor must be swept away. Militarism, in which states tax citizens to prepare to fight other states, is intolerable.

In terms of its theoretical foundations, libertarianism is uncompromising in its radicalism. In practice, however, not all libertarians were comfortable embracing the wholesale upheaval of existing institutions—and privileges. From its beginning, then, libertarianism has attracted a mix of radical and reactionary elements: those who were eager to follow the dictates of libertarian justice wherever they might lead, and those who saw in libertarianism a rationale for defending the status quo against change. The tension between progressive and reactionary elements, a tension within the very soul of libertarianism, is the major theme of this book.

The difficulty in reconciling these conflicting tendencies would become vivid in the twentieth-century United States, when the rise of international and expansionist socialism led many libertarians to align themselves with conservatives against their common threat. This is the version of libertarianism that we expect will be familiar to contemporary readers. The focus on socialism as a threat to liberty, notably in the writings of European immigrants such as Ludwig von Mises, F. A. Hayek, and Ayn Rand, led to the development of an American libertarianism starkly different in form from the nineteenth-century individualist anarchism of Benjamin Tucker and Lysander Spooner. That earlier form of libertarianism, born out of opposition to slavery, was radical to its core. Twentieth-century American libertarianism, by contrast, resembled far more the mix of radical and reactionary elements that characterized nineteenth-century French and British libertarianism than it did its own direct U.S. antecedent.

By the mid-twentieth century, the struggle against socialism came to dominate the libertarian worldview. As a result, for many libertarians of the Cold War era, *economic* liberty came close to representing liberty as such. For example, if facing a choice between supporting civil liberties or economic liberties, economic liberties always trumped—or so most libertarians of that era believed. This emphasis affected which threats to liberty the Cold War era libertarians were quick to spot and which they were slow to see (or, perhaps, could not see at all). This shift in emphasis, as we shall see, significantly shaped the way libertarianism is currently perceived.

A few words about our project. This book is a history of libertarian ideas. It offers neither a history of libertarian politics nor a history of the libertarian movement.[1] It is an *intellectual* history. Further, this book offers an intellectual *history* of libertarianism and not a philosophical defense. Our task, as we see it, is to report the ideas and arguments of libertarians just as we find them. Except for a few places where we explicitly say otherwise, we make no sustained attempt to strengthen old arguments or develop new ones.

Moreover, because this is a history of *libertarian* ideas, our treatment of nonlibertarian ideologies and figures will be brief. This book discusses the ideas of classical liberals like John Locke and Adam Smith insofar as those ideas influenced later libertarian thought. But this book does not intend to provide a thorough overview of those ideas, or of classical liberalism more generally. Similarly, while there are close connections between libertarianism and neoliberalism, as well as between libertarianism and the Austrian, Virginia, and Chicago schools of economics, the primary focus of this book is not the people or ideas associated with those movements and institutions.[2] True, this book may well be seen as a complement (or corrective) to the growing body of scholarship in these areas by showing their relationship to libertarianism. But it is libertarianism, and not these other areas, that is our concern.

Although this is a history, we have chosen not to organize the book chronologically. Instead, we have structured the book around a number of topics—poverty, anarchism, race relations, and so on—and devoted a chapter to each. For each topic, we explore how libertarians of different eras (and in different places) took divergent paths from common principles. By focusing on topics instead of chronology, our book seeks to *show* the history of libertarian thought rather than merely tell it.

Our topical approach will also make vivid the pluralist and idiosyncratic character of libertarian thinking. This will be a constant theme of our book: there is no single libertarianism. As we see it, libertarianism cannot be defined by any one set of necessary and sufficient conditions. Instead, libertarianism is best understood as a cluster concept. We see libertarianism as a distinctive combination of six key commitments: property rights, negative liberty, individualism, free markets, a skepticism of authority, and a belief in the explanatory and normative significance of spontaneous order. Chapter 1 introduces each of these six concepts, shows how libertarians interpret them, and explains how, when brought together into an integrated set, they form a distinct and recognizably libertarian approach.

Understanding libertarianism as an (integrated) cluster of related concepts helps us understand why the view could take such different forms in the hands of its various proponents. This is because, first, each of the concepts within that cluster is subject to a range of plausible interpretations. With respect to private property, for example, libertarians can disagree about what sorts of things a person may legitimately own, what particular rights over things are entailed by owning them, and in what circumstances (if any) property rights must give way to competing claims or interests. Second, libertarians can disagree about how the different elements of the cluster fit together. Are property rights *foundational* to the libertarian worldview? Or are they merely one important idea among many? Different interpretations of the six key concepts, and different ways of combining those concepts into an integrated whole, lead to divergent yet equally "libertarian" conclusions.

If this analysis is correct, then a common way of thinking about libertarianism is mistaken. It is often claimed that libertarianism is a simple ideology, the dictates of which can be logically deduced from first principles. There can be power in simplicity, and some people find libertarianism attractive precisely for that reason. By contrast, our analysis suggests that libertarianism is an inherently flexible ideology, one that can be developed (or bent) in different ways, depending on the interests, preoccupations, or social context of the theorist. Behind the mask of timeless logic, there is judgment work—with all the variable strengths and flaws that attend the exercise of that human capacity.

Most important, our approach helps explain why libertarianism has always contained a mixture of radical and reactionary elements. An emphasis on private property and skepticism of government power could be, and was, used by radical libertarians to argue that slavery is a uniquely grotesque violation of individual self-ownership, and must be abolished immediately. But those same ideas could also be, and were, used by later libertarians to defend Southern segregation against "tyrannical" attempts by the federal government to dismantle it.[3]

After introducing libertarianism in chapter 1, we turn to introducing the three major periods or waves of libertarian thought. The first, "primordial" era covers the latter half of the nineteenth century, with special focus on Britain, France, and the United States. The second "Cold War" era runs from the 1930s through the 1980s and mainly centers in the United States. Finally, and more tentatively, we discuss the emerging "Third Wave" of libertarianism.

The narrative arc of our history is easy to trace: emerging in the nineteenth century as an idealistic and progressive radicalization of classical liberalism, libertarianism had by the second half of the twentieth century taken on a more conservative, perhaps even reactionary, status quo–preserving cast. The current "Third Wave" period of libertarianism is marked by a struggle to define the future direction of libertarian thought, with tensions between historical libertarianism's radical and reactionary tendencies front and center.

The main body of our book, chapters 3–8, has a dual organizational structure. In each chapter, we explore how one of our six libertarian family *commitments* informs the libertarian response to one of six chosen political *topics*. For example, chapter 3, on the questions of land and labor, addresses these topics through the lens of the libertarian commitment to property. Chapter 4, on the topic of anarchism, also deals with the libertarian skepticism of authority. Chapter 5, on business, is also about the libertarian commitment to free markets. Chapter 6, on poverty, also discusses spontaneous order. Chapter 7, on race, does so in light of the libertarian commitment to individualism. And chapter 8, on global justice, examines that topic through the libertarian commitment to negative liberty.

Before we begin, we believe we owe our readers a word about the ideological perspective from which this book is written. We both have long identified ourselves as libertarians. Indeed, it was the attraction we feel toward many of the ideas and thinkers discussed in this book that led us to take up this project. We have spent almost a decade in conversation and in the study of these ideas. In some ways, the exploration has deepened our love of them, revealing new insights, fresh perspectives, and forgotten figures. In other ways, our attraction has been challenged, as libertarian arguments and outlooks that once seemed solid now appear weaker: historical study has a way of doing that, and to political ideologies of every hue.

Whether inspiring or disappointing, the history of libertarian ideas has never failed to surprise us. The intellectual tradition we thought we knew is deeper, richer, and more diverse than either of us expected. Exploring that diversity has led us to question many beliefs we once took for granted, and to better understand and appreciate libertarianism for what it is—the parts that are ugly, and the parts that are beautiful too. We hope this book can do the same for you.

CHAPTER ONE

What Is Libertarianism?

Origins of "Libertarianism"

"Libertarianism" is best understood as a family of political theories rather than a single theory. Like all families, the libertarian family has different branches, each with unique characteristics. Here we find a family line that carries the chin of a studious great-uncle. There, a branch with the dark eyes of a difficult aunt. Elsewhere, we find new lines begun by contemporary scholars developing versions of libertarianism all their own.

Imagine that we were asked to design facial recognition software to identify all members of the libertarian family. Is there a single idea, or set of commitments, that might be used to identify a view or thinker as *libertarian*?

The word "libertarian" is built on the word "liberty," so that might seem a promising place to begin. Indeed, this is where the name *did* begin. Its earliest uses in the late eighteenth century referred simply to one who believed in human liberty—not originally to *political* or *economic* liberty but rather to someone who believed in *liberty of the will*.[1] "Libertarian" denoted those who opposed the doctrine of "necessarianism" (what we would now call "determinism") and thus believed that human beings possess the power of free will.

Before long, the label migrated from metaphysics to social philosophy. The *Oxford English Dictionary* locates the first use of the word in the sense of "an advocate or defender of liberty (especially in the political or social spheres)" in England in 1796.[2] Similar references can be found scattered about the first half of the nineteenth century. Like many ideological labels, "libertarian" was used mainly as a pejorative for the views of *others*, rather than as a self-description, especially in the context of English debates over the French Revolution.[3]

So the term "libertarian" does have its origin in the concept of "liberty." But defining the libertarian as one who believes in liberty is helpful only if we have a shared understanding of liberty to fall back on. Unfortunately, we do not. As Montesquieu wrote, "There is no word that admits of more various significations, and has made more varied impressions on the human mind, than that of liberty."[4] The word "liberty" means radically different things to different people. And so if "libertarian" means merely "an advocate of liberty," we should expect great confusion when the term is embraced by those with few substantive political, moral, or philosophical commonalities. And confusion is precisely what we find.

Contemporary American libertarians who know the term only in reference to champions of capitalism such as Ayn Rand, Milton Friedman, and Murray Rothbard might be surprised to learn that the first individual to self-identify as a "libertarian" was a French *anarcho-communist*.[5] Joseph Déjacque, a nineteenth-century social agitator, argued that private property and the state were simply two different ways in which social relationships could become infused with hierarchy and oppression.[6] A consistent defender of liberty, Déjacque believed, must therefore seek the complete abolition of both. Déjacque popularized these ideas, and his new label for them, through his influential anarcho-communist newsletter, *Le Libertaire*, which he published out of New York from 1858 to 1861.[7] The label gradually caught on among anarchists in Europe and the United States and spread in the latter half of the nineteenth century from communist anarchists such as Déjacque (who opposed private property) to individualist anarchists such as Benjamin Tucker (who favored it). Both groups, however, saw opposition to the state as a necessary concomitant of individual freedom.[8]

The word "libertarian" also continued to be used in a broader sense, as a kind of antonym to "authoritarian" rather than as a label for any specific ideology, whether anarcho-communism or free-market capitalism. By the late nineteenth and early twentieth centuries this broader, anti-authoritarian sense became dominant. While the anti-statism of Déjacque and Tucker would remain an important element of libertarianism, the term also came to denote those who opposed the *excesses* of state authority without opposing the state *as such*.[9] By the early twentieth century, it was even used to refer to a kind of cultural support for liberty that was not directly concerned with the state at all—a precursor, perhaps, to the contemporary idea of "civil libertarianism."[10]

One early figure behind the contemporary meaning of the word was Charles T. Sprading, a prominent landowner and libertarian activist who lost much of his fortune in the San Francisco earthquake of 1906. In *Liberty and the Great Libertarians* (1913), Sprading used the word "libertarian" to describe a broad spectrum of anti-statist ideas and personalities.[11] He noted that the libertarians featured in his book were "chosen from all different political parties and economic schools" including "Republicans, Democrats, Socialists, Single-Taxers, Anarchists, and Women's Rights advocates."[12] So big was this libertarian tent that it could shelter both the "Individualist and the Communist." The crucial requirement, according to Sprading, is that advocates of these different ideologies must not attempt to impose their views on others by force.

> Plans voluntarily accepted by individuals or groups of individuals and not forced upon others are in no way a violation of liberty. They would be if others were forced to do so by the seizure of "all means of production and distribution," as the State Socialists purpose to do, thereby excluding non-conformers from their use. It is not the difference in taste between individuals that Libertarians object to, but the forcing of one's tastes upon another.[13]

With Sprading, we see the first self-conscious attempt to forge what we will describe in this book as the "Liberty Movement": a loose group of mostly U.S.-based intellectuals, businesspeople, and activists united in their support of free markets and limited government, despite deep disagreement on both the detailed nature of their ideal society and its philosophic and economic foundations. Throughout the first half of the twentieth century, and in some contexts still today, the term "libertarian" was often given a *broad meaning* that referred to all those affiliated with the Liberty Movement, including egoist defenders of the minimal state such as Ayn Rand, consequentialist advocates of "free-market anarchism" such as David Friedman, and neoliberal advocates of an international market economy such as David's father, Milton Friedman.

Although a few isolated intellectuals such as H. L. Mencken and Albert Jay Nock would adopt the term in the 1930s, it was not until the 1940s that the label would achieve widespread popularity. This was due largely to the work of Leonard Read, a California businessman and general manager of the Los Angeles branch of the U.S. Chamber of Commerce.[14] Read founded one of the first and longest-lasting institutions of the U.S. Liberty Movement: the Foundation for Economic Education (FEE). Since its inception in 1946, FEE has promoted a philosophy of free markets and limited government in a variety of ways, perhaps most significantly through its publication *The Freeman*.[15] FEE worked closely with most of the major figures in the postwar libertarian movement in the United States, including Ayn Rand, Rose Wilder Lane, Friedrich Hayek, Ludwig von Mises, and Henry Hazlitt.

Read is generally credited (and has credited himself) with popularizing "libertarian" as shorthand to refer to "the free market, private property, limited government philosophy and the moral and ethical tenets which underlie these institutions."[16] *The Freeman* published one of the earliest calls to embrace the name "libertarian" for the burgeoning free-market movement. In 1950, lamenting that the word "liberal" had been "corrupted" by leftists, Dean Russell called on his readers to "reserve for our own good use the good and honorable word 'libertarian,'" which he defined as the belief that "government should protect all persons equally against external and internal aggression, but should otherwise generally leave people alone to work out their own problems and aspirations."[17]

But while Sprading and Read had sought to broaden libertarianism into an ideological "big tent," its use in the latter half of the century cut in the opposite—and more exclusive—direction. Within the academy in the 1970s, Robert Nozick developed a reputation as libertarianism's leading philosopher, and his particular neo-Lockean, natural rights–based theory came to be identified, for many academics, with libertarianism as such. Outside the academy

Ayn Rand's books sold millions of copies,[18] and Murray Rothbard's energetic writing had raised him to prominence as "Mr. Libertarian" and one of the foremost influences on enduring libertarian institutions such as the Libertarian Party, the Cato Institute, and the Ludwig von Mises Institute. Like Nozick, Rand and Rothbard adopted a radical and moralistic approach that left little room for compromise with rival moral or pragmatic concerns. Rothbard in particular was quick to write people out of the libertarian movement who deviated from what he regarded as the purist forms of the doctrine. As a result, in many circles "libertarianism" took on what we will call its *strict meaning*, one that would coexist uneasily with the broad meaning attached to all those affiliated with the Liberty Movement. These divergent uses have led to endless and intractable debates over who does, and does not, count as a *real* libertarian.

Radical Classical Liberals

Libertarianism as a political ideology developed out of the works of writers such as John Locke, Adam Smith, and David Hume, all of whom today are described as "classical liberals." Like libertarians, those earlier liberals generally saw protection of individual liberty as the primary purpose of government. Also like libertarians, classical liberals held that respect for individual liberty imposed severe restrictions on the size and scope of government and afforded individuals wide latitude to conduct their personal and economic affairs as they wished.

For classical liberals, however, individual liberty was merely a strong *presumption*, not a moral absolute. Exceptions to the rule of laissez-faire could be justified to promote the public good.[19] Thus Adam Smith supported the prohibition of banknotes under five pounds in order to reduce the likelihood of fraud, along with a restriction on the exportation of grain to foreign markets under certain circumstances.[20] In the twentieth century, Friedrich Hayek condemned the "wooden insistence" of some liberals on the principle of laissez-faire and supported a number of deviations from it, including the state provision of "a certain minimum income for everyone . . . a sort of floor below which nobody need fall even when he is unable to provide for himself."[21] Similarly, some contemporary classical liberals such as Richard Epstein favor state provision of public goods and the restrained use of eminent domain in order to overcome certain collective action problems.[22] Still, while almost all classical liberals recognized exceptions to the presumption of liberty, most agreed with John Stuart Mill that "letting alone . . . should be the general practice; every departure from it, unless required by some great good, is a certain evil."[23]

As we will see in the next chapter, libertarianism in its strict form was born at the midpoint of the nineteenth century as a *radicalized version* of classical liberalism. Where classical liberals treated liberty as a strong but defeasible presumption, libertarians extolled it as a moral absolute. The principle of liberty, for libertarians, is universal in the scope of its application, covering persons of all ages, races, nationalities, and genders. Its moral force is definitive, overriding any and all other competing moral values, including the "public good" to which classical liberals so often appealed to justify state action.

As a general rule, strict libertarians are *rationalistic* and *monistic* in their approach to moral and political questions, while classical liberals were generally more *empiricist* and *pluralistic*. Many strict libertarians saw their entire political philosophy flowing logically from a single axiomatic principle: Spencer's law of equal freedom or Rothbard's "Nonaggression Principle," for example.[24] This often gives strict libertarian theories a more *systematic* character than their classical liberal antecedents. Practical policy questions, for them, could be resolved almost syllogistically, with the axiomatic principle serving as the major premise of the argument and a schematic description of the policy serving as the minor. If all forms of physical aggression are morally forbidden, and taxation is a form of physical aggression, then taxation is morally forbidden, QED.

For these libertarians, policy questions should be settled on the hard rock of *principle*, not the shifting sand of circumstance. Private property must be held as a moral imperative regardless of whether it happens to produce the desired results in particular circumstances. Further, because libertarians tend to have a relatively *monistic* theory of justice—because their system tends to rest upon a *single* fundamental principle—there is rarely any question of "balancing" moral principles against another. As a result, libertarian conclusions tend to arrive in *absolutist* form. Political philosophy is a matter of working out the logical implications of first principles, and with no competing principles or empirical contingencies to hold those implications in check, the authority of their pronouncements is absolute.

Strict libertarians are thus radicals by nature—both *conceptually* and *politically*. They are conceptual radicals in that they seek to resolve questions of contemporary politics by appeal to first principles. And since real-world politics almost never measure up to such principles, strict libertarians are soon led to political radicalism: the belief that existing institutions of society are deeply unjust and must largely be swept away. As we will see throughout this book, however, libertarian radicalism has always coexisted with a more conservative, even reactionary strand.

Libertarians tend to see their political conclusions flowing from one of two more foundational moral approaches.[25] Many of the best-known strict libertarians embraced a kind of neo-Lockean natural rights position, according to which each individual's ownership of his or her self is a moral absolute that undergirds a similarly absolute right to ownership in properly acquired external resources.[26] The deontic structure of this form of libertarianism— embraced by Robert Nozick and Murray Rothbard, among others—lends itself naturally to an uncompromising position. If libertarian rights are to be respected as a matter of absolute moral duty, then we need not concern ourselves with the consequences that a libertarian regime is likely to produce. If respect for individual rights means that existing social institutions must be radically revised, or if it means that some people will be much worse off than they are in the present system, then so be it. Such is the price of justice.

Consequentialist moral theories, in contrast, seem at first glance ill-suited to support a truly strict libertarian view. For even if private property and free markets do generally produce good consequences, it is hard to believe that they must always do so, in every imaginable circumstance. Consequentialists thus seem compelled to abandon their commitment to liberty whenever doing so might lead to some improved outcome, however slight the improvement.

Some libertarians argue that it was precisely the rise of utilitarianism in the late nineteenth century—and the corresponding decline in popularity of natural rights theories—that led classical liberalism to be replaced by the new, progressive liberalism of Hobhouse, Green, and Dewey.[27]

Nevertheless, there is no necessary incompatibility between consequentialism and strict libertarianism. The tension between the two results not from consequentialism as a moral philosophy per se but from the tendency of consequentialists to evaluate each policy empirically and on a case-by-case basis, endorsing libertarian policies when they "work" and rejecting them when not. A more indirect and *rationalistic* form of consequentialism, in contrast, evaluates the consequences not of specific policies but of general principles and retains its commitment to those principles even if they (seem to) fail in particular instances. So, for example, Herbert Spencer was as uncompromising a libertarian as any natural rights theorist, despite grounding his views on a kind of indirect utilitarianism.[28] A similar kind of rationalistic consequentialism can be found in the a priori economics of Ludwig von Mises and in Friedrich Hayek's epistemic and pragmatic case for "principles" over "expediency."[29]

In short, it is the rationalistic and (relatively) absolutist commitment to principle that gives strict libertarianism its radical edge and distinguishes it from more empiricist and pluralist forms of classical liberalism. Libertarian principles may derive from a belief in natural law, but they may also come from a belief in the general tendency of certain classes of actions and policies to produce consequences of a certain sort. Indeed, as we will see in chapter 3 and elsewhere throughout this book, there is often less of a gap than one might suppose between these two apparently quite distinct approaches.

A Note on Terminology

Libertarianism and classical liberalism are closely related, both historically and philosophically. But both of these terms are used in conflicting and potentially confusing ways.

As we have already seen, the term "libertarianism" is used in both a *strict* and a *broad* sense. In its strict sense, libertarianism refers to a radical political view which holds that individual liberty, understood as the absence of interference with a person's body and rightfully acquired property, is a moral absolute and that the only governmental activities consistent with that liberty are (if any) those necessary to protect individuals from aggression by others. Strict libertarianism emerged as a radicalized form of classical liberalism in the middle of the nineteenth century in the work of theorists such as Herbert Spencer, Frédéric Bastiat, and Lysander Spooner.

But the term "libertarian" is also used—sometimes by libertarians themselves and almost always in public discussions of libertarianism—in a broad sense to refer to anyone within what we have called the Liberty Movement: that loose group of intellectuals and activists united in their support of the broad goals of free markets and limited government. Friedrich Hayek, for example, is *not* a strict libertarian due to his philosophical methodology (broadly Humean and empiricist) and his policy positions (moderate and not radically anti-statist). But he *is* a libertarian in the broad sense. Murray Rothbard, by contrast, is a libertarian in both senses of the term.

"Classical liberalism" likewise varies in common use, referring to both a *historical* and a *contemporary* ideology. In the former sense, it denotes a view developed in the sixteenth through nineteenth centuries by figures such as John Locke, David Hume, and John Stuart Mill. That view, as we have seen, adheres to a strong but defeasible presumption of liberty and holds this presumption to impose strict (but not *radical*) limits on the proper scope of government. But "classical liberalism" is also used to refer to a contemporary view.[30] In this sense, the phrase is often self-consciously employed by individuals who identify with the Liberty Movement broadly construed but who wish to distinguish themselves from their strict libertarian allies in that movement. So, for example, Richard Epstein, Friedrich Hayek, and David Schmidtz are all classical liberals in this contemporary sense. They are therefore libertarians in the broad sense of the term, but not in the strict sense.

To confuse matters further, sometimes the individuals we are describing here as contemporary classical liberals are alternatively described as "neoliberals." This term, too, is used in a variety of conflicting and not always clearly defined ways. But as scholars such as Quinn Slobodian, Angus Burgin, and Kevin Vallier have argued, it does identify a recognizable political and economic worldview, with distinct sociological and philosophical characteristics.[31] Historically, the term "neoliberalism" arose in connection with the early days of the Mont Pelerin Society, especially from its founding in 1947 until the end of Milton Friedman's presidency of the organization in 1972. Founding figures of the society like Friedrich Hayek, Wilhelm Röpke, and Frank Knight sought to establish a solid intellectual foundation for a liberal and market-based society against the rising threats of socialism and fascism, while at the same time distancing themselves from what many both inside and outside the movement regarded as the discredited "laissez-faire" position of the nineteenth century. Unlike strict libertarians, neoliberals saw a robust role for the state to play alongside the market economy. Indeed, as Slobodian argues, neoliberals went even further than many classical liberals in holding that a central function of the state is to "encase" the market order, playing an active role in international affairs to open up markets and insulate them from democratic pressure.[32] Neoliberals thus were an integral part in the development of international institutions like the General Agreement on Tariffs and Trade and the International Monetary Fund, institutions for which more radical strict libertarians would have nothing but disdain.

These manifold distinctions can be confusing. But they also reflect something vital about modern politics. Friedman and Hayek, while not libertarians in the *strict* sense, really are best classified as libertarians in relation to the dominant political landscape. Compared to the sorts of policies that are in place in almost every jurisdiction in the world today, and compared to the views of most intellectuals about what those policies should be, the differences between a neoliberal like Friedman, a contemporary classical liberal like Loren Lomasky, and a strict libertarian like Ayn Rand are too minor to merit popular attention. But when we switch contexts—when we focus not on the general political landscape but

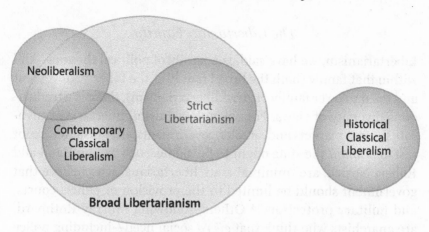

FIGURE 1. Venn diagram of the relationship between libertarianism,
neoliberalism, and classical liberalism.

on the Liberty Movement in isolation—the differences between
Friedman, Lomasky, and Rand jump out. Some contexts make it
appropriate to distinguish broad libertarianism from strict libertarianism, while others are better suited to broader labeling.

Because this book is an intellectual history of libertarianism,
and because both the strict and the broad uses of libertarianism
are common and often appropriate, we will discuss the ideas and
influence of contemporary classical liberals and some neoliberals as
well as those of strict libertarians.[33] We will not, however, devote
any significant attention to historical classical liberalism, though
its ideas share much with its contemporary form. We exclude historical classical liberalism since it does not qualify as "libertarian"
on *either* of the two senses of the term we have adopted. Historical classical liberals are not libertarians in the strict, philosophical
sense, and they were not part of the wider Liberty Movement that
has come to be identified today with broad libertarianism, for the
simple reason that such a movement did not yet exist. Based on
the self-identification of their respective members and in terms of
objective philosophical and sociological differences, there are solid
grounds for including contemporary classical liberals within the
purview of this book while excluding historical classical liberals. So
that is our approach.

The Libertarian Family

Libertarianism, we have said, is a family of political theories. And within that family (both the broad family of the Liberty Movement and the narrower family of strict libertarianism), there is a tremendous diversity of views. For example, while all libertarians advocate for free markets and smaller governments, they disagree about just *how small* the state ought to be. Some, such as Ayn Rand and Robert Nozick, are "minimal-state libertarians" who believe that government should be limited to the provision of police, courts, and military protection.[34] Others, following Murray Rothbard, are anarchists who think that *every* social need—including police protection, judicial determination, and even lawmaking itself—can be provided by competitive firms in an open market.[35] When we widen our lens to include libertarians in the broad sense such as Friedrich Hayek and Loren Lomasky, the diversity increases still more. Contemporary classical liberals typically hold that governments may, in some circumstances, extend beyond the strict limits of the minimal state to provide genuinely public goods including even "a comprehensive system of social insurance."[36]

Libertarians disagree with each other not just about "policy outputs" but also about "moral inputs."[37] Some, such as Milton Friedman, David Friedman, Ludwig von Mises, and Richard Epstein, ground their beliefs in broadly consequentialist appeals to human happiness and economic efficiency.[38] Others, such as Jan Narveson and James Buchanan, appeal to a contractarian logic in which libertarian political arrangements arise from self-interested agreement for mutual advantage.[39] Many libertarians, such as Lysander Spooner, Murray Rothbard, Robert Nozick, and Randy Barnett, are natural rights theorists of some sort.[40] Others, such as Douglas Rasmussen and Douglas Den Uyl, seek justification in Aristotelian principles of perfection.[41] Still others such as Ayn Rand and Tibor Machan—like Benjamin Tucker a century before them—ground their libertarian beliefs in a form of egoism.[42] And we could continue at length.

Given this variety, it is difficult, if not impossible, to define "libertarianism" in terms of a neat set of necessary and sufficient conditions. A better approach, we think, is to look for *patterns* in the beliefs held by all libertarians and to define libertarianism in terms of the more flexible notion of "family resemblance." In the remainder of this chapter, we identify and discuss six ideas that form the core of the libertarian worldview. We think of these ideas as *markers of membership* shared by everyone in the libertarian family, however else they may diverge. These six markers of libertarianism are private property, skepticism of authority, free markets, spontaneous order, individualism, and negative liberty. Unsurprisingly, libertarians interpret and express even these shared ideas in different ways. For strict libertarians, these six ideas tend to be held in a relatively absolutist and highly systematic form. For classical liberals, these principles are more contingent and defeasible. We begin with a sketch of each marker and then step back to see the libertarian profile that emerges when the six markers are considered as a set.

Private Property

A commitment to private property stands as perhaps the central defining feature of libertarianism. In terms of our facial recognition software, it is the nose on the libertarian face. Of course, nearly all political philosophers, including Marxists, allow *some* scope for private property, at least for personal items like clothes and books.[43] But libertarians distinguish themselves by the *scope* and the *weight* they assign to property rights.

Libertarians believe that we should be able to acquire rights of private property in *a distinctively wide array of objects*, including not only personal goods but productive capital as well. Indeed, many libertarians expand the scope still further, insisting that we should regard our own body parts as a kind of private (and alienable) property, or arguing that public property such roads, parks, and oceans should be converted to private property as well.[44]

Strict libertarians also differ—even from classical liberals—in the *moral weight* they assign to property rights. Indeed, the paradigmatic strict libertarian position is that property rights are nearly inviolable or absolute. For libertarians such as Murray Rothbard and Auberon Herbert, this means that each individual's property in their own person, labor, or possessions cannot be overridden for the sake of *any* other individual or social good, no matter how pressing.[45] By contrast, classical liberals (libertarians in the broad sense) hold that property rights may give way in certain situations of pressing social need or market failure, though even these theorists set a higher bar for overriding property rights than most other thinkers.[46] Classical liberals see property rights in much the same way that mainstream legal theorists view rights to free speech: while in certain situations they can give way, the presumption of the right can be overcome only in exceptional circumstances.

Strict libertarians often (though not always) describe property rights as foundational. Indeed, some hold that property rights are the *only* rights we have and that all other rights—rights to bodily integrity, free speech, and so on—are ultimately derived from a basic property right in one's person.[47] The basic moral right is a right of *self-ownership*. Since we each own our body, we own our labor too, and this gives us ownership of the fruits of our labor. Whatever property we legitimately acquire must ultimately be grounded in our own labor or in the labor of others and transferred to us by voluntary exchange or gift.[48]

Some libertarians argue from different but equally deontological grounds such as an appeal to negative liberty or to autonomy.[49] Others adopt consequentialist justifications, showing how private property replaces the zero- (or negative-) sum transactions of the commons with the positive-sum transactions of a market economy,[50] or explaining how rights of private property are instrumentally valuable in securing *other* important civil and political rights.[51] In truth, most libertarians help themselves to a rich buffet of different arguments for private property, believing that respect for property rights is both a moral duty *and* a wise social policy.[52] On this issue, libertarians have typically held, justice and utility go hand in hand.

The libertarian account of property faces distinct challenges, some of which we will explore in chapter 3. Many people balk at the absolutism of the libertarian view, especially as this seems to block the use of taxation to fund state activities they regard as desirable or morally mandatory. But the libertarian account also faces other problems, many originally raised over a century ago and still haunting it today. The nineteenth-century libertarian commitment to the ownership of one's labor, for example, was shared by many who identified themselves as socialists, and who saw the capitalist system of wage labor as running afoul of that commitment.[53] What, if anything, can justify wage-labor arrangements on the libertarian view? And what justifies the ownership of unimproved natural resources such as land, which are not the product of anyone's labor?[54]

Finally, how does libertarians' theoretical account apply to the actual distribution of property in society? It is one thing to specify a manner in which property *might* be justly acquired. It is quite another to show that the process of property acquisition in society actually conforms to those requirements. As we will see, the tension between defending the *actual* distribution of property and defending a *philosophically pure* distribution of property has given rise to conflict between the conservative and radical elements in libertarian thought.

Skepticism of Authority

Libertarians are skeptical of political authority for both moral and practical reasons. Practically, libertarians question whether officials and bureaucrats are either as *wise* or as *benevolent* as they claim—or are assumed—to be. Drawing on the work of Friedrich Hayek and others, libertarians doubt that political authorities have access to the "knowledge of the particular circumstances of time and place" necessary to effectively plan or regulate a complex and dynamic economy.[55] Libertarians also draw on the public choice tradition of James Buchanan and Gordon Tullock in noting that politicians and bureaucrats suffer from the same vanity, the same biases, and the same self-interestedness as the rest of us.[56] Politicians are ordinary human beings, and there is little reason to believe that they are better positioned to run our lives, or our workplaces, than we are ourselves.

But libertarians also challenge political authority in a more fundamental sense: they doubt that governments *have* authority in terms of possessing a moral claim to command and be obeyed. At minimum, governments lack the authority to do many of the particular things that they currently do. Government, libertarians believe, has no business—and no *right*—to involve itself in running a post office or subsidizing farmers or printing currency. It certainly has no rightful (monopoly) power to *prevent others* from doing the same. Such actions may be perfectly constitutional. But even if governments have the *legal* authority to pursue these policies, libertarians deny that they have the *moral* authority to do so. When law exceeds the boundaries established by morality, libertarians say, law becomes naked force, and nothing more.[57]

This skeptical attitude reflects a more fundamental belief about the nature of moral rights and duties common to libertarians. This belief, which we follow Jason Brennan in calling the "moral parity thesis," holds that governments and their agents have no rights that are not identical to or derivable from the rights of ordinary individuals.[58] In other words, all people—whether private actors or government agents—have the same basic (nonderivative) rights and duties, such that whatever is wrong for private citizens to do is (generally) wrong for an agent of the government to do as well.[59] The idea behind the moral parity thesis dates back at least to John Locke, who wrote that "the injury and the crime is equal, whether committed by the wearer of a crown, or some petty villain. The title of the offender, and the number of his followers, makes no difference in the offense, unless it be to aggravate it."[60] Since then it has been a recurring theme in the libertarian intellectual tradition, finding expression in the writings of Frédéric Bastiat, Lysander Spooner, Auberon Herbert, Murray Rothbard, Michael Huemer, and many others.[61]

Taken to its extreme, the moral parity thesis has radical implications for the nature of political authority. For if governments and their agents have only the same rights as ordinary citizens, then how can they tax us, or tell us what drugs or medicines we can consume, or regulate our economic behavior in ways that our neighbors cannot? The only way that such a right to rule over us *could* have come about is through consent—through one group of people agreeing to follow the commands of another. But most people never consented to a governing authority. The idea of a "social contract," to many libertarians, is a myth, a fiction that hides the true origin and nature of government in conquest and exploitation.[62] On this view, then, it seems to follow logically that *all* governments, even the most benign, are illegitimate. The pole of libertarian skepticism about political authority is anarchism.[63]

The debate between anarchist libertarians and "minimal-state" libertarians who believe that the government has the authority to protect individual rights through the monopoly provision of police, courts, and military—but nothing more—has long occupied these thinkers.[64] As we will see in chapter 4, this debate involves fundamental philosophical questions about consent, power, and the efficacy of state versus nonstate solutions to various social problems. In these debates, minimal-state libertarians such as Rand and Nozick find themselves precariously fighting a war on two fronts, arguing against the anarchists that states have the authority to engage in *some* coercive and monopolistic activities but also against classical liberals and everyone else who believes that states may permissibly do a little (or a lot) more. Whether a justification can be found for such a bright-line view of limited state authority remains one of the central questions of libertarian political theory.

Free Markets

Libertarians are famous for their enthusiasm about free markets. This too is a central philosophical commitment, deeply connected with the archetypical libertarian commitment to private property. Indeed, according to one libertarian argument, the liberty to trade freely with others is simply part of what is *entailed* by individuals' ownership of their bodies, their labor, and their justly acquired external goods.[65] If the authorities can forcibly prevent you from, say, renting out a room in your house, then those authorities are in some sense *part owners* of your house. If they can stop you from selling your labor to someone for a wage on which you both agree, then those authorities are part owners of *you*. Full self-ownership requires full freedom to trade.

For most libertarians, however, free markets are not only required as a matter of justice (understood as respect for property). Free markets are also a fountainhead of human well-being: a form of social organization that facilitates voluntary, decentralized, and mutually beneficial exchanges. These qualities are tightly connected: it is *because* market transactions will not take place unless both parties consent that both parties will tend to walk away from such transactions better off than they were before. On a small scale, such transactions allow individuals to improve their lives without making anyone else worse off. On a larger scale, the mutually beneficial nature of exchange allows market economies to create wealth on a massive scale. The basic physical building blocks of the universe might be finite but wealth is not. Wealth is a function of how those building blocks are arranged to satisfy our wants, not merely how many of those blocks there are. The potential of markets to produce economic growth is limited only by the boundaries of human ingenuity, which may well be limitless.[66]

Libertarians are radically committed to free trade. They are radicals in terms of the scope of *objects* that individuals should be permitted to trade on the market—not just automobiles and bread but kidneys, sexual services, methamphetamines, and perhaps even police services and courts. They are radicals in terms of the scope of *people* with whom individuals should be entitled to trade—not just those who live in the same political jurisdiction but all persons everywhere, no matter their nationality or creed. Finally, libertarians are radicals about the *freedom* that ought to govern trade. Ending the absolute prohibition on certain sorts of exchanges is not enough. Regulations on the quality of goods that can be sold, the labor conditions under which they are produced, the price that may be charged, and so on also limit freedom in ways that many libertarians find objectionable.

Despite its apparent simplicity, however, the libertarian position regarding free markets is complicated. It is not clear that libertarian principles require opposition to *all* regulations on market exchange. Prohibitions on fraud, for example, have been thought by many (but not all) libertarians to be consistent with—if not required by—the foundational libertarian commitment to voluntary exchange.[67] Restrictions on pollution are arguably needed to protect the property rights of third parties.[68] And so on.

Moreover, as with property rights, we might wonder what an *ideal* commitment to free markets means in a world falling well short of that ideal. If Walmart has already received millions of dollars in subsidies from the state (say, in terms of infrastructure such as the public highways on which Walmart's trucks ship their goods), does a commitment to free markets require libertarians to oppose taxes and regulations aimed at Bentonville? To what extent does defending the ideal of a free market mean defending the mix of free and regulated markets with which we actually find ourselves? Libertarians sometimes say that they are for *free* markets, not actually existing markets. Still, as in the case of property rights, radical and conservative elements within libertarianism sometimes diverge in the ways they attempt to bridge this difficult gap between theory and practice.

Spontaneous Order

Libertarians sometimes speak of the "miracle" of markets and market prices.[69] To the uninitiated, this can feel like jarring hyperbole. But libertarians often ask us to reflect more deeply on social structures that we too often take for granted. Consider the tremendous social coordination that goes into feeding a great metropolis like Paris: which foods will be produced, which ingredients used, how these will be transported, how restaurants will serve the dishes, and so on. When too little is brought to market, the people go hungry; when too much is produced, the produce rots. If any single person—or even a whole agency—were tasked with directing such a massive endeavor, the complexities would quickly overwhelm them. Yet, every day, Paris is fed. And *no one is in charge.*[70]

Libertarians appreciate how markets form *spontaneous order.* Spontaneous orders are forms of social organization which, in the words of the Scottish moral philosopher Adam Ferguson (1767), arise as "the result of human action, but not the execution of any human design."[71] Like the variety of food available to Parisians, spontaneous orders result from the intentional actions of human agents, whether acting in concert or alone. But no agent *designed* or even *foresaw* the overall order that would result from these actions. Spontaneous orders are *consensual* rather than coerced, *polycentric* rather than directed, and *emergent* rather than consciously designed.[72] Such forms of order are grown, not made. They arrive through evolutionary processes, not intentional design.

The market process of wealth creation, guided by the "invisible hand" channeling self-interest to the common good, is one form of spontaneous order.[73] But the idea of spontaneous order is much broader than the market. Language is a spontaneous order. So too is the common law.[74] So too are local norms that communities develop to help them cope with problems ill-suited to market solutions.[75] Markets sometimes fail, but libertarians insist that we cannot infer from the existence of market failure that state action is warranted. Spontaneous orders offer us ways of coping with externalities, and ways of addressing free-rider problems, without necessarily invoking centralized, coercive state action. The market is one component of a free society; it is not the whole of it.[76]

The idea of spontaneous order thus provides a *positive* account of how a free society can function, of how we can have "order without law." But it also provides a *negative* warning to those who seek to control society from the commanding heights of power. As Ludwig von Mises and Friedrich Hayek pointed out, socialist central planning failed because the planners lacked the knowledge to control an intricate and constantly changing economy. Human society is a complex ecosystem, and like all natural ecosystems, it is difficult to manage, much less control. When dealing with complex systems, the attempt to impose a consciously designed order from above often backfires. The unavoidable narrowness of our perspective and knowledge, combined with the reactions of those being controlled, often causes our interventions to yield consequences never intended or desired.[77]

Still, tensions emerge between libertarians' commitment to spontaneous order and their political radicalism. Respect for spontaneous order seems to counsel a certain deference to the grown institutions of social order—at the very least a healthy skepticism toward those who claim to know enough to radically redesign those institutions for the better. To some this suggests a conservatism at odds with at least the more radical forms of libertarian theorizing.[78] We should not be surprised, then, to find a certain degree of animosity between the champions of spontaneous order such as Friedrich Hayek and the nearly utopian radicals such as Murray Rothbard. As we will see later in this book, the libertarian respect for spontaneous orders becomes more complicated—and its moral valence more mixed—when we consider emergent cultural norms, especially norms that reinforce hierarchies of class, gender, and race.

Individualism

A commitment to individualism is at the core of libertarianism. Indeed, before the term "libertarian" caught on, many of the most intellectually active friends of liberty in Britain were simply known as "individualists."[79]

The individualism to which libertarians are committed can take different forms. Many libertarians are individualists in a normative sense, where this is understood to entail a commitment to the principle that each individual is an end in themselves. Libertarians take it to be morally significant that each of us is a separate person with our own life to live.[80] From this they infer that we are each a unique and incommensurable site of value in the world and that whatever value *groups* of individuals may have—whether nations, genders, or races—is wholly dependent on the value of the individuals who constitute it. Indeed, sometimes libertarians go further, arguing that every individual is the *only* source of value for themselves. Ayn Rand's ethical egoism may have taken an unusually extreme form, but she was not the first libertarian committed to this view.

Libertarians' normative individualism has political implications, in particular for their commitment to individual *rights*. Because they believe that all value resides in distinct, individual persons, libertarians deny the permissibility of sacrificing one individual for the "greater good." They typically resist policies that would impose costs on individuals, however few, in the attempt to generate greater benefits for some group, however large.[81] For similar reasons, normative individualism sets libertarians against victimless crimes. If the state wants to outlaw some activity—say, the dissemination of information about birth control, drug-taking, or unorthodox sexual behaviors—that activity must, at a minimum, be shown to be bad *for* someone and not merely what some philosophers have called a "free-floating evil."[82]

Partly as the result of their normative and political individualism, libertarians are also *methodological* individualists. Libertarians counsel that, in seeking to understand social phenomena, we must remember that it is only *individuals* who think, choose, and act. Adopting this perspective helps us develop a more realistic understanding of how state lawmaking works: states don't make laws; individual legislators with their own particular interests do.[83] More radically, methodological individualism helps libertarians pierce the *moral* mythology of the state. Most of us would never think it permissible for one individual to steal from his neighbor, even if he put the stolen money to perfectly good use. Why then, libertarians ask, is the action any more permissible when done by a *group* of individuals calling themselves a "government"? In this sense, individualism is deeply connected with the moral parity thesis, described above.[84]

Negative Liberty

Finally, libertarians all share a commitment to liberty. In keeping with their individualism, when libertarians talk about liberty, it is *individual* liberty that they have in mind. They care about the freedom of individual human beings, not of collective entities such as the community, the nation, or the race. Libertarians are especially concerned with *negative* liberty (freedom from) rather than *positive* liberty (freedom to).[85] While there may be a sense in which the person who cannot climb a mountain from lack of ability is not "free" to do so, libertarians will insist that this is not the relevant sense of freedom for political philosophy. Negative freedom, libertarians hold, is the only kind of freedom that may be properly *enforced* by the coercive power of law.[86]

But here the puzzles begin. For there are three quite different and not obviously compatible ways in which libertarianism might be related to liberty. The first we will call the *maximizing* approach, exemplified by Herbert Spencer's law of equal freedom, which holds that every individual should have "the freedom to do all that he wills, provided he infringes not the equal freedom of any other man."[87] This principle requires the sphere of each individual's liberty to be as large as possible, compatible with a similar liberty for others. Note that the *kind* of maximization involved here differs from that involved in utilitarian or other consequentialist approaches to morality. Utilitarianism counsels us to maximize *aggregate* happiness, in a way that allows losses for some individuals to be counterbalanced by gains to others.[88] By contrast, libertarians like Spencer aim to maximize the sphere of *each and every individual's* liberty, subject only to the limit imposed by the right of each other person to an equally extensive liberty. The libertarian understanding of freedom is not only negative but also *universalistic* and *compossible*.[89]

The second approach, which we will call the *property-based* approach, is somewhat less intuitive. We find this view most explicitly articulated in the writings of Murray Rothbard and other strict libertarians who start from the principle of individual self-ownership. For these thinkers, the idea of liberty is intimately connected with the idea of *rights*.[90] Freedom means being unconstrained in the exercise of one's rights. An individual who is prevented from exercising her right to speak at assembly is rendered unfree by that constraint, while the robber who is prevented from stealing a television is not. Freedom, on this view, is a *moral* concept with content filled out by the underlying theory of rights. For libertarians such as Murray Rothbard, that theory of freedom begins (and ends) with *property* rights.

Finally, some libertarians hold what we will call the *instrumental* approach. This approach—which tends to be more common among classical liberals than strict libertarians—argues that individual, negative liberty is valuable as a means to an end, where the end is usually specified in terms of utility or happiness. These views rely heavily on empirical claims as to the relationship between certain sorts of freedoms (e.g., free speech, freedom from certain sorts of economic regulation) and desirable outcomes. But for this very reason, this approach cannot easily sustain the *absolutist* stance toward liberty characteristic of strict libertarianism. One who takes an instrumental approach to liberty must always be open to the possibility that there will be some circumstances in which liberty turns out *not* to be the best means to one's end.

The Integrated Set

Beyond providing us with a mechanism for capturing the resemblance that defines the libertarian family, our six markers of membership also give a fuller picture of the libertarian worldview. They help us distinguish members of the libertarian family from other

rival theoretical families: conservatives, nationalists, social democrats, and communists alike. For while members of those clans may
affirm one or more of our six markers, members of the libertarian
family distinctively affirm all six ideas at once.

Significantly, libertarians typically see these ideas as a tightly
integrated system of thought, with each commitment being supported by, and lending support to, the others. Private property
rights, for example, support free markets. A commitment to negative liberty, combined with the idea that any system of rights must
be compossible, helps explain the libertarian emphasis on private
property rights. A skepticism of authority buttresses their individualism, and their individualism helps explain an emphasis on the
emergent structure of spontaneous order.

Earlier, we distinguished strict libertarians from the postwar
classical liberals whom we treat as libertarians by virtue of their
place within the Liberty Movement. Our markers-of-membership
model enables us to make additional, finer-grained distinctions
within both categories. Each marker can be affirmed in stronger
or weaker formulations. Rights of property, for example, can be
affirmed by libertarians simply as being *among* the weightiest of
rights—a position common among contemporary classical liberals.
Or, at the other pole, *every* right can be seen as being but a species
of property right. (On that reading, property rights are affirmed as
absolutes, in part, because property rights are the *only* rights there
are.) So too with spontaneous order: on weaker readings, such
orders are seen to play a vital and underappreciated role within
free societies, a theme common among twentieth-century classical liberals such as Hayek. By contrast, on stronger formulations,
spontaneous orders provide *all* the rules and institutions needed
for society to function (as with libertarian anarchism). Each marker
is itself a continuum, making available a wide range of intermediate
ways that each of our six common traits might be expressed.

Our "cluster character" approach has other advantages as well.
As mentioned above, some of our markers can also be interpreted
in ways that lead in conservative directions (and in stronger, or
weaker, ways). For example, if structural racism is in part a product
of spontaneous social processes, and if libertarians have a principled affinity for spontaneous processes, do libertarians sometimes

find themselves defending inherited racist structures—whether or not these libertarians themselves hold racist attitudes? While libertarians have historically been eager to distinguish themselves from conservatives (on a variety of issues), we will see that the boundary between libertarian and conservative doctrines is more fraught than libertarians like to believe.

As intellectual historians, we find all of this advantageous. Our markers-of-membership approach allows us to do more than simply flesh out our definition of libertarianism or distinguish the libertarian family from its rivals—though our approach helps with these tasks too. Just as important, our model allows us to make fine-grained but useful distinctions within the libertarian family. These similarities and differences enliven the story of libertarianism, to which we now turn.

CHAPTER TWO

Three Eras of Libertarian Thought

LIBERTARIANISM EMERGED IN the middle of the nineteenth century, first in Britain and France as a partially conservative reaction against the threat of socialism, and later in America as a radical and progressive movement opposed to slavery, war, and even (in some cases) capitalism itself. By the third decade of the twentieth century, the center of gravity of libertarianism had shifted heavily toward the United States, and the intellectual war against socialism had come to play a defining role in the libertarian worldview. As such, the libertarianism of twentieth-century America came to resemble more closely the somewhat conservative libertarianism of nineteenth-century Britain and France than the radical anarchism of its own nineteenth-century movement. But the fall of the Soviet Union at the end of the twentieth century, and with it the collapse of the centrally managed socialist state as a credible intellectual or political threat, undermined this source of identity. Without socialism to be against, what was libertarianism *for*? Would the libertarianism of the twenty-first century be marked by a return to its radical nineteenth-century roots? Or would it take a more conservative, perhaps even reactionary and nationalist turn?

This chapter traces the development of libertarian thought over three eras: the "primordial" libertarianism of nineteenth-century Britain, France, and United States; the "Cold War" libertarianism of the twentieth century; and the contested and tumultuous Third Wave of the present day.

Primordial Libertarianism

The markers of libertarian thought had all appeared before. Notably, Thomas Hodgskin's essay "The Natural and Artificial Right of Property Contrasted" (1832) offered insights about property, spontaneous order, and skepticism of authority that would become central tenets of the libertarian worldview, and Herbert Spencer produced twelve remarkable letters on "The Proper Sphere of Government" in 1842–43, to be later republished in his book *The Man versus the State*. Still, it was not until 1850—plus or minus a year—that an efflorescence of unmistakably libertarian writing emerged, including Gustave de Molinari's defense of market anarchism in "The Production of Security" (1849), Frédéric Bastiat's "The Law" (1850), and Spencer's libertarian synthesis, *Social Statics* (1851).

For the first time, libertarianism formed an intellectual *system*. These "primordial" libertarians distinguished themselves from earlier classical liberal influences by integrating all six of our core ideas into a unified framework of individualism, private property, skepticism of authority, free markets, spontaneous order, and negative liberty. Classical liberals had embraced these ideas as defeasible and sometimes conflicting presumptions. For strict libertarians, in contrast, they were complementary parts of an overarching and uncompromising system of liberty.

Why 1850? And why Britain and France? Two main factors explain why libertarianism came into existence when and where it did.

First, the libertarians of nineteenth-century Britain and France were able to draw on the experience of the Industrial Revolution at its height to inform their political and economic views. Mass urbanization, the rise of wage labor, and the concentration of capital made issues of property rights, contract, and capitalism central to political debates in a way that they simply could not have been before. Because of these enormous changes in the social context, there is something misleadingly anachronistic about describing prior figures as "libertarian," regardless of how devoted they were to ideas of "self-ownership" or "markets." What markets *meant*—how they shaped relations between workers and managers, and the kind of inequalities, mobility, and creative destruction to which they gave rise—simply changed too radically in the nineteenth century for us to be able to infer what earlier classical liberals such as John Locke, or even Adam Smith, would have had to say about them. Libertarianism, at least as understood as a theory defined partly by its support of "free markets," was an answer to a question that could not have been asked, or at least not asked with the same meaning, prior to the Industrial Revolution.

Second, and most important to our story, the mid-nineteenth century saw socialism rise as a cultural and intellectual force, especially in the European revolutions of 1848. Just as classical liberalism could only develop in reaction to political absolutism, so too strict libertarianism needed a foil against which it could identify and position itself. Both liberalism and socialism were universalizing, expansionist doctrines, claiming to bear truths applicable to all people, everywhere. Both offered a comprehensive vision built on moral and economic propositions. Had socialism restricted itself to small, voluntary associations—as with the Owenite communities in North America—the two views may have coexisted in peace.[1] (Indeed, as we shall see in chapter 4, libertarians too made room for experimental communities of all sorts.) But *state* socialism—socialism as a mandatory scheme of social organization under the power of a centralized state—challenged every aspect of liberalism.

Faced with the intellectual and political challenge of socialism, liberals responded in two different ways, generating a split in the liberal family and an ambiguity in the term "liberalism" that survives to this day. One response was *progressive liberalism*.[2] Following John Stuart Mill, progressive liberals adopted the idea that the state should actively encourage a just distribution of wealth.[3] Inspired by figures such as Proudhon and Robert Hale, progressives tended to regard private property as a constraint on freedom rather than as a means to securing it.[4] Following John Dewey and Augustus Comte, progressives also tended to see the scientific management of society and the economy as a proper, and perhaps inevitable, role of the state. On the whole, progressive liberals responded to socialism by adopting some of its core commitments (such as collective responsibility for the poor) while attempting to incorporate those commitments into a broadly liberal framework.

The remaining liberals, however, responded to the challenge of socialism not by softening their position but by hardening it. Decrying the despotism and scarcity to which they believed socialism would lead, libertarians began to stiffen their view and to resist the temptation to give a single inch to even the most reasonable-sounding pleas for larger government. For these thinkers, socialism was the logical end point of the compromises and exceptions earlier liberals had carved out from the presumption of liberty. As the nineteenth-century British libertarian Auberon Herbert put it, socialism is "the logical completion of our compulsory interferences, our restrictions of faculties, and our transfer of property by the easy ... process of the vote."[5] If liberalism were to survive, this group believed, it must be *radicalized*. Thus, first in Britain and France, and shortly after in America, libertarianism came into the world as classical liberalism's radical child.

BRITAIN

In the first half of the nineteenth century, Britain's long tradition of individualist thought was coming to fruition.[6] John Locke's *Second Treatise*, originally published in 1689, is famous for its influence on twentieth-century libertarians such as Murray Rothbard and Robert Nozick. But as we will see in more detail in the next chapter, Locke's ideas were already starting to take radical form in the nineteenth century through the ideas of Thomas Hodgskin, whose *Labour Defended against the Claims of Capital* (1825) and "The Natural and Artificial Right of Property Contrasted" (1832) used Lockean ideas about self-ownership and labor-mixing to launch a radical critique of state privilege and crony capitalism.[7]

More directly influential on the laws and politics of Britain were the writings of Jeremy Bentham, whose utilitarian framework called for the radical reform of existing social institutions in order to more effectively promote the happiness of all human beings—"the greatest good for the greatest number." For Bentham, that greatest good was most likely to be achieved under a system that left individuals substantially free to order their lives as they saw fit.

Bentham thus criticized Adam Smith (of all people) for being too half-hearted in his defense of laissez-faire, arguing that concerns about usury could not justify restrictions on individual freedom of contract.[8] Bentham argued (anonymously) that individuals should be free to engage in homosexual or other "eccentric pleasures of the bed."[9] And he argued that England's legal system should and could be made less corrupt, more democratic, and more responsive to the needs of the people—arguments that culminated, just days before his death, in the monumental Reform Act of 1832.[10] Bentham, along with his fellow Philosophical Radicals David Ricardo and James Mill, were also impassioned advocates of international free trade.[11] Their theoretical arguments against protectionism bore practical fruit in Richard Cobden and John Bright's successful campaign to repeal the Corn Laws in 1846.[12]

It was in this intellectual climate that Herbert Spencer published what might well be regarded as the first systematic treatise of libertarian thought: *Social Statics*. Published in 1851, *Social Statics* sought to replace Benthamite utilitarianism's weighing of costs and benefits with a political theory based on *principle*—a principle that could be derived from both theory and experience and then applied across a wide range of political issues in a rationalistic and nearly absolute manner. For Spencer, the guiding political principle was the law of equal freedom, which held that "each man shall have the greatest freedom compatible with a like freedom for others."[13] From this principle, Spencer derived a host of libertarian implications regarding freedom of contract, freedom of speech, the rights of women and children, and the strictly limited role of the state. Surprisingly, Spencer also concluded—contra Locke and Hodgskin— that private property in land was morally unjust. As we will see in the next chapter, this conclusion thrust Spencer into considerable political conflict with other libertarians of the day.

Still, *Social Statics* is in one important respect a less *political* book than it is often interpreted to be. Spencer wrote the text as an exercise in what contemporary philosophers would call "ideal theory." It described principles not for human beings as they actually *were* but as Spencer (optimistically, in 1851) believed they would eventually *come to be*. At that point in his life, Spencer saw humanity evolving toward ever greater perfection, and the purpose of *Social*

Statics was to set out "the law of the perfect man."[14] It is therefore a mistake to take the principles or conclusions set forth by Spencer in that book as offering practical guidance for Britons in the nineteenth century or Americans in the twenty-first. *Social Statics* was a theoretical exercise, not a guidebook for practical politics.

By the time *Social Statics* was published, however, Spencer's perspective already felt out of date. In 1848—the same year revolutions swept across Europe and Marx and Engels published their *Communist Manifesto*—John Stuart Mill published *Principles of Political Economy*, a book which over the course of its many editions would come to represent the trajectory of English political thought during the nineteenth century. Mill was in many ways the "intellectual heir" of Bentham, and his 1859 *On Liberty* set forth an impassioned defense of individual freedom against both state interference and oppressive social pressure. But Mill was no dogmatist in either morals or economics. Just as Mill tempered Bentham's hedonistic utilitarianism by incorporating an eclectic mix of pluralistic values, so too he moderated Bentham's case for laissez-faire in economics. With its distinction between the productive and distributive roles of markets and its apparent openness to Fourieristic socialism, Mill's *Principles* was seen by many contemporary and later readers to represent a definitive milestone in the decline of individualism, and the rise of collectivism, one that paved the way for later critiques of laissez-faire from Jevons, Cairnes, Sidgwick, Marshall, and others.[15]

As the British jurist A. V. Dicey noted in 1905, "It is . . . perfectly clear that from 1848 onwards an alteration becomes perceptible in the intellectual and moral atmosphere of England. . . . Nor can we now doubt that this revolution of thought tended in the direction of socialism."[16] Carlyle's *Latter-Day Pamphlets* (1850) heaped scorn upon the preachers of laissez-faire from the authoritarian right, while in the field of literature Kingsley's *Alton Locke* (1850) and Gaskell's *Mary Barton* (1848) undermined the moral authority of political economy from the humanitarian left. The middle class discovered poverty in its midst and learned of the frightful conditions faced by many workers as they moved from farms to factories.[17] The same humanitarian impulses that had motivated the followers of Bentham to push for laissez-faire in the first half

of the nineteenth century now pushed for government intervention to protect women and children from exploitation at work, to
regulate pay and working hours, and to make employers liable for
injuries suffered by their workers.[18] The greater freedom extended
to workers under the Trade Union Act of 1871 facilitated the growth
of labor unions and the expanded use of the strike as a tool for
wresting concessions from employers. In the "New Unionism" of
the 1880s, the trade union movement became increasingly political, with key leaders advancing explicitly socialist ideals and policy
agendas.[19]

British socialism tended to take a Fabian, gradualist form rather
than the revolutionary form it often took on the continent. But
this simply led those Britons most strongly opposed to socialism to
worry that any step in the *direction* of socialism had to be resisted
with the utmost urgency. The contemporary historian John Mason
summarizes:

> The debate over state socialism was essentially a debate among liberals
> about how far it was desirable to depart from laissez-faire. Individual
> liberty, private property and freedom of contract were the touchstones
> for the defenders of extreme *laissez-faire*. Any infringement of them
> was seen as the first step in an inevitable slide towards socialism. This
> might be called the germ theory of socialism, because it was felt that
> there was no way to contain the disease once it had taken hold.[20]

Increasing calls for state regulation and redistribution were seen
by individualists as a slippery slope: a "road to serfdom" with no
off-ramp. Edward Dicey expressed the worry in 1885: "if once you
desert the solid ground of individual freedom you can find no
resting-place till you reach the abyss of Socialism."[21] The response
of a certain group of individualists to this challenge was to *radicalize* their doctrine—to transform maxims of freedom, property, and
limited government from the rules of thumb that earlier classical
liberals had sought to balance among a set of other competing considerations into absolute rules admitting no exceptions. It was thus
largely in reaction against the perceived threat of socialism that
strict libertarianism, as a radical, rationalistic, and monistic theory of the state, first emerged in the second half of the nineteenth
century in Britain.

One can see this emergence in the evolution of Spencer's approach to political questions. Spencer's 1851 writings displayed both theoretical detachment and cautious optimism. By 1884, however, with the publication of his collection of essays, *The Man versus the State*, Spencer had become a pessimistic warrior fighting a rear-guard action. Gone was the belief in mankind's perfect future freedom, replaced by dire warnings about "The New Toryism" and "The Coming Slavery."[22] Gone, too, were his earlier speculations about the theoretical injustice of property in land, replaced by an earnest commitment to defend liberty and property against state intrusion.[23] In response to the socialists, Spencer's libertarianism took on a distinctly reactionary and conservative character.[24]

Spencer was not the only libertarian whose views migrated in a conservative direction toward the end of the nineteenth century. In the 1880s and 1890s, a group of self-described "Individualists" created the first real libertarian movement in Britain, complete with its own newsletters and book series supported by wealthy donors (an alliance characteristic of later libertarian movements as well).[25] The Liberty and Property Defense League (LPDL), founded in 1882 by Francis Charteris, the 10th Earl of Wemyss, was the most significant organization in this movement and the clearest exemplar of British libertarianism's reactionary attitude toward socialism.[26] Its membership and affiliations included intellectuals such as Wordsworth Donisthorpe and Thomas Mackay, politicians such as Auberon Herbert, and jurists such as Lord Bramwell, many of whose writings were collected in one of its most enduring products: a collection of essays titled *A Plea for Liberty*, edited and published by Mackay in 1891 with an introduction by Herbert Spencer.[27]

The League aimed to stop what it regarded as "a general movement toward State-Socialism."[28] Its mission statement announced that the League "opposes all attempts to introduce the State as competitor or regulator into the various departments of social activity and industry, which would otherwise be spontaneously and adequately conducted by private enterprise."[29] Toward that end, the League served as a kind of Chamber of Commerce, uniting various business interests in a "system of mutual defense" that monitored pending legislation for hostility to members' interests.[30] It fought against legislation regulating the working conditions of laundresses, against the expansion of the Poor Law, and against employers' liability for injuries suffered by their workers. The liquor and beer trade became an area of special interest for the League (and its financial backers), and it waged a number of battles against temperance and other restrictive measures.[31]

The League earned a reputation as a reactionary organization, one that represented the interests of wealthy earls and barons against the poorer laboring classes. Its membership roll did nothing to discourage this view. As a contemporary critic noted, just twenty-one members of the League owned between them over 2,100,000 acres of land in Great Britain.[32] In that light, the League's opposition to Irish land reform seemed to many less a consistent application of libertarian principles than a defense of self-interest.[33]

Wordsworth Donisthorpe, a Hobbesian positivist who helped found the British Chess Association, invented a moving picture camera called the Kinesigraph, and lived mostly off the wealth his family earned in the Yorkshire woolen industry, had always been something of an iconoclast who felt ill at ease with the LPDL's conservative bent. In 1887 he founded his own periodical, *Jus: A Weekly Organ of Individualism*. In 1888, Donisthorpe publicly disassociated with the League. That organization, Donisthorpe later noted, had never hesitated to speak up against "all State-interferences with the liberty of landowners, of pawnbrokers, of water companies, and, in short, of monopolists and property owners of every description."[34] But on issues involving *personal* liberty—on the repeal of the Contagious Diseases Acts, on compulsory vaccination, and on the Disestablishment of the Church of England—the LPDL was silent. "Half-hearted and one-sided individualism is not the doctrine we have set ourselves to preach," Donisthorpe proclaimed. "If the doctrine is good for anything, it is good for everything. A body which flaunts the flag only on suitable occasions, when the rich, the strong, and the privileged may benefit by the adoption of the principle, but which remains silent when it cuts the other way" is, Donisthorpe argued, incompatible with the independent course he hoped to take with *Jus*.[35]

Donisthorpe was not alone in his discomfort with the League. While the LPDL defended the interests of beer barons and landed aristocrats, another libertarian organization took a more progressive approach. The Personal Rights Association (PRA) had been founded by the professor of logic and economics J. H. Levy in 1871. Like the LPDL, it put out a series of books and pamphlets articulating and defending a broadly libertarian position. But unlike the LPDL, the focus of which was primarily economic and anti-socialist, the focus of the PRA was broadly social. Where the LPDL identified itself as a "system of mutual defense" for industry, the PRA set out to "uphold the principle of the *perfect equality of all persons before the law* and in the exercise and enjoyment of their Individual Liberty and Personal Rights."[36]

Both the LPDL and the PRA stood against state interference; both were shaped by their opposition to socialism. But the different grounds on which they chose to make that stand reveal a great deal about their priorities and about the different forms of social activism to which libertarian commitments can lead. The PRA had grown out of Josephine Butler's campaign to repeal the Contagious Diseases Acts, which allowed for the compulsory medical inspection of prostitutes in garrison towns.[37] Over the course of its existence, the PRA fought against protectionism and economic regulation, but also against vivisection and vaccination.[38] Rather than defending the rights of English landlords over Irish peasants, the PRA held that "private property in land—apart from improvements—is essentially incompatible with individualism."[39] For the LPDL, individualism was largely a conservative doctrine established to defend existing social hierarchies and privileges. For the PRA, libertarianism was a *progressive* force, one that took as a primary aim the liberation of oppressed and marginalized classes.

Although the LPDL continued into the 1920s, its last real campaign was its (spectacularly unsuccessful) struggle against "municipal socialism."[40] The PRA, too, long outlived its relevance, its influence dying with its founder J. H. Levy in 1913 (remarkably, the organization itself hung on until 1978). By the late 1880s, when Chancellor of the Exchequer William Harcourt announced "we are all socialists now," the first wave of British individualism was spent. A brief attempt to forge a "new individualism" on the basis of an amoral, Nietzschean egoism went nowhere.[41] By the dawn of the twentieth century, the British libertarian movement was effectively dead.

FRANCE

As in Britain, libertarianism in nineteenth-century France developed out of a long tradition of classical liberal thought.[42] Unlike in Britain, however, where a libertarian movement emerged out of an eclectic mix of jurists, businessmen, and philosophers, the development of French libertarianism was driven almost entirely by economists, whose approach was pervasively shaped by the conceptual framework of political economy.

The first French libertarians drew from two traditions of thought.[43] The first was an older native tradition of French economic thinking, represented by Richard Cantillon, the Physiocrats (especially François Quesnay), and Jacques Turgot. The second was the Anglo-Scottish tradition of Adam Smith, Jeremy Bentham, Thomas Malthus, and David Ricardo. These two traditions merged in the work of Jean-Baptiste Say, whose 1803 *Traité d'économie politique* introduced many of the themes that would be developed and radicalized at the middle of the nineteenth century.

Many of the most important of these developments derived from Say's analysis of economic production. While the Physiocrats had argued that agriculture was the only genuinely productive form of economic activity, Say argued that production was never really about the creation of new physical objects (since matter can be neither created nor destroyed) but simply the *rearrangement* of objects in a way that makes them more useful.[44] This provided a better explanation for why and when manufacturing activity is productive but also, crucially, allowed Say to argue (against the socialists) that productivity was a function of consumer value rather than workers' labor. Thus, for Say, merchants, entrepreneurs, and capitalists were as much engaged in economically productive activity as were manual laborers.

Say's analysis also allowed him to identify certain activity as *unproductive*: activity that consumes value but does not produce it. As we will see in chapter 5, Charles Dunoyer and Charles Comte would later develop this distinction into an original and radically libertarian theory of class and class conflict.

Say, Comte, and Dunoyer made seminal contributions to French liberal thought, but no one did more to synthesize and radicalize their ideas than Claude Frédéric Bastiat. Born in 1801 in the provincial town of Bayonne in southwest France, Bastiat spent his early life observing the tumult of post-Revolutionary Paris from afar, farming his deceased father's estate and tending to his ailing grandfather. In his spare time, Bastiat read widely in religion, literature, politics, and especially economics.[45]

Bastiat's life in a merchant family showed him firsthand the hardships that France's robust and ever-expanding system of tariffs imposed. Inspired by Smith and Say, Bastiat discerned the larger social implications of these policies, their connection to France's continuing economic hardship, and their link to deeper questions about the value of individual liberty.

In the 1840s, Bastiat discovered the writings of the English social reformer Richard Cobden. The effect was like a religious awakening. The struggle of Cobden's Anti-Corn Law League against protectionism in Britain (see chapter 8) inspired Bastiat to wage a similar battle against the tariff system in France. Bastiat wrote a book on Cobden's movement and traveled to Paris to have it published. He started his own free trade association, which drew crowds of over two thousand people to its meetings in 1846.[46] Most important, Bastiat began writing his own essays decrying the folly and destructiveness of protectionist policies.

Many of these essays were originally published in Bastiat's own newsletter, *Le Libre-Échange* (Free Trade). In one of the most famous pieces, Bastiat penned a fictitious petition from the candle-makers' guild to the government of France. The candlemakers complain that they are the victims of unfair competition from a foreign rival who, apparently, is in "a condition so far superior to ours for the production of light that he absolutely inundates our national market with it at a price fabulously reduced."[47] The rival, it is soon revealed, is none other than the sun. Bastiat, trusting his readers to see the folly of the proposal, has the candlemakers petition the government to protect their industry by "ordering the shutting up of all windows, skylights, dormer-windows, outside and inside shutters, curtains, blinds, bull's eyes; in a word, of all openings, holes, chinks, clefts, and fissures, by or through which the light of the sun has been in use to enter houses."

Like Cobden, Bastiat thought that free trade was integral to the liberal idea of peaceful cooperation between nations.[48] More generally, Bastiat saw free trade as an illustration of a broader idea that would become one the central themes in his economic thought: the harmony of interests that exists between individuals under conditions of freedom.[49] Where protectionists saw conflict between the interests of domestic and foreign producers, Bastiat saw exchanges that were good for producers—and, more importantly, consumers— in both countries. While socialists saw the interests of capital and labor as being in conflict, Bastiat argued that increases in the quantity of capital employed in a nation tend to increase, rather than diminish, the share of production that goes to workers. So long as producers must entice consumers to part with their money voluntarily, market exchange will be mutually beneficial. When trade is free, the interests of producers and consumers align.

Bastiat had sympathized with the critics of the July Monarchy, who saw it as an abuse of state power for the benefit of the bourgeoisie. But the February revolution of 1848, the socialist designs of Louis Blanc, and the agitation of even more radical and revolutionary factions on the streets of Paris led Bastiat to see the threat to liberty in France as both imminent and dire. In April 1848, Bastiat ran successfully for a seat in the Chamber of Deputies to combat what he saw as France's drift toward authoritarian socialism and to defend his vision of a free society.

His struggle against socialism led Bastiat to see laissez-faire—the cause to which he had dedicated most of his adult life—as merely one aspect of a broader conflict between freedom and coercion. "All forms of freedom are interrelated," Bastiat wrote. "Together they all constitute a systematic and harmonious whole."[50] Fighting tariffs was not enough. "Rather than the fact of free trade alone, I desire for my country the general philosophy of free trade. While free trade itself will bring more material wealth to us, the acceptance of the general philosophy that underlies free trade will inspire all needed reforms."[51]

Bastiat would develop his own systematic theory of the purpose and limits of government authority in one of his last major essays, "The Law," written just before his death in 1850.[52] Like other libertarians, Bastiat saw the morality of government activity as entirely co-extensive with the morality of *individual* activity.[53] Governments have no rights apart from those held by the individuals over whom they govern. It follows that governments should use force only in the single circumstance where *individuals* would have the same right: self-defense. According to Bastiat, then, the sole legitimate function of government is the "collective organization of the individual right of legitimate defense."[54] Its core duties were "few indeed: to preserve peace and order, to maintain national security, to render equal justice to everyone, and to undertake a few public works of national importance."[55]

Bastiat saw the socialist program—with its state-mandated wages, redistribution, and restrictions on trade—as a threat not merely to economic growth but to justice itself. By using coercion to achieve its goals, socialism violates the vital defensive function of the state. It also replaces the natural harmony of interests in a free market with an artificial *conflict* of interest. In setting up the state as a mechanism of redistribution and control, socialism incentivizes using the state to advance one's own interest at others' expense. This amounts to a system of legal plunder.[56] Under such a system, Bastiat wrote, "the state is the great fiction by which everybody endeavors to live at the expense of everyone else."[57]

Bastiat devoted most of the last part of his life to battling socialism. Against Louis Blanc, he argued that true fraternity could only be realized under a regime of individual liberty.[58] Against socialist challenges to the legitimacy of private property, Bastiat argued that the right to property is a moral principle with deep roots in the human nature.[59] And against Proudhon, Bastiat defended the moral and economic legitimacy of interest and profit.[60]

While sharply critical of the moral and economic theories of socialists on the left, Bastiat was no man of the right. His was a vision of progress and of expansive liberalization, with no room for the privileges and corruption of the ancien régime. In the Chamber of Deputies, Bastiat sat on the *left* side of the aisle with Proudhon and Blanc. Bastiat even rose to Blanc's defense when Blanc was put on trial for insurrection and conspiracy against the state.[61] Bastiat's principled commitment to individual liberty often confused his constituents and made him difficult to classify in terms of the dominant political categories of his time.

Other libertarians of the Paris School were equally hard to classify. Gustave de Molinari (1819–1912), born a Belgian, moved to Paris around the age of twenty-one to pursue a career as a journalist and a political economist. He quickly became affiliated with the Société d'Économie and Bastiat's Association for Free Trade, and took to Bastiat as a friend and mentor. Like Bastiat, Molinari worked to understand his time in terms of fundamental principles. Indeed, Molinari's commitment to economic rationality may have been even more radical than his mentor's—contemporaries waggishly referred to Molinari as "the law of supply and demand made into man."[62]

For Molinari, as for Bastiat, the economic perspective stood in sharp contrast to those taken by both the political left and the political right of his day. One of Molinari's most important books, *Les soirées de la rue Saint-Lazare* (1849), is written in dialogue form, with one character, The Economist, defending Molinari's vision of a free society against two rival perspectives: The Conservative and The Socialist.

Against The Socialist, who demands the abolition of private property, Molinari treats property and free exchange as absolute moral imperatives. Private economic liberties express man's mastery over his own person.[63] Against The Conservative and other defenders of inherited authority, Molinari has his Economist describe an emergent social order driven by voluntary and decentralized processes. Both rival views, according to Molinari, privileged the state, its plunder, and its conflicts. Molinari thought his own ideals conducive to individual liberty, cooperation, and peace.[64]

As in Britain, French libertarian thought in the mid-nineteenth century was infused with optimistic themes of progressive liberation. But French libertarianism also mirrored its British counterpart in becoming increasingly muted and pessimistic as the twentieth century drew near. Bastiat's premature death in 1850 preceded the fall of the Second Republic less than a year later. Though not without victories still to come—such as the Cobden-Chevalier free trade treaty of 1860—the cause of liberty in France was on the defensive. By the end of his life, Molinari prophesied that the twentieth century would be dominated by imperialism, protectionism, socialism, and war. While he hoped that the spirit of liberalism might be recovered, he grew increasingly worried that anti-liberal forces might destroy civilization itself.[65] As the historian David Hart notes, after Molinari's death in 1912, "only a few members of the 'old school' remained to teach and write—the economist Yves

Guyot, and the anti-war campaigner Frédéric Passy survived into the 1920s. The academic posts and editorships of the major journals were held by 'new liberals' or by socialists who spurned the laissez-faire liberalism of the 19th century."[66]

AMERICA

While Britain and France each had their own individualist traditions on which to draw, America seemed to have individualism written into its DNA. The radical ideas of John Locke were influential in the period leading up to the American Revolution. John Trenchard and Thomas Gordon's *Cato's Letters* used Lockean ideas to defend natural rights, constitutional restraints, the separation of powers, and the right to resist tyrannical government. Although written in Britain more than fifty years before American independence, their essays were widely read by the Founding Fathers and served to popularize a radicalized Lockeanism among the broader public.[67] And, of course, Jefferson's Declaration of Independence was heavily indebted to Locke—with some passages being taken almost verbatim from Locke's *Second Treatise*.[68]

As in Britain and France, it was not until the second half of the nineteenth century that libertarianism began to emerge as a radical and systematic set of ideas in the United States. But while the timing was similar, the nature and content of libertarian ideas developed in the United States were strikingly different. While libertarians in Britain and France defended their position through a mix of utilitarian and natural rights analyses, libertarians in the United States, at least by the end of the nineteenth century, almost all embraced a form of egoism. While libertarians in Britain and France mostly viewed the state as having some legitimate role to play in defending individual rights, libertarians in America were mostly anarchists. And, finally, while the labor theory of value played a negligible role in British and French libertarian thought, it was a dominant factor in the American approach to libertarianism, shaping not only their economic analysis but their entire social theory and political orientation.[69]

We cannot explain these differences with certainty, and they must not be overstated. For example, there existed in Britain a small individualist anarchist movement that bore strong similarities to the American libertarian movement.[70] Its influence, however, was minor. The big point is that the varied political contexts of the New World and Old did much to shape the libertarian movements to which they gave rise. Specifically, where the perceived threat of socialism spurred the development of British and French libertarianism, it played almost no role in America for the simple reason that socialism did not exist there as a viable *political* force. Socialism in nineteenth-century America—to the extent that it existed at all—was a utopian movement found in experimental communities and other voluntary forms of organization. It posed no threat to the dominant social order. There was no Fabian society working to gradually (but radically) transform the state and economy, no significant revolutionary socialist movement that threatened to seize control of the state by force.

But nineteenth-century America had something else that Britain and France did not: extensive slavery. Moreover, this was not the slavery of far-off empire but slavery next door, with all the heated debates and political turmoil this engendered. Given the connections between the abolitionist and libertarian movements of the time, and the character of the issues with which nineteenth-century American libertarians preoccupied themselves, we believe that it was slavery, far more than socialism, that shaped the character of the libertarian movement in nineteenth-century America.[71] We will explore the deep social, political, and conceptual ties between the libertarian and abolitionist movements in chapter 4. For now, our hypothesis is that while libertarianism in Britain and France emerged largely as a reaction against socialism, it was a reaction against *slavery* that gave rise to American libertarianism, and in particular to its distinctive attraction to egoism, anarchism, and the significance of labor.

Crucially, the first American libertarians saw the issue of slavery primarily through the lenses of *authority* and *property* rather than of *race*. Libertarians condemned slavery as an unjust usurpation of individual sovereignty and a denial of the individual's rightful entitlement to the fruits of their labor. The fact that it was *African Americans* being enslaved by *whites* seemed to play, for libertarians, no essential role in either their analysis of the injustice or their motivation for opposing it. For the nineteenth-century libertarians, slavery was merely a vivid venue of a larger struggle between freedom and authority.

Nevertheless, slavery shaped the way American libertarians thought and wrote about freedom. Slavery led American libertarians to see stealing another's labor, or the fruits of another's labor, as the paradigm of injustice and to proclaim each individual's sovereignty over his or her body and labor as a bedrock moral principle. Many were then led by analogy to view any *other* institution that imposed upon the individual's will as a usurpation of individual sovereignty, different from slavery only by degree. American libertarians thus embraced anarchism in rejecting the state's illegitimate claim to authority over the individual and embraced egoism in rejecting morality's (or moralists') illegitimate claim.

The distinctive character of late nineteenth-century American libertarianism can be seen most clearly in the pages of *Liberty*, a journal edited and published by Benjamin Tucker from 1881 to 1908.[72] Across its nearly thirty-year run, *Liberty* published essays by almost all of the most important figures in the American libertarian movement, as well as original articles and translations by Europeans. Its contributors debated the respective merits of egoism versus natural rights, the rights of children, the legitimacy of intellectual property, and the legitimacy of interest, profit, and rent. One need look no further than its masthead to see that *Liberty* represented a radically different approach to libertarianism from that embraced on the continent. The masthead of *Liberty* magazine was emblazoned with a quotation from Proudhon (whom Bastiat regarded as one of his chief rivals): "Liberty: not the daughter but the mother of order." The connection between *Liberty* and Proudhon ran deep. Tucker was deeply influenced by Proudhon's mutualism, and indeed translated and published a number of Proudhon's writings over the course of his career, including an 1876 translation of *What Is Property?*

As Wendy McElroy observes, contributors to *Liberty* were largely united on two main ideas: the sovereignty of the individual and cost as the limit of price.[73] The first of these ideas, which we will explore further in chapter 3, is roughly equivalent to the contemporary idea of self-ownership and derived from the anarchist social reformer Josiah Warren. The second idea, which we will look more closely at in chapter 4, also came from Warren and expresses a normative injunction based on the labor theory of value. Since labor is the source of all value, and since goods ought to be sold for no more than their true value, it follows that any price higher than the labor cost of the good or service being sold is unjust. Contributors to *Liberty* generally found profit, interest, and rent to be exploitative and unjust. At its birth, American libertarianism was radically anti-capitalistic.

As we will see, a commitment to individual sovereignty played an important role in the American abolitionist movement and drove many abolitionists to embrace anarchism as the logical end point of their opposition to authority. But while American libertarians almost universally shared this commitment, they disagreed on the *grounds*. Some, like John F. Kelly, Henry Appleton, and Lysander Spooner, embraced natural law reasoning.[74] Others, like Victor Yarros, based it on a Spencerian commitment to "equal freedom."[75] But the majority of *Liberty*'s contributors, including Tucker, rejected these approaches in favor of egoism. They were particularly influenced by the egoism of Max Stirner, a German theorist whose book *The Ego and Its Own* was first translated into English by Tucker in 1907.

Unlike the better-known egoism of the twentieth-century libertarian Ayn Rand, Stirner's variant was essentially amoral, holding that concepts such as "rights" and "obligations" are "myths" or "ghosts," and that the only true standard of right is sheer might, the ability to transform one's will into action.[76] The only rightful limits on one's will are those voluntarily chosen through contract.

Although some contributors to *Liberty*—including, at times, Tucker himself—followed this egoism all the way to its most extreme (and arguably repellent) conclusions, for the most part Tucker seemed to treat his egoism as a kind of metaethical principle that left his earlier normative beliefs in natural rights largely unchanged.[77] Tucker held that a "tacit" agreement exists among all men "not to trespass upon each other's individuality, the motive of this agreement being the purely egoistic desire for the peaceful preservation of his own individuality."[78] However, while this argument might plausibly ground duties of mutual noninterference among competent adults, it cannot account for such duties toward children, who are not parties to any contracts, tacit or otherwise. Tucker was forced by his more consistently Stirnerite correspondents to conclude that parents have no duties of either a positive *or* a negative sort toward their children. Until they reach the point of maturity, Tucker ultimately concluded, children are the property of their parents.[79]

Despite its egoistic framework, *Liberty* generally took a progressive stance on economic and political issues. *Liberty's* egoism was less a celebration of selfishness than an assertion of the sovereignty of the individual against external authorities. For the most part, it was the sovereignty of the poor and working classes that concerned the authors of *Liberty*, not the interests of the capitalists or landowners.

In a passage strikingly similar to Wordsworth Donisthorpe's criticism of the Liberty and Property Defense League, Tucker penned a scathing critique of Herbert Spencer. Reviewing Spencer's late essays "The New Toryism" and "The Coming Slavery," Tucker wrote that Spencer "is one of those persons who are making a wholesale onslaught on Socialism as the incarnation of the doctrine of State omnipotence carried to the highest power." But Tucker saw something inconsistent in Spencer's critique:

> Amid his multitudinous illustrations (of which he is as prodigal as ever) of the evils of legislation, he in every instance cites some law passed, ostensibly at least, to protect labor, alleviate suffering, or promote the people's welfare. He demonstrates beyond dispute the lamentable failure in this direction. But never once does he call attention to the far more deadly and deep-seated evils growing out of the innumerable laws creating privilege and sustaining monopoly. You must not protect the weak against the strong, he seems to say, but freely supply all the weapons needed by the strong to oppress the weak. He is greatly shocked that the rich should be directly taxed to support the poor, but that the poor should be indirectly taxed and bled to make the rich richer does not outrage his delicate sensibilities in the least. Poverty is increased by the poor laws, says Mr. Spencer. Granted; but what about the *rich* laws that caused and still cause the poverty to which the poor laws add?

Tucker's attention to the plight of the oppressed went further, insisting that "individualism must be supplemented by the doctrines of equity and courtesy." Tucker concludes his critique by conceding that, "while State Socialism is just as dangerous as Mr. Spencer pictures it, there is a higher and nobler form of Socialism which is not only not slavery, but which is our only means of rescue from all sorts and degrees of slavery."[80]

Thus, toward the end of the nineteenth century in America, socialism was regarded not only as *compatible* with libertarianism but as the most effective means of realizing freedom. *State* socialism was of course regarded by all libertarians as an unmitigated evil. But late in the nineteenth century, it was still possible for American libertarians to distinguish between *voluntary* and *coercive* socialism and to recognize the former as at least compatible with if not positively required by their creed.

In the twentieth century, all of this changed.

Cold War Libertarianism

In February 1926, twenty-one-year-old Alisa Rosenbaum arrived in New York City. She had left St. Petersburg on a visa to visit relatives in Chicago. But she had no intention of ever returning to her native Russia. Rosenbaum vividly remembered the day in 1918 when her father's chemistry shop had been seized by armed soldiers in the name of "the people." That shop had been built by decades of work and sacrifice by her father and family. In a moment, it was gone. The incident taught Rosenbaum something she would never forget—for all its language of equality and fairness, communism in practice amounted to little more than brute force and centralized power. She had to get out.

Arriving in America, Rosenbaum was ready to start a new life. After visiting relatives in Chicago, Rosenbaum moved to Hollywood, had a fortuitous run-in with Cecil B. De Mille, and started writing for his studio under the new name she had given herself upon arriving in America: Ayn Rand.[81]

Rand would go on to become one of the most influential figures in the development of twentieth-century libertarianism. Like Rand, the libertarian movement in the twentieth century would largely find its home on American soil. While the nineteenth century witnessed significant developments in libertarian thought in Britain and France, in the twentieth century many of the most important contributors to libertarian ideas followed Rand in moving to America, thus giving credence to the misleading twentieth-century notion that libertarianism was a distinctly American ideology.

Long before she realized precisely what sort of political-economic system she was *for*, Rand knew what she was *against*. In 1936 she published her first novel, *We the Living*, a scathing critique of Soviet communism. The novel traces the devastating impact of the authoritarian regime on a single family. But as her notes for the novel reveal, Rand was already beginning to see politics in more universal and abstract terms. Communism, she noted, was simply the logical end point of the more fundamental philosophical idea of collectivism.[82]

Rand's next and more famous novel, *The Fountainhead*, sought to present what Rand regarded as the moral antithesis of collectivism—individualism. And eventually, in *Atlas Shrugged*, that commitment to individualism would evolve into a full-throated celebration of laissez-faire capitalism. But throughout her career, Rand would remain hypervigilant against the threat of communism and its philosophical precursors. In 1941, she wrote an essay titled "To All Fifth Columnists," intended to attract like-minded intellectuals to an organization aimed at the defense of individualism. In it she proclaimed that "totalitarianism had already won a complete victory in many minds" and warned American businessmen that "the money, home, or education you plan to leave [your children] will be worthless or taken away from them. Instead, your legacy will be a Totalitarian America, a world of slavery, of starvation, of concentration camps and firing squads."[83] Her "Screen Guide for Americans," published in 1947, sought to advise the movie industry on how to detect and avoid communist messages in films. Later that year, she testified in front of the House Un-American Activities Committee.[84]

The American political climate could hardly have been less receptive to Rand's ideas. The New Deal was pitched as salvation from deprivation. The Soviet Union still appeared to many as an economic and social success. Rumors of Stalin's brutality were dismissed by journalists such as Walter Duranty in the pages of the *New York Times*. High-profile visitors to the USSR credulously reported communists' progress in everything from poverty reduction to the elimination of mental illness.[85] A number of these visitors went on to play important roles in the presidential administration of Franklin Delano Roosevelt.[86]

Yet Rand was not entirely alone in fearing collectivism. Roosevelt's New Deal, in particular, generated a number of critics among business and intellectual elites. The essayists H. L. Mencken and Albert Jay Nock shared Rand's disdain for collectivism, not to mention her admiration for the ideas of Friedrich Nietzsche. Rand even sought out such individuals with the hope of building a movement of "reactionaries."[87] And while those relationships almost always ended badly, she gained from them ideas and influences that would later prove vital for her own work. Nock, for instance, sometimes described himself as a "Spencerian Individualist," and it was his republished version of *The Man versus the State* that introduced Rand to Spencer's strident anti-socialism.[88]

Isabel Paterson, a well-connected columnist for the *New York Herald Tribune*, developed a friendship with Rand that would serve Rand as a "virtual graduate school in American history, politics, and economics."[89] Through Paterson's guidance, Rand became acquainted with other opponents of the New Deal, including Rose Wilder Lane, a freelance journalist and the daughter of *Little House on the Prairie* author Laura Ingalls Wilder.[90] Like most of Rand's relationships, the friendship between Rand, Paterson, and Lane was turbulent. Still, the three women profoundly influenced each other and, as a result, influenced the development of twentieth-century libertarianism.[91] Indeed, just as 1850 was a calendric milestone for the first generation of European libertarians, so 1943 would be a critical year for Cold War libertarianism. That single year saw the publication of Rand's *Fountainhead*, Lane's *The Discovery of Freedom*, and Paterson's *The God of the Machine*.

Despite her tremendous later influence, Rand's early attempts to build a movement of "reactionaries" never bore fruit. That task fell to Leonard Read. Head of the Los Angeles Chamber of Commerce, in 1946 Read founded the Foundation for Economic Education (FEE)—the arguably first major libertarian organization of the

Cold War era.[92] FEE hoped "to educate for liberty on every level." It published a magazine called *The Freeman* that opposed union violence and extolled the virtues of the free market. FEE gave away or sold over half a million copies of Henry Hazlitt's *Economics in One Lesson* and Bastiat's "The Law."[93] And it introduced Americans to up-and-coming libertarian economists like Ludwig von Mises and Friedrich Hayek.

The impact of Read's organization on twentieth-century libertarianism can hardly be overstated. It served as a bridge between libertarian intellectuals and wealthy donors in the business community, many of whom were far from ideologically pure advocates of laissez-faire. But in their opposition to the New Deal and the American labor movement and, above all, in their abhorrence of socialism, they found many points of connection with libertarianism. These connections served as the foundation for an uneasy alliance between conservatives and libertarians that would last most of the twentieth century and shape the character of libertarian thought in that era.

Anti-socialism was central to the early work of both Mises and Hayek, and crucial in establishing their reputation among a broader audience in the United States. Mises, for instance, developed some measure of fame by arguing in his 1922 book *Socialism: An Economic and Sociological Analysis* that the centralized economic planning favored by state socialists was not merely wrong-headed but *impossible* since, in the absence of market prices, socialism lacks any method for calculating the trade-offs necessary for economic decision making.[94] Later, in his 1944 book *Bureaucracy*, Mises would argue that the idea of a "third way" between capitalism and socialism was a chimera: "Capitalism means free enterprise, sovereignty of consumers in economic matters, and sovereignty of the voters in political matters. Socialism means full governmental control of every sphere of the individual's life. . . . There is no compromise possible between these two systems."[95]

Such strident libertarianism was unusual among economists at the time, even among the Austrian school that Mises represented. In its native Vienna, the Austrian school of economics had been opposed to socialism. But it had hardly been dogmatic in its defense of laissez-faire. Early Austrians supported progressive taxation on grounds of the diminishing marginal utility of wealth and supported targeted state intervention in the economy.[96] It was only upon its migration to America that the Austrian school took on a distinctively libertarian flavor, especially through the work of Mises.

Fleeing war-torn Europe in 1940, Mises eventually landed a job at the Graduate School of Business at New York University (NYU) in 1945. In 1948, he began running a seminar that served to spread his free-market ideas to an American audience. But Mises's dog=matic libertarianism soon alienated him from his colleagues at NYU, the broader economic profession, and even many of his fellow Austrian economists. The scholarly impact of Mises's NYU seminar never approached that of the similar seminar Mises had run in his native Vienna that had produced such notable students as Friedrich Hayek, Oskar Morgenstern, Fritz Machlup, Felix Kaufman, and Alfred Schultz. In contrast, the NYU seminar often drew as many businessmen and political activists as aspiring academics. In 1949, Mises's official position at NYU was not renewed, and he was forced to rely on private funding from the Volker Fund, which allowed the seminar to continue until 1969, four years before his death at ninety-two.

A vehement opposition to socialism also characterized the work of Mises's student Friedrich Hayek. Hayek's first work of social criticism, *The Road to Serfdom* (1944), is popularly perceived to have argued that any deviation from pure laissez-faire would lead to totalitarianism. As the economist and Hayek biographer Bruce Caldwell has argued, however, this interpretation makes little sense.[97] After all, Hayek himself endorsed *many* deviations from laissez-faire in *The Road to Serfdom* and explicitly claimed that "nothing has done so much harm to the liberal cause as the wooden insistence of some liberals on certain rough rules of thumb, above all the principles of *laissez-faire*."[98] What Hayek was arguing against in 1945 was not the welfare state but the kind of state management of the economy that many Western countries had adopted as a temporary measure during wartime but which socialists and some sympathetic economists sought to extend to a permanent measure. It is the embrace of socialism, not the welfare state, that Hayek thought sets a nation off down the road to serfdom. As Hayek would later put it: "The dispute between the market order and socialism is no less than a matter of survival. To follow socialist morality would destroy much of present humankind and impoverish much of the rest."⁹⁹

After a disappointing start (*The Road to Serfdom* was rejected by three publishers before being accepted by the University of Chicago Press), Hayek's book found an eager audience among American readers.¹⁰⁰ Henry Hazlitt gave it a glowing review in the *New York Times*. *Reader's Digest* published an abbreviated version, exposing Hayek's ideas to millions. General Motors even commissioned a cartoon version of the book for its workers in its "Thought Starter" series. In 1945, Hayek left his academic home at the London School of Economics to do a book tour in the United States. There, he made connections that led to an academic appointment on the Committee on Social Thought at the University of Chicago.

Like Rand and Read before him, Hayek dreamed of creating an organization devoted to libertarian principles. With help from the Volker Fund, this dream was realized in 1947 and the Mont Pelerin Society held its first meeting in Switzerland.¹⁰¹ Hayek's group had a decidedly more academic character than Read's—the purpose of Mont Pelerin was not to propagandize libertarianism to the masses but to study and refine it among the elite. All of the participants at the initial meeting—Karl Popper, Milton Friedman, Ludwig von Mises, Frank Knight, and others—shared a commitment to classical liberal values of individual freedom and limited government. But some held these values more strongly than others. Milton Friedman would later recall one point during the meeting when the discussion turned to the appropriateness of government action to affect the distribution of income.

> I particularly recall a discussion of this issue, in the middle of which Ludwig von Mises stood up, announced to the assembly "You're all a bunch of socialists," and stomped out of the room, an assembly that contained not a single person who, by even the loosest standards, could be called a socialist.¹⁰²

As the libertarian movement grew over the course of the twentieth century, disagreements such as these multiplied. Disputes were particularly sharp between those who took a classical liberal and consequentialist perspective and those taking a more rationalistic and absolutist approach. For example, in 1946 the Foundation for Economic Education published a pamphlet on rent control by Milton Friedman and George Stigler, titled "Roofs or Ceilings?"[103] In it, the two free-market economists set forth an argument that has now become commonplace among critics of rent control: by placing an artificial ceiling on the price of rental housing, rent control reduces supply and therefore fails to achieve its stated objective of making it easier for people to find an affordable home. Ayn Rand, who was closely associated with FEE at the time, was incensed. In an eight-page letter to an associate of Leonard Read's "replete with exclamation points and capitalized sentences," she fumed, "Not one word about the inalienable right of landlords and property owners . . . not one word about any kind of principles. Just *expediency*. . . . and humanitarian . . . concern for those who can find no houses."[104] She dismissed Stigler and Friedman as "two reds"[105] and condemned the pamphlet as "the most pernicious thing ever issued by an avowedly conservative organization."[106]

One also sees divisions in the different paths taken by Mises's students. Hayek's libertarianism was scholarly in its presentation, broadly consequentialist in its moral foundations, and (relatively) moderate in its political implications. Murray Rothbard, in contrast, who studied with Mises in his NYU seminar, would develop and promulgate a version of libertarianism that was far more popular in its orientation, deontological and absolutist in its morality, and radical in its implications.

In many ways, Rothbard is unique among twentieth-century American libertarians. For one thing, he drew ideas from an unusually wide range of historical sources. While Read and Paterson had drawn fairly directly on the nineteenth-century English and French traditions of Spencer and Bastiat, Rothbard was virtually alone in looking for insights in the nineteenth-century American tradition of Tucker and Spooner.[107] Indeed, Rothbard almost single-handedly introduced these thinkers, with their anarchism, their radicalism, and their anti-corporatism, to a new generation of libertarians.

Rothbard was also distinctive in his attitude toward socialism, and in the priorities and alliances that characterized his political thought and activity. At times, Rothbard's approach more closely resembled that of his nineteenth-century American predecessors than it did his fellow twentieth-century libertarians. For example, while most libertarians regarded socialism as the ideological opposite of their view, Rothbard held that the real antithesis of libertarianism was not socialism but *conservatism*. As we will see more fully in chapter 5, Rothbard saw socialism as a "mixed" system that sought to achieve liberal goals of freedom and peace through conservative means of statism and hierarchy.[108] While state socialism was certainly something that libertarians ought to reject, Rothbard thought that it would be a mistake to view it as the primary threat to libertarian freedom. It would be an even *greater* mistake to do what many libertarians of the twentieth century actually did: compromise one's libertarianism in an alliance with conservatives in order to combat socialism.

Rothbard's influence on the libertarian movement was immense and multifaceted. He refined and popularized Misesean economics in his enormous *Man, Economy and State* (1962). He developed and spread libertarian views on politics and philosophy in *For a New Liberty* (1973) and *The Ethics of Liberty* (1982). He developed provocative revisionist views on the history of economic thought and economic history in *An Austrian Perspective on the History of Economic Thought* (1995) and *America's Great Depression* (1963). And he spread his own distinctive brand of libertarian commentary on current issues through his editorship of a number of journals and newsletters, including *Left and Right: A Journal of Libertarian Thought* (1965–68), the *Libertarian Forum* (1969–84), and the *Journal of Libertarian Studies* (1977–95). He was even the subject of a relatively sympathetic profile on libertarianism in the *New York Times* in 1971.[109]

Rothbard also cultivated a group of followers, including several other participants from Mises's NYU seminar such as Ralph Raico, George Reisman, and Leonard Liggio. The group met regularly during the 1950s and early 1960s in Rothbard's small West 88th Street apartment, calling themselves "The Circle Bastiat."[110] Bruce Goldberg, then a graduate student in philosophy at Princeton University, was also a frequent attendee. A former Trotskyist, Goldberg was described by Raico as "a fervent missionary, for whatever views he might hold at the time."[111] Once converted to libertarianism, Goldberg set to spreading libertarian ideas among fellow students back at Princeton. He tried his luck with George Will, who was studying political science. But he found more lasting and significant success with another philosopher whom he eventually managed to convince to spend an evening at Rothbard's apartment. Six years later, Robert Nozick would write in the acknowledgments of his libertarian treatise, *Anarchy, State, and Utopia*, that it was "a long conversation . . . with Murray Rothbard that stimulated my interest in individualist anarchist theory."[112]

Nozick's book was divided into three parts. The first part ("Anarchy") aimed to refute Rothbard's anarcho-capitalist position by showing how a minimal state could emerge from a state of nature via an "invisible hand" process without impermissibly violating anyone's rights. The second ("State") sought to argue that the minimal state was the *most* extensive state that was permissible—that any more extensive state would necessarily violate rights. Finally, the third part ("Utopia") cast the minimal state as an inspiring "framework for utopia" under which individuals could pursue various visions of the good life and the good society through voluntary cooperation with others.

While there is little direct engagement with socialism in Nozick's book—the second part is mainly dedicated to refuting Rawlsian "distributive justice" rather than Marxian socialism—the focus is nevertheless quite similar to the dominant trend of Cold War libertarian thought. In concentrating narrowly on the two issues of political authority and distributive justice, Nozick's book places questions about the relationship between the state and the economy at the core of libertarianism, to the exclusion of social issues of the sort that had concerned American libertarians in the nineteenth century. In terms of the theory, of course, there is nothing to prevent a reader from applying Nozick's libertarianism to issues of women's rights or sexual or religious freedom. But Nozick himself hardly mentions such issues. Even the one economic issue that had most concerned nineteenth-century American libertarians—the rights of laborers against politically privileged capitalists and landlords—is given scant attention in Nozick's text. Thus, Nozick did little to challenge either the exclusive economic focus or the generally rightward drift of twentieth-century libertarian thought. Indeed, by setting the terms of the academic conversation about libertarianism for decades to come, Nozick arguably reinforced those qualities as definitive of libertarianism as such.

Third Wave Libertarianism

We have argued that beginning in the late nineteenth century in Britain and France, and beginning in roughly the third decade of the twentieth century in the United States, libertarianism defined itself largely in opposition to state socialism. This opposition shaped the issues on which libertarians chose to focus and the political alliances libertarians formed in pursuit of those issues. Libertarians saw state socialism as the antithesis of freedom—as metaphorical, if not literal, "slavery" or "serfdom." So dire was this threat perceived to be that it came to dominate their writing and activism. Earlier nineteenth-century concerns over social liberties such as women's rights and sexual freedom were consigned to the margins of libertarian interest. Even those economic liberties that veered too close to the socialist agenda were marginalized, such as workers' rights or the injustice of landownership.

When the Berlin Wall fell in 1989, libertarianism was thus thrown into an identity crisis. If libertarianism was anti-socialism, and socialism was discredited, what was left of libertarianism?[113] The question would not be easily resolved. Multiple reinterpretations of libertarianism have emerged in the decades since the fall of Soviet communism. Some of these overlap in their aims and methodologies, others are sharply incompatible with others, but none has yet risen to dominance. So far, the Third Wave of libertarianism has been marked, more than anything else, by active contestation.

This section will identify three distinct strands in Third Wave libertarian thought. Each of them challenges, in some way or another, the narrow Cold War focus on economic issues and the challenge of socialism. But like Cold War libertarianism, each identifies itself largely in terms of its opposition to some perceived threat to liberty. In some cases, the shift involves elevating to primacy some threat that had played a supporting role for the Cold War libertarians—the threat of war, or of crony capitalism. In other cases, the perceived threat is one that had previously gone largely unrecognized or unaddressed—economic insecurity or an alleged erosion of the cultural values on which freedom rests.

The first strand of Third Wave thought emerged in 1990, when Llewelyn Rockwell Jr. published a manifesto for what he called paleo-libertarianism. Founder and president of the Ludwig von Mises Institute, Rockwell argued that libertarianism should seek a new alliance with the political right.[114] Unlike the Cold War alliance with the right, however, which had been based on the idea that libertarians were "economically conservative and socially liberal," Rockwell sought to move libertarianism in the direction of *cultural* conservativism. Seeking to free libertarianism of the "libertine muck" of 1960s-style moral relativism, paleo-libertarianism was a call for a libertarianism committed to the preservation of "Western culture," deference to "social authority—as embodied in the family, church [and] community," and "objective standards of morality, especially as found in the Judeo-Christian tradition." Two years later, Murray Rothbard would lend his name to the movement and spell out what he took to be the policy implications: slash welfare, abolish racial privileges such as affirmative action, "Crush Criminals," "Get Rid of the Bums," "End the Fed," "Defend Family Values," and "America First."[115]

Around the same time, a new form of libertarianism with a very different orientation began to stir, especially among academics. During the late 1980s, philosophers such as Loren Lomasky, David Schmidtz, and Gerald Gaus developed views that featured all or almost all of the markers of libertarianism we identified in chapter 1: a commitment to strong rights of private property, individualism, negative liberty, spontaneous order, free markets, and a skepticism of political authority.[116] Yet these theories differed sharply from the Randian, Nozickian, and Rothbardian forms of libertarianism that dominated the Cold War era. Broadly speaking, they were more empiricist, more pluralist, and more consequentialist. Most significantly, they were more willing to take seriously, and sometimes even endorse, ideas and policies that had generally been associated with academic theories on the political left: the importance of democratic legitimacy, the moral value of equality, and even the need for a limited form of redistributive welfare state.

It was not until the late 2000s and early 2010s, however, that these ideas were more identified as a distinct school of thought and pursued by a new generation of scholars and students. In 2011, Matt Zwolinski started "Bleeding Heart Libertarians," a blog devoted to "Free Markets and Social Justice." The next year, John Tomasi published *Free Market Fairness*, a book largely devoted to reconciling the free market ideas of Friedrich Hayek with the liberal egalitarianism of John Rawls. Meanwhile, Students for Liberty, an organization of student libertarian clubs founded in 2008, was exploring issues of intersectionality, structural inequality, racism, heterosexism, and a host of other stereotypically "progressive" issues in discussion groups, blogs, and conferences.

Similar ideas were developing outside of academia too. In 2006, Cato Institute vice president for research Brink Lindsey published an article in the *New Republic* titled "Liberaltarians." In it, Lindsey called for a new political alliance between libertarians and democrats grounded, at the philosophical level, in "some kind of reconciliation between Hayek and Rawls."[117] Will Wilkinson, Lindsey's colleague at Cato, signed on to the idea, dubbing the hoped-for philosophical fusion "Rawlsekianism."[118] Both left Cato soon after, presumably for what was then viewed as libertarian apostasy. But both would continue to pursue and develop this fusionist idea, culminating in 2014 with the formation of the Niskanen Center, a think tank devoted to translating liberal/libertarian fusion from abstract philosophy into concrete public policy.

Many orthodox libertarians criticized the Bleeding Heart movement for being too far to the left—or for not being "libertarian" at all. However, yet another group of libertarians sometimes took issue with them for being not *sufficiently* leftist. The contours of the ideological landscape here can be confusing, in part because some of the key figures in this movement—Roderick Long and Gary Chartier, for instance—were active contributors to the Bleeding Heart Libertarian (BHL) blog. Without question, there is a greater affinity between this group and BHL than there is between BHL and paleo-libertarianism. But, on the whole, "left libertarianism," or as it is sometimes more descriptively called, "left-wing market anarchism," is best conceived of as a distinct strand of Third Wave thought.

Unlike BHL, which, as the label "neoclassical liberals" suggests, can be thought of as a development of the classical liberalism of Smith, Hume, and Hayek, left-libertarianism is self-consciously a revival of the individualist anarchism of Molinari and Tucker. Where BHL tends to be empiricist, pluralist, and consequentialist, left-libertarianism tends to be rationalist, monist, and absolutist. Indeed, from a philosophical perspective, there is not much difference between left-libertarianism and the Cold War libertarianism of Rand, Rothbard, and Nozick (almost all left-libertarians reject Tucker's Stirnerite egoism). The main differences are not philosophical but empirical. Left-libertarians believe, first, that capitalism as it currently exists is unjust *by libertarian standards*. Second, they believe that a society based on truly "freed markets" would be one in which many traditionally left-wing goals of equality, worker autonomy, and decentralization of power would likely be achieved (see chapter 5). The main debates between Third Wave libertarians, *within the academy*, have been between the more moderate and empiricist Bleeding Hearts and the more rationalist left-libertarians.

But what about paleo-libertarianism? By 2007, Rothbard was dead, and Rockwell declared that he was no longer a paleo-libertarian.[119] But the belief that libertarianism fits more naturally with political conservativism than with liberalism would live on. Conservative libertarians insist that the libertarian commitment to freedom does not and cannot stand alone, and that culture, religion, and morality matter to give meaning to freedom, to define its limits, and to sustain the formal and informal institutions necessary for its preservation. These philosophical beliefs would lead them to attack the more common libertarian embrace of an "open borders" immigration policy, to reject the attempts of more left-leaning libertarians to make peace with certain aspects of the welfare state, and, in some instances, to support Donald Trump in both 2016 and 2020 as the candidate who would allegedly do the most to advance liberty overall. People disaffected with the political status quo—some espousing racist, xenophobic, and conspiracist worldviews—have been staking claims on the dark edges of the libertarian movement.

From a wider historical perspective, the contestation that marks contemporary libertarianism is no surprise. Between each of our three eras of libertarianism, and often within each era too, we find active struggles to define what "libertarianism" really is. The best way to deepen our understanding of this great historical struggle—between libertarianism's radical and reactionary elements—is to see it in action. Let's begin.

CHAPTER THREE

Land, Labor, and Ownership

THE RIGHT OF PRIVATE PROPERTY

Dominium Sui

In 1539, a hundred and fifty years before Locke's *Second Treatise*, the Dominican theologian Francisco de Vitoria delivered an important lecture at the University of Salamanca.

Since the early sixteenth century, Spain's brutal conquest of the New World had been built on the murder and enslavement of American Indians and the theft of their land and possessions. Under the notorious encomienda system, Spanish colonists were "given" a number of American Indians, ostensibly for the latter's "protection" (hence "encomienda" from the Spanish *encomendar*, meaning "to entrust"). In theory, colonists were to shelter the natives from intertribal violence and instruct them in the Catholic faith. In practice, the Indians were put to hard labor and their families subjected to torture, amputation, and even death.

Vitoria's lecture asked whether the moral law permitted Spanish missionaries to baptize the children of Indian nonbelievers against the wishes of their parents. But to answer this question, Vitoria saw that he must address a more fundamental concern: What is the moral status of the Indian?

Many of Vitoria's contemporaries assumed that Indians were the moral equivalent of animals. This meant that virtually *any* kind of ill treatment was justifiable. True, the Indians were human in a biological sense. But biology could not fully settle the moral question. Many Scholastics of Vitoria's time accepted Aristotle's doctrine of "natural slavery," according to which a certain "lower sort" of persons were "by nature slaves," such that it is "better for them as inferiors that they should be under the rule of a master."[1] As Juan de Sepulveda had written earlier in defense of the Spanish conquest: "The Spaniards rule with perfect right over the barbarians who, in prudence, talent, virtue and humanity are as inferior to the Spaniards as children to adults, women to men, the savage and cruel to the mild and gentile, the grossly intemperate to the continent, I might almost say as monkeys to men."[2]

For Vitoria, however, the intelligence or stupidity of the Indians was beside the point. Their fundamental moral status derived not from their wits but from the essential nature of the Indians as rational creatures. The Indians had the potential to be fully rational, Vitoria argued, but this natural potential had not been developed. As a result, though the Indians "seem to us insensate and slow-witted," this was due not to their nature but to their environment, to their "evil and barbarous education."[3] Fundamentally, Indians and Spaniards shared the same rational human nature. Because of that common rationality, they shared the same moral status:

> Every Indian is a man and thus is capable of attaining salvation or damnation. Every man is a person and is the master of his body and possessions. Inasmuch as he is a person, every Indian has free will and, consequently, is the master of his actions.[4]

Vitoria drew a striking political conclusion from this moral argument. Since Indians are humans, he reasoned, they are *self-owners*. As self-owners, they are capable of acquiring rights of ownership over the land on which they labor and live.[5] Therefore, Vitoria concluded, even if Indians are "barbarians," they nevertheless "undoubtedly possessed as true dominion, both public and private, as any Christians. That is to say, they could not be robbed of their property, either as private citizens or as princes, on the grounds that they were not true masters [*ueri domini*] . . . nor can they be counted among the slaves."[6] If the Spanish wished to acquire the land of the Indians, Vitoria argued, they could justly acquire it only through the same method they would use with any other human being: voluntary, mutually beneficial trade.[7]

The American Indian thus shared with the Spaniard the basic moral status of *dominium*, a concept that is often translated as "mastery," as in the quotation above. But as this quotation illustrates, *dominium* is an ambiguous concept.[8] Sometimes the term is used in a purely descriptive sense to refer to a kind of control or mastery of one's body or behavior. Thus, human beings have *dominium* in exercising free will and controlling their own behavior in ways that brute animals, or rocks and trees, cannot. Other times, however, *dominium* is used to refer not merely to control but to *rightful* control. In this sense, *dominium* is a normative concept. It expresses not only that one possesses control over the object of one's *dominium* but that it would be morally wrong for others to interfere with that control. *Dominium* in this sense is what we now refer to as a property right or "ownership." And *dominium sui*, or dominion over one's self, is what we would now describe as self-ownership.

These two senses of *dominium*—the descriptive and the normative—were related in Scholastic thought: it is *because* human beings have *dominium* in the sense of self-mastery or free will that they have *dominium* in the sense of self-ownership. To use more contemporary language, our nature as autonomous individuals gives us rightful claims to prevent others from treating us in certain ways without our consent.[9] Human beings are not means to the ends of others but ends in themselves.

Libertarian Self-Ownership

The idea that each of us has rightful dominion over our own body, and that it is therefore wrong for other individuals (or the state) to use that body without consent, would become one of the central principles of nineteenth- and twentieth-century libertarian thought, especially in what we have called "strict libertarianism."[10] The idea first surfaced in the United States in the mid-nineteenth century under the label "sovereignty of the individual."[11] According to

Josiah Warren, whose writings would have a profound impact on both Benjamin Tucker and John Stuart Mill:

> Society must be so converted as to preserve the SOVEREIGNTY OF EVERY INDIVIDUAL inviolate. That it must avoid all ... arrangements which will not leave every individual at all times at liberty to dispose of his or her person, and time, and property in any manner with which his or her feelings may dictate, WITHOUT INVOLVING THE PERSONS OR INTERESTS OF OTHERS.[12]

As we will see in the next chapter, the idea of individual sovereignty would play a significant role in the early American anarchist movement, especially in its connections with abolitionism. After all, to assert that each individual is sovereign over his or her self is to deny that any other individual or group has that claim. Just as individual sovereignty provides a point from which to push back against claims of authority made by masters over slaves, so too it provides grounds to push back against the claims of husbands over wives and of governments over citizens.

In the late nineteenth-century writings of the Spencerian Member of British Parliament Auberon Herbert, this idea of rightful dominion would receive its most notable early expression in the language used by libertarians today: self-ownership. In his "Principles of Voluntaryism," Herbert wrote:

> We hold that the one and only one true basis of society is the frank recognition of these rights of self-ownership; that is to say, of the rights of control and direction by the individual, as he himself chooses, over his own mind, his own body, and his own property, always provided, that he respects the same universal rights in others. We hold that so long as he lives within the sphere of his own rights, so long as he respects these rights in others, not aggressing by force or fraud upon the person or property of his neighbors, he cannot be made subject, apart from his own consent, to the control and direction of others, and he cannot be rightfully compelled under any public pretext, by the force of others, to perform any services, to pay any contributions, or to act or not to act in any manner contrary to his own desires or to his own sense of right. He is by moral right a free man, self-owning and self-directing; and has done nothing which justifies others, for any

convenience of their own, in taking from him any part, small or great, of his self-ownership.[13]

Of course, the idea of self-ownership, if not the phrase itself, had received its most influential expression a little over two centuries earlier, in the writings of the English philosopher John Locke.[14] In his *Second Treatise*, Locke wrote that "every man has a property in his own person: this no body has any right to but himself." From this principle, Locke went on to claim that each individual owns his or her own labor and, therefore (and within certain limits), what he or she *produces* with that labor. Locke's concept of self-ownership thus sanctioned an individual's ownership not only over his or her own body but over the land, animals, and other parts of the external world as well. We will explore the connection between self-ownership and world-ownership later in this chapter.

Locke's discussion of self-ownership and property rights would have an enormous influence on twentieth-century libertarianism, especially through the writings of Robert Nozick and Murray Rothbard.[15] But why should we accept that individuals are self-owners? Locke himself simply asserts the principle, and the arguments offered by later libertarians have often been disappointingly weak. Auberon Herbert, for instance, argued that "the great natural fact of each person being born in possession of a separate mind and separate body implies ownership of such mind and body by each person, and rights of direction over such mind and body."[16] But Herbert's argument was subject to devastating criticism by the more empirically minded British Individualist J. H. Levy:

> Why does the separate mind and body of the adult man imply one thing and the separate mind and body of the horse or child imply another? . . . I shall certainly not accept such a "philosophic basis for individualism," because "no other deduction" of the same sort "is reasonable." There is no deduction at all, but a gross and palpable *petitio principii*. The fact that an *ethical* principle is derived from a *single* "natural fact" is sufficient to discredit it with those who know what deduction means. We are here in the region of "high *priori*" mediævalism, not in that of modern scientific logic.[17]

In *For a New Liberty*, Murray Rothbard presented his own, equally problematic, argument for the principle of self-ownership.[18] Rothbard claims that there are three, and only three, possibilities regarding ownership of the self. Either (1) every individual is a full self-owner, (2) "a certain class of people, *A*, have the right to own another class, *B*," or (3) "everyone has the right to own his own equal quotal share of everyone else." Claim (2) "contradicts itself," according to Rothbard, because it proclaims that some humans have human rights of self-ownership while others lack them; it also "violates the basic economic requirement for life" because it allows some individuals to live parasitically at the expense of others. Claim (3), on the other hand, "rests on an absurdity" insofar as it holds that people are entitled to partial ownership of others but not of themselves; it is also impractical insofar as no one could survive if they required permission from all other persons before taking any action. Also, "if a world of zero self-ownership and one hundred percent other ownership spells death for the human race, then any steps in that direction also contravene the natural law of what is best for man and his life on this earth." Since (2) and (3) are unacceptable, we are left with (1), universal full self-ownership, by default.

This argument faces a host of difficulties.[19] Rothbard claims to find contradictions where there are none, relies on specious claims of slippery slopes, and, most seriously of all, ignores relevant alternatives to his three enumerated possibilities. That there are such alternatives should be obvious since virtually all of us inhabit one: we live under legal systems that respect neither "full self-ownership" nor universal communism. The structure of ownership in our societies is complex, composed of a wide range of rights that individuals may or may not have over a given object.[20] So the relevant question is not merely *whether* individuals own themselves or not but *how* and in *what respects* individuals own themselves, and how and in what respects their rights over themselves must be limited by the claims of others.

Perhaps the most promising argument for self-ownership is one that, ironically, does not actually mention the phrase "self-ownership" at all. In the first part of *Anarchy, State, and Utopia*, Robert Nozick makes an argument for what he calls libertarian side-constraints on the basis of an appeal to "the separateness of persons."[21] By "side-constraints," Nozick means to convey that respecting rights is not itself a goal to be maximized (e.g., by violating one person's rights in order to save ten other people from having *their* rights violated) but rather a limitation on the means we can take in order to pursue our goals. And by *libertarian* side-constraints, Nozick means that the content of these side-constraints is limited to protecting individuals from aggression by others.

Like his colleague and philosophical rival John Rawls, Nozick situates his own argument against classical utilitarianism.[22] He notes that utilitarianism allows for the sacrifice of the individual in order to advance the interests of the many but retorts that

> there is no *social entity* with a good that undergoes some sacrifice for its own good. There are only individual people, different individual people, with their own individual lives. Using one of those people for the benefit of others, uses him and benefits the others. Nothing more.[23]

It is one thing for someone to incur a cost now for the sake of later gain; moral balancing *within* a person's life is commonplace and morally unproblematic. Moral balancing *between* persons, however, is different entirely. Since the utilitarian does not seem to draw any distinction between these cases, Nozick concludes that utilitarianism "does not sufficiently respect and take account of the fact that [each individual] is a separate person, that his is the only life he has."[24]

Moreover, Nozick continues, the separateness of persons also entails that we should embrace libertarianism's austere account of the content of our rights. The force of Nozick's appeal to the separateness of persons draws on the Kantian notion that individuals are ends in themselves, not mere means for the advancement of others' ends. But if we really take that idea seriously—seriously enough to resist what Nozick calls the "powerful intuitive force of the end-state maximizing view"—then we have little ground to resist the libertarian "nonaggression principle": the conclusion that no individual may be sacrificed for another.

Nowhere in this argument does Nozick use the phrase "self-ownership," but the upshot of his position is difficult to distinguish from that of Herbert or Rothbard. Indeed, just a little later in

Anarchy, State, and Utopia, Nozick asks us to think of his theory of rights in the following way: "A line (or hyperplane) circumscribes an area in moral space around an individual. Locke holds that this line is determined by an individual's rights, which limit the actions of others."[25] Within the line, individuals are free to order their actions as they see fit, without seeking the permission of anyone else. Other individuals are, by and large, not permitted to cross that line without the individual's consent. And that is really all there is to the idea of self-ownership:

> The central core of the notion of a property right in X ... is the right to determine what shall be done with X; the right to choose which of the constrained set of options concerning X shall be realized or attempted. .... This notion of property helps us understand why earlier theorists spoke of people as having property in themselves and their labor. They viewed each person as having a right to decide what would become of himself and what he would do, and as having a right to reap the benefits of what he did.[26]

Libertarians continue to debate the extent of this right to control oneself, particularly on the question of whether one has the right to *alienate* that right by voluntary contract. Could an individual voluntarily sell him- or herself into slavery? Some libertarians say, along with Nozick, that the answer is "yes."[27] Part of what it means to own something, on this view, is having the right to sell it, or rent it out, or give it away for free. Others, however, regard self-ownership as an *inalienable* right, a normative claim grounded in the metaphysical nature of the individual as an autonomous being.[28] If self-ownership is part of your *nature* as a human being, then you cannot give it away any more than you can give away your nature as a rational being.

There is also significant disagreement among libertarians regarding the extent to which self-ownership constitutes an *absolute* bar against impositions by third parties. How, for instance, should libertarians deal with the problem of environmental pollution? If self-ownership is absolute, then even the smallest impositions of toxins, or benign but unwanted substances, or even perhaps light or sound waves constitute an impermissible infringement. However reasonable some constraints on pollution may be, an absolute prohibition on all "spillovers" of this sort seems incompatible with human social coexistence.[29]

Almost all strict libertarians, however, see self-ownership as the bedrock for their support of free-market capitalism and their opposition to state socialism. Following Locke, such libertarians typically perceive a neat chain of reasoning by which respect for self-ownership entails property rights in external resources, and by which respect for property rights (both external and internal) entails the legitimacy of capitalist economic arrangements. Likewise, libertarians claim that the socialist attack on capitalism must ultimately require a denial of self-ownership; and the denial of self-ownership is, to a greater or lesser extent, the endorsement of slavery.[30] "All socialism involves slavery," wrote Herbert Spencer in 1884, and the intensity of that slavery depends only on "how much is [each person] compelled to labour for other benefit than his own, and how much can he labour for his own benefit?"[31] Nozick similarly observed that "seizing the results of someone's labor is equivalent to seizing hours from him and directing him to carry on various activities. . . . [T]his process whereby they take this decision from you makes them a *part-owner* of you; it gives them a property right in you. . . . These principles involve a shift from the classical liberals' notion of self-ownership to a notion of (partial) property rights in *other* people."[32]

Of course, the claim that socialist redistribution entails a denial of self-ownership assumes that property rights in external resources like land and money can be derived from individuals' property in themselves. Whether and to what extent this is so is a matter of dispute even among libertarians. To see why, let's turn to an examination of the surprisingly complicated connection between labor and property in libertarian thought.

The Fruits of One's Labor

As we saw in the last section, some libertarians believe that socialist redistribution requires a denial of individual self-ownership. And some socialists agree. But not everyone who supports the redistribution of land or wealth rejects self-ownership. Indeed, in the nineteenth century a sharp split emerged between two camps of broadly libertarian theorists, each of which endorsed a strong form of self-ownership but disagreed regarding the implications of self-ownership for property in natural resources, especially land. For those familiar with libertarianism primarily through its contemporary varieties, this split illustrates one of the most surprising features of libertarianism as it manifested in the nineteenth century. During that period, in both Britain and in the United States, self-identified libertarian *socialists* were almost as common as the more familiar libertarian advocates of capitalism.

How did this split arise? As we have seen, many of the most influential libertarians in the nineteenth century followed John Locke in holding that every individual is a self-owner.[33] This view, which we will label here the "orthodox" libertarian position, further holds that because we own ourselves, we can also own external resources though the "mixing" of our labor. As John Locke famously explained the idea:

> The labour of his body, and the work of his hands, we may say, are properly his. Whatsoever then he removes out of the state that nature hath provided, and left it in, he hath mixed his labour with, and joined to it something that is his own, and thereby makes it his property. It being by him removed from the common state nature hath placed it in, it hath by this labour something annexed to it, that excludes the common right of other men: for this labour being the unquestionable property of the labourer, no man but he can have a right to what that is once joined to, at least where there is enough, and as good, left in common for others.[34]

But the metaphor of mixing one's labor with material resources would prove to be more mysterious than enlightening, and many later libertarians would either reject it outright or avoid its use altogether. As Robert Nozick would later ask, "If I own a can of tomato juice and spill it in the sea so that its molecules (made radioactive, so I can check this) mingle evenly throughout the sea, do I thereby come to own the sea, or have I foolishly dissipated my tomato juice?"[35] Thus, Lysander Spooner, whose position on property rights was largely (though not entirely) in line with that of Locke, chose to avoid the language of mixing in favor of the more straightforward idea that creators are entitled to that which they create. "Every man,"

Spooner wrote, "so far as, consistently with the principles of natural law, he can accomplish it—should be allowed to have the fruits, and all the fruits of his own labor."[36] Later in the twentieth century, Murray Rothbard and his followers would characterize original appropriation in terms of "homesteading."[37]

Spooner's and Rothbard's accounts of property differ from Locke's in another important respect. In the passage quoted above, Locke qualifies the right of appropriation by noting that it pertains "at least where there is enough, and as good, left in common for others." And later in his discussion of property, Locke claims that an individual's property rights are limited by a moral imperative to avoid waste:

> As much as any one can make use of to any advantage of life before it spoils; so much he may by his labour fix a Property in: whatever is beyond this, is more than his share, and belongs to others.[38]

Locke has generally been interpreted in these passages as placing certain provisos on the legitimate appropriation of natural resources.[39] Labor-mixing can generate property rights only if enough and as good is left for others, and only if that which is appropriated does not go to waste. Spooner and Rothbard, in contrast, clearly and unambiguously attach no such provisos to their views.[40] For these latter theorists, it would not be unjust for an individual or group of individuals to appropriate *all* of the available land and leave nothing for others. Whether such a view is consistent with libertarians' fundamental commitment to individual liberty and self-ownership is a matter about which there has been considerable and ongoing debate.[41]

Alongside these "orthodox" libertarian views, however, developed a variety of "heterodox" positions. These positions are all recognizably libertarian insofar as they affirm both a strong commitment to individual self-ownership and a deep skepticism of state authority as fundamentally incompatible with individual self-ownership. Nevertheless, they diverge from libertarian orthodoxy by denying the legitimacy of private property in land (and sometimes in *anything*) and by their strong moral criticism of capitalism in general, and wage labor, interest, profit, and rent in particular.

Indeed, a significant portion of these heterodox thinkers went so far as to identify themselves as *socialists*.

The idea of libertarian socialism will no doubt strike many contemporary readers as paradoxical, perhaps especially because we earlier described the rise of libertarianism as in part a *reaction* against socialism. But the term "socialism," like many other political concepts, carried with it a very different connotation in the nineteenth century than it does in twentieth-century and contemporary discourse. In particular, it is important to bear in mind that the figures we are discussing were writing well before socialism had become the organizing principle of large, centralized states like the Soviet Union and China. Those states, and their despotic, authoritarian character, became for many twentieth-century libertarians the paradigm by which all discussions of socialism were to be understood. And, understood in this way, the idea of a libertarian socialist is paradoxical indeed.

In the nineteenth and early twentieth centuries, however, it was much more common to conceive of socialism as a social ideal that could be implemented voluntarily, in the absence of state coercion. Thus, in one of his more famous essays, Benjamin Tucker was able to express his agreement with what he described as the "bottom claim of Socialism" that "labour should be put in possession of its own."[42] The view from which Tucker wished to distance himself and his fellow libertarians was not socialism but *state* socialism—"the doctrine that all the affairs of men should be managed by the government, regardless of individual choice." Socialism as such is compatible with liberty; it is only when socialism is implemented by the coercive monopoly of the state that it becomes problematic.

Heterodoxy among libertarians took a variety of different forms, not all of which can accurately be described as "socialist." And the variety of forms of heterodoxy is explained by the variety of different *reasons* for heterodoxy. To simplify what was truly a diverse and colorful intellectual landscape, we can classify the reasons for dissent from libertarian orthodoxy into three distinct categories: historical, economic, and moral. For reasons we will soon see, the economic argument for heterodoxy no longer has much influence among libertarians. The historical and moral arguments, on the other hand, remain influential to this day, and we will return to them later in this chapter.

Historical Arguments

Let us begin with the historical considerations. Libertarians in the Lockean tradition operate with what Robert Nozick called a historical conception of justice.[43] They believe that the justice of any particular distribution of resources depends on the process by which that distribution came about, and not on any structural features of the distribution such as how equal or unequal it may be. So long as each item of property in society was obtained through a just process of initial appropriation and transferred voluntarily from one owner to the next, the chain of title is legitimate and the resulting overall distribution is just. On Nozick's view, "whatever arises from a just situation by just steps is itself just."[44] The process consecrates the product.

The problem, as several prominent nineteenth-century libertarians noticed, is that the property arrangements of the actual capitalist societies they inhabited clearly did *not* arise "from a just situation by just steps." As Herbert Spencer wrote, in a scathing critique of Locke's doctrine of property,

> It can never be pretended that the existing titles to such property are legitimate. Should anyone think so, let him look in the chronicles. Violence, fraud, the prerogative of force, the claims of superior cunning— these are the sources to which those titles can be traced. . . . Could valid claims be thus constituted? Hardly. And if not, what becomes of the pretensions of all subsequent holders of estates so obtained?[45]

Thomas Hodgskin similarly devoted one of his most famous works to denouncing most legally recognized property rights as "artificial" rather than "natural" rights, since their basis lay in force and conquest rather than the only true source of entitlement: human labor.[46]

Hodgskin, but not Spencer, drew the anti-capitalist conclusion implicit in this reasoning. If the legitimacy of capitalist society depends upon the pedigree of the property rights on which it is based, and if that pedigree is flawed, then the legitimacy of capitalism disappears. Capitalism might still be justifiable in principle; one could *imagine* a capitalist society in which property rights were generated consistently with libertarian principles of peaceful appropriation and transfer. But if no *actually existing* capitalist society meets this standard, the justification of capitalism is relegated to theoretical possibility, divorced from life in the real world.

Economic Arguments

But while the historical argument for heterodoxy left the door open for the justification of capitalism in principle, the economic argument allowed no such leeway. In this argument, labor once again plays a central role. We have already seen how Locke and his followers believed that labor can give individuals original title over a previously unowned resource. Let us call this the *labor theory of entitlement*. Many libertarians have also subscribed to the belief that labor, and labor alone, confers *economic value* on a resource. We will call this idea the *labor theory of value*.

By the nineteenth century, the labor theory of value already had a long and distinguished pedigree in the classical liberal tradition, finding its most influential expressions in Adam Smith's *Wealth of Nations* and David Ricardo's *Principles of Political Economy*. Even in Locke, though, the idea was present, and this played an important role in his justification of property:

> it is labour indeed that puts the difference of value on every thing . . . I think it will be but a very modest computation to say, that of the products of the earth useful to the life of man nine tenths are the effects of labour: nay, if we will rightly estimate things as they come to our use, and cast up the several expences about them, what in them is purely owing to nature, and what to labour, we shall find, that in most of them ninety-nine hundredths áre wholly to be put on the account of labour.[47]

What troubled the nineteenth-century libertarians who accepted both the labor theory of entitlement and the labor theory of value was the existence of parasitical classes who appeared to consume the value produced by others' labor without laboring themselves.[48]

Here, for example, is how Thomas Hodgskin described landlords who lived on the rents of their tenants:

> The mere landowner is not a labourer, and he never has been even fed but by violating the natural right of property. Patiently and perseveringly, however, has the law endeavoured to maintain his privileges, power, and wealth. To support the government the aristocracy has sometimes made laws trenching on its own privileges, but after enforcing submission to government, the next object of the law has been to preserve the dominion and power of the aristocracy over the land.[49]

Hodgskin leveled a similar critique at capitalists. Capitalists, at least in their capacity as mere owners of capital, earn their money not through labor but through their possession of a scarce resource needed by others. Of course, a capitalist, like a landlord, might *also* earn money through labor—by overseeing the firm, attracting investors, selecting tenants, and so forth. And to whatever wealth they earn through their labor, they are entitled. But since the wealth they earn qua capitalists or landlords is not due to any *value* they create, the only way they are able to secure that income is through coercion. Landlords and capitalists are thus, on Hodgskin's view, parasites who survive only by capturing the coercive power of the state and using it to support their illegitimate, privileged position.[50] Views such as these earned Hodgskin the label of "Ricardian socialist" for reasons that are at least intelligible if not fully compelling.[51]

Benjamin Tucker, too, subscribed to a version of the labor theory of value, along with the idea (made famous by Marx) that laborers produce "surplus value" (value over and above that which they receive in exchange for their product) and that this surplus value is appropriated by various powerful elites within society.[52] Like Hodgskin, Tucker saw these elites as ultimately deriving their power from the state. But Tucker went beyond Hodgskin in identifying not merely rent paid on land but also profit, interest, and intellectual property rights as sources of this "usury."[53] Of these, Tucker saw the money monopoly as most fundamental. By maintaining a monopoly on the issuance of currency, the state created an artificial scarcity of money that Tucker believed inflated its price (the interest rate). Artificially high interest rates prevented workers from obtaining the capital needed to become independent entrepreneurs and thus forced them into wage labor where they would again be taken advantage of by capitalists.[54]

Many libertarians still hold to the labor theory of entitlement. The labor theory of value, however, was largely discredited by the marginalist revolution in economics and has few adherents among libertarians or, for that matter, their critics.[55] Of course, it remains possible to criticize capitalists and landlords on the grounds that their wealth is in some way ill-gotten. But the grounds of this critique can no longer be based on the bankrupt claim that labor is the only source of economic value.

Moral Arguments

In addition to historical and economic objections to the orthodox libertarian position on property rights and capitalism, some libertarians raised purely moral objections. The most famous of these took aim at Locke's contention that by mixing one's labor with the land, one could come to wield private ownership over it. Henry George, in his best-selling *Progress and Poverty*, claimed that even if one accepts the Spoonerian idea that creators are entitled to that which they create, this does nothing to establish the case for private property in land since, of course, the land itself was not created by anybody.[56] According to George, while individuals do own themselves and own their labor, their self-ownership rights fail to give rise to property in land (contra Locke) and are indeed positively *incompatible* with it.[57]

> The recognition of individual proprietorship of land is the denial of the natural rights of other individuals. . . . For as labor cannot produce without the use of land, the denial of the equal right to the use of land is necessarily the denial of the right of labor to its own produce. If one man can command the land upon which others must labor, he can appropriate the produce of their labor as the price of his permission to labor. . . . The one receives without producing; the others produce without receiving.[58]

Thus, according to George, landlords hold no just title to their land. Society would be within its rights if it set about immediately "abolishing all private titles, declaring all land public property, and letting it out to the highest bidders."[59] But this would involve a great shock to existing social practices and a great extension of governmental machinery. And this for no real purpose, since justice could be just as fully achieved by leaving land in the hands of those who currently claim to "own" it and confiscating not the land itself but only the *economic rent* that those owners derive from it—the "part of the produce that accrues to the owners of land . . . by virtue of ownership."[60] This confiscation would be the basis of the Georgist "Single Tax," so-called because George believed that the revenue generated by it would be sufficient to fund all of the proper functions of government and thus allow for the abolition of all other taxes.

George was not the first to articulate this argument. In 1775, the English schoolmaster and political pamphleteer Thomas Spence delivered a speech titled "The Real Rights of Man" in which he claimed that to deny the joint right of every individual to the free use of the earth would be equivalent to "denying them the right to live."[61] Thomas Paine put forward a similar argument in his 1797 pamphlet "Agrarian Justice."

Perhaps more surprisingly, Herbert Spencer himself set forth a strikingly similar argument in the first (1851) edition of *Social Statics*, writing that laborers are only entitled to the extra value their labor imparts to the land, not the land itself.[62] The land belongs to society as a whole, and society can and should assert its right, especially since doing so would, in Spencer's view, "cause no very serious revolution in existing arrangements." All that would be required, thought Spencer, was a "change of landlords."

> Separate ownerships would merge into the joint-stock ownership of the public. Instead of being in the possession of individuals, the country would be held for the great corporate body—Society. . . . [W]ithout any infraction of the law of equal freedom, an individual may lease from society a given surface of soil, by agreeing to pay in return a stated amount of the produce he obtains from that soil.[63]

Partly due to the clarity of his expression, and partly due to the tremendous fame he would acquire in the latter part of the nineteenth century, Spencer's presentation of this idea would become extremely influential, inspiring not only later theoreticians such as

Henry George (who cited Spencer frequently and approvingly in *Progress and Poverty*) but also a great deal of interest from the general public. The relevant chapter from *Social Statics* was frequently reprinted and distributed as a stand-alone pamphlet by Georgist political groups such as the English Land Restoration League.

Spencer, however, was not entirely comfortable with the use to which his arguments were put by such groups and often complained that the position he set out in *Social Statics* had been misunderstood and misapplied. When he issued a revised edition of the book in 1892, many of those in the land-reform movement who had valorized him were shocked to find that the chapter titled "The Right to the Use of the Earth," which contained Spencer's arguments against the legitimacy of property in land, had been cut altogether.[64]

Spencer felt misunderstood partly because *Social Statics* was, as we have seen, written as an exercise in what philosophers would today call "ideal theory" and not as a guide to immanent political reform. But the later Spencer found other problems with his 1851 views as well. In his updated treatment of property in his 1891 *Principles of Ethics*, he argued that the law of equal freedom did not require any fundamental changes to the existing system of land tenure at all, since the communal ownership of the land was already implicitly recognized in the right of the state to take private property for public use, provided compensation was paid.[65]

Spencer himself never regarded his position on the morality of the land issue to have changed, writing that he "adhere[d] to the inference originally drawn [in *Social Statics*], that the aggregate of men forming the community are the supreme owners of the land."[66] However, as he explained in 1893 in a letter to one of his American followers, he had changed his mind about whether the community's rightful ownership should be *exercised* by actually claiming ownership of all the land. In 1851, he had thought such an exercise would be both in accordance with justice and beneficial to the community as a whole. By 1893, however, he felt that the costs of the required compensation to landowners for all their improvements to the land beyond its natural state would be prohibitively high, such that the transaction would cost the community more than it would gain. Moreover, he professed to have lost much of what little faith he had in the effectiveness of government, concluding that a "system of public administration, full of the vices of officialdom, would involve more evils than the present system of private administration."[67]

Spencer's change of heart may have been more a matter of practical politics than philosophical reflection. As the nineteenth century waned, Spencer became increasingly conservative and pessimistic. Socialism's threat was imminent. For Spencer, movements for land reform (such as the Irish Land Act of 1881) were proxy battles in the struggle against socialism, which required resistance through organizations such as the Liberty and Property Defense League, an organization with which Spencer was aligned but to which he could never convince himself to fully sign on.[68]

Henry George, meanwhile, was not impressed. In a lengthy treatise denouncing Spencer as a "perplexed philosopher," George described Spencer's new position on land reform as "intellectually and morally beneath contempt."[69] Nevertheless, despite his criticism of Spencer and his advocacy of the nationalization of economic rent, George defended his own libertarian credentials, writing that within the line circumscribed by *properly* designated property rights,

> I have always opposed government interference. I have been an active, consistent, and absolute free-trader, and an opponent of all schemes that would limit the freedom of the individual. I have been a stauncher denier of the assumption of the right of society to the possessions of each member, and a clearer and more resolute upholder of the rights of property than Mr. Spencer. I have opposed every proposition to help the poor at the expense of the rich. I have always insisted that no man should be taxed because of his wealth, and that no matter how many millions a man might rightfully get, society should leave to him every penny of them.[70]

George's philosophy was immensely influential in the United States in the late nineteenth and early twentieth centuries. *Progress and Poverty* sold millions of copies and achieved a popular readership unheard of for a treatise on political economy. George narrowly missed being elected mayor of New York City on two separate occasions. And while his ideas have always been controversial and hotly contested, they have inspired a line of thinkers and activists that includes the twentieth-century libertarian Albert Jay Nock, con-temporary left-libertarian academics such as Hillel Steiner, and the popular "geo-libertarian" movement of today.[71]

Other libertarians were more radical than George in their departure from Lockean orthodoxy. For example, Tucker rejected not only the natural rights framework on which Locke based his position but also the idea that a single act of labor could estab-lish a permanent individual property right in land.[72] For Tucker, following in the footsteps of the French anarchist Pierre-Joseph Proudhon and the American libertarian socialist J. K. Ingalls, the only legitimate property is that rooted in continued occupancy and use. This "mutualist" position, according to Tucker, requires the protection "of all people who desire to cultivate land in the posses-sion of whatever land they cultivate, without distinction between the existing classes of landlords, tenants, and laborers, and the positive refusal of the protecting power to lend its aid to the col-lection of any rent whatsoever."[73] According to Tucker, this view has the advantage of tying property in land *more* closely to labor than the orthodox Lockean view, insofar as it rules out the possibil-ity of "absentee landlords" and other owners who may never have worked a single day on the land they own. Moreover, the mutualist position required no complicated machinery of state—or indeed, in Tucker's view, any state at all—to enforce. Unlike the Georgist position, which requires the state to assess and collect the economic rent of all properties, the mutualist view creates an absolute right of the owner to his or her land, so long as that right is maintained by occupancy and use.

Property in Ideas

Even among libertarians agreed upon the principle of self-ownership, there is thus considerable disagreement regarding the implications of this principle for the justice of existing property claims in external resources. But even this disagreement pales in comparison with the controversy among libertarians regarding the legitimacy of property in *ideas*.

In the nineteenth century, both Herbert Spencer and Lysander Spooner argued that intellectual property was a requirement of justice, resting on the same foundation as property in tangible goods. For Spencer, as we have seen, that foundation was the law of equal freedom.[74] He held that since one who acquires new knowledge through his own mental labor does not in any way restrict the freedom of others to do the same, "it follows that he has a *right* to so claim [his original ideas]; or, in other words, such ideas are his property."[75] Indeed, Spencer argues, the case for property in ideas is in at least one respect *stronger* than the case for property in tangible goods, "since that which constitutes [the former's] value is exclusively created by the worker."[76] That is, unlike material goods created from natural resources, the creation of ideas takes nothing from the common stock of humankind. Thus, Spencer concludes, there is no obvious reason why the *duration* of intellectual property should not be at least as long as that of tangible property. In other words, property in ideas should be permanent and bequeathable.[77]

Spencer's argument vacillates somewhat uneasily between appeals to the idea of equal freedom and appeals to the role of mental *labor* in justifying intellectual property. One might wonder, for instance, why the principle that "each man shall have the greatest freedom compatible with the like freedom of all others" should not imply that ideas should be open to all, since by the nature of ideas one person's use of an idea does not at all diminish another's ability to use it.[78] By contrast, Lysander Spooner's argument for intellectual property makes no reference to the idea of equal freedom and relies solely on the Lockean view that individuals are entitled to a property right in that which they create or discover.

Spooner's essay "The Law of Intellectual Property" sets forth not merely a theory of intellectual property but also a theory of property in general. In its broad outlines, it is strongly and explicitly Lockean, though as we have seen Spooner rejects both the Lockean metaphor of "labor-mixing" and the idea of any restrictive proviso on original appropriation.

For Spooner, it does not matter whether we regard ideas as created (as in the case of books or music) or discovered (as in the case of physical laws of nature). If the former, then "the right of property in them belongs to him, whose labor created them; on the same principle that any other wealth, created by human labor, belongs right fully, as property, to its creator, or producer." If the latter, then the right of property follows from the principle of first possession.[79] In either case, the right of property in one's ideas is "a natural and absolute right—and if a natural and absolute, then necessarily a perpetual, right."[80] Indeed, according to Spooner, "so absolute is an author's right of dominion over his ideas, that he may forbid their being communicated even by the human voice, if he so pleases."[81]

Spooner stands virtually alone among the late nineteenth-century American anarchists in his strident defense of intellectual property rights. Though debate on the topic raged for three years between 1888 and 1891 in the pages of *Liberty*, the vast majority of libertarians associated with that periodical were firmly opposed to the morality of both copyrights and patents.[82] Benjamin Tucker, in particular, was vehement on the issue, dismissing Spooner's essay on intellectual property as "the only positively silly work which ever came from Mr. Spooner's pen."[83]

For Tucker, intellectual property rights were a form of usury, one of the "four monopolies" enabling authors and inventors to "extort from the people a reward enormously in excess of the labour measure of their services,—in other words, in giving certain people . . . the power to exact tribute from others for use of this natural wealth, which should be open to all."[84] Nor can intellectual property be grounded in ownership of one's body or one's mental labor. It is true, as Spooner claimed, that others "cannot force [a man] to give his ideas to them," but this is not because the individual has any property in his ideas. Rather it is because he has a *power* to keep the idea private, which power is protected by other (genuine) rights, such as "the right of inviolability of the person, the right of privacy of domicile, and the right of contract."[85]

For Tucker, property as an institution emerged to address a certain sort of problem—the problem of scarcity. Because different people with different desires have conflicting uses for scarce resources, we need some method for determining who gets what. Ideas, however, are not scarce. Ideas can be used "by any number of individuals in any number of places at precisely the same time, without in the slightest degree impairing the use thereof by any single individual."[86] Property in ideas therefore serves no useful end and, in fact, is positively harmful insofar as it limits society's ability to derive maximum benefit from useful ideas by encouraging their widest possible spread and use.

Moreover, Tucker denied that there was any principled distinction to be drawn between copyrights and patents. Henry George had argued that copyrights were permissible, since the ideas involved there were pure acts of creation; but he rejected patents, which involved mere discoveries of preexisting laws of nature.[87] Tucker, in response, claimed that "the same argument that demolishes the right of the inventor demolishes the right of the author." The writing of literature is no more an act of pure creation than the invention of a new machine, for both merely involve the rearrangement of preexisting materials—words in the one case, physical objects in the other.[88]

Among twentieth-century libertarians, the debates over intellectual property mostly played out along the lines opened up by Spencer, Spooner, and Tucker, though by the end of the century the opponents of intellectual property greatly outnumbered proponents, at least among strict libertarians. Ayn Rand stands out as the main libertarian proponent of strong intellectual property rights, while Murray Rothbard, Tom Palmer, Roderick Long, and Stephan Kinsella have written extensively against them.[89] On the whole, libertarians with a more consequentialist moral framework, such as Ludwig von Mises, Friedrich Hayek, and Milton Friedman, were more supportive of certain varieties of intellectual property than their Lockean brethren.[90] As we shall see in the next section, an approach to property rights rooted in the ideas of Mill and Hume has played an influential role in the development of this line of libertarian thought, one that both challenges and, perhaps, strengthens the better-known Lockean approach.

A Different Libertarian Approach to Property

The ideas and debates concerning property discussed in this chapter have thus far arisen within a broadly Lockean form of strict libertarianism. For those who embrace this approach, the idea of property plays a fundamental, almost axiomatic role in libertarian thought. Self-ownership is seen as a basic natural right, and the rest of libertarian theory is essentially just a spelling-out of the implications of consistently respecting that right. Self-ownership implies property rights; property rights imply free exchange; and free exchange implies a strictly limited state (if any state at all).

There is, however, another approach to libertarianism, one with origins not in seventeenth-century England but eighteenth-century Scotland, and in particular the ideas of the philosopher and historian David Hume. On this approach, property rights are not natural but artificial. They are social constructs developed to help people solve recurring problems of social life, problems springing from the self-ishness, limited generosity, scarcity, and instability of possession that characterize human social existence.[91] And while the libertarians who use this approach view property as a particularly important construct, they do not view property rights as having the same axiomatic, absolute status as do those in the Lockean tradition. This sort of libertarianism is more pluralistic in its methodological and normative approaches and, as a consequence, less absolutist with respect to any particular idea or value, including property rights.

The starting point for this approach is the eighteenth-century utilitarian moral philosopher William Paley's observation that without rules to determine who gets what in a world of scarce resources, "war and waste, tumult and confusion, must be unavoidable and eternal." Indeed, Paley gave particular importance to one sort of "tumult and confusion," drawing a lesson from his observation of how people treat things that no one owns:

> A cherry-tree in a hedge-row, nuts in a wood, the grass of an unstinted pasture, are seldom of much advantage to anybody, because people do not wait for the proper season of reaping them. Corn, if any were sown, would never ripen; lambs and calves would never grow up to sheep and cows, because the first person that met them would reflect, that he had better take them as they are, than leave them for another.[92]

Paley had identified what the twentieth-century ecologist Garrett Hardin would later famously call the "tragedy of the commons."[93] Self-interested people just don't have much incentive to care for resources they don't own. Unowned resources see too much use and too little investment, as both the costs of one's use and the benefits of one's investments are largely *externalized*. Why not overuse when it is mostly other people who suffer the consequence? Why invest when others reap most of the benefit?

The Plymouth Colony in early America learned this lesson through hard experience. Due to the insistence of its English financiers (the Merchant Adventurers corporation), Plymouth's founding required that all property be held in common for the first seven years.[94] Whatever crops were grown, whatever game was hunted, and whatever fish were caught would all be thrown into a common pool from which anyone could draw. This, it was thought, would maximize corporate profits and allow the settlers to repay their debt quickly. Once the debt was paid, the common stock would be divided into private parcels and the settlers could work for themselves.

Within three years, however, this "common course" experiment had failed disastrously. Governor William Bradford wrote in his journal:

> [the system of common ownership] was found to breed much confusion and discontent and retard much employment that would have been to their benefit and comfort. For the young men, that were most able and fit for labour and service, did repine that they should spend their time and strength to work for other men's wives and children without any recompense. The strong, or man of parts, had no more in division of victuals and clothes than he that was weak and not able to do a quarter the other could; this was thought injustice.[95]

The colony's corporate-imposed communalism was producing a tragedy of the commons. So in 1623 Bradford did what he thought was necessary to bring that tragedy to an end: he unilaterally broke the contract with the financiers and assigned the families of the colony private ownership over their own individual plots of land. The result, according to Bradford, was an immediate and dramatic change in the colonists' attitudes and behavior. The establishment of private plots

> made all hands very industrious, so as much more corn was planted than otherwise would have been by any means the Governor or any other could use, and saved him a great deal of trouble, and gave far better content. The women now went willingly into the field, and took their little ones with them to set corn; which before would allege

weakness and inability; whom to have compelled would have been thought great tyranny and oppression.[96]

In the case of Plymouth Colony, then, the tragedy of the commons was resolved by an explicit order establishing private property in land and other valuable resources. We should be cautious, however, in generalizing too broadly from this one particular case. The establishment of private property is not the only solution to the tragedy of the commons, nor is it even the only solution to which libertarian thinkers have drawn attention.[97] More importantly, the *process* by which private property was established in the case of Plymouth Colony—the express command of a political authority—is both historically anomalous and, in an important way, quite unrepresentative of the Humean strain of libertarian thought we are now considering.

Hume thought that rational people marked by the circumstances of justice would quickly see that it was to their advantage to enter into a kind of "convention" in order to

> bestow stability on the possession of those external goods, and leave every one in the peaceable enjoyment of what he may acquire by his fortune and industry. By this means, every one knows what he may safely possess.[98]

Hume was careful, however, to emphasize that by "convention" he did not mean anything like an *explicit agreement* or *promise*. What drives the development of property institutions in most cases is not conscious deliberate design but

> only a general sense of common interest; which sense all the members of the society express to one another, and which induces them to regulate their conduct by certain rules. I observe, that it will be for my interest to leave another in the possession of his goods, *provided* he will act in the same manner with regard to me. He is sensible of a like interest in the regulation of his conduct. When this common sense of interest is mutually express'd, and is known to both, it produces a suitable resolution and behaviour. And this may properly enough be call'd a convention or agreement betwixt us, tho' without the interposition of a promise; since the actions of each of us have a reference to those of the other, and are perform'd upon the supposition, that something is to be perform'd on the other part.[99]

Property is conventional, then, in the same way that two men pulling the oars of the boat regulate the pace of their rowing by convention, or in the same way that the development of language, or the adoption of gold and silver as money, is governed by convention.[100] In each of these cases, individuals coordinate their activity without any explicit agreement to coordinate, and often without either the *intention* to coordinate or the *understanding* of what form such coordination will ultimately take. The rules of coordination emerge from the interaction of many different individuals, rather than being imposed by design from above (as happened in Plymouth).

For libertarians in the Humean tradition, property rights are a manifestation of spontaneous order.[101] And in some ways, it is the spontaneity of the process, rather than the precise nature of the institutions that ultimately emerge from that process, that such libertarians regard as most significant. The Humean emphasis on decentralized solutions to social problems can therefore seem to diverge quite sharply from the Lockean emphasis on property as a universal, natural human right. Consider, for example, the influential discussion of property from the contemporary Humean libertarian David Schmidtz.[102] Much of that discussion touches on what are by now well-known libertarian themes, such as the ability of private property to address the tragedy of the commons and the way in which the original appropriation of previously unowned resources can benefit later generations even more than it benefits appropriators themselves.[103] But Schmidtz emphasizes that private property is not a unique or universal solution to the problems of scarcity and rivalrous use. Thus, Schmidtz (along with other Humean libertarians) cites approvingly the work of Harold Demsetz, showing how an unregulated commons can function when populations are small and resources are abundant, as with the indigenous tribes of the Labrador Peninsula prior to the advent of the fur trade.[104] He cites the work of Robert Ellickson, showing how communal property arrangements can, under certain circumstances, effectively manage resources in a way that allows for both significant flexibility and the spreading of individual risk.[105] Schmidtz also cites the work of Elinor Ostrom, the first woman to win the Nobel Prize in Economics, who discusses in detail the various ways in which communities have arrived at voluntary, decentralized methods for effectively avoiding the tragedy of the commons.[106]

For Schmidtz, as for Hume, property rights are a means to an end, not a natural, inalienable right. And the end toward which they are a means is "mutual advantage." As Eric Mack describes this idea in his excellent primer on libertarianism, "general compliance with certain principles of justice engenders a cooperative social and economic order that is advantageous to all of its members."[107] In the twentieth century, the most influential libertarian in this tradition was the Austrian economist and social theorist Friedrich Hayek, whose approach to questions of property and justice was self-consciously indebted to that of Hume.[108] And Hayek, like Hume before him, saw property rights and other institutions of a liberal society as crucial tools allowing individuals to live together in conditions of scarcity, diversity, and disagreement.

Property rights solve these problems, according to Hayek, by carving out a kind of moral space in which individuals can make their own decisions without needing to seek permission from anyone else. *We* do not have to decide what the insides of *our* homes will look like—whether they will all have televisions or not, whether richly or sparsely decorated, and so on. Instead, *I* get to decide what the inside of *my* house will look like, and *you* get to make the same decision for *yours*. Even if our aesthetic or pragmatic values clash, we can both have things our way.

Hayek argued that this system of "several property" allows individuals to use the knowledge they have of their own particular circumstances to advance their ends.[109] In any complex society, most of the knowledge necessary to coordinate activity and utilize resources effectively is dispersed. Each individual knows certain "particular circumstances of time and place" that other individuals lack and that cannot possibly be collected and utilized by a central authority.[110] What are the soil conditions on my farm? How much extra storage space do I have in my railway cars? Do I have a spare room that I could rent out for extra income? In order to ensure that this dispersed knowledge is used effectively, it is imperative that decision-making authority be dispersed as well. And this is precisely what private property allows.

Property rights also serve as an indispensable foundation for the development of trade, the division of labor, and the emergence of market prices.[111] Together these have made possible that complex interpersonal coordination and cooperation that characterizes modern life, as well as the stunningly dramatic increases in wealth and improvements in living standards that have accompanied it.[112]

People differ from each other not only in their knowledge of economic conditions but in their values. And here, too, it is impossible for any central planner to devise a scheme that can adequately account for this diversity. Thus, for Hayek, private property accommodates "the multiplicity of separate and incommensurable ends of all its separate members."[113] As he explains,

> It is as much because we lack the knowledge of a common hierarchy of the importance of the particular ends of different individuals as because we lack the knowledge of particular facts, that the order of the Great Society must be brought about by the observance of abstract and end-independent rules.[114]

Rights of private property are thus closely connected with the libertarian value of *freedom*. If property is best understood as a kind of jurisdiction over some portion of the world—the right to make authoritative, unilateral decisions in disposing with that part of that world—then to have a property right *just is* to be free to use that thing as one wishes. And to be free to use something as one wishes means having a property right in it. For this reason, Hayek called private property "an essential condition for the prevention of coercion," even if it is not the *only* condition.[115] To have a property right—in one's home, one's land, one's self—is to have the right to make the final say, without being subject to the dominating will of another.

Humean Solutions to Lockean Problems

We saw earlier in this chapter how the "orthodox" Lockean libertarian position faces two remaining challenges once the economic objection falls along with its labor theory of value. The first of these objections, found in the work of Thomas Hodgskin and others, draws on the observation that many existing titles to land are rooted in unjust theft and violence rather than honest labor. The second objection, found in the work of Henry George and elsewhere, claims that even honest labor cannot justify valid titles in land, since land itself is not the product of labor but its necessary input.

Orthodox libertarians have tended to respond in one of two ways to the problem of historical injustice, each of which faces its own particular challenges. One approach has been to brush off concerns about historical injustice as irrelevant, since the victims are either all dead or impossible to identify. Here, for example, is Herbert Spencer's dismissive response to the claims of the English Land Restoration League in an 1894 letter to the *Daily Chronicle*:

> My argument in *Social Statics* was based upon the untenable assumption that the existing English community had a *moral* right to the land. They never had anything of the kind. They were robbers all round: Normans robbed Danes and Saxons, Saxons robbed Celts, Celts robbed the aborigines, traces of whose earth-houses we find here and there. Let the English Land Restoration League find the descendants of these last, and restore the land to them. There never was any equity in the matter, and re-establishment of a supposed equity is a dream. The stronger peoples have been land-thieves down to the present hour.[116]

Spencer's follower Auberon Herbert argued similarly that

> if land was taken from Saxon by Norman, it had been previously taken by Saxon from Briton, and by Briton from the long-headed race.... [A]ncient history therefore ... gives no true title for another taking of the land, since it discloses no true previous title existing anywhere. If property has been stolen, and restitution has to be made, you must be able to show the person from whom it has been stolen, and to whom it is to be restored.[117]

The problem with these arguments is that, pragmatic as they may appear, they are entirely inconsistent with the strict libertarian approach to justice and property. A doctrine based on a historical conception of entitlement cannot dismiss history as irrelevant simply because it is inconvenient. Moreover, while it is true that no solution to the problem of historical injustice will be perfect, we cannot avoid imperfection through inaction. For to do nothing, in this context, is to affirm and enforce a property arrangement that we know to be the product of injustice, and thereby to entrench and extend that injustice.

Indeed, some radical libertarians made precisely this point. Lysander Spooner, for instance, argued that the mere passage of time could never right the injustice of past thefts:

> Every successive holder not only indorses all the robberies of all his predecessors, but he commits a new one himself by withholding the lands, either from the original and true owners, or from those who, but for those robberies, would have been their legitimate heirs and assigns.[118]

Similarly, Murray Rothbard argued that because states necessarily acquire their property through unjust means, any property held by the state is illegitimate and subject to reappropriation, preferably by the people who actually *worked* on the property (though anybody other than the state would do in a pinch). Thus ownership of state-run universities should be ceded to the faculty and/ or students; ownership of General Dynamics—a corporation deriving much of its income from defense contracts with the federal government—should be turned over to the individuals who work there; and so on.[119]

Of course, making restoration is both pragmatically difficult (in identifying the perpetrators and victims of injustice, or their heirs) and morally problematic (if, as seems likely, significant costs of the reparations will fall on innocent persons). Spooner and Rothbard's radical libertarian position on this issue is thus, while perhaps more consistent than the conservative approach taken by Spencer and Herbert, no more fully satisfactory.

Here is where the Humean approach can perhaps help. Historical injustice poses such a problem for the Lockean libertarian because, for those in this camp, property rights are meant to reflect a natural and nearly absolute moral right.[120] But this is not how the Humean account asks us to think about property, or indeed about justice more generally. Property rights, on the Humean view, aren't meant to be a deep reflection of some kind of underlying natural entitlement. They are a social convention designed to solve a certain kind of pervasive social problem.

For the Humean, we need property rights to prevent conflict over scarce resources. Property rights serve their purpose by making clear what is *mine* and what is *yours*, for it is only once such boundaries are drawn and publicly recognized that people can safely approach each other for mutually beneficial cooperation and trade.

In order for property rights to serve this purpose, they must be established on the basis of clear, fixed, and generally accepted *rules*. But not just any rules. A rule requiring that everybody ought to get exactly what they deserve, while perhaps pleasing to our intuitive sense of justice, would be disastrous as a social policy. Such a rule would not *settle* conflict but provoke it.[121] A rule that held that "every one continue to enjoy what he is at present master of" seems to have less to recommend it from the perspective of ideal morality;[122] who winds up with what in the historical distribution of wealth is often determined as much by injustice and brute luck as it is by labor and voluntary trade. But for a Humean, these contingent social facts matter a great deal. Such are the human sentiments, writes Hume, that custom

> not only reconciles us to any thing we have long enjoy'd, but even gives us an affection for it, and makes us prefer it to other objects, which may be more valuable, but are less known to us. What has long lain under our eye, and has often been employ'd to our advantage, *that* we are always the most unwilling to part with; but can easily live without possessions, which we never have enjoy'd, and are not accustom'd to.[123]

This means that recent injustices naturally lead to conflict in a way that more distant ones do not. In the words of the contemporary Humean libertarian David Schmidtz:

> Dwelling too much on the past is wrong for the same reason that ignoring the past altogether is wrong: Excess in *either* direction reduces stability in transactions, thus making it harder to go forward in peace. A routine title search when buying a house (to verify that the seller's holding of the deed is in fact uncontested) is one thing; going back as many centuries as the land has been occupied is another.[124]

The Humean position thus arrives at a conclusion similar to the relatively conservative libertarianism of Herbert and the later Spencer, but with a more principled basis for that position than orthodox Lockeanism can supply.

Similar considerations underlie the Humean case for property in land. Hume is skeptical of the Lockean idea that labor-mixing can provide a clear standard to govern the original appropriation of previously unowned objects.[125] Does the first person who lands on a desert island come to own the whole thing or just the part within his immediate possession? Hume rejects the idea that questions like this can be answered by a rationalistic appeal to natural rights. But he also rejects the claim that our inability to find a rationalistic justification of first possession means that we should reject the practice altogether. We cannot have property without some rules for original appropriation, and we cannot have civilization without property. Once we have that civilization, some form of property tax along the lines suggested by Henry George might well turn out to be defensible. But if so, that justification will be due to the way in which that tax serves important social goals in a cost-effective way, not because original appropriation is a kind of theft that needed to be compensated for.

Not So Different After All

The Humean account provides a moral foundation for property rights that avoids the pitfalls of the Lockean approach. But the Humean approach has problems of its own. If property rights avoid the tragedy of the commons, incentivize production, and facilitate social coordination, these are good reasons to favor *some* kind of private property arrangement over either the unregulated commons or a centrally planned economy. But can these essentially consequentialist considerations really ground the kind of *strict* and *robust* property rights that distinguish the libertarian view from more social democratic forms of liberalism?

Many libertarians have doubted it. Murray Rothbard routinely criticized utilitarianism as incapable of providing "an absolute and consistent yardstick" with which to defend rights of property against the state. The utilitarian "will only use a principle, at best, as a vague guideline or aspiration, as a tendency which he may choose to override at any time." When utilitarianism came to surpass natural rights as the dominant approach to defending liberalism in the late nineteenth century, according to Rothbard, the libertarian creed was "fatally compromised" and succumbed to the new era of Progressive liberalism.[126]

The Humean approach to property can defend property rights only if those rights are the most effective way of promoting overall social utility. In situations where property rights do not promote utility, Humeanism requires that we abandon them. At first, then, the Humean approach appears to be *too* sensitive to consequences to ground a robust libertarian commitment to property rights.

The Lockean, natural rights approach to property, on the other hand, counsels respect for property *no matter what*. The distinctive characteristic of rights, after all, is that they forbid certain actions and policies *even if* the consequences of performing and enacting those actions and policies would be tremendously beneficial. The Lockean approach, then, appears to be *not sensitive enough* to consequences to provide a rationale for property rights that is *plausible*.

But these common characterizations are too simplistic, both as accounts of what Locke and Hume themselves wrote and as accounts of how their ideas have been used by later libertarians. A closer and more attentive reading reveals that the supposed differences between these two approaches are not nearly as great as may have first appeared. In short: the Lockean approach to property is significantly *more* sensitive to consequences than is typically assumed, and the Humean approach is significantly *less*.

Let's start by taking a closer look at the Lockean account of property. While Locke thought that labor-mixing was *necessary* to acquire previously unowned resources, he apparently did not think it was *sufficient*. Why, after all, should the fact that *you* spent some time working on some land give *me* a reason to respect your right to exclusive use of it? Locke thought that this challenge could be met *if* it could be demonstrated that an act of appropriation was not "any prejudice to any other man."[127] If my claiming a piece of land as my own doesn't make you any worse off, in other words, then you don't have any real grounds for complaint. And so long as my act of appropriation satisfies the so-called "Lockean proviso" of leaving "enough, and as good, in common for others," Locke thought that this condition would be satisfied.[128]

But Locke also took pains to demonstrate that under ordinary circumstances, the conversion of resources from the common stock to private use, far from setting back the interests of other people, instead *advances* them.

> He who appropriates land to himself by his labour, does not lessen, but increase the common stock of mankind: for the provisions serving to the support of human life, produced by one acre of inclosed and cultivated land, are (to speak much within compass) ten times more than those which are yielded by an acre of land of an equal richness lying waste in common. And therefore he that incloses land, and has a greater plenty of the conveniencies of life from ten acres, than he could have from an hundred left to nature, may truly be said to give ninety acres to mankind: for his labour now supplies him with provisions out of ten acres, which were but the product of an hundred lying in common.[129]

For Locke, the moral justification of property turns not merely on whether an individual has "mixed his labor" in the right way but on the *social consequences* of property rights. To be sure, social consequences do not matter for Locke in the same way that they would for, say, a straightforward utilitarian. Locke highlights the benefits of private property to show how appropriation does not worsen anyone's condition. This differs considerably from the utilitarian goal of showing that, on the whole, the benefits of property outweigh its harms. Locke recognized that property rights do not simply follow from individual self-ownership in any kind of direct way. Self-ownership is one of the considerations relevant to defending property. But it is only one consideration among many. Locke, like Hume, recognizes that property is an inherently *social* phenomenon, so its moral justification also must be social in nature.

Much the same is true of Locke's most famous libertarian follower, Robert Nozick. Nozick, too, hinges the case for private property on the social effects of a system of property rights. This he does by endorsing a modified Lockean proviso which holds that "a process normally giving rise to a permanent bequeathable property right in a previously unowned thing will not do so if the position of others no longer at liberty to use the thing is thereby worsened."[130] Nozick, apparently like Locke, believes that "the free operation of a market system will not actually run afoul of the Lockean pro-viso."[131] And, again like Locke, Nozick defends this claim by appeal-ing to

> the various familiar social considerations favoring private property: it increases the social product by putting means of production in the hands of those who can use them most efficiently (profitably); experi-mentation is encouraged, because with separate persons controlling resources, there is no one person or small group whom someone with a new idea must convince to try it out; private property enables people to decide on the pattern and type of risks they wish to bear, leading to spe-cialized types of risk bearing; private property protects future persons by leading some to hold back resources from current consumption for future markets; it provides alternate sources of employment for unpop-ular persons who don't have to convince any one person or small group to hire them, and so on.[132]

Even for Nozick, then, an important element in the moral justifi-cation of private property is an appeal to the beneficial social con-sequences that property rights produce. This is hardly what one would expect from a theorist who is supposed to have rationalisti-cally deduced an absolute right to private property from the funda-mental axiom of self-ownership.

But not only do beneficial social consequences form an impor-tant part of the justification of private property for Nozick; they also set an important *limit* to that justification. Nozick's version of the Lockean proviso is not a one-time-only principle, to be applied at the moment of original appropriation and then forgotten. Even after the original appropriation is complete, the proviso continues to cast a "historical shadow" on all future uses of the appropri-ated property that "excludes [the owner's] transferring it into an agglomeration that does violate the Lockean proviso and excludes his using it in a way, in coordination with others or independently of them, so as to violate the proviso by making the situation of others worse than their baseline situation."[133] To illustrate this point, Nozick offers the example of a water hole in the desert.[134] Someone who owns the only source of water in a desert—even if they came into the position of a monopolist through no fault of their own—is forbidden from using it in a way that makes others worse off than they would have been in a world where that appropriation (or perhaps appropriation in general) had not taken place.[135]

For both Locke and Nozick, then, the nature and extent of the justification of private property are shaped by its social consequences. Far from advocating property rights "though the heavens fall," their endorsement of private property seems both predicated and *contingent* on a prediction that the heavens will *not* fall. And while this is not the position of *everyone* in the Lockean tradition—especially for strict libertarians such as Lysander Spooner, Edward Feser, and Murray Rothbard who deny the existence of any proviso constraining original appropriation—it is certainly a dominant theme in that tradition.[136]

While the Lockean approach is more consequence sensitive than is commonly appreciated, the Humean approach, in turn, is less consequence sensitive. For Humeans, beneficial consequences give the institution of property its point. But the consequences that matter are not the consequences of this or that particular instance of property but the consequences of the system in general. Hume writes:

> However single acts of justice may be contrary, either to public or private interest, 'tis certain, that the whole plan or scheme is highly conducive, or indeed absolutely requisite, both to the support of society, and the well-being of every individual. 'Tis impossible to separate the good from the ill. Property must be stable, and must be fix'd by general rules. Tho' in one instance the public be a sufferer, this momentary ill is amply compensated by the steady prosecution of the rule, and by the peace and order, which it establishes in society. And even every individual person must find himself a gainer, on ballancing the account; since, without justice, society must immediately dissolve, and every one must fall into that savage and solitary condition, which is infinitely worse than the worst situation that can possibly be suppos'd in society.[137]

Hume explains that even if there are particular instances in which violating property rights might produce better consequences than not doing so, the overall *system* of property rights still produces much better consequences than would its absence. But why should this matter? What is the relevance of this point if the decision before us is not whether to adopt such a system but rather whether *given* the background existence of such a system, we should intervene to regulate or abridge the rights of property in this particular case? Why stick to the rules when the rules don't work?

Partly the answer rests on the knowledge that our authorities can't always be trusted to *know* when the rules don't work. Legislators might think they can do more good by intervening in the existing system of property rights than they could by respecting it. But this is often a mistake, a product of focusing too much on the "seen" effects hoped for to the neglect of the "unseen" and unintended consequences such interventions often produce.[138] As Hayek would later observe, this leads to an epistemic bias in favor of regulation:

> Since the value of freedom rests on the opportunities it provides for unforeseen and unpredictable actions, we will rarely know what we lose through a particular restriction of freedom. Any such restriction, any coercion other than the enforcement of general rules, will aim at the achievement of some foreseeable particular result, but what is prevented by it will usually not be known. The direct effects of any interference with the market order will be near and clearly visible in most cases, while the more indirect and remote effects will mostly be unknown and will therefore be disregarded. We shall never be aware of all the costs of achieving particular results by such interference. And so, when we decide each issue solely on what appears to be its individual merits, we always overestimate the advantages of central direction.[139]

For Hayek, individual liberty and well-being depend on society's being governed by firm and fixed rules.[140] Violating those rules in the name of expediency is a bad idea—not because the rules have divine or natural authority but simply because, as Herbert Spencer noted long before, the direct pursuit of expediency is rarely expedient.[141]

Lockean and Humean libertarians thus converge on common conclusions from different directions. Both believe that we should understand property rights (and justice more generally) in terms of a set of *rules*; both agree that these rules derive (at least some of) their justification from the general consequences they produce; both also believe that the application of those rules to particular circumstances should not (in the ordinary run of cases) be contingent on the consequences of that specific application.

Indeed, it would not be too great a stretch to say that both kinds of libertarians converge in a belief in *natural law*. Traditionally, this term has been reserved exclusively for libertarians in the Scholastic/Lockean tradition who hold that human beings are, by their nature, governed by a moral law emanating from the Divine Creator. Hume, though certainly no Scholastic, was not embarrassed to speak of stability of possession, transference by consent, and the performance of promises as "the three fundamental laws of nature."[142] Adam Smith, Hume's contemporary in the Scottish Enlightenment, described his preferred legal system as "the obvious and simple system of *natural* liberty."[143] More recently, libertarians such as Randy Barnett have defended a secular and broadly Humean understanding of natural laws as empirical generalizations about the ways in which certain kinds of behaviors conduce (or fail to conduce) to human happiness.[144] Similarly, John Hasnas has written of an "empirical theory of natural rights" in which certain rights *emerge* as "natural" from the long history of humanity's efforts to resolve and minimize social conflict in peaceful and cooperative ways.[145]

We should not overstate our case. A Humean/indirect consequentialist approach to property rights is still likely to diverge in some cases from a Lockean/deontological one. But divergence about a small number of "hard cases" should not blind us to the more significant convergence of these two streams of libertarian thought. This convergence is not *merely* a case of reaching a common set of conclusions for radically different reasons. The Lockean and Humean approaches to property converge not just on conclusions but on an underlying rationale as well. The justificatory roots of the two sides of our libertarian family tree—Locke's strict libertarian side and Hume's classical liberal side—are distinct but entwined.

In our introductory chapter, we identified a commitment to strong rights of private property as a defining feature of libertarianism. Property rights play an important role both in shaping the structure of libertarians' philosophical theory and in generating some of their most significant (and controversial) political conclusions.

Philosophically, what distinguishes libertarian accounts of property is not merely that they hold private property rights to be legitimate but the uniquely wide scope and great weight (sometimes even *absolutism*) they give those rights. Libertarians believe in rights not just to personal property like clothes and houses but in a broad range of goods including productive property, in wildlife, roads, and, at the most fundamental level, one's own body.

The libertarian commitment to property rights generates some of the theory's most striking, controversial, and inspiring practical conclusions. Historically, a commitment to self-ownership provided one of the most compelling grounds for denouncing the enslavement of the American Indians. As we shall soon see, that same argument would later play a leading role in the emancipatory struggles of slaves and women during the nineteenth century, as well as undergirding the libertarian opposition in the early twentieth century to imperialism and to the nationalist concept of "total war."

But the radical implications of full self-ownership are far from fully realized. After all, if you fully own your own body, then on what grounds could others legitimately prohibit you from smoking marijuana, or from selling your sexual labor or even your kidney? Here, as elsewhere, libertarians promise that respect for property rights would not only better accord with the demands of justice but also relieve unnecessary suffering caused by the state's suppression of those rights. Libertarians advocated legalizing marijuana long before it became popular to do so. So too, libertarians say that decriminalizing prostitution will bring an end to the shameful spectacle of poor women (and men) being abused by pimps or johns, or sent to jail, simply because they sell a service that others think ought only to be given away. Allowing individuals to sell their kidneys means more kidneys available for those who desperately need them and fewer people dying on waiting lists or leading lives crippled by the grueling demands of dialysis.[146] Libertarians take property rights to lengths where others fear to tread. Indeed, as Robert Nozick notes in the opening words of *Anarchy, State, and Utopia*, "so strong and far-reaching are these rights that they raise the question of what, if anything, the state and its officials may do."[147]

If property rights are as widespread and as stringent as libertarians claim, is there *any* room left for legitimate state activity? Or is the most consistent libertarian position the one embraced by Lysander Spooner, who wrote that "*All taxes*, levied upon a man's property for the support of government, without his consent, are mere robbery; *a violation of his natural right to property*"?[148] If libertarian property rights mean that taxation is illegitimate, and taxation is necessary for the existence of government, then where does this leave the libertarian theory of the state?

In the next chapter, we will explore what some libertarians believe is the most consistent and principled conclusion to draw from libertarian premises: anarchism.

CHAPTER FOUR

Demystifying the State

LIBERTARIAN ANARCHISM

Lysander Spooner's Post Office

For many libertarians, the U.S. Postal Service represents everything wrong with government. Monopoly power. Mediocre service. Inflated prices. But even high prices—which have outpaced inflation over the last half century by 50 percent—can't compensate for inefficient management and bloated pensions, especially as more of us turn to email and cheaper, faster forms of communication. As a result, the post office regularly runs massive deficits and periodically considers suspending weekend deliveries altogether. In private sectors of the economy, most products and services get better and cheaper with each passing year. The U.S. Postal Service, by contrast, seems to offer ever higher prices and ever worse service.

Things weren't so different 150 years ago. The mid-nineteenth century saw dramatic improvements in canals, turnpikes, and railroads, all of which led to cheaper transportation costs and lower prices across the economy. Postal rates, however, remained stuck at the same high levels. In 1840, it cost 18 ¾ cents to send a letter from Boston to New York, and 25 cents to send one all the way to Washington, D.C.[1] To illustrate the absurdity of these prices: the cost to send a quarter-ounce letter from Boston to Albany was only slightly less than what the Western Railroad charged to ship a two-hundred-pound barrel of flour.[2]

Public dissatisfaction soon led to subversion. Despite Congress making it illegal for private citizens to "take up, receive, order, dispatch, carry, convey or deliver any letter or letters, packet or packets, other than newspapers for hire or reward," Americans discovered ingenious ways to work around the government's postal monopoly.[3] Some sent newspapers—which could be mailed at a cheaper rate—with secret messages encoded in the underlined letters of words. Others disguised packages of letters as merchandise and sent them using a private express company.[4]

A few enterprising contrarians launched their own private mail services to compete with the Postal Service. They kept overhead low by having mail carriers hire a ride on the local steamboat or stagecoach, which helped them offer better service—personal delivery instead of mandatory pickup at the local post office—for around half the price. Because competing with the post office was illegal, most such businesses operated in secret and purely at the local level.

Until Lysander Spooner.

Spooner was never one to shy away from conflict. As a twenty-seven-year-old would-be lawyer, one of his first public campaigns took on the government of his home state of Massachusetts. The state's licensing laws required noncollege graduates to study for five years in a lawyer's office before being admitted to the bar, as opposed to only three years for college graduates. Since at that time a college education was almost entirely classical rather than practical in nature, it remained a luxury largely out of reach for the working class. Seeing the Massachusetts rule as a form of class discrimination, Spooner campaigned for its repeal: "No one has ever dared advocate, in direct terms, so monstrous a principle as that the rich ought to be protected by law from the competition of the poor."[5] Spooner's arguments proved victorious, and in 1863 the restriction was repealed by the Massachusetts legislature.

In the U.S. Postal Service, Spooner saw another case of the government illegitimately suppressing competition in order to benefit a small and politically powerful class of persons at the expense of a larger but politically weaker group. The post office subsidized unprofitable, sparsely populated routes in the South by charging higher rates in the urban North. Why, wondered Spooner, must a factory worker in Chicago pay more so that a wealthy landowner in

Virginia might pay less? The government also used its monopoly to suppress unpopular speech: the Comstock Laws, passed later in 1873, made it illegal to disseminate information about birth control through the mail.[6] From a libertarian perspective, the postal monopoly was multiply immoral: it furthered the goal of regressive redistribution, by the unjust means of restrictions on individuals' freedom of labor, contract, and expression.

Lysander Spooner decided to do something about it. Like others, Spooner established his own private mail delivery service: the American Letter Mail Company. Unlike anyone else, though, Spooner's mail company would operate on an interstate scale—and without the veil of secrecy. Indeed, Spooner positively *welcomed* government scrutiny. Prior to starting operations, Spooner wrote to the Postmaster General and noted his intentions, his address, and his readiness "at any time to enter suit."[7] His advertisement on the front page of the *New York Daily Tribune* promised not only to "carry letters by the most rapid conveyances, and at the cheapest rates," but, most important for Spooner's purposes, to "thoroughly agitate the questions, and test the Constitutional right of the competition in the business of carrying letters."[8]

Spooner came ready for a fight. Attached to his letter to the Postmaster General was a twenty-page pamphlet titled "The Unconstitutionality of the Laws of Congress, Prohibiting Private Mails."[9] His core argument was simple. While Article 1, Section 8 of the Constitution *permitted* the government to establish a post office, nowhere had the document authorized Congress to *prohibit* private post offices. Spooner claimed that these were distinct powers: "The simple grant of an authority, whether to an individual or a government, to do a particular act, gives the grantee no authority to forbid others to do acts of the same kind."[10]

Characteristically, Spooner saw in this issue a congruence between the fundamental law of the Constitution, the moral requirements of natural law, and considerations of expediency. For Spooner, the point was not merely that the Constitution did not *happen* to give the government the authority to suppress private mail delivery. More fundamentally, any such grant of authority would conflict with natural law and thus conflict with the moral foundation of constitutional authority itself. Individuals have the

"natural right . . . to labor for each other for hire." Since our governments "profess to be founded on the acknowledgement of men's
natural rights, and to be designed to secure them," we must interpret the law in such a way as to be consistent with those rights.[11] A
prohibition of private mail delivery would violate the natural right
to labor, and to sell labor or hire the labor of others. The prohibition on private mail was therefore a violation of natural law, and
prima facie unconstitutional.

Happily, moral duty also aligned with expediency. Market competition, Spooner argued, naturally draws forth "the most active
physical powers, and the most ingenious mental ones." Government monopolies, however, inevitably become tools of patronage
by which the friends and relations of those in power rest "secure
in the enjoyment of warm nests, large salaries, official honors
and power, and presidential smiles." About government officials,
Spooner continues:

> They take office to enjoy its honors and emoluments, not to get their
> living by the sweat of their brows. They are too well satisfied with their
> own conditions, to trouble their heads with plans for improving the
> accustomed modes of doing the business of their departments—too
> wise in their own estimation, or too jealous of their assumed superior-
> ity, to adopt the suggestions of others—too cowardly to innovate—and
> too selfish to part with any of their power, or reform the abuses on
> which they thrive.[12]

The government acted swiftly to protect its monopoly. Because
each letter carried by the American Letter Mail Company constituted a separate legal offense, Spooner was soon overrun with law-
suits and legal fees. One of Spooner's agents was arrested and found
guilty of transporting mail on a postal road of the U.S. government.
The government warned the railroads and other transportation
firms that their lucrative government contracts would be cut off if
they continued to do business with Spooner.

This quickly proved too much, and after just half a year Spooner
was forced to close his business.[13] His legal argument, however,
proved more difficult to dispatch. In a Circuit Court decision exon-
erating one of Spooner's agents, Supreme Court Justice Joseph

Story found serious legal deficits in the government's claim to a monopoly.[14] Ultimately, however, those deficits would go unchallenged. With the looming threat of a Supreme Court case and with postal revenues continuing to decline, the Postmaster General eventually caved and asked Congress for help. On March 3, 1845, Congress cut the rate for mailing a letter less than 300 miles to 5 cents—a reduction of over 70 percent.[15] Rates were cut again in 1851 to a level that would earn Spooner his lasting title: "Father of the Three Cent Stamp."

In one sense, Spooner's arguments against the postal monopoly were quite limited. He focused on a single, mundane function of government, and he claimed not that the government should avoid this function altogether but merely that it ought not prevent *others* from engaging in it too. Spooner's lifelong arguments against the constitutionality of slavery likewise appeared narrowly legalistic in nature. In both cases, however, the logic of Spooner's arguments contained a veiled, underlying radicalism.[16] If the government had the authority to provide postal service but not to prohibit others from doing so, could not the same be said of *other* services that government provides? Consider, for instance, the government's police power. If the state has the authority to establish a police force, does this entail that private individuals are forbidden from establishing their *own* police services as fee-for-service businesses? If people become dissatisfied with the government's courts, could the law legitimately prohibit them from establishing private, competing courts of their own?

Spooner took seriously the American belief that governments derive their just powers entirely from the consent of the governed.[17] "Government" is nothing more than a voluntary association among individuals. But if this is so, then shouldn't those same individuals be able to create *other* associations when doing so would better suit their needs?[18] Shouldn't the government be just one voluntary association among many? Following Max Weber, government has often been defined in terms of its monopoly on the use of force.[19] But if we accept Spooner's logic, the legitimacy of any state monopoly becomes suspect. And if government is necessarily monopolistic, the question then becomes: why have government at all?

The Logic of Anarchism

The term "anarchism" did not come into widespread use until the mid-nineteenth century, when Pierre-Joseph Proudhon became the first person to announce to the world: "I am an anarchist."[20] Before Proudhon, the term had been occasionally used but, like many ideological labels, only as a way of describing (and thereby condemning) other people's beliefs. Indeed, as George Smith has documented, prior to the nineteenth century it was a common argumentative strategy to discredit the premises of one's intellectual opponents by showing that their consistent application led to anarchism.[21]

> For centuries the epithet "anarchy" served the same function in political debates that "atheism" served in religious debates. If one could show that the theory defended by one's adversary logically entailed anarchy, then that theory stood condemned and nothing more needed to be said against it.[22]

To take one early example, consider the critiques leveled by Sir Robert Filmer (1588–1653) against those systems premised on the "supposed natural equality and freedom of mankind."[23] Filmer hoped to rebut those who concluded from these premises that legitimate government must be grounded in consent. He noted that it would be impossible for everyone in the *whole world* to give their consent to a single king. If political society is to be practicable, consent must operate on a more localized basis, with different groups consenting to the formation of different political communities: you consent to your king; I consent to mine.

But if consent is the basis for political society, how should the *boundaries* of political society be drawn? With this question, Filmer put his finger on a serious quandary for consent theorists that puzzles philosophers to this day:

> Since nature hath not distinguished the habitable world in kingdoms, nor determined what part of a people shall belong to one kingdom and what to another, it follows that the original freedom of mankind being supposed, every man is at liberty to be of what kingdom he please. And every petty company hath a right to make a kingdom by itself; and not

only every city but every village and every family, nay, and every particular man, a liberty to choose himself to be his own king if he please.
And he were a madman that being by nature free would choose any
man but himself to be his own governor. Thus to avoid the having but
of one king of the whole world, we shall run into a liberty as having as
many kings as there be men in the world, which upon the matter is to
have no king at all, but to leave all men to their natural liberty—which
is the mischief the pleaders for natural liberty do pretend they would
most avoid.[24]

A world in which every individual can be king by withholding
his consent from others is a world with no kings at all: it is anarchy. If liberal premises entail anarchic conclusions, then *obviously*
those liberal premises must be rejected.

At least, that was the lesson that Filmer drew from this logic.
But logic alone rarely settles political debate. One philosopher's
modus tollens is another's *modus ponens*.[25] For if liberal premises logically entail anarchism, then one will be led to reject liberal
premises *only if* one takes the falsity of anarchism as a given. If,
instead, one begins with a confident belief in liberal premises, then
the same logic will lead to the rejection not of freedom and equality
but of the state.

We find precisely this kind of logical jiujitsu in Herbert Spencer's *Social Statics*. In a chapter called "The Right to Ignore the
State," Spencer uses Filmer's own logic to reach the exact opposite
conclusion:

> As a corollary to the proposition that all institutions must be subor-
> dinated to the law of equal freedom, we cannot choose but admit the
> right of the citizen to adopt a condition of voluntary outlawry. If every
> man has freedom to do all that he wills, provided he infringes not the
> equal freedom of any other man, then he is free to drop connection with
> the state—to relinquish its protection, and to refuse paying towards its
> support. It is self-evident that in so behaving he in no way trenches
> upon the liberty of others; for his position is a passive one; and whilst
> passive he cannot become an aggressor. It is equally selfevident that
> he cannot be compelled to continue one of a political corporation,
> without a breach of the moral law, seeing that citizenship involves pay-
> ment of taxes; and the taking away of a man's property against his will,

is an infringement of his rights. Government being simply an agent employed in common by a number of individuals to secure to them certain advantages, the very nature of the connection implies that it is for each to say whether he will employ such an agent or not.[26]

Spencer would later distance himself from the radicalism of this passage,[27] and his followers likewise held their individualist anarchist fellow-travelers at arm's length.[28] But Spencer never attempted to refute the logic of his earlier argument, nor is it obvious that he even rejected that logic himself.[29]

Another illustration of the ambiguity of the Filmerian logic is found in one of the first anarchist tracts published in the English language: an essay written in 1756 by the father of modern political conservatism, Edmund Burke. In *A Vindication of Natural Society*, Burke, writing anonymously, set forth an extended critique of political society. The state, he argued, is born from conquest and bloodshed. The state inevitably becomes something worse than "the most disorderly Anarchies," in part by giving violent men the power to enact their violence on a wider and even deadlier scale.[30]

The problem, Burke noted, is not merely that the state sometimes falls into the hands of wicked men:

> In vain you tell me that Artificial Government is good, but that I fall out only with the Abuse. The Thing! the Thing itself is the Abuse! Observe, my Lord, I pray you, that grand Error upon which all artificial legislative Power is founded. It was observed, that Men had ungovernable Passions, which made it necessary to guard against the Violence they might offer to each other. They appointed Governors over them for this Reason; but a worse and more perplexing Difficulty arises, how to be defended against the Governors? *Quis custodiet ipsos custodes?*[31]

Later anarchist thinkers would read this passage with delight, seeing in Burke's essay a forceful and eloquent expression of their own deeply held beliefs. William Godwin, whose book-length defense of anarchism would be published in 1793, credited Burke with anticipating many of his arguments and called the *Vindication* a work of "incomparable force of reasoning and lustre of eloquence."[32] In 1858, a British follower of the American anarchist Josiah Warren would reprint Burke's essay and praise it as "a serious and earnest denunciation of State Governments, under whatever name or form they may exist."[33] In the twentieth century, Murray Rothbard would celebrate the document as "a very sober and earnest treatise" on the anarchist thesis that "*any and all* government, and not just specific forms of government," is to be denounced.[34]

One might wonder how a conservative like Edmund Burke could author such a pamphlet. Burke would go from arguing that Reason (with a capital "R") favors anarchy to defending the rights of government against the rationalistic, revolutionary liberalism of Thomas Paine. How could the famed author of *Reflections on the Revolution in France* also have written *A Vindication of Natural Society*?

Murray Rothbard concluded that the elder Burke must have been faking it. Concerned to protect the future of his parliamentary career, Burke publicly adopted views better suited to the masses, however far they might be from his truer anarchistic beliefs.[35] But Rothbard's interpretation is implausible. In the second edition of the pamphlet Burke added a preface to highlight the satirical nature of the work. And even a moderately careful reading of the *Vindication* alongside Burke's other writings gives ample evidence against Rothbard's reading.[36] Burke's *Vindication* might not have been very *good* satire; but satire it clearly was.

But this, in a way, is precisely the point. Whether one reads Burke's work as satire or as an earnest anarchist tract depends not as much on the logic of the text itself as it does the assumptions one brings to the text. The logic, after all, is the same either way. Whether it leads to anarchism or conservatism depends on which set of beliefs one holds as sacred, or absurd.

As a final illustration, consider the disputes over American slavery in the nineteenth century. Today we remember that conflict mostly in terms of the political struggle for equal freedom. But the movement to end slavery had important *philosophical* dimensions as well. More than any other challenge in American history, the struggle over slavery brought into relief the conflict between freedom and authority. Debates about slavery forced conscientious Americans to think carefully about the meaning of those concepts and their practical implications.

Critics and defenders of slavery both engaged in such reflection. On the anti-slavery side, abolitionists argued that slavery amounted to a wrongful usurpation of authority that could rightfully be claimed only by God. Every human being, wrote William Lloyd Garrison, has an inalienable right to liberty. Every person has "a right to his own body—to the products of his labor"[37]—and slavery was the ultimate usurpation of this right.

Garrison's opposition to slavery was based on simple moral principles, but the logic of those fundamental principles could not be contained once set loose. Slavery may unjustly usurp authority, but it is far from the *only* unjust usurpation of authority by man over man. Slavery allows some human beings to force other human beings to act against their will. So too does government. Slavery allows some human beings to seize the product of others' labor without consent and without compensation. So too does government. Garrison and fellow radical abolitionists like Henry Wright were not long in reaching the conclusion that these premises suggest:

> God has a Government & Man has a government. These two are at
> perpetual *War* . . . Man is trying to subject his fellow men to himself . . .
> God gave to man dominion over all beasts & fowls & fish. But this does
> not *satisfy*. Man is not content to rule over animal creation. He would
> get dominion over man. He tries all arts to obtain this end. *I regard all
> Human Governments as usurpations of God's power over Man.*[38]

For Garrison and Wright, slavery was a paradigmatic case of a general problem: the unjust claim of authority by man over man. Once they recognized this, radical abolitionists began to attack unjust authority in *all* its forms. This led them first to nonresistance— the idea that the individual use of force against any human being, even in self-defense, was illegitimate—and ultimately to anarchism and its characteristic belief that *governments*, based as they are on force, are illegitimate as well.[39]

Meanwhile, nineteenth-century defenders of slavery such as J. H. Hammond attacked the abolitionist argument at its root. In a debate with the English abolitionist Thomas Clarkson, Hammond claimed that coercive authority is a necessary feature of civilized societies. Nonresistant abolitionists who sought to abolish coercion altogether were paving the way for disaster:

> In what country or condition of mankind do you see human affairs regulated merely by the law of love? ... [I]n every turn of your argument against our system of slavery, you advance, whether conscious of it or not, radical and revolutionary doctrines calculated to change the whole face of the world, to overthrow all government, disorganize society, and reduce man to a state of nature—red with blood, and shrouded once more in barbaric ignorance.[40]

Similar arguments appeared in the writings of George Fitzhugh and John Calhoun. In a world in which all men are *not* created equal it is necessary that some human beings have authority over others if society is to avoid chaos and disorder. Northern "free" states had taken this logic only halfway, establishing government but denying that body the full authority it needs. The result, Fitzhugh argued, was the worst of both worlds: Northern blacks are subject to the worst abuses of slavery under the factory system with none of the corresponding benefits, while Northern capitalists had all of the authority of slave owners with none of the corresponding responsibilities.[41]

These debates revealed sharp disagreements about human equality, the proper scope of government, and, of course, the place of African Americans in a mostly white and largely racist society. Nevertheless, underlying these disagreements is a fascinating convergence of moral logic. For the radical abolitionists, government and slavery shared essentially the same moral status. Since slavery was immoral, so too must be government. Southerners like Hammond and Fitzhugh agreed that government and chattel slavery shared the same moral status. To them, however, it was obvious that government was necessary and good. Thus, so too must be slavery.

Driven by this logic, many of the most prominent libertarians in late nineteenth-century America began as abolitionists, gradually radicalizing to embrace free thought, free love, and individualist anarchism. Lysander Spooner, as we have seen, went from arguing that slavery was unconstitutional to arguing that the Constitution itself had no authority when checked by the standard of natural law. Ezra and Angela Heywood married in 1865, after having met while engaged in abolitionist activism, but went on to found *The Word*, a periodical dedicated to libertarian labor reform and free love.[42] Moses Harman, too, was an outspoken abolitionist—to the point where the pro-slavery county of Crawford, Missouri, once threatened to run him out of town due to his unpopular beliefs.[43] All of these individuals had a profound influence on Benjamin Tucker, who encountered their lectures as a young man at the New Bedford Lyceum in Massachusetts.

For these libertarians, slavery was understood primarily as a conflict between freedom and authority. The *philosophical* dimension of slavery gripped them, but the racial and sociological dimensions of slavery seem largely to have gone unnoticed. For this reason, libertarians were quick to leap from abolitionism to other issues that shared a similar formal structure. But for the same reason, libertarians were slow to see what others regard as the most significant moral dimensions of the American experience with slavery, or its aftermath (see chapter 7).

Lucifer the Light-Bearer

On September 19, 1886, Lillian Harman and Edwin Cox Walker were wed in a small house in Valley Falls, Kansas. The two had met in 1882 when Edwin was hired to work for the newspaper run by Lillian's father, Moses Harman. Edwin and Moses got along well, and Moses both approved of their romance and participated in the marriage ceremony.

However, the conventional elements of Lillian and Edwin's relationship end here. Lillian and Edwin were both committed anarchists, as was Lillian's father. The newspaper at which they worked was a radical free-thought journal titled *Lucifer the Light-Bearer*. And Lillian and Edwin's wedding ceremony was anything but ordinary.

No priest or justice of the peace was present at the ceremony. Moses Harman presided and made clear from the outset that the "autonomist" principles accepted by all parties present were incompatible with both the ceremonies and structures of traditional

Christian marriage. Traditional marriage, he argued, prioritized the interests of the husband over his wife's, despite the fact that it was the woman who stood to gain or lose considerably more from the union. Legal marriage compelled woman to merge her individuality "as a legal person into that of her husband, even to the surrender of her name, just as chattel slaves were required to take the name of their master." Of this suppression of personal autonomy, Moses Harman would have no part. Though he consented to Lillian's marriage, he refused to "give her away." Instead, Harman declared: "I wish her to be always the owner of her person, and to be free always to act according to her truest and purest impulses, and as her highest judgment may dictate."[44]

Edwin and Lillian likewise used the ceremony to reaffirm their own commitment to individual autonomy. Edwin, for his part, renounced the patriarchal "marital rights" to which the legal institution of marriage entitled him, insisting that in agreeing to marry him, Lillian "has not alienated a single natural right. She remains sovereign of herself, as I of myself, and we severally and together repudiate all legal powers conferred upon husbands and wives."[45] Lillian likewise affirmed her individuality and insisted that it was her duty to retain her full maiden name. "I love you," she whispered to her husband, "but I will not be tied to you."[46]

The State of Kansas did not look kindly upon this unusual union. Two days after their wedding the couple was jailed for violating the Kansas Marriage Act of 1867, which forbade any couple to present themselves as being "married" without state sanction. Lillian Harman was sentenced to forty-five days in jail, and Edwin— who was not yet divorced from his first wife, with whom he had two children—was sentenced to seventy-five days for the more serious crime of adultery.[47]

This would not be the last time the Harmans' anarchist principles led them into conflict with state authorities. Like other anarchists before him, Moses Harman would find himself routinely harassed by the federal government acting under the authority of the Comstock Laws, which prevented the distribution of "obscene" material through the mail.[48] In 1886, Harman published a letter from a Tennessee physician, Dr. W. G. Markland, which relayed a story of marital rape in explicit, though clinical, detail. For this,

Harman was arrested and tried on 270 violations of the Comstock Laws. Because of a technicality, Harman would wind up serving only a few months of his five-year sentence. But similar charges, and more jail time, would continue to haunt Harman for the rest of his life.

For Moses and Lillian Harman and Edwin Walker—as for so many in the anarchist movement of late nineteenth-century America— the struggle against state authority was just one part of the broader struggle against unjust authority *as such*.[49] As we saw earlier, it is no accident that William Lloyd Garrison and Henry Wright saw a strong connection between abolitionism and anarchism. These movements were unified by a common philosophical opposition to unjust authority, as well as by a set of overlapping social connections. Those overlapping connections embraced not only anarchism and abolition but a host of other progressive, anti-authoritarian social movements such as labor reform, free thought, and free love.[50]

Writing in response to a correspondent in the pages of *Lucifer* in 1886, Harman expressed a common anarchist sentiment in viewing these seemingly disparate issues as parts of a greater whole:

> Every Freethinker is an Anarchist in matters of religion. Mr Gibson allows no archy (government) to dictate to him what he shall believe and what not believe. Some Freethinkers go a little farther and deny the right of any archy to dictate to them in matters of food, drink, literature, pictures, statuary, etc. We of the Lucifer office follow the logic of free thought further still. We deny the right of any archy to dictate to us in the domestic or sex-relations; we repudiate the right of any government to exercise sovereign power over the individual in trade or commerce, in the issue of legal currency or legal tender, in the control of public lands, etc. In short, we maintain that the denial of the sovereignty of God through kings and priests implies and necessitates the affirmation of the sovereignty of the individual by conceding, that there can be no rightful sovereignty of a state or nation over that individual. He who is a subject cannot, at the same time be a sovereign.[51]

For Harman and his fellow anarchists, the cause of human liberation was an unbroken whole, demanding freedom from unjust authority of every kind. Ecclesiastical authorities who claimed to speak for God were no less tyrannical than political authorities who claimed to speak in the voice of the People. And for these authorities to be overthrown, the world would first have to *recognize* the tyrants for what they are. An essential task of the anarchist was thus to expose false authorities, to show that the emperor—or the cleric, or the landlord—has no clothes.

Demystifying the State

Consider the following hypothetical scenario, constructed by the contemporary philosopher Michael Huemer:

> You live in a small village with a crime problem. Vandals roam the village, stealing and destroying people's property. No one seems to be doing anything about it. So one day, you and your family decide to put a stop to it. You take your guns and go looking for vandals. Periodically, you catch one, take him back to your house at gunpoint, and lock him in the basement. . . .
>
> After operating in this way for a few weeks, you decide to make the rounds of the neighborhood, starting with your next door neighbor. As he answers the door, you ask, "Have you noticed the reduction in crime in the last few weeks?" He nods. "Well, that is thanks to me." You explain your anticrime problem. Noting the wary look on your neighbor's face, you continue. "Anyway, I'm here because it's time to collect your contribution to the crime prevention fund. Your bill for the month is $100."[52]

How might your neighbor respond to such a demand? What if you did not merely request payment but demanded it, threatening to lock *him* in your basement if he does not comply?

In such a scenario, Huemer suggests, most people would reasonably regard *you* as a criminal. Perhaps you have a right to use some force to protect yourself and others from criminals. But it is doubtful that you have the right to unilaterally imprison people who no longer pose any immediate threat. You almost certainly do *not* have the right to use threats of violence to exact payment for your "services" from your neighbors.

Why, Huemer asks, do matters change when the state, rather than some private individual, acts in this way? How can it be morally right for the state to do that which is wrong for an individual? States claim the right to do much more than simply prevent crimes against person and property. They claim the right to decide which drugs can be produced, sold, and used; which words and images can be broadcast over the public airwaves; which course of study people must complete before offering their services for hire; which wages must be paid for certain kinds of labor; and so forth. Further, they claim the right to enforce their dictates through fines, imprisonment, and, ultimately, violence. How ought your neighbor to respond if you tried to do all of *that*?

Most people believe that there is something unique about the state. Of course it would be wrong for *you* to treat your neighbors in these ways, but it's different when the government does it. The government, most people believe, has the *authority* to engage in these activities, an authority that ordinary individuals lack. Most people believe such things—but not everyone. As we have seen, a broad skepticism of authority is one of the defining features of libertarianism, and nowhere is this skepticism more pronounced than among libertarian anarchists.

Libertarian anarchism blossomed in America in the late nineteenth and early twentieth centuries, especially among the "Boston Anarchist" group headed by Benjamin Tucker.[53] Their arguments often began with the observation that governments are mere collections of individuals. As Victor Yarros, the Boston anarchist and follower of Herbert Spencer, formulated it:

> "The community," or "the State," is an abstraction, and an abstraction has neither rights nor duties. Individuals, and individuals only, have rights.[54]

Notice what this implies. If "government" is merely a shorthand way of referring to a group of individuals, and if individuals are the only entities that possess rights, then it follows that governments have no rights above and beyond the rights of the individuals who constitute it:

> If the community cannot rightfully compel a man to do or refrain from doing that which private and individual members thereof cannot legitimately force him to do or forego, then compulsory taxation

and compulsory cooperation for any purpose whatever are wrong in principle, and government is merely another name for aggression. . . . There is one ethical standard, not two; and it cannot be right government to do that which would be criminal, immoral, when committed by individuals.[55]

Fellow Bostonian Lysander Spooner drew the lesson more forcefully:

It is self-evident that no number of men, by conspiring, and calling themselves a government, can acquire any rights whatever over other men, or other men's property, which they had not before, as individuals. And whenever any number of men, calling themselves a government, do anything to another man, or to his property, which they had no right to do as individuals, they thereby declare themselves trespassers, robbers, or murderers, according to the nature of their acts.[56]

In these passages Huemer, Yarros, and Spooner affirm what we call the *moral parity thesis*: governments have no rights that are not identical to or derivable from the rights of ordinary individuals. Stated in the abstract, this sounds unremarkable. But one of the contributions of libertarianism has been to reveal the radical implications of this seemingly commonplace notion. If we take seriously the idea that government agents are just ordinary human beings— with no special moral status—then it seems to follow, as Murray Rothbard put it, that "War is Mass Murder, Conscription is Slavery, and Taxation is Robbery."[57]

These claims are hard for most people to swallow. Taxation certainly doesn't *look* much like robbery. Agents of the state don't *look* much like robbers: they wear suits, carry briefcases, and wield pens and forms rather than guns or knives. But these outward appearances, libertarians claim, obscure the true reality of the state. Despite the bureaucratic formality, despite the pomp of office, despite the misleading talk of democratic rule and a supposed "social contract," all government is based on *force*. If you refuse to pay taxes, you'll first get a letter or phone call. Then men in suits show up at your door. If you persist in ignoring their demands, the men in suits will be replaced by men with guns. And the men with guns will not be ignored.

Thus, writes Murray Rothbard, "the libertarian . . . is almost completely like the child in the fable, pointing out insistently that the emperor has no clothes."[58] What does government look like, stripped of its respectable guise? "Simply think of the state as a criminal band," says Rothbard, "and all of the libertarian attitudes will fall logically into place."[59]

For the libertarian anarchists, the state is a criminal organization supported by a powerful mythology. For most of us, the culture of state authority is one we are born into and never bother to question. It is reinforced with parades, anthems, pledges of allegiance, honorific titles, and the monumental architecture of government buildings.[60] Belief in political authority takes on the status of what many libertarians describe as a "figment of the imagination" or a "mass superstition."[61] This, libertarians believe, is the real key to human unfreedom. As the historian of anarchism William Reichert writes:

> All anarchists, however they may be classified as to their economic or philosophical beliefs, agree on the fundamental proposition that human slavery starts and ends with myth. Man as a political animal is the product of countless generations of development wherein he has progressively enslaved himself by fettering his reason with the chains of superstition and fear. . . . Man's greatest enemy in this regard has been himself.[62]

If myth is what gives rise to human slavery, then *demystification* must be one of the key strategies for human liberation. Libertarian anarchists have thus long seen their main intellectual task as exposing the true nature of the state. Once the false *belief* in state authority has withered, they hold, the thing itself will cease to exist, for force alone could never keep a people in bondage. The sixteenth-century French philosopher Étienne de la Boétie, for whom Murray Rothbard had a deep admiration, expressed the idea in a striking passage on the nature of monarchical tyranny:

> He who thus domineers over you has only two eyes, only two hands, only one body, no more than is possessed by the least man among the infinite numbers dwelling in your cities; he has indeed nothing more than the power that you confer upon him to destroy you. Where has

he acquired enough eyes to spy upon you, if you do not provide them yourselves? How can he have so many arms to beat you with, if he does not borrow them from you? The feet that trample down your cities, where does he get them if they are not your own? How does he have any power over you except through you? . . . From all these indignities, such as the very beasts of the field would not endure, you can deliver yourselves if you try, not by taking action, but merely by willing to be free. Resolve to serve no more, and you are at once freed. I do not ask that you place hands upon the tyrant to topple him over, but simply that you support him no longer; then you will behold him, like a great Colossus whose pedestal has been pulled away, fall of his own weight and break in pieces.[63]

The libertarian insight here follows from methodological individualism: governments are, in the final analysis, nothing more than the individuals who constitute them. From this it follows that governments have no more *power* than those same individuals, nor any greater *authority*.

But this is not the way that most nonlibertarians have seen things. Of course, *some* states can be oppressive—absolute monarchies or dictatorships, for example. But in a genuinely democratic society the government *is* the people. If democracies involve the people ruling themselves—if it merely involves *self*-rule—doesn't that solve the problem of legitimate political authority?

Democratic Authority?

Libertarians in general, and anarchists in particular, have for the most part been unimpressed with the purported authority of democratic self-governance. Following Mill, libertarians believe that phrases such as "self-rule" fail to express "the true state of the case." Rather, "the 'people' who exercise the power are not always the same people with those over whom it is exercised; and the 'self-government' spoken of is not the government of each by himself, but of each by all the rest."[64]

For anarchists like Benjamin Tucker, government is "invasion, nothing more or less."[65] If government's laws invade the sovereignty of citizens, then it really doesn't matter whether those laws are enacted by one individual or by ten thousand. In a similar vein, Robert Nozick famously asked his readers to consider the "Tale of the Slave," in which a series of situations are presented beginning with a slave "completely at the mercy of his brutal master's whims" and gradually proceeding by a series of incremental steps to a situation resembling pure democracy. At what point in this process, Nozick asks his reader to consider, did the slave cease to be a slave? Nozick, as was his wont, left his own question unanswered. But Herbert Spencer, who originally developed the example that Nozick would later make famous, was (as was *his* wont) more direct: "The degree of his slavery varies according to the ratio between that which he is forced to yield up and that which he is allowed to retain; and it matters not whether his master is a single person or a society."[66]

Some libertarians regarded democratically enacted laws as *worse* insofar as they make ordinary citizens an accomplice in acts of invasion. In a debate with Victor Yarros—who had argued that voting just *might* be permissible in some circumstances if it would result in an unjust law being defeated—Benjamin Tucker responded by insisting that voting is *always* aggression. We cannot be sure, Tucker claimed, that the politicians we elect will vote for nothing but libertarian measures, and even if we could, our candidate "would necessarily draw a salary out of funds gathered by compulsory taxation" and the ballots with which we voted would be printed and counted by that same illegitimate taxation.[67]

Democratic governance would pose no theoretical problem for libertarians if citizens had genuinely consented to it. Libertarians believe that many, if not all, of our rights can be waived by consent. If individuals voluntarily agreed to follow the law and pay their taxes through some form of "social contract," then democratic government would no more trouble a libertarian than, say, a homeowners association or a membership in the local Rotary Club.

But the idea of a binding social contract is one that libertarians have almost universally rejected. The most influential attacks on this idea were penned by Lysander Spooner, first in his 1870 essay "No Treason," and then in his 1887 "Letter to Grover Cleveland."[68] In "No Treason," Spooner concisely makes the case against the social contract (in the form of the U.S. Constitution):

> The Constitution has no inherent authority or obligation. It has no authority or obligation at all, unless as a contract between man and man. And it does not so much as even purport to be a contract between persons now existing. It purports, at most, to be only a contract between persons living eighty years ago. . . . Those persons . . . are all dead now. . . . *And the Constitution, so far as it was their contract, died with them.* They had no natural power or right to make it obligatory upon their children.[69]

In other words, nobody actually alive today has given (or even been asked for) their actual consent to the Constitution or any other purported social contract. And as for the idea that individuals have *tacitly* consented to the document, the libertarian response is best summed up by Robert Nozick's quip that "tacit consent isn't worth the paper it's not written on."[70]

Nor can democracy be justified by the beneficial *consequences* it is likely to produce. The consequentialist critique of democracy is especially common among contemporary libertarians, who point to the ignorance and irrationality of average voters as a partial explanation for the poor policy outcomes produced by democratic countries like the United States.[71] But it has a long pedigree in a strand of libertarian thinking about the limited capacity of the average person to reflect and engage thoughtfully with political matters.[72] And these concerns about voter competence are buttressed by considerations explored in chapter 5 regarding the ways in which democratic institutions have a tendency to be captured by special interests at the expense of the public good.

The most that many libertarians will concede to democracy is that it is less bad than alternative forms of political organization.[73] Democracy can be justified merely as a (highly imperfect) means to an end, where that end typically includes protecting personal freedom. As Herbert Spencer put the point in an 1867 letter to John Stuart Mill:

> The unhindered exercise of faculties by each, limited only by the equal claims of others, is that which the right of voting serves to obtain and to maintain. This is the real liberty in comparison with which the right of voting is but a nominal liberty.[74]

Libertarian support for democracy is thus purely instrumental and, accordingly, highly contingent; democracy should be embraced only if the available alternatives prove worse for individual rights.

Consider the struggle for women's suffrage in Britain and the United States in the late nineteenth century. Many prominent libertarians doubted that extending the franchise was required, or even permitted, by their fundamental political principles. Libertarians such as Tucker and Yarros saw voting as an inherently aggressive act and believed that *no one* ought to have the right to vote. So they saw no principled case for extending the vote to women. "The women are not entitled to the ballot not because they are women," wrote Yarros, "but because the ballot is not something which can be claimed by any one under the highest law of social existence,— equal freedom."[75] Lysander Spooner was even more emphatic, writing that women "have just as good a right to *make* laws as men have, and no better: AND THAT IS JUST NO RIGHT AT ALL."[76]

Herbert Spencer, whose 1851 *Social Statics* contained a remarkably progressive chapter on the rights of women and an advocacy of "universal suffrage," argued in his 1867 letter to Mill that giving women the right to vote should be regarded as an "ultimate" aim but not an "immediate" one. Voting is a means to an end, and so the crucial question for Spencer was whether giving women the right to vote in the present circumstances would be an effective means toward the end of realizing a society of equal freedom.[77] Spencer concluded that it would not since, in his view, "women, as a mass, are habitually on the side of authority" and thus would use their vote to restrict liberty rather than expand it.[78] For Spencer, women's suffrage was required neither as a matter of principle nor as an effective means toward political liberty.

An example from more recent South American history illustrates the libertarian ambivalence toward democracy. In 1977 and 1981, Friedrich Hayek made two visits to Chile.[79] At the time, Chile was under the rule of the dictator Augusto Pinochet, who had seized power in a military coup from the Marxist regime of president Salvador Allende in 1973. Since taking power, Pinochet had instituted a series of economic reforms aimed at countering the country's rampant inflation and unemployment. Many of these reforms were devised or supported by the "Chicago Boys," a group of young Chilean economists who had trained under Milton Friedman at the University of Chicago with support from the U.S. State Department's "Chile Program." Pinochet set Chile on a course to be a real-world test case of many libertarian policy ideals: private savings accounts for retirement, universal school vouchers, even privatized roads and water. At the same time that free-market reforms were implemented, however, the Pinochet regime was engaging in brutal political repression against socialists and other political critics. In 1991, Chile's Truth and Reconciliation Commission would report that, during Pinochet's dictatorship, at least 40,000 Chileans were subject to political imprisonment, 2,095 were executed, and 1,102 had "disappeared."[80]

When Hayek was invited to Chile in 1977, he was riding a crest of fame from winning the Nobel Prize in Economics in 1974. Hayek had long been admired in libertarian and conservative circles for his iconoclastic book *The Road to Serfdom*. Hayek's more recent books, *The Constitution of Liberty* and *Law, Legislation, and Liberty*, had established his reputation as a leading theorist of free-market ideals. The Chilean authorities plausibly hoped that Hayek's visit might lend legitimacy to their own free-market reforms and thus to Pinochet's unconstitutional regime.

Like the parade of other free-market scholars who visited Chile in those years, Hayek was impressed with what he saw in Chile. The market reforms appeared to be producing the desired effect, with the stage being set for Chile to enjoy economic growth rates that far outstripped those of its Latin American neighbors. "The direction of the Chilean economy is very good," Hayek noted in an interview with *El Mercurio*, adding that "the effort the country is taking is an example to the world." As for the fact that Chile was run by a dictatorship, Hayek seemed not to be terribly concerned, noting that "unlimited" democracy was not a system that he in any way supported.[81] Hayek would return to this theme during his 1981 visit in another interview with the same newspaper. There, he said that

as long-term institutions, I am totally against dictatorships. But a dictatorship may be a necessary system during a transitional period. Sometimes it is necessary for a country to have, for a time, some form of dictatorial power. As you will understand, it is possible for a dictator to govern in a liberal way. And it is also possible for a democracy to govern with a total lack of liberalism. I personally prefer a liberal dictator to a democratic government lacking liberalism.[82]

What ultimately mattered for Hayek was that individual citizens enjoy the economic and personal freedoms of liberalism. Democracy, as he wrote elsewhere, "is essentially a means, a utilitarian device for protecting freedom."[83] Hayek hoped and believed that Chile's "transitional" dictatorship would ultimately pave the way for the reemergence of democratic institutions. But those institutions would not be valuable in themselves but only insofar as they safeguarded the liberties of individual citizens.

For libertarians in general, and for anarchists in particular, democratic political institutions hold no special, intrinsic authority. Their value is instrumental. Libertarians who allow a somewhat larger role for the state tend to be more appreciative of democracy: for Ludwig von Mises, democracy is the only political system that is able to achieve the conditions necessary for peaceful coexistence in a pluralistic world.[84] But this raises an important question: If democracy is a system of peaceful social organization, and anarchists reject that system, by what principles (moral or otherwise) is an anarchist society to be organized?

The Stateless Society

William Godwin's *Enquiry Concerning Political Justice* (1793) is arguably the first sustained elaboration and defense of philosophical anarchism. However, Godwin's *Enquiry* exhibits two defects that have long plagued anarchist thought.

The first is a lack of clarity regarding the institutional structure(s) of a stateless society. Like Burke (on whose *Vindication* he drew), Godwin made a compelling case for the essential evil of the state, condemning it as "a usurpation upon the private judgment and individual conscience of mankind" and calling for "the dissolution ... of [this] only perennial cause of the vices of mankind."[85] But, again like Burke, Godwin had very little to say about just what exactly a society without a state would look like. How, for instance, will an anarchist society deal with the problem of violent crime?

Without the state and its police—both of which will have been eliminated because of their fundamentally coercive character—what prevents *private* individuals from coercing each other and possibly subjecting each other to a much worse tyranny than they had ever suffered at the hand of the state?[86]

Godwin suggested that such problems could be dealt with by juries that would act as advisory bodies in "adjusting controversies." But, as the libertarian anarchist historian David Hart has noted, Godwin's proposal seems highly impractical.[87] As envisioned by Godwin, such juries would have only the powers of criticism and ostracism, not physical compulsion. But without the force to capture and extract compensation from criminals, how could they ever fulfill their function? Why should criminals listen to them?

Godwin's answer was that criminals would listen to juries because that would be the reasonable thing to do. Criminals would be reasonable, he thought, because there would be no corrupting state influences around to make them *unreasonable*:

> Simplify the social system in the manner which every motive but those of usurpation and ambition powerfully recommends; render the plain dictates of justice level to every capacity; remove the necessity of implicit faith; and we may expect the whole species to become reasonable and virtuous.[88]

Thus, the first problem in Godwin—and with early anarchist thought more generally—is a lack of specificity on the kinds of institutions that an anarchist society would need to address what Locke described as the "inconveniences" of the state of nature.[89]

A second defect compounds the first and is evident in the passage just quoted: too often, when anarchists *did* try to describe how a stateless society would work, their predictions relied on radical changes in human nature. William Batchelder Greene, whom Reichert has described as the "chief philosopher of the anarchist idea in 19th century America," thought that individuals were capable of infinite evolutionary development. Once the state was abolished, claimed Greene, the "basic character of humanity as we have known it throughout history would be transformed."[90] Herbert Spencer similarly believed that the eventual perfection of man could be deduced from universal law; that humans would ultimately develop to a point where the state would no longer be necessary; and that each individual would view her own welfare as inseparable from the welfare of all human beings.[91]

Spencer thought that human perfection would have to wait for evolution to run its long, slow course. But not all anarchists were willing to tolerate imperfection in their own time. Josiah Warren, often described as the "first American anarchist," sought to combat social evil directly and immediately by withdrawing from political society and establishing an alternative community based on true moral and economic principles.[92]

Warren's attraction to this strategy was shaped by his experience with Robert Owen, a socialist reformer who had established his own utopian society at New Harmony, Indiana, in 1825.[93] Warren played an active role in planning and founding Owen's experimental community, and moved to New Harmony with his wife and baby daughter shortly after its establishment with high hopes for its success. Warren's optimism was short-lived: less than a year and a half later, New Harmony was near collapse. Warren blamed the failure on the community's suppression of individual autonomy. Owen's powerful personality and micromanaging leadership kept residents from feeling that the community was theirs. Given the socialist organization of tangible resources, residents lacked private ownership as well. This lack of ownership, in Warren's view, stifled individual initiative, dissipated responsibility, and failed to provide an adequately protected space for individual self-expression. He wrote:

> It appeared that it was nature's own inherent law of diversity that had conquered us . . . our "united interests" were directly at war with the individualities of persons and circumstances and the instinct of self-preservation . . . and it was evident that just in proportion to the contact of persons or interests, so are concessions and compromises indispensable.[94]

Humbled but undaunted by his experience at New Harmony, Warren went on to participate in several other experimental communities of his own and others' creation before embarking upon his most famous venture: the community of Modern Times. Warren created Modern Times in 1851 on Long Island, New York, in close association with fellow anarchist Stephen Pearl Andrews. Both men set out the theoretical foundations on which the community was to be based in two important works of nineteenth-century American anarchist thought: Warren, in his 1846 *Equitable Commerce*, and Andrews in his 1851 *Science of Society*.

Warren and Andrews agreed on two basic points. The first concerned respect for what they called "individual sovereignty." According to Warren, society could only succeed when due respect was paid to the individuality of its members: the only true basis for society, he wrote, is "FREEDOM to differ in all things, or the SOVEREIGNTY OF EVERY INDIVIDUAL."[95] Second, Andrews and Warren both affirmed the so-called "labor cost principle": the idea that the just market price of goods was equivalent to the labor necessary to produce those goods. In other words, someone who spends four hours plowing a field should be paid the equivalent of four hours of someone else's labor—nothing more, and nothing less. On this view, profit, interest, and rent are all forms of unjust economic usurpation and ought to be abolished from a just society.

The labor cost principle was not unique to Warren and Andrews. Indeed, as we saw in chapter 3, it was something of a mainstay of nineteenth-century anarchist and radical thought that was developed in different directions by Marx, Proudhon, and Benjamin Tucker.[96] What is unique—and uniquely fascinating—about Warren was his commitment to putting the principle into practice. In 1827, Warren established the Time Store in Cincinnati, Ohio. The basic idea was simple: instead of buying and selling goods with money, the Time Store would buy and sell with hours of labor. A customer who wanted to buy a sack of grain from the store could either purchase it with a direct exchange, giving the shopkeeper a good that cost an equivalent amount of labor to produce, or give the clerk a "labor note" promising to "repay an equal amount of time, in the customer's occupation, to the shopkeeper." But it was not just the labor of the producer of the good that required compensation. The shopkeeper, too, exerted labor in making the exchange. Items in the store were marked up 7 percent to compensate for the labor required to bring them to market. An additional surcharge was added to cover the time spent performing the transaction. Warren describes the scheme:

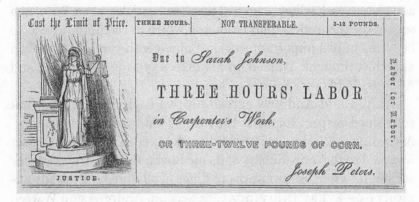

FIGURE 2. Sample labor note from the Cincinnati Time Store. Scanned from Josiah Warren, *Equitable Commerce: A New Development of Principles* (New York: Fowlers and Wells, 1852).

A clock was in plain sight to measure the time of the tender in delivering the goods which was considered one-half of the labor, and purchasing, etc., the other half. An index resembling the face of a clock was fixed just below it; and when the tender commenced to deliver goods, he was to set the index to correspond to the clock; the index would stand still while the clock would run on, and a comparison of the two would see how much time had been employed.[97]

The Time Store operated successfully in Cincinnati for about three years. Warren and Andrews hoped that Modern Times would serve to implement the ideas of equitable commerce more fully. Unfortunately, controversy over more scintillating matters soon overshadowed the economic relationships within that community.

Warren's commitment to individual sovereignty meant that he was willing to tolerate any form of alternative lifestyle among his residents, so long as it did not forcefully infringe upon the sovereignty of others. Once word of this principle got out, Modern Times was beset by hordes of both curiosity-seekers and "crochets," as Warren described them, who brought some "particular hobby" that would result in the total and immediate salvation of the world and all in it.[98] Some advocated (and practiced) various forms of free love; some nudism; others adopted bizarre nutritional practices, such as the woman who adopted a diet of nothing but beans. "She tottered about a living skeleton for about a year," noted Warren, "and then sank down and died (if we can say that there was enough left to die)."[99] Modern Times itself did not survive long under such an influx. For his part, though, Warren stayed true to principle—regardless of how peculiar, offensive, or ill-conceived were his residents' schemes of life, he rejected the use of force to compel them to change.

From State to Market

Skepticism of authority is one of the defining elements of libertarian thought, one that finds its most forceful expression in the libertarian anarchists we have surveyed in this chapter. Another defining element of libertarianism is an appreciation for the free market. For most of the anarchists we have covered so far, these two elements never came together. Indeed, for some anarchists, like the early Herbert Spencer, the connection seems never to have come to mind. Spencer embraced a kind of philosophical anarchism in holding that individuals have a right to "ignore the state." Yet Spencer had little to say about how individuals might organize themselves *outside* the state, apart from a somewhat vague reference to the idea of a "mutual-safety confederation," and thus did not seriously consider the role market mechanisms might serve to facilitate social organization.[100] Other anarchists, such as Josiah Warren, explicitly *rejected* the idea of a market economy based on prices determined by individuals' subjective preferences, and denounced interest, profit, and rent as usurious and unjust. In no case prior to the mid-nineteenth century did any anarchist propose the market as a *substitute* for the state.

The first such proposal was put forward in 1849 by the Belgian-born economist Gustave de Molinari. In an article published in the *Journal des Économistes* titled "Dé la production de la sécurité" (The Production of Security), Molinari formulated what has since become known as "market anarchism": the idea that the state should be abolished and that police and military protection, along with every other good or service, should be provided through market mechanisms.[101]

Molinari's reasoning was seductively simple. The sort of protection traditionally offered by states, he reasoned, is merely a service.

By the mid-nineteenth century, many thinkers had become comfortable with the idea that goods and services are best provided through the competitive discipline of markets. Why should the protective services traditionally provided by the state be any different?

According to Molinari, the science of political economy had established two fundamental truths. First, that "in all cases, for all commodities that serve to provide for the tangible or intangible needs of the consumer, it is in the consumer's best interest that labor and trade remain free, because the freedom of labor and of trade have as their necessary and permanent result the maximum reduction of price." Second, that "the interests of the consumer of any commodity whatsoever should always prevail over the interests of the producer." It followed from these two truths "that the production of security should, in the interests of the consumers of this intangible commodity, remain subject to the law of free competition." Additionally, "no government should have the right to prevent another government from going into competition with it, or to require consumers of security to come exclusively to it for this commodity."[102]

Molinari thought protection ought to be sold on the competitive market by private firms. These firms would act like insurance companies: customers would pay a premium that varied with the value of the resources they wished to protect, in return for which they would be offered protection for their persons and property and full compensation for any harms they might suffer from criminal behavior. Like modern insurance companies, Molinari's protective agencies would take steps to keep their risks as low as possible, requiring customers to refrain from criminal or risky behavior, perhaps to install locks on their doors, and to submit to other "constraints . . . to facilitate the discovery of wrongdoers."[103]

Such a system might appear ill-suited to the needs of the poor. If protection is only to be provided to those willing and able to pay the price, won't the poor be left vulnerable to crime? Worse, won't the poor be vulnerable to the predation of the rich, who might use their wealth to purchase violence for *aggressive* rather than for purely defensive purposes? Whatever the merits of this critique, this is certainly not how Molinari imagined his system working. Indeed, his primary motivation was to oppose the monopolistic system of centralized government *in order* to protect "the most wretched and degraded man."[104] Molinari believed that most of the objectionable elements of market competition that socialists attributed to capitalism were really the result "not [of] liberty but [of] the absence of liberty, [of] monopoly, [of] servitude."[105] While we might speculate that a system of open competition would lead to the exploitation of the poor, Molinari observed, we need no speculation to see the fate of the poor under monopoly:

> Under such a system, we know what would result. The large shareholders and those property owners in possession of the franchise would govern society for their own profit. The law which should protect all citizens equally would serve to increase the property of the strong shareholders at the expense of the weak. Political equality would be destroyed.[106]

Still, Molinari's proposal for the private provision of protection was not well received, even by his fellow radical liberals in the Société d'Économie Politique.[107] When that group devoted its October 10, 1849, meeting to discussing Molinari's paper, the general consensus was that Molinari had gone too far. Frédéric Bastiat, whose own libertarian analysis of politics, "The Law," would be published the following year, thought that violence could only be legitimate when it was exercised by a "supreme power" to wield a monopoly on its use. The radical libertarian class theorist Charles Dunoyer charged that Molinari had been led astray by "the illusions of logic" and argued that a system of competing protection agencies would lead to "violent struggles." In one of the most interesting and penetrating critiques, Charles Coquelin argued that market competition could not be relied on to *produce* peace because it *presupposes* peace:

> Competition is simultaneously an engine of activity and of order; it subjects everything to rule; it places each person and each thing in its place: yes, but *on one condition*. That is that fraud and violence be banned from human transactions: otherwise, farewell to order, farewell to rule; there is no longer anything but chaos and confusion. Speak then of competition to people who hold a sword at your kidneys or a pistol at your throat. The necessary condition for competition to take place, is that the sword return to its sheath and the pistol to its holster. That, sir, is what you forget.[108]

Anarcho-Capitalism

Molinari's radical proposal drew few allies in his day. Indeed, Molinari himself would apparently reconsider his position, arguing in 1899 that military and police services are "naturally collective" and therefore the proper object of governmental monopoly and compulsion.[109] Nevertheless, Molinari's basic idea—that state services should be provided privately through competitive markets—never really disappeared.

The idea sometimes seems to have been rediscovered independently, with no evidence of direct influence from Molinari. We have already noted Herbert Spencer's brief allusion to the idea of a "mutual-safety confederation." Spencer's follower Auberon Herbert developed this idea further by claiming that once government loses its grip on monopoly power, "every want that we have will be satisfied by voluntary combination," and "voluntary protection associations" will emerge to provide for people's need for security.[110]

> The state should compel no services and exact no payments by force, but should depend entirely upon voluntary services and voluntary payments . . . it should be free to conduct many useful undertakings . . . but . . . it should do so in competition with all voluntary agencies, without employment of force, in dependence on voluntary payments, and acting with the consent of those concerned.[111]

But the view that most closely resembled Molinari's in its reliance on a distinctively *economic* justification for anarchism was that of the Belgian botanist Paul Émile de Puydt. In 1860, de Puydt proposed a system of "panarchy," in which those dissatisfied with existing political arrangements could obtain a kind of political "divorce" and register, without the burden of changing their physical location, for the protection of a new government of their own choosing. Such a system, de Puydt believed, would amount to "free competition in the business of government," in which one could "move from republic to monarchy, from representative government to autocracy, from oligarchy to democracy, or even to Mr. Proudhon's anarchy—without even the necessity of removing one's dressing gown or slippers."[112]

Neither Spencer, nor Herbert, nor de Puydt went as far as Molinari in envisioning protective services as being provided by "fully professional business organizations whose prices would be determined on the market by competition."[113] That idea, which now goes by the label "anarcho-capitalism," is now commonplace among libertarian anarchists.[114] But it appears to have been Molinari's distinctive intellectual contribution, and the lineage of the present idea can be traced back to him quite directly.

The first libertarian to rediscover Molinari and explicitly revive his economic analysis of protection in a stateless society was Benjamin Tucker. In 1904, Tucker's anarchist periodical, *Liberty*, favorably reviewed Molinari's *The Society of Tomorrow*.[115] Tucker's own analysis of defensive services under anarchy was essentially the same as Molinari's:

> Defence is a service, like any other service; . . . it is labor both useful and desired, and therefore an economic commodity subject to the law of supply and demand; . . . in a free market this commodity would be furnished at the cost of production; . . . competition prevailing, patronage would go to those who furnished the best article at the lowest price.[116]

But Tucker went further than Molinari in making not merely an economic but also a *moral* argument for anarchism. Like Spooner in his critique of the postal monopoly, Tucker insisted that a state monopoly on protection was not just inefficient but also unjust insofar as it did not itself rest upon true individual consent, and indeed *prohibited* individuals from exercising consent to form protective associations of their own liking.

This union of moral and economic analysis would later receive its most forceful and influential expression in the twentieth-century writings of Murray Rothbard. More than any other recent libertarian, Rothbard is responsible for developing and popularizing the doctrine of market anarchism and exploring the ethics and economics of a stateless society. Unlike Tucker, who based his ethical analysis on a form of Stirnerite egoism, Rothbard grounded his moral case for anarchy on a secularized Thomistic theory of natural moral law. Since the state necessarily aggresses against the (property) rights of its subjects, the state is morally illegitimate—a "criminal band" writ large.[117] For the same reason, any individual or organization in a stateless society that violated the natural rights of others would be criminal as well. Even under anarchism not just anything could be bought and sold on the market; a stateless society, in Rothbard's view, would have a kind of "basic legal code" specified by principles of natural law. This code would differentiate between legitimate *defensive* services and illegitimate *aggressive* services that would properly be outlawed (that is, forcefully prohibited by other legitimate defensive agencies).[118]

Rothbard's belief in the existence of an objective legal code reflects his rationalist approach to political morality. Characteristic of the strict libertarian tradition, Rothbard's rationalism sets him apart from libertarian anarchists who took a more empirical and pluralistic approach to the question of law in a stateless society. For these libertarians, "law" is best understood as something distinct from "legislation," law being a phenomenon that can evolve—and often has evolved—in a decentralized, spontaneous fashion to help people peacefully settle disputes and avoid conflict.[119] From this perspective, it is not merely law *enforcement* that we should expect to see privately provided in a stateless society but law *creation* as well. Libertarians in this tradition note that the content of law developed under the Law Merchant, for instance, was a contextually appropriate response to the demands of European merchants in the eleventh century and quite different in content and purpose from the Canon Law in existence during the same period.[120] In this vein, David Friedman has argued that a market-like system of law creation could serve to satisfy the different needs that different individuals and communities have for legal rules, without presupposing the existence of a single right answer specified by natural law.[121]

Nevertheless, Rothbard's formulation of anarchist theory had tremendous influence. Prior to Rothbard, the vast majority of libertarians were not anarchists. Ayn Rand, the most influential libertarian of Rothbard's era, was openly hostile to anarchism, dismissing it as a mere "floating abstraction" and arguing that a stateless society "would be at the mercy of the first criminal who came along and who would precipitate it into the chaos of gang warfare."[122]

Under Rothbard's influence, though, Rand's ideas began to face serious challenges from within the libertarian movement that blossomed in the United States during the latter half of the twentieth century.

For example, Roy Childs was a radical anarchist essayist with deep sympathies toward Rand's philosophy of "Objectivism." In 1969, at the age of twenty, Childs published what would go on to become his best-known work, "An Open Letter to Ayn Rand." Childs sought to convince Rand and her followers that anarchism, not statism, was the system most compatible with respect for individual rights. Childs's core argument was compact: any government that sought to enforce its monopoly on the use of force by violently suppressing competing protective services would itself be initiating force and thereby violating individual rights.[123]

Moreover, if not for Murray Rothbard, the leading academic libertarian philosopher of the twentieth century might never have turned his attention to the problem of anarchism. As we saw in chapter 2, Robert Nozick credited a "long conversation . . . with Murray Rothbard" for stimulating his interest in anarchist theory, an idea that he would spend the first third of *Anarchy, State, and Utopia* (1974) trying to rebut.[124] Nozick wanted to take seriously the anarchist claim that "in the course of maintaining its monopoly on the use of force and protecting everyone within a territory, the state must violate individuals' rights and hence is intrinsically immoral."[125] As such, he begins his story in the same place as Rothbard does—with individuals in a state of nature trying to meet their need for security by hiring the services of a variety of private protective associations. Nozick's core thesis in the first part of his book is that out of a situation like this, a minimal state could emerge via a kind of *invisible hand* process. That is, a minimal state could come about without anybody's *designing* it or *contracting* into it or, crucially for Nozick's view, without anyone's rights being violated in the process.

Nozick's account of how this process might take place is long and philosophically complicated. But the main steps in the argument involve showing that (1) the plurality of protective associations in the state of nature would converge into a single Dominant Protective Association (DPA), due to network effects, economies of scale, and similar considerations;[126] (2) "independents," who are not paying clients of the DPA, would remain free to protect their rights through their own individual action, but in doing so would impose upon others the unjustifiable risk of being mistakenly subject to wrongful coercion;[127] (3) in order to protect its clients from this risk, the DPA may justifiably prohibit independents from self-help enforcement; but (4) because doing so seriously disadvantages independents who are not necessarily violating anyone's rights, the DPA owes compensation for this prohibition; (5) this compensation can take the form of providing them with the protective services of the DPA at a discounted cost, at which point the DPA will then satisfy the two essential requirements of statehood, namely, monopoly of force within a territory and universal protection of all individuals within the territory.

Nozick's argument was impressive in its philosophical creativity and sophistication. But few anarcho-capitalists were convinced by it. Indeed, each of its five main claims has been subjected to considerable and persuasive criticism. For example, some, such as the contemporary libertarian philosopher Eric Mack, have doubted the claim (1) that the DPA would form a natural monopoly in the state of nature. Why couldn't multiple independent protection associations operate while coordinating their activities around a core set of common standards, in much the same way that different cell phone companies do?[128] Others have challenged the idea in (3) and (4) that individuals may be justly prohibited from risky but non-rights-violating activity so long as compensation is paid, noting that this involves a shift from a "property" to a "liability" model of rights that sits uneasily within Nozick's overarching libertarian framework.[129] Finally, as both Murray Rothbard and Roy Childs argued, there is something strange about the idea in (5) that *if* the independents may be prohibited from engaging in self-help protection as long as compensation is paid, then this compensation could take the form of discounted access to the DPA's services. In other words, independents who want to avoid the DPA and protect themselves will be compensated for being rendered unable to do so by being given membership in . . . a state. Precisely the condition they wished to avoid.[130]

Nozick rejected Rothbard's anarcho-capitalism in favor of "minimal-state" libertarianism: the view that government may legitimately exercise a monopoly on physical violence but only to protect individual rights by preventing the initiation of physical force. After the publication of *Anarchy, State, and Utopia*, however, Nozick moved on from political philosophy to other topics, leaving the many scholarly criticisms of his libertarian vision unanswered. Indeed, Nozick himself would later reflect that "the libertarian position I once propounded now seems to me seriously inadequate," leading most readers to conclude that *even Nozick*—the twentieth century's greatest academic champion of libertarianism—had eventually come to realize its defects and abandon it.[131]

While it is true that Nozick's attention moved from political philosophy after *Anarchy, State, and Utopia*, it is not true that he abandoned political philosophy altogether. In a rarely mentioned essay titled "Free Enterprise in America" in the 1976 *Britannica Book of the Year*, Nozick supplemented *Anarchy*'s philosophical justification of the minimal state with a historical and economic analysis of the nature of capitalism. In his 2001 book *Invariances* Nozick described voluntary cooperation as the "core principle of ethics," arguing that the negative duties of noninterference (which he terms the "ethics of respect") are "all that any society should (coercively) demand."[132] Most important, in 2002, in the final interview before his death, Nozick noted that "rumors of my deviation (or apostasy!) from libertarianism were much exaggerated." His political views had evolved, he explained, but were still within the "general framework of libertarianism."[133] Nozick was a member of the libertarian family until the end.

What's in a Name?

Intriguingly, despite their radical anti-statism, neither Gustave de Molinari nor Auberon Herbert was ever willing to call himself an "anarchist."[134] Molinari, for instance, saw himself as an opponent of the *state* but not of *government*. He used the term "state" to refer to existing governmental bodies that overstepped their boundaries and prevented competition by force. By contrast, the term "government" did not necessarily imply monopoly. Hence Molinari could say that he was not opposed to government; indeed, he claimed to favor the multiplication of it.[135] Herbert, too, thought that some entity was necessary to "use force to restrain force" and thus refused to classify anarchy, which he regarded as a creed opposed to all government, "among the creeds of liberty."[136]

Are these merely semantic differences? If we define "government" as necessarily possessing or claiming a kind of monopoly on the use of force, then Molinari and Herbert were indeed opposed to government and hence were anarchists. If, on the other hand, monopoly is merely an *accidental*, unnecessary property of governments, then Molinari and Herbert were not. But in that case, the disagreement between Molinari and Herbert on the one hand and self-professed anarchists like Tucker and Rothbard on the other is merely about how to use words, and not about anything of substance.

But perhaps there is more to it. After all, it's not just that Molinari and Herbert refused to call *themselves* anarchists. Many contemporary anarchists of the left-wing variety refuse to identify them as anarchists too.[137] For these writers, opposition to the state is an important *component* of anarchism but not the whole of it. To be a true anarchist, one must oppose not only the state but also capitalist private property and the exploitation of man by man.

Why must these phenomena be rejected? Because, for the anarchist who follows Proudhon, property is a form of theft or coercion. And exploitation is made possible only because some individuals wield illegitimate coercive power over others by controlling the means of production. Thus the real issue underlying the apparently terminological debate might be whether there is *any* place in society for coercion or whether it must be eliminated altogether—not just in the state but also in the workplace, in the family, and in the system of private property more generally.

For some anarchists such as Tolstoy and Garrison, and later anarchists in the socialist tradition, anarchism means opposition to coercion as such. But the libertarian anarcho-capitalists we have discussed in this chapter seek no such lofty goal. They believe that force and violence are a necessary part of society and that their use can be morally appropriate, *so long as that violence is used in the defense of what they regard as individual rights*. Force exercised in defense of private property is one thing. Force exercised to limit or redistribute property rights is quite another.

So here we find a real, substantive dispute, one that underlies and explains the various terminological disputes we see between libertarian and socialist anarchists. Is the use of violence in defense of individual property rights legitimate? Or is it merely another *form* of usurpation, different in scale but not in kind from the usurpation exercised by the state? Is a hierarchical workplace in which workers are directed in the most minute detail of their speech, dress, and behavior fundamentally a form of voluntary, cooperative association? Or is it a form of tyranny, a state writ small? Questions like these bring to light some of the most fundamental commitments and tensions not just of libertarian anarchism but of libertarian thought more broadly. Is libertarianism genuinely committed to the freedom of all, or only to the freedom of some? Is the libertarian faith in the free market based on a sound moral principle, or is it a mere rationalization for the power of the capitalist ruling class? We take up these questions in our next chapter.

CHAPTER FIVE

Big Business and Free Markets

AT THE START of the 1960s—the decade of Freedom Riders, the Stonewall uprising, and *The Feminine Mystique*—Ayn Rand asked an audience to think about persecution in a somewhat . . . different way.

> If a small group of men were always regarded as guilty, in any clash with any other group, regardless of the issues or circumstances involved, would you call it persecution? If this group were always made to pay for the sins, errors, or failures of any other group, would you call that persecution? If this group had to live under a silent reign of terror, under special laws, from which all other people were immune, laws which the accused could not grasp or define in advance and which the accuser could interpret in any way he pleased—would you call that persecution? If this group were penalized, not for its faults, but for its virtues, not for its incompetence, but for its ability, not for its failures, but for its achievements, and the greater the achievement, the greater the penalty—would you call that persecution?[1]

The group living under this "silent reign of terror," according to Rand, consisted not of political dissidents or some oppressed religious sect. The group described here—the group referenced in the title of the talk as "America's Persecuted Minority"—is none other than "the American businessman," especially the *big* businessman.[2]

Rhetorical flairs aside, many people think Rand's position reveals a core truth of libertarianism: libertarians are ideologically committed to taking the side of big business in its eternal fight against government regulation. After all, in a liberal market economy, government regulations aim to rein in business, to protect consumers and ensure that the economy operates on fair terms; libertarians say such regulations violate the natural rights of the business leaders. So why *shouldn't* libertarians regard economic elites as a persecuted minority, as victims of class warfare—even if the savvier among them refrain from saying so in polite company?

This image of libertarianism as the friend of big business looms large in the popular mind, and Rand is just one of many libertarians who lend credence to this view.[3] In this chapter we hope to show that Rand's position toward big business and government is actually a minority view in the libertarian intellectual tradition. As we show, defending free markets does not entail a defense of big business, and indeed their commitment to truly free markets often makes libertarians the *enemies* of big business and economic elites. On the other hand, business elites have often provided economic support to libertarian causes. The story of the relationship between big business and the defenders of free markets is more complicated, and more interesting, than defenders and critics of libertarianism assume.

Murray Rothbard—Radical Leftist

Just four years after Rand published her paean to the American businessman, another libertarian would express a rather different view toward big business, regulation, and the free market. In his essay "Left and Right: The Prospects for Liberty," Murray Rothbard would draw on largely forgotten ideas and figures to set an agenda for libertarianism that continues to shape—and polarize—the movement to this day.

Murray Rothbard was no stranger to Ayn Rand. In the late 1950s, Rothbard was briefly admitted into Rand's "Collective," a small group of dissidents who met in Rand's living room on Saturday nights to discuss philosophy, current events, and, especially, Rand's new novel, the mammoth *Atlas Shrugged* (1957). Rothbard's membership in the Collective allowed him to read Rand's novel before it was published, and his response—rather uncharacteristically—was overwhelmingly positive. *Atlas Shrugged*, Rothbard declared, was quite simply "the greatest novel ever written."[4] This response stood in sharp contrast to his evaluation of Rand in a letter written three years earlier: "George Reisman has commented, and I think most astutely, that Ayn's system is a perfect engine of complete totalitarianism, but that Ayn herself is a libertarian out of an irrational prejudice, and that fifty years from now some smart Randian disciple will see the implications and convert the thing into a horrible new Statist sect." Never one to mince words, Rothbard concluded: "life in a Randian Rationalist society would be a living hell."[5]

As he would document later in his scathing essay *The Sociology of the Ayn Rand Cult*, and in his more humorous but equally biting one-act play *Mozart Was a Red*, Rothbard did indeed eventually come to see life in Rand's inner circle to be an (apartment-sized) living Hell. But this was in many ways a conflict of personalities, not principles.[6] On a wide range of issues in philosophy, economics, and politics, the views of Rand and Rothbard aligned. Rand's novels celebrated business as an embodiment of the virtue of productivity, the capacity of the human mind to transform the world in ways that improve the human condition. Her heroes were men and women who lived by the principle that they must offer the best within them to those they hoped to win as customers. Traders, on this vision, are people who encounter one another on equal ground. In the free market, traders can look one another in the eye and, in the words of Rand's character Francisco D'Anconia, exchange "value for value."[7]

In her fiction, however, Rand also recognized that business could operate on different principles. Instead of exchanging value for value—which requires constantly striving to offer better products at lower prices—some businesses find it easier to undermine or bypass their customers' independent judgment through deception or force. In *The Fountainhead*, Rand describes how weak and contemptible characters such as Peter Keating win clients not by designing better buildings or offering lower prices than genuine architects such as Howard Roark but by playing to customers' irrational deference to his presumed authority. Most tellingly, Rand's arch-villain, the lobbyist and eventual bureaucrat Wesley Mouch, earned his wealth and power by helping hapless businessmen like Orin Boyle beat their competition through government force rather than entrepreneurial acumen.

But when Rand then went on to praise the business leaders of her day as victims of class warfare, Rothbard saw her as being in the grip of a myth about American history. This myth, which Rothbard thought especially common among conservatives and libertarians, caused free marketers to forget one of their own most fundamental principles: governmental power corrupts. According to Rothbard, the myth goes like this:

> America was, more or less, a haven of laissez-faire until the New Deal; then Roosevelt, influenced by Felix Frankfurter, the Intercollegiate Socialist Society, and other "Fabian" and Communist *conspirators* engineered a revolution which set America on the path to Socialism, and, further on, beyond the horizon, to Communism. The present-day libertarian who adopts this or a similar view of the American experience, tends to think of himself as an *extreme right-winger*; slightly to the left of him, then, lies the Conservative, to the left of that the middle-of-the road, and then leftward to Socialism and Communism.[8]

What's wrong with this story, Rothbard claimed, is just about everything. First, he argued, it is wrong about historical detail. While there was indeed much for libertarians and some conservatives to dislike in Roosevelt's so-called New Deal, it was "not a *revolution* in any sense." Rather,

> its entire collectivist program was anticipated: proximately by Herbert Hoover during the depression, and, beyond that, by the war-collectivism and central planning that governed America during the First World War. Every element in the New Deal program: central planning, creation of a network of compulsory cartels for industry and agriculture, inflation and credit expansion, artificial raising of wage rates and promotion of unions within the overall monopoly structure, government regulation and ownership, all this had been anticipated and adumbrated during the previous two decades.[9]

The myth also misunderstands the nature of business regulation during the Progressive Era. The great bulk of Progressive regulation, Rothbard argued, was not *intended* to benefit the poor and working masses, nor did it have that effect in practice. Instead, New Deal regulation was largely crafted in response to *demand* from business elites. These regulations therefore catered to the interests of big business. They did so by using the power of the regulatory state to hinder any would-be challengers to the economic status quo. Powerful business leaders were more committed to profits than any abstract principles of fair competition. They leapt at the chance to help draft regulations and saw the pro-regulatory climate of the New Deal as an opportunity to cement their dominant market positions. This new thicket of regulations would shelter them from the gales of economic change that Joseph Schumpeter would later call "creative destruction."

Rothbard agreed with the socialist historian Gabriel Kolko that regulation during the Progressive Era amounted to "The Triumph of Conservatism."[10] Contrary to popular belief, Kolko argued, the first decades of the twentieth century were a time of "intense and growing competition" in most areas of industry.[11] Failing to combat this through mergers and acquisitions, many firms turned to government regulation instead. According to Kolko, the hallmark regulatory developments of the Progressive Era were built for economic elites and political insiders. Most of the country's major banking interests supported the creation of the Federal Reserve. Its policies soon consolidated and cemented the power of those interests by granting special, legally entrenched privileges to a select few banks. The Federal Trade Commission, among other things, established rules of "fair competition" that protected established firms from the unseemly (but effective) tactics of their upstart competitors, and thus won strong support from the National Chamber of Commerce.[12]

Finally, and most significantly, Rothbard argued, the myth is wrong about the relationship between socialism, conservatism, and libertarianism. According to the myth, libertarianism and socialism lie on opposite extremes of the political spectrum, with mainstream conservatism falling in between them as a kind of confused middle ground. But this misunderstands both the historical and the philosophical relationships. Historically, libertarianism has its origins in Western Europe as a form of liberalism, an ideology of "hope, of radicalism, of liberty, of the Industrial Revolution, of progress, of humanity." As a progressive, humanist doctrine, libertarianism aligned itself *against* the conservative ideology of "reaction . . . hierarchy, statism, theocracy, serfdom, and class exploitation of the Old Order."[13] Over time, Rothbard argues, liberalism lost its radical edge, thanks in part to its embrace of a utilitarian ethics (as opposed to a more radical and, for Rothbard, sounder natural law ethics) and a strategy of gradual evolutionary (as opposed to revolutionary) social change.[14]

Socialism emerged to fill the void left by liberalism's moderation. But according to Rothbard, socialism too failed—at least in its dominant, statist variety—and wound up as the actual "middle of the road" ideological movement. The reason for this is that socialism sought "to achieve Liberal *ends* by the use of Conservative *means.*"

> Socialism, like Liberalism and against Conservatism, accepted the industrial system and the liberal *goals* of freedom, reason, mobility, progress, higher living standards for the masses, and an end to theocracy and war; but it tried to achieve those ends by the use of incompatible, Conservative means: statism, central planning, communitarianism, etc.[15]

Contrary to popular mythology, then, socialists and libertarians actually have more in common with each other than they do with their common ideological enemy, conservatism. In their different ways, each opposes the society of status, stagnation, and hierarchy that conservatism represents. According to Rothbard, libertarians and socialists disagree mainly about the best *means* of bringing about their shared moral *goals* of liberty, prosperity, social progress, and the like.

Of course, this way of framing the issue is at least partially misleading, even on Rothbard's considered view. For libertarians and socialists disagree not merely about means but about the more fundamental ends that those means are meant to achieve. The term "liberty," for example, means something different to postwar libertarians such as Rothbard than it did to socialists such as Marx or Bakunin. As a rough generalization, the former tend to think of liberty in the "negative" sense to mean freedom from coercion;

the latter think of liberty in the "positive" sense, a state of affairs in which people are effectively able to act and pursue whatever projects they wish. Here again, agreement on verbal signifiers can easily obscure underlying philosophical conflict.

Still, Rothbard was right to stress that libertarians and socialists had *more* in common than was typically recognized by either side. By pointing this out, Rothbard hoped to lay the foundations for a new strategic alliance between libertarians and the left. This alliance, developed in Rothbard's new journal *Left and Right: A Journal of Libertarian Thought* (1965–68) and in books like Ronald Radosh and Murray Rothbard's *A New History of Leviathan* (1972), and carried on by thinkers such as Leonard Liggio and Karl Hess, would draw on and develop many of the natural points of convergence.[16] Rothbard hoped, for example, that opposition to the perceived imperialism of American foreign policy and to the conscription of American soldiers would resonate especially with the young, who were increasingly drawn to various left-wing movements such as Students for a Democratic Society.

Rothbard also thought that libertarians and the left could make common cause of their opposition to "political" or "crony" capitalism (sometimes called "corporatism"). Crony capitalism is a system in which, under the guise and rhetoric of "free markets," certain powerful corporate interests are subsidized, cartelized, and insulated from market competition by the coercive power of the state. Crony capitalism is an alliance between, on the one hand, politicians eager to advance their own careers and, on the other, corporate leaders eager to hinder their would-be competitors in the market. It is a game of insiders. As such, it is a game as likely to be played by adherents of one political party as much as any other. No matter who occupies the privileged position of power, the losers are the outsiders—not just the upstarts with new ideas but especially the common, ordinary people wanting better products at better prices, as only a genuinely free market can produce.

If the left had in mind *crony capitalism* when decrying the evils of capitalism—an easy confusion, argued Rothbard, since that was precisely what the capitalist economy of the United States amounted to, laissez-faire rhetoric notwithstanding—then they were perfectly correct in judging capitalism to be deeply immoral.

If the left made any mistake, it was in thinking that *this* was the sort of system that libertarians defended. In fact, Rothbard and others argued, libertarians and socialists alike had ample reason to vigorously oppose capitalism of the corporatist variety.

In emphasizing libertarianism's opposition to crony capitalism, and by looking for points of political alliance with the left, Rothbard was drawing on a long tradition of libertarian thinking. Let's now examine the roots of Rothbard's ideas by returning to early nineteenth-century French classical liberal thought. We'll then consider how ideas from these French thinkers continue to nourish the libertarian movement today.

Liberalism against Privilege: Nineteenth-Century French Liberal Thought

On October 26, 1686, the government of France outlawed the importation of printed cotton textiles (calicos) from India and declared the printing of imitation calicos in France illegal. Calicos were considered a threat to the old French linen, woolen, and silk industries. Leaders of those industries complained that competition from calicos reduced demand for their products, created unemployment, and drove bullion out of the country. French consumers, on the other hand, adored the new fabrics and eagerly put them to use in clothing, curtains, bedcovers, and upholstery. Strong demand for calicos, combined with certain exceptions to the prohibition on import for the East India Company, made enforcement difficult. But the old manufacturers fought tenaciously to preserve their privileged place in the French economy. They found eager support in the French government.

In the face of popular resistance, restrictions tightened. In 1688, restrictions on imports were extended to white cottons. In 1689, the government announced that its army of *intendants* (informants) would begin searching merchants' businesses for the prohibited calicos, and it gave orders to seize and burn all calicos that had not been declared and earmarked. Finally, in 1700, the government forbade even the *personal* possession of calicos. According to one historian, "agents of the government were soon peering into coaches or private houses and reported that the governess of the marquis de Chormoy had been 'seen at her window clothed in calico of a white background with big red flowers, almost new' or that the wife of a lemonade-seller had been seen in her shop in a *casaquin* of calico."[17] Personal possession led to confiscation and a fine of 150 livres. For the tailors and merchants who violated the law, the fine was 3,000 livres. According to at least one account, the penalties were sometimes much more severe: the historian Eli Heckscher claims that "on one occasion in Valence, 77 people were sentenced to be hanged, 58 were to be broken upon the wheel [and] 631 were sent to the galleys." Heckscher puts the costs of prohibition at some 16,000 lives.[18]

The fight against calicos, while unusually colorful in its details, was not unrepresentative of economic policy in late seventeenth-century France. In 1694, the French government prohibited the manufacture, sale, and possession of buttons made of wool or any fabric other than silk. This came at the behest of the *boutonniers-passementiers* whose handmade silk buttons were threatened by changes in fashion and technology. So eager was the French government to protect this venerable industry that it not only granted the request for prohibition but also gave the button-makers' guild the right to search tailors' shops in order to ferret out illegal buttons. The button-makers tried to press their advantage, asking the government to extend their right of search to private homes and arrest anyone found sporting nonsilk buttons on the street. But this, at least, the government found going a stitch too far.

Despite this setback, protectionist regulations throughout the economy flourished. Regulations against half-beaver hats aimed to increase the consumption of beaver; the making of woolen stockings on looms or frames was prohibited in order to protect hand knitting; the production and sale of so-called "English lace" was entirely banned. Each of these restrictions was thought necessary not only to protect French industry from unjust and/or dangerous competition but to protect consumers from purchasing clearly inferior-quality goods.

These economic policies of late seventeenth-century France were largely the invention of one person: Jean-Baptiste Colbert, French minister of finance under Louis XIV from 1665 to 1683. Under Colbert's reign, the French state took an unprecedented role in managing the economy. Unlike today's advocates of regulation, though, Colbert did not justify his actions in terms of protecting the vulnerable from business's rapacious quest for profit. For Colbert, the purpose of regulation was not to *constrain* business but to *promote* it. Or, at least, to promote those elements of the business sector that were seen as essential to the development of a strong French nation.

Colbert's policies constituted the height of French *mercantilism*, a system that today's students of economics know mostly (if at all) as Adam Smith's intellectual foil in *The Wealth of Nations*. Contemporary economics texts describe mercantilism in terms of an unwarranted focus on the promotion of a country's exports relative to its imports.[19] But as the case of Colbert demonstrates, mercantilism was about more than the creation of a favorable balance of trade. It was, as Rothbard argued, more broadly "a comprehensive system of state building, state privilege, and what might be called 'state monopoly capitalism.'"[20]

Mercantilism is more readily understood in terms of policy than ideology; interest groups mattered more to the development of mercantilism than abstract political philosophy or economic theory. What little theory the mercantilists did develop was largely a sham devoted to hiding this fact. In the words of Jacob Viner, mercantilist "theory" consisted mostly of

> writings by or on behalf of "merchants" or businessmen, who had the usual capacity for identifying their own with the national welfare. . . . The great bulk of the mercantilist literature consisted of tracts which were partly or wholly, frankly or disguisedly, special pleas for special economic interests. Freedom for themselves, restrictions for others, such was the essence of the usual program of legislation of the mercantilist tracts of merchant authorship.[21]

Mercantilist policy was the messy and sometimes contradictory product of a struggle among elites. Merchants fought for favorable regulations; bureaucrats wanted to advance diplomatic goals, strengthen their own political position, and, quite often, enrich themselves and their friends.[22] The policy tools used for these aims varied but frequently included wage and price controls (including *maximum* wage laws), long apprenticeship requirements, tax breaks, subsidies, and even honorific grants of nobility status.

The most significant method employed by the mercantilists was the grant of "privilege." This conferred monopoly power on some favored producer, which carried with it a variety of special rights including, usually, the exclusive right to manufacture and/or sell certain kinds of goods within a specified region.[23] Such monopolies were allegedly needed in order to protect key industries from foreign competition, ensure that goods met certain specified standards of quality, spur employment, and secure a favorable balance of trade. In reality, grants of privilege often endowed some favored courtier or raised revenue for the state.[24] Indeed, grants of monopoly under Colbert swelled to such an extent that revenue from their sale replaced taxation as the state's main source of income, accounting for more than half of all funds received.[25]

Mercantilist policies often failed to live up to expectations. Protecting favored industries against foreign and domestic competition slowed innovation and productivity gains. Wage controls and apprenticeship requirements hindered labor mobility, making the economy rigid and unable to adapt to changing circumstances. Fixation on a favorable balance of trade blocked the natural growth of specialization in pursuit of comparative advantage and kept consumers from enjoying cheaper (and often higher-quality) foreign-made goods.

Protection for politically favored firms did more than slow economic growth. It also changed how existing wealth was distributed. Under mercantilism, the success of a firm depended on the extent to which its interests coincided with those of the ruling political classes. Because the political classes were populated by those with wealthy, aristocratic backgrounds, mercantilism tended to have a regressive distributional effect, further concentrating wealth and power among those who already had the most.[26]

It was against this backdrop of mercantilist policy, and the extremes of Colbertism in particular, that a revolution in liberal thought began to take shape in the late eighteenth and early nineteenth centuries.[27] The most famous product of this revolution, of course, was Adam Smith's *Inquiry into the Nature and Causes of the Wealth of Nations*, published in 1776. Its fourth book presented a lengthy and devastating critique of the "mercantile system" in which Smith took mercantilists to task, both for the conceptual confusion of identifying wealth with money and for the grossly inefficient policies stemming from this belief. But while Smith's book stands largely on its own in our historical memory, it was certainly not the only (and perhaps not even the most compelling) expression of liberal dissatisfaction with the status quo.

Liberals criticized mercantilism not only for its *inefficiency* but also for its manifest *injustice*.[28] One of the most important figures to make this moral argument was the French economist Jean-Baptiste Say. Today, Say is known among economists almost exclusively for his defense of what has come to be called "Say's Law," and even that idea is known to most only through John Maynard Keynes's famous (and arguably inaccurate) reformulation of it—that "supply creates its own demand."[29] But Say's Law was only one of many ideas developed in Say's most famous work, his 1803 *Treatise on Political Economy*, and the significance of the law for Say and other early French liberals is almost entirely unappreciated. Say argued that a correct understanding of the relationship between production and consumption was not some arcane point of macroeconomic theory but was necessary to understand some of the most fundamental truths in economics. In particular, Say placed these concepts at the center of a theory of social class and class struggle. This theory, which would be developed at greater length in Say's later work and by his followers Charles Comte, Charles Dunoyer, and other members of the French Industrialist School, would have a profound impact on later libertarian thinkers, most notably Albert Jay Nock and Murray Rothbard. Perhaps most surprisingly, this early theory of class struggle would influence the author of the most famous class theory ever developed: Karl Marx.

To better understand this, let us put aside the technical details of Say's Law and take note of its spirit. The underlying point of the law for Say was to supply an answer to those who thought that governments should encourage consumption. In Say's time, many experts believed that free markets would tend to overproduce, leading to a glut of products and painful economic corrections. Accordingly, these theorists thought, government policies that discouraged production were not necessarily a bad thing and might sometimes be positively desirable.

Say, by contrast, believed that in the absence of distorting governmental interference, there could never be too much production. Government should thus never discourage production, nor should it encourage nonproductive consumption.[30] To produce, after all, was simply a matter of taking "a product in one state and putting it into another in which it has more utility and value."[31] And it is only because, and to the extent that, individuals produce utility and value that they are able to consume the products of others. Production creates the wealth that is necessary for consumption, and between producers and consumers there exists a natural harmony of interests.

Crucially, this relationship obtains only when exchanges are *voluntary*. The requirement that exchange be mutually consensual helps ensure that trade only takes place when it is in the interest of both parties. Trade will be in the interest of both parties when they receive more utility than they give up. In order to acquire goods from others through trade, one will have to bring to the table goods of one's own that are valuable enough to make the deal worthwhile to one's trading partner. One will, in other words, have to produce.[32]

None of these claims holds true in the case of *nonvoluntary* "exchanges." If A can seize B's goods without B's consent, then A has no incentive to offer B any valuable consideration in exchange. Person A *might* engage in productive activity anyway, with his own resources or with resources seized from B. But if he has the power to take goods from others by force then there is no *need* for him to produce at all. He can live as a purely unproductive consumer, living entirely off others' labor. He can exist, in other words, as a parasite. Here there exists not harmony but a stark conflict of interests.

This idea formed the key insight in the class theory of Say and his followers in the Industrialist school. Governments claim unique authority to seize wealth with or without consent, and this means that those who can bend state power toward their interests need never produce. As Say's follower Charles Comte wrote,

> What must never be lost sight of is that a public functionary, in his capacity as functionary, produces absolutely nothing; that, on the contrary, he exists only on the products of the industrious class; and that he can consume nothing that has not been taken from the producers.[33]

A corollary follows: the harmony of interests possible between individuals does *not* exist between individuals and their government. More significantly, even this harmony among individuals can be destroyed when their interactions are mediated by the coercive power of government. As Say noted,

> If one individual, or one class, can call in the aid of authority to ward off the effects of competition, it acquires a privilege and at the cost of the whole community; it can then make sure of profits not altogether due to the productive services rendered, but composed in part of an actual tax upon consumers for its private profit; which tax it commonly shares with the authority that thus unjustly lends its support. The legislative body has great difficulty in resisting the importunate demands for this kind of privileges; the applicants are the producers that are to benefit thereby, who can represent, with much plausibility, that their own gains are a gain to the industrious classes, and to the nation at large, their workmen and themselves being members of the industrious classes, and of the nation.[34]

Frédéric Bastiat would elaborate on Say's ideas. In his 1850 essay "The Law," Bastiat identified two ways in which men can supply themselves with the goods necessary to life and happiness. They can *labor*, applying their faculties to the improvement of natural resources, or they can *plunder*, seizing and consuming the products of the labor of others. Because men are naturally inclined to avoid pain, and because labor is often painful, we should expect men "to resort to plunder whenever plunder is easier than work."[35] The purpose of the law, for Bastiat, is to suppress plunder. But the power that governments must claim in order to effect this suppression can also be used to *perpetuate* plunder. And we should expect that government power *will* be so used whenever it affords those who wield it an easier way of acquiring wealth than productive labor. Societies thus tend to evolve into systems of legal plunder. In societies where this process is not stopped, the law will increasingly be used to benefit those who administer it, along with any merchant, guild, or special interest with the resources to curry favor with them.

Society, for the French Industrialists, is thus divided into two great classes: one productive; the other plundering. The productive class consists of laborers, including not just manual laborers but intellectual laborers, managers, and even capitalists.[36] The plundering class consists almost exclusively of the agents of government and those who are dependent upon coercive transfers for their support. In the next section, we will explore the way in which this class analysis was adopted and developed by later libertarian theorists. But it is worth noting that the analysis appears to have had a more immediate impact on, of all people, Karl Marx. In a letter to his American follower Joseph Weydemeyer, Marx wrote that

> no credit is due to me for discovering the existence of classes in modern
> society or the struggle between them. Long before me, bourgeois his-
> torians had described this class struggle and bourgeois economists, the
> economic anatomy of the classes.[37]

The two most prominent bourgeois historians Marx named were François Guizot and Augustin Thierry, the latter of whom was a close associate of Charles Comte and Charles Dunoyer, with whom he had worked at the Industrialist journal, *Le censeur européen*.

The liberal theory of classes expressed by Comte and Dunoyer does not find much expression in Marx's most famous theory of class, in which the laboring proletariat is exploited by the capital-owning bourgeoisie by virtue of the latter's ability to extract surplus value from the former. But though this line was never fully developed, Marx sometimes hints at a different class theory—one that sits more comfortably with the libertarian analysis initiated by Comte and Dunoyer.

Marx's pamphlet *The Eighteenth Brumaire of Louis Bonaparte* describes the French state as an "appalling parasitic body, which enmeshes the body of French society like a net and chokes all its pores." The French state, Marx argued, snatched every common interest from society and made it "an object of government activity, from a bridge, a schoolhouse and the communal property of a village community to the railways, the national wealth and the national university of France." Competing political parties, rather than posing any genuine threat to this takeover, instead merely "contended in turn for domination [and] regarded the possession of this huge state edifice as the principal spoils of the victor."[38]

Friedrich Engels offers a similar analysis in his preface to *The Civil War in France*:

Society had created its own organs to look after its common interests. . . . But these organs, at whose head was the state power, had in
the course of time, in pursuance of their own special interests, transformed themselves from the servants of society into the masters of society. . . . Nowhere do "politicians" form a more separate and powerful
section of the nation than precisely in North America (i.e. the United
States). There, each of the two major parties which alternately succeed
each other in power is itself in turn controlled by people who make a
business of politics. . . . It is in America that we see best how there takes
place this process of the state power making itself independent in relation to society . . . we find two great gangs of political speculators, who
alternately take possession of the state power and exploit it by the most
corrupt means and for the most corrupt ends—the nation is powerless
against these two great cartels of politicians who are ostensibly its servants, but in reality dominate and plunder it.[39]

We see here a fascinating overlap between libertarian and Marxist theories of business, exploitation, and the state. *Both* theories
assert that a pervasive source of injustice in society is business's
tendency to use the coercive power of government to advance its
own private interests at the expense of the general interest of society. They differ, however, in their diagnosis of the source of this
injustice and their prescription for its cure. Marxists find the fault
in private property and demand its abolition. Libertarians, in contrast, blame an overly expansive state and call for its constraint.
But as we shall see, libertarians share with Marxists and other leftists two other important beliefs: first, the actual workings of our
political/economic system place disproportionate political power in
the service of corporations and other powerful economic interests,
and second, that this merging of economic and political power is a
source of pervasive injustice.

Rent-Seeking and Radicalism in
the Twentieth Century

Twentieth-century libertarian thought would develop the class theory of Say, Comte, Dunoyer, and Bastiat in two different ways: first,
by *radicalizing* it into a full-fledged theory of class and of the state;

and second, by *systematizing* it into a rigorous and well-developed school of economic thought. While interconnected in various ways, these two developments were largely independent in terms of their cast of characters, their methodology, and the substance of their ideas. This section treats them each in turn. We begin chronologically, with the radicals.

Though he does not appear to have been directly influenced by the nineteenth-century French liberal economists—he does not refer to them in this book or anywhere else in his writings—the key writings of Albert Jay Nock bear the greatest resemblance to the class theory of Say, Comte, Dunoyer, and Bastiat. Of particular relevance is Nock's 1935 classic *Our Enemy, the State*, which developed that class theory into a distinctively *libertarian* critique of the state in general and of the redistributive and regulatory programs of the New Deal in particular.

The most significant influence on Nock was Franz Oppenheimer, a German sociologist whose "conquest theory" of the state added a historical dimension to the economic class theory of Say and his followers. Oppenheimer thought that the origins of the state are to be found not in a "social contract" but in violence and conquest. The origin and function of the state are completely de-romanticized:

> The State, completely in its genesis, essentially and almost completely during the first stages of its existence, is a social institution, forced by a victorious group of men on a defeated group, with the sole purpose of regulating the dominion of the victorious group over the vanquished, and securing itself against revolt from within and attacks from abroad. Teleologically, this dominion had no other purpose than the economic exploitation of the vanquished by the victors.[40]

States are established by force to enrich those who can exert it. The state may often find it convenient to confer benefits upon its subjects: protection from internal and external aggression, perhaps the occasional road or aqueduct. But such benefits only further the state's pursuit of its own interests.

Once state power is established, individuals and groups within it will struggle to control it for their own purposes. Recall Bastiat's earlier analysis of plunder versus labor as two means of satisfying one's desires, and note the similarity in Oppenheimer:

There are two fundamentally opposed means whereby man, requiring sustenance, is impelled to obtain the necessary means for satisfying his desires. These are work and robbery, one's own labor and the forcible appropriation of the labor of others.

Oppenheimer describes the first of these as "the economic means" and the second as "the political means." He writes: "wherever opportunity offers, and man possesses the power, he prefers political to economic means for the preservation of his life."[41]

For Nock, plunder was not merely an accidental but an essential feature of the state. The state is not "a social institution administered in an anti-social way. It is an anti-social institution administered in the only way an anti-social institution can be administered, and by the kind of person who, in the nature of things, is best adapted to such service."[42] In referring to the state as "anti-social" Nock means not merely to suggest that the state is dangerous or that it produces harmful effects. Rather, borrowing an idea from Thomas Paine, Nock means to suggest that the state is *literally* anti-social.[43] The state obtains its vital force by taking it from society: as the former grows stronger and more all-encompassing, the latter necessarily withers and atrophies.

Like Marx, Nock held that the essentially exploitative nature of the state persisted throughout numerous changes in its outward form and its justifying ideology. The shift from feudalism to industrial capitalism, for instance, involved a variety of developments in the formal institutions, rhetoric, and public perception of the state. But it involved no change in its nature as an instrument of plunder. This "revolution" merely changed the *identity* of the holders of state power, along with certain changes in the *mechanisms* by which they used state power to enhance their own power, wealth, and status.

> The feudal State, and the merchant-State, wherever found, merely took over and developed successively the heritage of character, intention and apparatus of exploitation which the primitive State transmitted to them; they are in essence merely higher integrations of the primitive State.[44]

While feudalism relied on a system of corvée labor, the merchant system employed "tariffs, concessions, rent-monopoly, and the like."[45] But these were merely different *forms* of exploitation. So long "as the organization of the political means is available—so long as the highly-centralized bureaucratic State stands as primarily a distributor of economic advantage, an arbiter of exploitation, so long will" the instinct of men to use the political rather than the economic means to enrich themselves prevail.[46]

Of course, the *rhetoric* of the American merchant class was replete with paeans to laissez-faire and "rugged individualism." But for Nock, such phrases were "imposter terms"[47] that disguised the true nature of the American political-economic system. In reality, the phrase "laissez-faire" was inaccurate both as a description of the way the American economic system *actually* functioned and as a description of the way the merchant classes *wanted* it to function. The typical merchant did not want a "night watchman" state. Rather, he wanted a state that would

> redistribute access to the political means, and concern itself with freedom and security only so far as would be consistent with keeping this access open. . . . He was not for any essential transformation in the State's character, but merely for a repartition of the economic advantages that the State confers.[48]

Nock's analysis here is consistent with the views of Benjamin Tucker, which we explored in chapter 3. Tucker, like Nock, believed that many of the most objectionable features of the American "capitalist" economic system were in fact the product of *too little* competition, not too much. They resulted from monopolies that were established by—and could only be sustained through—*state* intervention in the competitive marketplace: in particular the state monopoly on money, illegitimate state-granted monopolies on land, monopolies sustained by tariffs, and monopolies sustained by patents and other forms of intellectual property.

Tucker and Nock's radical followers have developed and expanded their ideas, in part by continuing and honing the analysis of the relationship between contemporary capitalism, big business, and state-granted special privileges. Rothbard, for instance, devoted a substantial section of his *Power and Market* to a discussion of grants of monopolistic privileges, writing that "although a monopolistic grant may openly and directly confer a privilege and exclude rivals, in the present day it is far more likely to be hidden or indirect, cloaked as a type of penalty on competitors, and represented as favorable to the 'general welfare.'"[49] Rothbard then lists not four but fourteen species of monopolistic grant, including not just obvious instances such as the compulsory codes of the New Deal NRA but also more obscure cases such as licensing laws (which restrict entry into markets by means of fees, educational requirements, and other means), safety codes (which privilege existing methods of production over radically new ones), and minimum wage laws (which restrict lower-skilled workers from competing for jobs on the basis of their willingness to accept a lower wage).

Implicit in Rothbard's analysis is a point emphasized by certain of his contemporary followers, especially those who classify themselves as "left-libertarians" or "left-wing market anarchists." Capitalism as it exists in America (and most everywhere else) is *not* a fully free-market system. It is a system of liberal corporatism, also described as "neo-mercantilism, interest-group liberalism, neo-fascism, corporate liberalism, political capitalism, military State capitalism, State monopoly capitalism, and corporate syndicalism."[50] On this view, libertarians who defend the current system as if it *were* a purely free market—who argue, for instance, that we should refrain from criticizing Walmart because in a free market Walmart only makes a profit by making its customers better off— are making a terrible mistake. They are falling into the error that Kevin Carson has described as "vulgar libertarianism" and Roderick Long as "right-conflationism."[51] It is true that libertarian theory provides no grounds for criticizing Walmart *if* it makes its profits only by engaging in voluntary mutually beneficial trade with its customers. The mistake is in supposing that this is the (only) way that Walmart actually makes its profits. In reality, Walmart's profits are at least partially dependent upon a whole host of state-sponsored privileges, from publicly subsidized roads and transportation costs, to Wagner Act restrictions on the methods of organized labor, to outright government subsidies and grants.[52]

The distinguishing feature of contemporary left-libertarians is not the radicalism of their fundamental philosophical commitments; their belief in strong forms of self-ownership and private property *is* radical, but they share this with other strict libertarians on the "right." Rather, left-libertarian radicalism distinguishes itself in its views on how contemporary capitalism actually functions. It undermines the widely held belief that America is a society *mostly* governed by libertarian, free-market principles, or that it *was* governed by such principles during some Golden Age in the past until that freedom was snuffed out by progressive, anti-business, pro-labor reformers. The reality is that American capitalism is a system characterized by class conflict, coercion, and exploitation.

It is thus only superficially surprising that left-libertarians are attracted to neo-Marxist and New Left historical revisionism, especially the work of scholars such as Gabriel Kolko, William Appleman Williams, James Weinstein, Lloyd C. Gardner, Martin Sklar, Ronald Radosh, and David Eakins. Despite their ideological differences, left-libertarians and leftist revisionist historians share one important belief: many of the putatively "progressive" reforms enacted in the United States during the early part of the twentieth century were a sham. Neo-Marxists think the reforms shambolic because they failed to attack the core injustice of capitalism, instead perpetuating that injustice by furthering the interests of the capitalist ruling class. Left-libertarians, on the other hand, saw progressive reforms as an unjustified deviation *from* capitalism, disguised by reference to a common good they were neither intended nor able to advance. Left-libertarians saw in the findings of the neo-Marxist historians empirical support for their normative conclusions. After all, if the powers of big government will inevitably be corrupted to serve the interests of the capitalist classes, then perhaps the solution is not an even *bigger* government (as the Marxists propose) but a "totally free market" in which the power of government to regulate economic affairs (for good or ill) is eliminated entirely.[53] In the words of Joseph Stromberg:

> The one solution that will not create more monopoly lies in the repeal of all laws regulating the economy and the reduction of the State to the much-maligned "night watchman State" of classical liberalism. . . . Not only would the new monopolies be thus precluded, but the former monopolists, now stripped of their privileges, would be forced to serve the consumers better than their competitors, or face the deterioration of their previously protected positions.[54]

Outside the realm of libertarian intellectuals and activists, the left-libertarians have so far been little read and have had little direct influence on public discourse. But many of their insights have been formalized and developed in a field that *has* had tremendous influence: public choice economics.

The key insight of public choice economists, especially as developed in the work of Gordon Tullock and James Buchanan, was that individuals in their capacity as political actors could be analyzed in the same way, and on the basis of the same assumptions, as individuals in their capacity as market actors. In other words, just as standard economic theory presents a model of market actors as persons who are largely motivated by self-interest, and whose capacity for altruism is severely limited (especially toward relatively distant or unknown persons), public choice economics makes the same basic assumptions about political actors—about voters, politicians running for and serving in elected office, bureaucrats, and so on.[55] The result of this analysis was a highly deflationary view of politics—a view of politics "without romance."[56]

Like the left-libertarians and the neo-Marxist revisionists, public choice economists paint a picture of the origin of regulation that is very different from the one most people accept. On their account, private interests are far more influential than considerations of the common good. But unlike the class analyses that neo-Marxists (always) and left-libertarians (sometimes) employ, the public choice analysis proceeds from a thoroughly individualistic methodology. Class analyses such as Marx's, as Mancur Olson noted, failed precisely by focusing exclusively on the interests of classes as a whole, and thereby neglecting the contrary incentives of different members of those classes.[57] As Russell Hardin summarizes, such theories begin by correctly noting that "it would be in the collective interest of some group to have a particular result, even counting the costs of providing the result," but then stumble in inferring from this fact that "it would be in the interest of each individual in the group to bear the individual costs of contributing to the group's collective provision."[58] This inference fails, of course, by ignoring the now well-known free-rider problem, a problem that becomes apparent only once we move away from the idea of classes as fundamental explanatory concepts in social science and instead take up the perspective of methodological individualism.

Public choice theorists argue that once we take up this perspective, and once we make the assumption that political actors are no different in their fundamental motivations and capacities than human actors in any other context, we are led naturally to certain conclusions about the likely origin of political regulation. Consider, first, the relationship in which those charged with creating and enforcing regulation stand with respect to the potential *costs* of that regulation. In almost every case, the vast majority of those costs are borne by others: by taxpayers, by consumers, by workers, and by firms.[59] Political actors have little prudential reason to take these costs seriously—say, by weighing them against potential benefits in order to determine whether the regulation is, on net, worthwhile. This is especially true when the political actor derives significant private *benefits* from the outcome—when this appeases some important lobbying group, for example, or when a vote can be used to obtain a reciprocal vote from another lawmaker at a future date. When the benefits of regulation are *internalized* to political actors and costs are largely *externalized* onto third parties, public choice economics teaches us that we should expect such regulation to be enacted even when it subverts the public interest.[60]

The ability of political agents to externalize costs represents one source of socially inefficient regulation. The *distribution* of costs and benefits among nonpolitical actors represents another. As Mancur Olson observed, the benefits of legislation often concentrate in a small group while its costs disperse widely. This has vital implications for collective action. Imagine a policy that imposed a cost of $10 on one hundred people and conferred a benefit of $70 on ten people. Such a policy is socially inefficient; it results in a deadweight loss of $300. Nevertheless, the ten individuals who benefit have strong incentives to devote significant resources lobbying for it—up to $70 each. Cumulatively, of course, the hundred people who pay for the policy have even greater resources at stake. But because their individual costs are so small, and because the costs of coordinating and mobilizing such a large, dispersed group of people are high (and subject to the free-rider problem), the incentive for any particular individual to devote significant resources to combating the policy is negligible. The result? David Friedman explains:

> Special interest politics is a simple game. A hundred people sit in a circle, each with his pocket full of pennies. A politician walks around the outside of the circle, taking a penny from each person. No one minds; who cares about a penny? When he has gotten all the way around the circle, the politician throws fifty cents down in front of one person, who is overjoyed at the unexpected windfall. The process is repeated, ending with a different person. After a hundred rounds everyone is a hundred cents poorer, fifty cents richer, and happy.[61]

These examples describe a phenomenon that public choice economists call *rent-seeking*. Rent-seeking refers to the investment of resources in nonproductive (or nonoptimally productive) uses in order to attain some special position or monopoly power.[62] Rent-seeking can hurt societies in two ways. First, they lose out on the potential benefits that could have resulted, had the resources spent on rent-seeking been put to productive use instead. Second, rent-seeking can lead to public policies that benefit special interests rather than society as a whole. This is clearest in the phenomenon described by George Stigler as "regulatory capture," in which a regulatory process or policy designed to serve the interests of society as a whole is instead "captured" by the very entity that was supposed to be the *object* of the regulation.[63]

Examples of regulatory capture are easy to find, once one looks past the defensive rhetoric of regulatory policies to see who actually gains and loses from their implementation. Consider occupational licensing. Most people in the United States are familiar with occupational licensing in medicine and law, where permission to practice is granted only after training and testing approved by the American Medical Association or the American Bar Association, respectively. But few people realize how widespread occupational licensing actually is. Not just doctors and lawyers but cosmetologists, massage therapists, barbers, auctioneers, and even interior designers are subject to licensing requirements. Indeed, over 1,100 different jobs are now licensed in at least one state in the United States.[64]

The ostensible purpose of occupational licensing is to ensure that goods and services provided on the market are safe and of high quality. But the licensing boards that devise and implement the rules are made up of practitioners in that very same field. Public choice economics provides a compelling account of what is likely to happen in such a scenario. Lawyers, for instance, support strict licensing requirements for attorneys because those requirements erect barriers to entry into the field, thus giving the dominant professional organization and its members a degree of monopoly power and the ability to reap artificially high profits. Legislators, in turn, are willing to give the American Bar Association these special privileges because the costs of the policy (higher prices for legal services) are borne by the third parties, while the benefits (financial contributions and votes from the legal profession) are internalized to the legislator. Public safety, in most cases, is little more than window dressing used to publicly justify a policy that is actually designed to advance the self-interest of current providers at the expense of both consumers and potential (but currently unlicensed) providers.[65]

If Libertarianism Isn't Pro-Business, Why Is Business Pro-Libertarian?

So far, this chapter has suggested that it is a mistake to characterize libertarianism as a "pro-business" ideology. Libertarians—at least at their most radical—support *fully* free markets, and these often antagonize business interests, especially at well-established firms that fear competition from newer upstarts.

Still, if our thesis is true, it raises a puzzle. If libertarianism is *not* a pro-business ideology, why has it drawn so much financial support from the business community? Most readers of this book are familiar with the activities of Charles and David Koch, whom Jane Mayer famously characterized in her 2016 book, *Dark Money*, as "the primary underwriters of hard-line libertarian politics in America."[66] And not without some reason. The Koch brothers have given a great deal of money to libertarian organizations such as the Institute for Humane Studies, Americans for Prosperity, *Reason* magazine, George Mason University's Mercatus Center, the Cato Institute, and a growing number of smaller centers and individual scholars at universities throughout the United States. In so doing, they have had a tremendous influence on the character of the contemporary libertarian movement.

Nor are the Kochs unique in this respect. Indeed, for almost as long as a libertarian movement has existed, it has drawn significant financial support from the business community. From 1947 until 1963, the William Volker Fund, under the management of Harold Luhnow, funded a variety of libertarian individuals and projects in ways that would have a tremendous impact on late twentieth-century libertarianism. In 1945, the Volker Fund helped secure and fund a position for Ludwig von Mises at New York University, which he would hold until his retirement in 1969 and would use to assemble and train some of the leading intellectuals in the postwar American libertarian movement.[67] Later, in 1948, the Volker Fund financed Friedrich Hayek's first academic position in the United States on the Committee on Social Thought at the University of Chicago.[68] It supported the formation of the Mont Pelerin Society; it helped (along with the John M. Olin Foundation) launch the academic discipline of law and economics; and it even paid libertarian intellectuals such as Rose Wilder Lane and Murray Rothbard to work as "talent scouts," scouring newly published books and journals to discover promising new thinkers for future opportunities.[69]

But even prior to the twentieth century, and even outside the context of the United States, libertarian organizations drew financial support from the business community. We have already seen how in late nineteenth-century England, the Liberty and Property Defense League brought together a coalition of manufacturing and agricultural interests to defend "individualism" and laissez-faire against the threat of "overlegislation," trade unionism, and socialism.[70] Railway interests threatened by pro-union legislation, liquor and beer companies fearing prohibition, and landowners concerned about the possible appropriation of their property all found in the League an organization that could mobilize to defend their interests and a willing cadre of intellectuals to supply a theoretical basis for their political ideals.[71] And before the Liberty and Property Defense League, there was Richard Cobden and the Anti-Corn Law League, which received substantial support from English manufacturers in Manchester, some of whom saw the restrictive tariffs on grain as driving up the cost of their workers' food and thus driving up the wages they had to pay for labor.[72]

The alleged financial connection between business and the libertarian movement is thus no figment of the progressive imagination. Still, it must be given some perspective, for several reasons. First, while it is true that the libertarian movement has received a substantial proportion of its financial support from business, it is *not* true that business has devoted anything close to a substantial proportion of its financial resources to libertarianism. According to Brian Doherty, "no more than $125 million" is spent per year (as of 2007) on "explicitly libertarian think tanks, advocacy groups, political parties, or publications."[73] By way of comparison, approximately $1.5 *billion* was raised and spent during the 2015–16 U.S. election cycle. And this makes sense, even on the assumption that businesses' donations are driven entirely by their financial self-interest; investment in a fringe ideology such as libertarianism must be expected to yield a much worse return than, say, investment in one of the two dominant political parties. Even if it were true that libertarians' political vision aligned better with business interests than that of the Republicans or Democrats, this fact surely must be discounted by their much smaller chance of actually obtaining the political power necessary to realize that vision.

This leads to a second, more crucial point: the libertarian vision often does *not* align with the interests of business. Take, for example, the case of Murray Rothbard, whose career was marked by a number of schisms and breaks, both with fellow libertarian intellectuals and with their corporate sponsors. The Volker Fund was happy enough to support Rothbard in writing his economic treatise, *Man, Economy and State*, the great bulk of which was merely a restatement and refinement of Ludwig von Mises's economic treatise *Human Action*.[74] But the final chapter, which applied the logic of Mises to make the case for anarcho-capitalism, was too much for Volker, and they insisted that he cut it.[75] Later, in 1980–81, Rothbard became embroiled in a heated dispute with the other two cofounders of the Cato Institute, Charles Koch and Edward Crane, over their push to move the organization in a more mainstream direction and deemphasize the radical Austrian economic approach favored by Rothbard. In 1980, Charles's brother David ran as the Libertarian Party's vice-presidential nominee on a platform that Rothbard deemed far too moderate but nevertheless still only managed to get a little over 1 percent of the popular vote. Rothbard charged that Koch and his running mate, Ed Clark, had "sold their souls—ours, unfortunately, along with it—for a mess of pottage, and they didn't even get the pottage."[76] The next year Rothbard was fired from his position at the Cato Institute.[77]

As we have seen throughout this book, strict libertarianism is a radical political ideology that counsels sweeping changes to the political and economic status quo. Strict libertarians are thus not terribly enamored of big business, and so it should be no surprise that the feeling is largely reciprocal.

The situation changes when it comes to more moderate forms of libertarianism. "Neoliberals" in particular, especially those economists associated with the Mont Pelerin Society, have tended to enjoy a more favorable relationship with the business community. Professionally, their expertise as economists has opened doors to the halls of power that have remained closed to philosophers like Nozick and social critics like Nock. And ideologically, as Quinn Slobodian has demonstrated, the neoliberal focus on the importance of economic growth and prosperity (as opposed to the strict libertarian focus on justice and individual rights) led them to place a high value on the interests of the business community and to counsel policy recommendations that would facilitate their growth and international expansion.[78] Here, again, we see a tension between more radical and more conservative branches of the libertarian family.

Libertarianism and the Labor Movement

Those who perceive libertarianism as an inherently pro-business ideology often also believe it to be an ideology opposed to the interests of labor, and especially to the interests of *organized* labor. If the interests of business and labor are inherently antagonistic then, it is supposed, libertarians, being aligned with the former, must necessarily be opposed to the latter.

As we have already seen, however, things looked different in the nineteenth century. In the United States, Benjamin Tucker saw the struggle for workers' rights as not only compatible with but central to his libertarianism. Along with other libertarian notables such as Ezra Heywood, Josiah Warren, and Lysander Spooner, Tucker was actively involved in the New England Labor Reform League. For these libertarians, the struggle to ensure that workers received the full product of their labor was the core element of their platform of economic reform, and worker organization and education played a central role in pursuing it.[79]

Similarly, in France, Gustave de Molinari devoted both theoretical and practical energies toward efforts to improve the conditions of labor, developing a system of labor exchanges which, he believed, would improve workers' wages by making the labor market more competitive.[80] And in Britain, Thomas Hodgskin devoted much of his early journalistic career to the labor issue, culminating in his 1825 book, *Labour Defended against the Claims of Capital*, which argued that English law unjustly deprived workers of the fruits of their labor by means of legal privileges given to capitalists, and legal impediments placed on labor, such as the Combination Laws that rendered certain forms of worker organization illegal. Wordsworth Donisthorpe, for his part, motivated by horror at what he saw as the exploitation of the working class, devoted a great deal of his career to developing and promoting the idea of "labor capitalization," an idea that essentially amounted to a proposal to replace the system of wage labor with one consisting of worker-owned and worker-managed cooperatives.[81]

Still, even in the nineteenth century libertarianism's ties to organized labor were complex. On the one hand, the right of workers to form unions appeared to follow naturally from the right of free association, and from the right of any individual or group of individuals to negotiate in the marketplace on behalf of their own interests. On the other hand, many libertarians worried that the methods unions used to advance the interests of their members were exclusionary and ultimately harmful to both consumers and nonunion workers. As Auberon Herbert wrote in 1891:

> The more a union could restrict the admission of members into the trade by limiting the number of apprentices . . . the more it could for the moment . . . keep up or raise its rate of wages. . . . The effect of all restriction is to diminish production and raise prices . . . a state of things, which was good for it, but bad for all others.[82]

In addition to such economic objections, there was (especially in Britain) a growing moral concern over the means employed by the

"New Unionism." Rather than free association, unions increasingly relied on coercion to achieve their ends: privately through worker strikes, publicly through state regulations enacted on the union's behalf. In either case, nineteenth-century libertarians regarded such coercion as a hypocritical betrayal of the true spirit of "association." As Herbert Spencer wrote in 1891, "While their members insist on their own freedom to combine and fix the rates at which they will work (as they are perfectly justified in doing), the freedom of those who disagree with them is not only denied but the assertion of it is treated as a crime."[83]

In theory, the libertarian position on labor unions is straightforward: unions are permissible when and insofar as they are voluntary, impermissible when and insofar as they are coercive. In practice, matters are far less clear. For example, George Howell, a British Member of Parliament and writer for the Liberty and Property Defense League, took that League to task for what he perceived to be a double standard in their supposedly absolutist commitment to liberty.

> The Liberty and Property Defence League of to-day is regarded by many as carrying to the very extreme the principle of non-interference by law in matters of "contracts of service" in the realm of labour. The adherents of this school appear to be inclined to appeal to philosophical principles only in so far as they are protective of their own interests. This is not perhaps intentional, but proceeds from forgetfulness of what they owe to earlier legislation and regulation. They protest, and in many cases rightly, against the enactment of fresh restraints on individual liberty, but they are not enthusiastically eager to part with advantages which earlier legislation has conferred upon the class from which the members of that school are drawn.[84]

In other words, if state coercion has already been used to illegitimately advance the interests of *employers*, then it is not obvious even on libertarian principles that state coercion to advance the interests of *employees* is unjust. Libertarian principles clearly prohibit the initiation of coercion, but (as we saw in chapter 3) the precise conditions under which coercion is permissible for purposes of retaliation or rectification have always been less clear.

Similar debates can be found over current American "Right to Work" laws. These laws prohibit contracts between employers and

employees that make payment of union dues a condition of employment.[85] Many conservatives and libertarians supported Right to
Work laws on the grounds that they protect workers from being
forced to pay for a union that they might not support. However, as
other libertarians such as Milton Friedman pointed out, Right to
Work laws protect this "freedom" only by interfering with employers' freedom of contract.

> Given competition between firms, there seems no reason why employ-
> ers should not be free to offer any terms they want to employees. . . . If
> in fact some employees would prefer to work in firms that have a closed
> shop and others in firms that have an open shop, there would develop
> different forms of employment contracts, some having the one provi-
> sion, others the other provision.[86]

If voluntary associations are permissible and coercion is wrong,
then Right to Work laws seem just as impermissible on libertarian grounds as laws that limit the maximum number of hours that
employers can ask their employees to work. The only real difference
is that the former laws seem intended to advance the interests of
business, while the latter appear designed to advance the interest
of workers.

However, as George Howell pointed out in the nineteenth century,
it is one thing to say what libertarian principles would require in the
realm of ideal theory. It is another to say what they require in a world
where violations of libertarian principles have already taken place.
Thus, Friedrich Hayek argued that Right to Work laws were justifiable, though perhaps only as a second-best policy.

> If legislation, jurisdiction, and the tolerance of executive agencies
> had not created privileges for the unions, the need for special legisla-
> tion concerning them would probably not have arisen in common-
> law countries. But, once special privileges have become part of the
> law of the land, they can be removed only by special legislation.
> Though there ought to be no need for special "right-to-work laws,"
> it is difficult to deny that the situation created in the United States
> by legislation and by the decisions of the Supreme Court may make
> special legislation the only practicable way of restoring the principles
> of freedom.[87]

Hayek's position illustrates a difficulty in the application of libertarian principles. If the initiation of coercion is wrong, but coercion for purposes of rectification is sometimes permissible, how do we distinguish between the two in practice? Hayek's argument depends upon the claim that prior state coercion had stacked the deck in favor of unions. But as left-libertarians such as Kevin Carson have pointed out, the government has actually done a great deal to *weaken* unions in the United States, too.[88] Sorting out who coerced whom first and who is thus justified in coercing *back* seems a hopelessly complicated task, not to mention one that is ripe for special pleading on behalf of one's favored class.

What Libertarians Do Like about Business

Libertarianism cannot accurately be described simply as "pro-business." Why are libertarians so often caricatured as such? No doubt some of the blame falls on libertarians themselves. In their rush to defend the ideal of free markets, libertarians such as Rand too quickly overlook the ways in which actually existing markets are unfree. This lends a reactionary quality to the response of libertarians to critics from the left. If the anti-capitalist left condemns big business and supports unions, then libertarians must defend big business and attack unions. The enemy of our enemy is our friend.

But if libertarians bear some responsibility for the public misunderstanding of their position, certainly some of the blame must be laid on the detractors. If leftist critics of libertarianism think that ours truly is a free-market system, then it's easy to see why libertarian defenders of markets would be flagged as apologists for big business. But this is simply the vulgar libertarian mistake in reverse: for strict libertarians, free markets are an ideal yet to be achieved, not a status quo to be defended.

Still, behind these mistakes lies an important truth. Libertarians really *do* find much to admire about business. This admiration is no accident: it is a natural expression of their fundamental empirical beliefs and value commitments. Libertarians, for example, maintain that voluntary exchange is a positive-sum game. Adam Smith noted in his *Wealth of Nations* that the butcher, the baker, and the brewer provide us with our dinner not because they care about us but because they care about themselves.[89] But however selfish businesspeople may be supposed, in a free market they can only entice us to hand them our money by offering us something we perceive as more valuable in return.

This analysis proceeds on the assumption that exchange is voluntary. In a world of imperfectly free markets, this assumption will not always be met. But just as we should not exaggerate the extent of our freedom, so too should we not exaggerate our constraints. Despite a panoply of subsidies, taxes, and regulations, it remains generally true that businesses only succeed in the long run if they provide customers with added value. And if this is true, no one need apologize for making an honest profit. Making a profit is not an anti-social activity that ipso facto obligates one to "give something back" to the community, as though the profit one earned was something that came at the community's expense. Rather, the fact that one has made a profit is typically some evidence that one has *already given* to the community—that the goods and services offered were judged by consumers to offer more value than they cost. The libertarian industrialist Charles Koch has called this "good profit" since, in a genuinely free market, business success only results from providing real benefits to one's customers and partners.[90]

On an individual level, libertarians find much to admire about businesspeople. This is especially true of entrepreneurs, a class that libertarians (especially those in the Austrian tradition) interpret broadly to include those who seek profit by being alert to unrealized opportunities.[91] Successful entrepreneurship requires intelligence and creativity and a bit of good luck. While entrepreneurial innovations can be painful or disruptive in the short term,[92] they can eventually lead to the massive and widespread improvements in individual well-being of the sort we have had over the last several hundred years. Entrepreneurship acts as the engine of economic growth, and economic growth is the indispensable condition of increased well-being for the masses.

This defense may leave us disquieted. Yes, if economic development requires business activity, then perhaps we must tolerate it. But if it brings development at the cost of sacrificing mutual *respect* between persons, then markets take on the tragic cast of a necessary evil. Do markets really conflict with mutual respect? Libertarians think not. Indeed, many libertarians see markets as an important *source* and *forum* for respect. The market, as Voltaire observed, can encourage individuals of various ethnic and religious backgrounds to work together despite their different and often divisive backgrounds.[93] And while overlooking a person's religion in order to maximize one's own profit might not quite *itself* be the ideal equality of which philosophers dream, it is certainly an important advance over open religious conflict. It is a step *toward* the kind of mutual respect for which philosophers hope. Financial incentives can provide individuals with the motive to work closely with each other. Repeated interactions in the market can foster a kind of trust and respect that easily spills over into other contexts. No wonder, then, that early liberals were wont to associate markets with a variety of moral virtues. As Montesquieu wrote, "Commerce is a cure for the most destructive prejudices; for it is almost a general rule that wherever we find agreeable manners, there commerce flourishes; and that wherever there is commerce, there we meet with agreeable manners."[94]

But what about the poor? However much markets might encourage respect, toleration, and peace, if markets mean that "the rich get richer and the poor get poorer," then many will regard markets as morally bankrupt. This is especially true regarding the *libertarian* vision of markets, in which businesses are set free to pursue their self-interest, untrammeled by regulation or redistribution. Can libertarianism cope with the problem of poverty? In the next chapter, we will see how they have tried.

CHAPTER SIX

Poverty and Spontaneous Order

IN 1878, Phillips Thompson published his satirical "The Political Economist and the Tramp," a poem decrying the "Social Darwinism" he associated with Adam Smith and Herbert Spencer and its view of market life as ruthless competition:

> ... Dost thou know, deluded one,
> What Adam Smith has clearly proved,
> That 'tis self-interest alone
> by which the wheels of life are moved?
> This competition is the law
> By which we either live or die;
> I've no demand thy labor for,
> Why, then, should I thy wants supply?
> And Herbert Spencer's active brain
> Shows how the social struggle ends;
> The weak die out the strong remain;
> 'Tis this that nature's plan intends. . . . [1]

Libertarianism's critics have repeated these charges ever since. Their critiques operate on two levels: at the "micro" level of individual human actions, libertarians valorize the pursuit of self-interest; at the "macro" level of human society, libertarians see society as a Darwinian battlefield for separating the strong from the weak.[2] At both levels, defenders of market society are found wanting.

In response to this double-barreled critique, libertarians point out that many in their tradition fought explicitly on behalf of the poor and the marginalized. In the 1600s, proto-libertarians such as the English Leveller John Lilburne pioneered the view that each person matters, no matter their station at birth. In his own day, Adam Smith was criticized by Thomas Malthus and others for being *overly* concerned with the poor. Richard Cobden's concern to improve the condition of workers drove his struggle against the Corn Laws (see chapter 8). More recently, Milton Friedman and F. A. Hayek insisted that their libertarian program was the most effective means—indeed, the only means—for lifting people out of poverty.

Still, the "cold-hearted" label continues getting stuck to libertarians—and it remains stuck no matter how eagerly generation after generation of libertarians have sought to scrub it off. In this chapter, we examine how members of the libertarian family have addressed the problem of poverty, in different ages and in different places. We begin by examining the central charge from Thompson's poem: that libertarians are Social Darwinists.

Survival of the Fittest

From its first appearance around 1900, the phrase "Social Darwinism" has been used almost exclusively to describe the ideas of *other people*.[3] Our research turned up not a single libertarian who claimed themselves an adherent. As intellectual historian Donald Bellomy has argued, the phrase "Social Darwinist" seems primarily to connote disagreement. The object of that disagreement drifts over time; Social Darwinism has served as a shorthand for ideas that were, variously, militaristic, racist, supportive of eugenics, indifferent to the plight of the poor, or excessively biological in their view of humanity.[4]

It was not until the 1940s that Richard Hofstadter made the phrase famous by applying it to the doctrine of laissez-faire. Hofstadter's particular targets were Herbert Spencer and Spencer's American contemporary, the Yale social scientist William Graham Sumner.[5] First in the pages of the *New England Quarterly* and later in his influential book *Social Darwinism in American Thought*, Hofstadter deployed the term in a forceful critique of libertarian trends in American thought.[6]

For Hofstadter, like others before him, the primary meaning of "Social Darwinism" was to express contempt for ideas he disliked. And Hofstadter passionately disliked the idea of laissez-faire. A former member of Columbia University's Communist Party group, Hofstadter wrote to friends that he "hate[d] capitalism and everything that goes with it."[7] In Spencer and Sumner, Hofstadter found thinkers who stood for everything he detested, in part because they opposed what he himself prized: a progressive economy directed by enlightened expert rule. According to Hofstadter, Spencer and Sumner found in the Darwinian idea of a struggle for existence "a new sanction for economic competition" and in "the survival of the fittest a new argument in opposition to state aid for the weak."[8]

Hofstadter's charge had enough plausibility to stick. Both Spencer and Sumner had indeed drawn social lessons from the new science of evolution; Spencer himself played a significant role in the development of that science. And when it came to discussing our social obligations toward the poor and the weak, both thinkers had the unfortunate tendency to invoke broadly evolutionary ideas in a way that seemed almost designed to invite uncharitable readings. Consider the following lines from Spencer's *Social Statics*:

> Nature demands that every being shall be self-sufficing. He on whom his own stupidity, or vice, or idleness, entails loss of life, must, in the generalizations of philosophy, be classed with the victims of weak viscera or malformed limbs. In his case, as in the others, there exists a fatal non-adaptation; and it matters not in the abstract whether it be a moral, an intellectual, or a corporeal one. Beings thus imperfect are nature's failures, and are recalled by her laws when found to be such. Along with the rest they are put upon trial. *If they are sufficiently complete to live, they do live, and it is well they should live. If they are not sufficiently complete to live, they die, and it is best they should die.*[9]

Sumner, too, had a knack for the memorably offensive phrase. In warning against the "socialists and sentimentalists" who seek to "regulate in any way the struggle of interests under liberty," he wrote:

> If we do not like the survival of the fittest, we have only one alternative and that is the *survival of the unfittest*. If A, the unfittest to survive, is

about to perish and somebody interferes to make B, the fittest, carry
and preserve A, it is plain that the unfittest is made to survive and that
he is maintained at the expense of B, who is curtailed and restrained
by just so much. This process, therefore, is a lowering of social development and is working backwards, not forwards.[10]

Passages such as these lead many to conclude that Spencer and
Sumner were, *at best*, indifferent to the plight of the poor. If this
indifference was motivated by the belief that economic competition
worked to sort the "fit" from the "unfit," these passages support the
common charge of Social Darwinism as well.

Unlikely as it may seem, though, a careful examination of
Spencer and Sumner's views supports neither charge. Libertarians have often stressed this fact, partly (one suspects) to improve
the image of their own view.[11] But others, too, have concluded
that Spencer and Sumner got a bad rap. After decades of post-
Hofstadter revisionary scholarship, the dominant position among
mainstream intellectual historians holds that neither Spencer nor
Sumner was a "Social Darwinist" in any meaningful sense of the
phrase.[12]

The central problem is that critics such as Hofstadter misunder-
stand what Spencer and Sumner mean by "fitness." To the modern
ear—and in Hofstadter's own usage—that phrase suggests a moral
endorsement of violent and cunning struggle and an approval of its
results. If the rich succeed while the poor fail, it must be because
the rich are "fit" and the poor are not. It is *good* that the rich flourish; it is *good* that the poor die out. Read this way, the Social Darwinist concept of the "survival of the fittest" becomes a normative
principle.

For Spencer and most others of his era, however, appeals to "the
survival of the fittest" were purely *descriptive* in nature. To label
an organism as "fit" was to make a largely formal statement about
its adaptation to the conditions of survival in a particular environment. It did *not* imply a normative judgment about the value of the
organism or the goodness of its survival. Indeed, Spencer himself
actively sought to discourage such a misunderstanding:

> The law is not the survival of the "better" or the "stronger." . . . It is
> the survival of those which are constitutionally fittest to thrive under

the conditions in which they are placed; and very often that which, humanly speaking, is inferiority, causes the survival.[13]

Crucially, this fitness is *relative*. The traits that constitute fitness for one environment or stage of human development might be wholly inappropriate for another. Indeed, Spencer believed that human beings were in the process of a transition between two radically different stages of development and that their moral codes, economic institutions, and political systems were adjusting accordingly.

Human societies were evolving, Spencer thought, from *militancy* to *industrialism*. The former mode of social organization fit well those periods of history marked by frequent violent conflict. Organization was centralized and hierarchical; coercion drove compliance. This was necessary, Spencer argued, to mobilize the persons and resources needed to carry out the primary purpose that these societies emerged to fulfill: offensive and defensive war. Industrial societies, on the other hand, emerge out of the peace and security that earlier militant forms of society made possible. Freed from the constant necessity of fighting and preparing to fight, industrial societies could afford to devote their attention to the protection of individual liberty. In this context, the powers of government could be restrained by institutions of representative, decentralized government and economic laissez-faire.[14]

On a normative level, Spencer and Sumner were first and foremost libertarians, not Social Darwinists. As libertarians, they were committed in principle to opposing the initiation of force in all its forms. Such a commitment is incompatible with the kind of "might makes right," "law of the jungle" philosophy associated with the phrase "Social Darwinism." Indeed Spencer's law of equal freedom expressly prohibits forceful aggression by the strong against the weak:

> If every man has freedom to do all that he wills, provided he infringes not the equal freedom of any other man, it is manifest that he has a claim to his life: for without it he can do nothing that he has willed; and to his personal liberty: for the withdrawal of it partially, if not wholly, restrains him from the fulfillment of his will. It is just as clear, too, that each man is forbidden to deprive his fellow of life or liberty: inasmuch as he cannot do this without breaking the law, which, in asserting his

freedom, declares that he shall not infringe "the equal freedom of any other." For he who is killed or enslaved is obviously no longer equally free with his killer or enslaver.[15]

On a range of social issues, Spencer and Sumner defended the weak and vulnerable not in spite of but precisely *because* of their libertarian commitments. For example, their principled commitment to nonaggression led them to be more consistent opponents of military imperialism than moderate liberals such as John Stuart Mill and other early progressives. Both Spencer and Sumner spoke out against state power being used to support the interests of the wealthy and well-connected at the expense of the masses.[16] Both would have been horrified by the coercive programs of eugenics later put into practice through restrictions on immigration, economic controls, compulsory sterilization, and other measures grossly incompatible with libertarian principles.[17] Both were staunch advocates of workers' right to unionize (or *not* to unionize, a right maintained by each individual worker).[18] Both defended the equal rights of women in an era when this was an unpopular stance, and Spencer even wrote sympathetically about the rights of children.[19]

Yet both Spencer and Sumner generally opposed state aid to the poor. Sometimes they were even charged, unjustly, with opposing *voluntary* charity.[20] Why?

Their skepticism can partly be explained by the Victorian distinction between "poverty" and "pauperism."[21] Poverty referred to an external condition of want and need: a lack of material stuff. Pauperism, by contrast, denoted a corruption of the soul or mind: a defect of character. As we shall see, English libertarians of the nineteenth century were particularly concerned by programs intended to fight poverty—such as systems of outdoor relief—that often failed and led to pauperization. Poverty worried them not only because it signifies a lack of access to material goods but because it leads to dependency and thus to a diminution of people's liberty.

Victorians routinely distinguished between the deserving and the undeserving poor. Spencer and Sumner recognized that people could become poor through no fault of their own. But sometimes a difficult life results from a person's own poor choices. Spencer and Sumner thought that compelling others to support such persons using the power of the state was both ineffective and unjust: ineffective because money alone cannot help those whose poverty stems from irresponsibility; unjust because forced aid penalizes the prudent and rewards the reckless. This latter argument played a prominent role in Sumner's 1918 essay "The Forgotten Man," a tribute to the "clean, quiet, virtuous, domestic citizen, who pays his debts and his taxes" and who is rewarded for his virtue by being forced to subsidize others' vices.[22]

On grounds of both justice and expediency, then, these Victorians found even well-meaning state aid to be generally objectionable. But Spencer and Sumner also feared that many—perhaps most—government policies were *not* well-meaning. The true guiding force of most state policy, Spencer wrote, is the self-interest of the legislators who create it: "It is a tolerably well-ascertained fact that men are still selfish. And that beings answering to this epithet will employ the power placed in their hands for their own advantage is self-evident."[23] Because legislators' self-interest generally aligns with the interests of the wealthy and powerful—not those of the poor and weak—legislation tends toward continued oppression.[24]

Neither Spencer nor Sumner intended their arguments to counsel against all efforts to assist the poor. They objected not to charity as such but rather to *coercive* or *injudicious* charity. Compulsory aid and aid that actually *harms* the poor are condemned by considerations of both morality and expediency. But Spencer and Sumner believed that effective aid, especially to those who have fallen on hard times through no fault of their own, is an essential component of a good society—a moral virtue that ought to be encouraged.[25]

At the most basic level, Spencer and Sumner's objection to state-based approaches to poverty was rooted in the idea of social complexity. Social complexity, and the problems of unintended consequences that result, would play an increasingly important role in libertarian thought during the twentieth century, especially in the work of Friedrich Hayek. Indeed, the concept of social complexity can serve as a kind of organizing principle for the libertarian approach to poverty. On the negative side, social complexity explains why coercive state programs are unlikely to be effective at helping the poor. And positively, complexity explains why the best engine for lifting people out of poverty runs on the fuel of individual liberty and the principle of voluntarism in human affairs.

Drawing on insights from Scottish Enlightenment thinkers such as Hume and Smith, Spencer and Sumner viewed society as a complex network of individuals, organizations, and causal relationships. In an industrial society their interactions far exceeded the grasp of human senses or intellect. "In a simple society," Sumner wrote, "all the parts of the organization lie bare to view." The causal, economic, and moral relations between persons can be observed by all "in their visible operation."[26] In a complex industrialized society, however, we comprehend these relationships only through our imperfect understanding of abstract, general laws. At best such laws reveal the *usual* effects of policies on a *limited* range of persons. But regarding the *total* effect of our policies, we remain ignorant. The larger and more complex a society becomes, the more reason we have to be skeptical of top-down, one-size-fits-all solutions.

Complexity requires that we evaluate policies not by their intentions but by their results. While social reformers "enjoy the satisfaction of feeling themselves to be more moral or more enlightened than their fellow-men," they are in reality, Sumner thought, "only more ignorant and more presumptuous than other people."[27] They fail to appreciate that

> every action inside of the social organism is attended by a reaction, and ... this reaction may be spread far through the organism, affecting organs and modifying functions which are, at the first view of the matter, apparently so remote that they could not be affected at all. ... Therefore, if we set to work to interfere in the operation of the organism, with our attention all absorbed in one set of phenomena, and regulate our policy with a view to those phenomena only, we are very sure to do mischief.[28]

For Spencer, the attempt to stamp out social problems using targeted legislation was like trying to straighten a wrought-iron plate with a hammer:

> It sticks up a little here towards the left—"cockles," as we say. How shall we flatten it? Obviously, you reply, by hitting down on the part that is

prominent. Well, here is a hammer, and I give the plate a blow as you advise. Harder, you say. Still no effect. Another stroke? Well, there is one, and another, and another. The prominence remains, you see: the evil is as great as ever—greater, indeed. But this is not all. Look at the warp which the plate has got near the opposite edge. Where it was flat before it is now curved. A pretty bungle we have made of it. Instead of curing the original defect, we have produced a second. . . . The required process is less simple than you thought. Even a sheet of metal is not to be successfully dealt with after those common-sense methods in which you have so much confidence. What, then, shall we say about a society? "Do you think I am easier to be played on than a pipe?" asks Hamlet. Is humanity more readily straightened than an iron plate?[29]

Thus the attempt to prevent drunkenness by placing restrictive licenses on the sale of gin inadvertently leads to black markets, new forms of crime and violence, and a net *increase* in the production and consumption of liquor.[30] Thus the attempt to ensure affordable housing by mandating various requirements of structure and space leads the poor to be priced out of the rental market and crowded together in unregulated quarters "unfit for human habitation."[31] Or, to take a more contemporary example, the attempt to render banking secure by means of legislative restrictions and guarantees leads lenders and borrowers alike to act recklessly. After all, if the state stands ready to pick up the tab for their extravagance, why should borrowers exert much effort to assess the stability of potential lenders? And why should lenders expend much effort in *being* stable? As Spencer wrote, "the ultimate result of shielding men from the effects of their folly, is to fill the world with fools."[32]

Spencer's negative case against state aid foreshadows libertarians' arguments ever since. But let us also consider the positive libertarian argument: that instead of coercive state programs, we should fight poverty by enlisting the ideals and institutions of liberty. Here, too, the concept of spontaneous order remains central.

Pencils, Coats, and Crimson Cloth

Viewed against the long sweep of history, poverty seems a fixed feature of the human experience. As John Maynard Keynes observed in 1929: "From the earliest times of which we have a record—back, say, to two thousand years before Christ—down to the beginning of the eighteenth century, there was no very great change in the standard of life of the average man living in the civilized centers of the earth. Ups and downs, certainly. Visitations of plague, famine, and war. Golden intervals. But no progressive violent change."[33] But starting in the late 1700s, with the birth of liberal ideas, a new phenomenon stirred the leading business and cultural centers of the West: economic growth.

Economists describe this macro-historic change as the "hockey stick" model of per capita growth. The long flat handle of the stick represents those eons with little change described by Keynes. But a sudden "violent change" begins at the heel of the hockey stick—the early 1700s, especially in liberalizing countries such as Holland and Britain—and then runs nearly straight up. The rate of growth has been especially pronounced in the United States. The economist Angus Maddison estimates that starting in 1820, the average rate of growth in the United States has been 2 percent—a small number that, through compounding, has produced a dramatic change in the standard of living for ordinary people. On Robert Fogel's calculations, for example, in 1875 the average American family spent about three-fourths of its income on food, clothing, and shelter. By 1995 that rate had dropped to less than 15 percent. Michael Cox and Richard Alm estimate that in 1938 Americans owned one car per every 4.4 persons; in 1960, one per every 2.4; and by 2003; one per 1.26. Dierdre McCloskey calls these fundamental changes in the human experience the "Great Fact." As McCloskey notes, no competent economist denies it.

This Great Fact features prominently in libertarians' positive arguments on poverty. As the great twentieth-century development economist (and libertarian) P. T. Bauer puts it: "Poverty has no causes. Wealth has causes." It is no accident that systematic economic growth began and accelerated largely in parallel with classical liberal ideas such as society by consent, freedom of expression, and individualized rewards for innovation and hard work.[34] The spectacular improvement in the material condition of ordinary people resulted not from any great benefactor or goodwill and solidarity among the masses. Far from relying on some Revolution of Good Intentions, this particular engine of human improvement relies on self-interest and the spontaneous orders it creates. It requires not even an *awareness* that good is being done.

In 1705, a scandalous poem called "The Grumbling Hive, or, Knaves Turned Honest" slipped anonymously into the leading literary circles of London. The poem, composed by Bernard de Mandeville, describes a thriving community of bees. Previously driven by avarice and desire for personal gain, the bees are suddenly made virtuous. As a result of this "improvement," alas, their economy collapses. The surviving bees retreat to a hollow tree, where they scratch out their remaining days. The poem inverted Christian teachings by insisting that vices such as greed and avarice, and not virtues such as self-sacrifice and concern for others, lead to general prosperity. As Mandeville describes the former glory days of the hive, when vice prevailed: "The worst of all the multitude / Did something for the common good."

Contemporary libertarians often first learn of spontaneous orders from Leonard Read's classic 1958 essay, "I, Pencil," which follows Adam Smith's near-equally famous example of the "woolen coat" from two hundred years before. Both describe the fantastic feat of coordination required to produce ordinary items. Less known is that both examples follow a still-earlier discussion in Mandeville concerning the production of crimson cloth.[35] In the *Fable*, Mandeville writes: "What a Bustle is there to be made in several Parts of the World, before a fine Scarlet or crimson Cloth can be produced." He lists the many craft-trades that are required to produce the cloth, and still others that are needed to make the tools for its manufacture. Global coordination is required to produce even the crimson colorant:

> How widely are the Drugs and other Ingredients dispers'd thro' the Universe that are to meet in one Kettle! Allum indeed we have of our own; Argol we might have from the Rhine, and Vitriol from Hungary; all this is in Europe; but then for Saltpetre in quantity we are forc'd to go as far as the East-Indies. . . . While so many sailors are broiling in the Sun and sweltering with Heat in the East and West of us, another set of them are freezing in the North to fetch Potashes from Russia.[36]

Consumer goods are not the only products of spontaneous processes. Mandeville notes that social traditions and even whole systems of rules often emerge through unwitting action. Regarding the precepts of English common law, for example, Mandeville writes: "there are very few, that are the work of one man, or of one generation; the greatest part of them are the product, the joint labor of several ages." He continues: "The Wisdom I speak of, is not the offspring of a fine understanding, or intense thinking, but of sound and deliberate judgement, acquired from a long experience in business, and a multiplicity of observations." Social knowledge is primarily a product of experience and the observation of the particularities of time and place, not of abstract reason or grand social plans. Evolutionary ideas first developed by proto-libertarians such as Mandeville to explain social phenomena would be picked up much later by Darwin and applied to problems of biology.[37]

The creation of social rules, like the production of a swath of crimson cloth, is a fabulous cooperative achievement. Most miraculous to Mandeville was that such coordination is achieved peacefully, indeed freely. He invites us to imagine a different productive process in which some great tyrant, desiring a piece of crimson cloth, attempts to compel all these various laborers to serve a need. This despot would meet such resistance from so many places that, no matter how great his power, he could never accomplish it. Yet in real-life crimson cloth gets produced as a matter of course, without anyone being forced to that end and without any of the key participants—miners, accountants, sailors, shepherds, and so on—having any notion that one end product of their labor will be fine pieces of crimson cloth. The cloth is produced not only voluntarily, Mandeville observes, but *unknowingly*.

Though cooperative labor produces social benefits, no individual needs to undertake his daily work with such ends in mind. Instead, each works with an eye to his own interest: "every one Works for himself, how much soever he may seem to Labour for others."[38] This world of competitive commerce rests upon an operational assumption that has an egalitarian feel: the assumption that all participants, no matter their social rank, have interests of their own that are worthy of being looked out for. Seventy years after Mandeville, Adam Smith would pick up this analytical assumption and build it into the base of the new science of economics.

On the opening page of *The Wealth of Nations*, Smith describes his visit to a pin factory. Ten people, each working alone, might produce a total of 10–20 pins in a day. But by dividing the tasks and working as a team, they routinely produce 48,000 pins a day—a massive increase in productivity. This might not seem significant when the products are simple pins. But when this same peaceful, cooperative approach of dividing labor is turned to the production of pencils and penicillin, rivets and roofing materials, corn and copper, and eventually televisions, automobiles, air-conditioners, and smartphones, the productive implications are staggering.[39] Market society *in and of itself* lifts us from poverty. As Mandeville put the point: "THUS Vice nurs'd Ingenuity, / Which join'd with time and industry, / Had carry'd Live's Conveniences, / It's real Pleasures, Comforts, Ease, / To such a Height, the very Poor / Liv'd better than the Rich before, / And nothing could be added more."[40]

For Smith, as for Mandeville, self-interest inclines our species toward exchange: we want to trade, and we want rules and norms that help those trades go smoothly. Nobel laureate Vernon Smith, the founder of experimental economics, has called this our "capacity for social exchange."[41] Human beings, left free, will relentlessly seek institutions that make possible positive-sum interactions. Adam Smith's biting critique of mercantilism sprang directly from his idea that any institutional system that restricted the God-implanted drive to exchange was unnatural. Smith writes: "It is the industry which is carried on for the benefit of the rich and the powerful, that is principally encouraged by our mercantile system. That which is carried on for the benefit of the poor and indigent, is too often, either neglected, or oppressed."[42] Mercantilist systems stunt the human propensity to exchange, and in so doing benefit the few at the expense of the many.

Smith argued that, without unjust interventions, an institutional system favorable to our natural sociability would "establish itself of its own accord." That system would emerge thanks to a natural harmony of individual interests that can be achieved when free exchange is protected. The sovereign has just three duties within Smith's "system of natural liberty": to guard against foreign invasions, to protect individuals from injustices, and to erect "public works." The system of natural liberty protects the natural sociability of humankind. If allowed to arise and operate, this system would unleash the energy and talents of humans and channel them across the natural world to the greater benefit of all. In Smith's famous proto-libertarian formulation: "Little else is requisite to carry a state to the highest degree of opulence from the lowest barbarism, but peace, easy taxes, and a tolerable administration of justice; all the rest being brought about by the natural course of things."[43]

As Jacob Viner observes, in *The Theory of Moral Sentiments* (1759) we find Smith at his most optimistic about the natural harmony of the economic order. His subsequent *Wealth of Nations* (1776) attends more closely to the gaps between freely pursued individual action and the common good. Not surprisingly, Smith now sees a greater role for the state in shoring up the spontaneous system of exchange. Along with state support for schooling, Smith now allows "progressive" taxes on luxury vehicles as well as taxes on house rents and more.[44]

We find echoes of all these classical liberal ideas in the libertarian thinking of the twentieth century, though in predictably stronger formulations. Writing in the wake of the Progressive Era, Mises emphasized the assumptions of human sociability that underlay market society: "Social man as differentiated from autarkic man must necessarily modify his original biological indifference to the well-being of people beyond his own family. He must adjust his conduct to the requirements of social cooperation and look upon his fellow men's success as an indispensable condition of his own."[45] Later, in *Human Action* (1949), Mises complained that the New Liberals—simply because they supported the creation of state-based agencies to fight poverty—"arrogate to themselves the exclusive right to call their own program the program of welfare." This he considered "a cheap logical trick."[46] After all, according to Mises, the central finding of praxeology is that capitalism alone benefits property owners and every productive class, while simultaneously benefiting consumers too. In Mises's characteristically uncompromising formulation: "Any increase in total capital raises the income of capitalists and landowners absolutely and that of workers both absolutely and relatively. . . . The interests of entrepreneurs can never diverge from those of consumers."[47]

Ayn Rand sharpened Smith's sociable "self-interest" into a pointed doctrine of selfishness. The unleashing of egoistic ambition within a system of free markets produces greater achievements than any planner could achieve. The unfolding of these spontaneous processes unintentionally—and yet with Misesean inevitably—raises the living standard of every productive member of society. Good intentions have no role here. Rand writes: "The skyline of New York is a monument of a splendor that no pyramids or palaces will ever equal or approach. But America's skyscrapers were not built by public funds or for a public purpose: they were built by the energy, initiative and wealth of private individuals for personal profit. And, instead of impoverishing the people, these skyscrapers, as they rose higher and higher, kept raising people's standard of living—including the inhabitants of slums, who lead a life of luxury compared to the life of an ancient Egyptian slave or of a modern Soviet-Socialist worker."[48]

As Rand takes care to note, life for workers in a libertarian society is not merely better than it was for Egyptian slaves or Soviet workers. As a matter of deduction from man's nature as a rational agent, capitalism is objectively identifiable as the *best possible* social arrangement: "[Capitalism] creates optimum social conditions for man to respond to the challenges of nature in such a way as to best further his life. It operates to the benefit of all those who choose to be active in the productive process, whatever their level of ability."[49]

Other Cold War libertarians, notably Friedrich Hayek and Milton Friedman, followed Smith more closely in giving the state an important—though carefully limited—role in fighting poverty. Friedman, for example, follows the main libertarian principle that individual liberty, not state action, best reduces poverty: "The extraordinary economic growth experienced by Western countries during the past two centuries and the wide distribution of the benefits of free enterprise have enormously reduced the extent of poverty in any absolute sense in the capitalistic countries of the West."[50] Still, Friedman says, poverty is in part a relative phenomenon. While charity and other nonmarket forms of social cooperation can help fill the gaps created by the general rise of market society (on which, see the following section), there is also a role for state action in setting what Friedman calls "a floor under the standard of life of every person in the community."[51]

Hayek also supported a limited welfare state. Over the course of his career, from *The Road to Serfdom* (1944) to the final volume of *Law, Legislation, and Liberty* (1979), Hayek consistently claimed that something like a basic income was compatible with, and perhaps required by, a free society.

> The assurance of a certain minimum income for everyone, or a sort of floor below which nobody need fall even when he is unable to provide for himself, appears not only to be wholly legitimate protection against a risk common to all, but a necessary part of the Great Society in which the individual no longer has specific claims on the members of the particular small group into which he was born.[52]

What form should state-backed welfare programs take? Though departing from spontaneous processes, Friedman looked for a form of state aid that we might call *as spontaneous as possible*. Instead of a host of problem-targeted state programs (housing, food, medical care), Friedman suggested that the state provide needy individuals with the flexible good of cash through a negative income tax. Such an approach helps individuals *as individuals* rather than as members of groups (say, the elderly as a group, or farmers as a group). Just as important, this approach allows individuals to improve their situation by working through the market rather than by distorting it, with all the unintended consequences such approaches entail.[53]

Charles Murray used this type of argument in his proposal that the American welfare state be replaced by a guaranteed income.[54] In 2012, on some calculations, the federal government spent more than $668 billion on over *one hundred and twenty-six* anti-poverty programs.[55] When you add in the $284 billion spent by state and local governments, that amounts to $20,610 for every poor person in America. Each one of those anti-poverty programs comes with its own bureaucracy and its own Byzantine set of rules. Many of them also impose a variety of demeaning, intrusive, and paternalistic requirements on recipients in a vain attempt to distinguish between the "needy" and "non-needy" poor. For libertarians such as Charles Murray who are concerned to reduce the size, cost, and intrusiveness of government, there is a certain appeal to scrapping the whole system and replacing it with a $10,000 payment to each and every adult in the country—a poverty relief measure so simple that it might be administered by a computer program.[56]

Mutual Aid: Darwin Again

For those of us who grew up in a welfare state, it is easy to imagine that, before the state got involved, there were no effective social welfare programs at all. But welfare historians such as David Green,[57] Dave Beito,[58] P.H.J.H. Gosden,[59] and Simon Cordery[60] tell a different story. Prior to the advent of the welfare state in the early twentieth century, welfare was often provided voluntarily through complex emergent structures of mutual aid. These tapped different motivations than those we have considered thus far: rather than simple self-interest, mutual aid societies also relied on reciprocity, solidarity, and feelings of mutual concern.

These societies often began informally. Neighbors in the public house might decide over a pint to contribute to a common fund, which could be tapped by any member in need. Among the first of such societies was the Incorporation of Carters, founded in Leith, Scotland, in 1555. The Incorporation consisted mainly of a simple lockbox into which members made small contributions at regular intervals. By pooling resources, members found a way to insure each other against risks of job loss and precarity, or against sudden expenses such as a sickness in the family or the costs of a funeral. Clubs like these sprang up all over the British Isles. They came in a great variety of sizes, with differing rules, purposes, and benefit structures.

Many early clubs were organized as "dividing societies." On this simple model, a balance would grow throughout the year, with dividends being disbursed to all members annually (typically at Christmas). Without a large endowment, though, these societies were sometimes short of cash in times of need, and the annual approach to membership struggled with members who became injured or fell into long-term sickness. The rules of the various friendly societies evolved in response to such problems. It became common for societies to carry balances from year to year and to guarantee membership and benefits over longer periods. Societies experimented with different rules and learned from the experiments of others.

From the beginning, mutual aid societies were important sites of civic engagement for working people. The lodges were self-governing; most decisions were made by a show of hands or voice vote. Membership provided an impetus, and opportunity, for the working class to develop skills of deliberation and oratory. Members took pride in membership. Along with their social welfare function, lodges were often a central feature of people's social lives.

Friendly societies soon evolved into larger and more permanent forms of union. The early nineteenth century saw an explosive growth of English mutual aid societies in size, number, and variety. To further disperse risk, many local aid societies eventually merged into federations known as affiliated orders. By 1874, when a Royal Commission on Friendly Societies was established, there were thirty-four affiliated societies in England with over a thousand members each. The two largest such societies, the Manchester Unity of Oddfellows and the Ancient Order of Foresters, eventually boasted nearly a million members between them. As the orders adopted these larger federal structures, their range of welfare services broadened. Along with funeral benefits and help to the short-term unemployed, affiliated orders increasingly provided medical care for members *and* their families. With a larger pool of financial resources, some orders offered long-term financial support to the widows and children of deceased members, and special programs such as grants to people who needed to travel to find work. Medical welfare became a major emphasis of lodge activity. It became common for each lodge to hire its own medical doctor or team of doctors. Doctors typically were paid a per capita fee each month in exchange for visiting sick lodge members. In large towns, some orders went beyond simply hiring doctors to establishing hospitals for members' care.

As these voluntary welfare societies grew in scale, their original ideal of direct democracy became unwieldy. Still, their democratic *ethos* remained. In place of direct discussion some lodges adopted referendums. Some instituted governing branches among which the responsibility for governance would rotate on an agreed-upon schedule. Soon representative assemblies were established. Eventually, the largest groups developed a three-tiered federated structure: national branch, regional district, local unity. Voluntary mutual aid societies had become national in scope.

When Alexis de Tocqueville toured the United States in 1831, he observed that Americans already had developed the busy habit of creating and joining voluntary associations. David Beito estimates that by 1920 some 18 million Americans voluntarily belonged to mutual aid societies, an astonishing 30 percent of all adults.[61] Membership in labor unions of the time, by contrast, rarely included even 10 percent of the working population.

Beito distinguishes between secret societies and fraternal insurance organizations (though functionally these may overlap). Secret societies such as the Masons, Elks, and Oddfellows focused on social and informal aspects of mutual aid. Rather than strictly specified benefits, they aimed to build an ethos of service—first to fellow lodge members and then to the wider community. Based on strong norms of responsibility, secret societies generally avoided written contracts or specific guarantees of welfare benefits: "'As a rule,' as the historian Lynn Dumenhill has written, 'Masonic spokesmen were dismayed by the possibility that men joined Masonry for mercenary reasons, and they repeatedly emphasized that one of the Masonic pledges included the oath that the initiate had not been influenced by the desire for personal gain.'"[62] Members knew, though, that should they fall into need, fellow members would offer help, even hiring outside specialists when necessary. While groups like the Masons usually worked informally, they had such power that they sometimes embarked on more visible projects. For example, during the late nineteenth and early twentieth centuries, Masonic lodges built orphanages and care facilities for older members.

Fraternal insurance societies had an even greater influence on the provision of social welfare in America. While sharing many of the rituals of the secret societies, these organizations offered members formal insurance policies. Originally focusing on the payment of death benefits (a lump sum that could be as large as a full year's wages), the societies increasingly moved into medical and accident insurance. Beito notes that before the Depression the fraternal organizations dominated the medical insurance market. Strictly commercial competitors lagged far behind. Beito suggests that the superiority of the fraternal model was based on its better ability to handle the problem of "moral hazard." With impersonally administered health insurance, people face the moral hazard to exaggerate their illnesses or seek more medical attention than they need, knowing that others will bear some of the cost. Unlike private companies (and unlike later government models), fraternal societies could combat moral hazard by drawing on member solidarity and their sense of mutual responsibility. Beito quotes a study of fraternal societies by the Social Insurance Commission of California: "the 'mutual benefit' nature of the societies undoubtedly counteracts the tendency to malinger. Persons who might be unscrupulous in dealing with a commercial company are apt to be more careful when dealing with an organization whose financial condition is a matter of direct concern to themselves."[63]

These self-help organizations gave working people a class consciousness distinct from the "reformers" from the middle and upper classes. As the intellectual historian Peter Ryley observes, "There was a strong working-class attachment to the idea of the 'free-born Englishman' that saw compulsion and regulation as an imposition." There was pride in being independent of government and of binding together with fellow workers. Indeed, Ryley continues: "The existence of self-help organizations, owned and controlled by their members, was one of the reasons why it has been suggested that the call for social reform and state welfare originally emanated from the middle, rather than the working, classes."[64]

The system was not without serious moral flaws; developed in a largely patriarchal and racist culture, the largest organizations typically restricted membership to white males. Nonetheless, mutual aid societies played an important role in the experience of marginalized groups including women, immigrants, and, especially, African Americans. Women-only membership societies such as the Ladies of the Maccabees enrolled huge numbers, in part by offering benefits such as maternity insurance. Immigrants were especially enthusiastic members of mutual aid societies. Along with much-needed support for the newly arrived, these groups celebrated ethnic pride with festivals and summer camps for children that sustained cultural traditions. And according to the sociologist Howard Odum, African Americans joined mutual aid and fraternal societies at a greater rate than any other racial or ethnic group. Indeed, Odum estimates that in 1910, the total African American membership in lodges equaled or exceeded their total church membership. It was not uncommon for towns in the South with five hundred black residents to have fifteen to twenty mutual aid lodges. Over 90 percent of Black residents in northern cities such as Philadelphia held fraternal insurance policies, topping even the 80 percent rate among white Philadelphians. The oldest African American mutual aid society, the Prince Hall Masonic Order, boasts a remarkable roll call of members: Adam Clayton Powell Jr., Oscar DePriest, Thurgood Marshall, Carl Stokes, Booker T. Washington, and W.E.B. Du Bois.[65]

Fighting Poverty with Liberty

When libertarian historians such as Beito and Palmer point to friendly societies as part of the "libertarian" solution to poverty, this does not mean that mutual aid participants were themselves libertarians (as the roll of the Prince Hall Order makes vivid). Still, many members of cooperative and charitable organizations did work from explicitly libertarian premises, most notably in Victorian England.

The most important such "welfare" organization was the Charity Organisation Society (COS). Established in London in 1869, the COS set up committees in each Poor Law district with the official aim of coordinating charitable activity. Led by free-market advocates such as Thomas Mackay (of the Liberty and Property Defense League), C. S. Loch, and Helen Bosanquet (wife of the idealist philosopher Bernard Bosanquet), the COS was a mainly middle-class effort aimed at reawakening the virtues of hard work and personal responsibility among the poor, virtues they saw as having been weakened by an excess of charitable activities. More specifically, the leaders of the COS thought welfare initiatives should remain true to the spirit of the Poor Law Amendment of 1834, which discouraged use of public relief by making tax-funded workhouses less attractive than jobs in private, for-profit industries. According to the COS organizers, the spirit of individual self-reliance so essential to a free society had been eroded by the increase in outdoor relief— that is, the distribution of meals and other goods to anyone who walked up and claimed a need. Their solution was to place specially trained experts at the gates of charity to sort the deserving poor from the undeserving, and so to reinvigorate a sense of personal agency across even the lower levels of Victorian society.

According to the social historian J. W. Mason, "The great ideal of the C.O.S. was to make charity a science by reconciling the spirit of traditional Christian charity with the teachings of political economy."[66] Thomas Mackay provided the clearest conceptual defense of the principles of the COS, framing the debate with the new rising class of progressive reformers as a contest between a free, individualist view of social order and a socialist one. Mackay defined individualism as "the rule of conduct which obliges each individual man to adapt his instincts, habits and character to his surroundings. These surroundings in civilized life are governed by economic laws, which though not of inflexible rigidity are yet more permanent in their nature than human nature." By contrast, he defined socialism as "the instinct which induces man to reject, unconsciously for the most part, Nature's offer of safe conduct, and to submit themselves, in their search for happiness, to the guidance of groups and associations of men."[67]

During the first years of the COS, the moral remedy of self-reliance offered by Mackay and his associates was fairly widely accepted, at least among its middle-class practitioners and supporters. But as the 1870s wore on, the more radical, class-based socialist analysis of poverty grew more prominent in public discussions. Against that rising tide, libertarian reformers such as Mackay, Loch, and Bosanquet insisted that the problem of human need, in the context of a fast-growing industrial economy, remained essentially an *individual* problem, an issue of virtue or vice. Individually, each person had to choose whether to work and make their own way or to "free ride" on the work of others. Moreover, effective charity required moral gatekeepers, middle-class experts positioned to instruct the poor on how to support themselves. As Beatrice Webb and other progressives raised the profile of structural and class-based analyses, the leaders of COS doubled down on their individualistic, case-by-case approach. These case-workers saw the importance of individual virtue and so were skeptical of abstractions such as social class. As C. S. Loch put it: "The more we trace social difficulty or individual misfortune to special causes—incompetence, misjudgment, want of foresight, physical inability—the less do we care for the generalization implied in the antithesis 'rich and poor', the less does [that antithesis] meet our increasing knowledge of facts."[68]

As in England, the libertarians in mid-nineteenth-century France also faced a rising socialist challenge. French socialists called for wholesale structural change away from "capitalism" and its component parts: private property, profit from wage labor, rents on land, and interest on loans. In response, libertarians of the Paris School such as Frédéric Bastiat, Michel Chevalier, and Gilbert Guillaumin insisted that statist restrictions on liberty were the true cause of poverty. From articles published in *Le Libre-Échange* (which included some future classics from Bastiat) to the many books published by Guillaumin (including Chevalier's 1849 ode to American liberty, *La liberté aux États-Unis*), the Parisians made the case for extensive private liberty, especially in economic life. Insisting that every individual has a right to earn a living, these writers argued against laws that prevented workers from moving about the country to choose new jobs and industries. They advocated for lifting the restrictions on the movement of capital and goods so that benefits from the division of labor could be enjoyed by all. Inspired by Richard Cobden and John Bright's successful campaign to remove the Corn Laws in England, Bastiat leveled some of his heaviest criticism at the French system of import tariffs that violated the natural rights of producers and consumers—whatever their nationalities—to exchange. Further, since tariffs often targeted basic goods such as grains and clothing materials, they effectively functioned as a tax on the poor. Worse still, as in England, the tariffs largely benefited the landed elites by keeping prices for their crops artificially high. In sum, the leaders of the Paris School argued that France needed fewer restrictions on trade, not more—and more individual liberty, not less.[69]

In both nineteenth-century England and France, then, libertarians centered their arguments on individual agency, while their socialist rivals advanced a structural analysis of poverty and turned to the state for solutions. This makes the contrast with American libertarianism of the time particularly striking. In the United States it was libertarians such as Lysander Spooner and Benjamin Tucker who promoted a structural analysis of the "social problem." Instead of seeking out state solutions, however, the American individualists saw the state as the *cause* of the structural problem of poverty.

In "Poverty: Its Illegal Causes and Legal Cure" (1846), Spooner argued that poverty is not inevitable and that existing inequalities cannot be explained by differences of virtue and vice, ability and lack of ability. Instead, he wrote, the persistence of poverty primarily resulted from "arbitrary and unjust legislative enactments, and false judicial decisions, which actually deprive a large portion of mankind of their right to the fair and honest exercise of their natural powers, in competition with their fellow-men."[70] Spooner identified a number of specific policies that contributed to this injustice, including artificial limits on the collection of debts from corporate bodies—limits that benefit "privileged debtors" at the expense of society as a whole.[71] But Spooner directed his most severe criticism at restrictions on free competition in banking and interest. These laws restrict the availability of capital, Spooner argued, which in turn keeps poor laborers from purchasing land or starting a business. They are thus left with no alternative but to work for someone else, a position that Spooner (like Donisthorpe) believed kept them trapped in long-term poverty.[72]

Legal restrictions that set a maximum rate of interest, for example—so-called "anti-usury" laws—may be well-intentioned. But their effect is to make it difficult for the poor, who are by definition more risky borrowers, to obtain (legal) loans. Again, the general tendency of the existing system is to concentrate wealth among the financial elite. As Spooner says:

> The loanable capital of society is monopolized almost entirely by those few, those very few, who wish to borrow, and can offer the most approved security; while the mass of those, who have not capital of their own, but who, if left free to make their own contracts, would be able to obtain a portion sufficient to employ their own hands upon, are now, for the want of capital on which to bestow their labor, compelled

to sell their labor to those who have, by means of the usury laws, monopolized the capital.[73]

Usury laws hurt the working poor. But they do not actually help the prosperous either. After all, those with capital to lend would prefer to be allowed to lend it at the highest rate of interest the market can bear. Because market conditions are constantly changing, any state-mandated interest cap will inevitably prevent mutually beneficial loans from being made. From where, then, does support for such laws arise? Here as elsewhere, Spooner displays a keen awareness of the way state institutions are vulnerable to capture by special interest, a line of thinking that, a hundred years later, would be formalized by libertarians in the public choice school of economics, most notably James Buchanan and Gordon Tullock. Anticipating Director's Law, Spooner notes that usury laws are supported by neither the rich nor the poor but by the middle-class businessmen "who control the legislation of the country, and who, by means of usury laws, can sparge money from those who are richer, and labor from those who are poorer than themselves—and thus make fortunes."[74]

In a democratic republic, one might imagine that ordinary workers would use the power of the vote to weaken the property rights of the rich and better their own condition. But Spooner saw that the poor never win at politics. So long as the state has the power to violate the rights of citizens, "so long will [property] be perpetually infringed, invaded, and denied, by innumerable legislative devices of the cunning and the strong, which a large portion of society, the ignorant, the weak, and the poor, can neither ferret out, nor resist."[75] Once the idea of equal rights before the law is abandoned, Spooner would later observe, "the boldest, the strongest, the most fraudulent, the most rapacious, and the most corrupt, men will have control of the government, and make it a mere instrument for plundering the great body of the people."[76]

How, then, to create a genuinely free political economy? Spooner's answer: break the state-supported monopolies. He writes: "The result ... would be, that the future accumulations of society, instead of being held, as now, in large estates owned by a few individuals while the many were in poverty, would be distributed in small estates among the mass of the people." Existing large estates would be scattered over the course of a generation or two. "Afterwards, we should see no such inequalities in the pecuniary conditions of man as now exist." Spooner claimed that the system of liberty would work toward both an increase in total wealth (in part because people work harder and more creatively for themselves) and a more equal distribution of that wealth (since capital could now flow freely). Spooner did not repudiate the Victorian ideal of individual responsibility. But his approach situates personal agency within a social structure made more prosperous, and more equal, through the protection of liberty. As he notes: "Some few incompetent or improvident individuals might always be poor; but there would be no such general poverty as now prevails among those who were honest, industrious and frugal."[77]

Spooner was not alone among American libertarians in calling for structural economic reform. Between 1881 and 1908, contributors to *Liberty* magazine routinely expressed a sympathy for workers and skepticism toward existing capitalism that equaled the intensity of any of the socialists. Frank Brooks comments: "The individualist anarchists who wrote on economics in *Liberty* essentially had a liberal mind and a socialist heart."[78]

In his introduction to the inaugural issue of *Liberty*, Benjamin Tucker deplored "the appalling problems of poverty, intemperance, ignorance, and crime." The cause of these conditions, Tucker argued, was "usury," a term he used to refer to practices made possible only by state-granted monopolies—notably monopolies concerning the use of land and the extension of credit. As we saw in chapter 3, Tucker argued that workers are owed the full value of their product (that "labor should be one's own"). But, like other anarcho-individualists of the Boston school, Tucker also rejected rents for land and interest on loans. As he put it: "Here, as usual, the State is the chief of sinners." Ground rent only exists because the state collects rents and enforces existing titles, which are themselves historically rooted in fraud or worse. Without state support for land monopolies, Tucker reasoned, "the land would be free to all, and no one could control more than he used."[79]

Tucker's views on interest were similarly extreme. Interest on loans exists, he claimed, because the state sanctions only the currency that it circulates and unjustly prohibits all others. Without this monopoly on the creation of money, "credit would be free to all, and money brought under the law of competition, would be issued at cost." Tucker says this system of state-granted monopoly is "the serpent gnawing at Labor's vitals, and only Liberty can detach and kill it." He concludes: "Give laborers their liberty, and they will keep their wealth."[80]

We must note one lacuna in this radically idealistic and progressive vision. With slavery being abolished in the United States only in 1865, poverty continued to oppress many recently freed slaves. We know that libertarians such as Spooner led the fight to end slavery, recognizing the practice as an extreme violation of individual sovereignty and the right to the fruit of one's labor. Still, even with Spooner, we find no *specific* discussion of how his poverty-fighting reforms might affect the freed slaves. Indeed, in our search of *Liberty* magazine (1881–1908), we find not a single discussion of this issue; references to "slaves" or "slavery" refer to the evils of the coercive state, rhetorical flourishes that will be familiar to readers of Rothbard or Rand. Given how nineteenth-century libertarianism was shaped by abolitionism, we can easily imagine libertarians of the era insisting that their structural reforms would help all citizens, including freed Blacks. Nonetheless, this silence on the issue might lead contemporary readers to wonder: even among these radically progressive American libertarians, to what degree did Black poverty matter?

By the turn of the twentieth century, both libertarian visions—progressive and idealistic in America; conservative and econometric in England and France—proved too weak to resist the rising tide of statist thinking. The strict anti-statism of the Boston libertarians was too radical for their fellow New Englanders, while the virtue-based approach of the Victorian libertarians, arguably, was not radical enough (by the 1880s, critics lampooned the COS approach as "Cringe or Starve"). As for the friendly society movement, even at the peak of its membership and scale, voluntary connections proved no match for the coercive power and expansive capacity of the great accomplishment of twentieth-century statism: the welfare state.[81] The radical individualism of the nineteenth-century libertarians slipped from public view and was soon all but forgotten.

Bleeding Heart Libertarians

Twentieth-century libertarians opposed the expanding welfare state in part because they rejected the moral ideal on which it was founded: social justice. They gave both theoretical and political reasons for doing so. On a theoretical level, strict libertarians such as Nozick argued that justice is a historical concept. For Nozick, whether a distribution is just or unjust depends *entirely* on how it came about—"Whatever arises from a just situation by just steps is itself just."[82] Inequality as such is morally irrelevant. Efforts by the state to achieve "social justice" through redistribution will only *create* injustice by depriving people of resources to which they were historically entitled. Above and beyond those micro-level entitlements, there is simply no such thing as macro-level (social) justice or injustice.[83]

While Hayek and Friedman allowed a slightly larger redistributive role for the state, they stood with Nozick in firmly rejecting the leftist theory of social justice. Friedman, for example, claimed that a free-market society would tend toward not only greater wealth but also greater material equality than all other historical systems. Yet he went out of his way to emphasize that this leveling should not be viewed as an achievement of justice; rather, relative wealth equality is "a desirable by-product of a free society, not its major justification."[84] More systematically, two years after the publication of Rawls's *Theory of Justice*, Hayek published *The Mirage of Social Justice*. According to Hayek, only products of human intentionality can properly be called "just" or "unjust." But since the actual distribution of goods and opportunities arose spontaneously, calling that distribution "just" or "unjust" (as advocates of social justice often do) would be a logical error. Indeed, in the context of a free society, Hayek calls the phrase "social justice" a piece of incoherent nonsense, much like the phrase "a moral stone."

Libertarians of Hayek's era also had political reasons for rejecting the idea. By 1960, it had become a common rhetorical practice on the left to describe Great Society programs (Medicaid, Medicare, food stamps, etc.) as requirements of social justice. Hayek bitterly criticized the political use of "social justice" as an "open-sesame" term for expanding state power, leading America step-by-step away from a society of free and responsible individuals down the road to serfdom. The libertarian alliance with conservatives of this era—Barry Goldwater, Margaret Thatcher, and Ronald Reagan, among others—was largely founded on a common rejection of statist demands for "social justice," whether undergirding calls for Great Society programs at home or full-on communism abroad.

In recent decades, however, some libertarians have begun to challenge this way of thinking. The emergence of "bleeding heart libertarianism" in the early twentieth century can be traced to a combination of factors—some theoretical and some more practical and political. We, the authors of this book, are widely seen as members of the bleeding heart movement; Tomasi's *Free Market Fairness* was the first book-length attempt to combine private economic liberty with social justice; Zwolinski founded and edited the Bleeding Heart Libertarians blog that served for a decade as the primary forum for "BHL" debates. Like many others in the BHL movement, we both finished graduate school after the fall of the Soviet Union and attended workshops organized by the Institute for Humane Studies, a group with an interdisciplinary approach to limited government that incorporated history, economics, and practical public policy. As graduate students in philosophy, we both entered our profession after the Great Debate between Rawls (for social justice) and Nozick (for rights-based libertarianism) had already been decided—with the Rawlsians, who dominated the editorial boards of major journals, very much on top. (Political philosophy courses of the era that featured Rawls and Nozick were typically taught as "Rawls and why Nozick was wrong.") This created for many of us a kind of disjunct in our thinking, along with a yearning to make something new of the Cold War libertarian creed.

More practically, the bleeding heart movement began at a time when libertarians had grown disillusioned with the libertarian-conservative alliance. In 2006, one libertarian blogger summed up the situation: "The long and tragic alliance of libertarians with the right against the spectre of state socialism is coming to a close, as it served no purpose after the fall of the Soviet Union and so-called 'conservatives' have subsequently taken to letting their true big-government-on-steroids colors fly. . . . It's time for libertarians to stop fighting the left and take up the challenge of *leading* the left."[85] That same year, Brink Lindsey published an article in the *New Republic* called "Liberaltarians." Widely recognized as the official start of the bleeding heart movement, Lindsey called for a new political alliance between libertarians and Democrats. But Lindsey realized that for this "new kind of fusionism" to last beyond the current election cycle, it needed deeper foundations. To succeed, he wrote, liberaltarianism needed to be a movement with intellectual coherence. What was needed was "a movement that, at the philosophical level, seeks some kind of reconciliation between Hayek and Rawls."[86] Will Wilkinson, Lindsey's colleague at the Cato Institute, dubbed this hoped-for philosophical fusionism "Rawlsekianism."[87] Both Lindsey and Wilkinson subsequently left Cato, presumably for what was then libertarian apostasy.[88] But the bleeding heart libertarian movement had been born.

At first glance, the prospects for fusing ideas from Rawls and Hayek might seem bleak: one advocated expansive state powers in pursuit of social justice, the other limited government and respect for private economic liberty. The history of the relationship between Hayek and Rawls, however, provides more context.

In 1965, Hayek wrote a letter from Freiberg to James Buchanan. Hayek begins by noting that he and Buchanan share an interest in understanding "the rules of conduct which are the foundation for a free society." Then, remarkably, Hayek states: "the only modern philosopher from whom I have received some help in this is John Rawls of M.I.T." Hayek recommends that Buchanan study an important early article by Rawls in which he argued that justice is a property of institutions rather than of particular distributions. In an analysis that was neither historical nor patterned, Rawls's focus on institutions was a kind of middle ground, judging institutions by their distributions not at any given moment but over the course of time, say, a generation or two. In his letter of reply a week later, Buchanan likewise expressed his approval of Rawls's institution-based approach to justice: "I agree that he is doing the most interesting work in philosophy and I hope that he has some impact."[89]

A decade later, Hayek reaffirmed his agreement with Rawls on this crucial point. In *The Mirage of Social Justice* (1973), Hayek directed concentrated fire upon the phrase "social justice" as it was used in popular political discourse. In the political arena, Hayek observed, appeals to "social justice" were typically marshaled to forcibly direct goods to some favored group or other—a process that, if unchecked, threatened the impersonal rules upon which the Great Society had been built. While vigorously attacking this popular use of social justice, Hayek noted that "social justice" was sometimes differently employed in learned conversations: not as a property of particular distributions but as a process-independent standard for evaluating the system of impersonal rules itself.[90] While open to the scholarly usage, Hayek preferred the term "justice" to the phrase "social justice."

This explains why Hayek describes his differences with Rawls as "more verbal than substantive."[91] At the conclusion of his critique of "social justice" as used in popular discourse, Hayek returns to this point: "there also exists a genuine problem of justice in connection with the deliberate design of political institutions, the problem to which Professor John Rawls has recently devoted an important book."[92]

So Hayek, Buchanan, and Rawls converged upon the idea— crucial to any theory of social justice—that we may properly evaluate entire rule systems as just or unjust. But there is more. For these men also shared ideas about the method by which the proper standard of evaluation might be identified and even, perhaps, about what sort of material distribution justice required.

By the late 1950s, Buchanan had grown impatient with the unreflectively consequentialist reasoning employed by many economists and social scientists. He wished to provide his own political theory a contractarian foundation. Without such a foundation, Buchanan feared, his conclusions about political action might seem mere "free-floating irrelevancies."[93] How might such a foundation be secured?

Writing with Gordon Tullock in 1962, Buchanan proposed a device he dubbed the "veil of uncertainty."[94] To model the moral equality of citizens, Buchanan and Tullock proposed that we imagine individuals selecting among various candidate constitutional rules from a position that rendered each uncertain what place they might have in the resulting social order, thus being unable to "predict with any degree of certainty whether he is more likely to be in a winning or a losing coalition on any specific issue" that might arise within any of the candidate rules.[95] Buchanan ran his "veil of uncertainty" argument at a lower level of idealization than the more famous argument later developed by Rawls; on Buchanan's model, parties are modeled as selecting among specific constitutional rules, or sets of such rules, rather than selecting between rival moral principles. Still, as Buchanan later noted, the "veil of uncertainty" anticipated, and shared, many of Rawls's motivational assumptions. By modeling contracting parties as making choices behind a veil, Buchanan explained, "[each imagined contracting party] will tend to agree on arrangements that might be called 'fair' in the sense that patterns of outcomes generated under such arrangements will be broadly acceptable, regardless of where the participant might be located in such outcomes."[96] As within Rawls's schema, this device captured a special concern for the least well-off in a system, since it leads parties "to concentrate on choice options that eliminate or minimize prospects for potentially disastrous results."[97]

Hayek appears to have considered a similar idea as early as 1940. Living in London during the Blitz, Hayek received letters from friends around the world offering to place his young children with some (then-unknown) families in their country, where they would remain if orphaned by the bombing. Hayek reports that this real-life experience led him to a general methodological principle: "we should regard as the most desirable order of society one which we would choose if we knew that our initial position in it would be determined purely by chance (such as the fact of our being born into a particular family)."[98] Regrettably, Hayek never worked out the implications of this idea. He turned his attention instead to central problems in economics proper and, when he returned to political writing years later, developed a political theory upon quasi-consequentialist foundations. While Buchanan did pursue a contractarian strategy, he did not seek to secure the scheme of basic liberties itself on such a foundation, much less consider their distributional implications.[99]

Still, it is intriguing to note these moments of convergence between Hayek and Buchanan, two of the premier libertarians of the twentieth century, and Rawls, the great champion of social justice. Like most thinkers on the left, Rawls thought that the pursuit of social justice required a large regulatory and redistributive state (and possibly even the eradication of private productive property). But our history suggests that great libertarians of the mid-twentieth century came close to offering a rival account of social justice of their own—even if none of them liked the term.

On March 3, 2011, Matt Zwolinski launched his Bleeding Heart Libertarians blog with the masthead "Free Markets & Social Justice." Noting that libertarians are not known for their sympathy for distributive or social justice, Zwolinski wanted to create a forum for academic philosophers who nonetheless were attracted to both sets of ideas. Even if rules and distributions emerge spontaneously, their spontaneity does not prevent us from asking whether they are just, and whether we might wish to change them in some ways. As Zwolinski wrote in his opening post: "What we have in common on this blog is an appreciation for market mechanisms, for voluntary forms of cooperation, for property rights, and for individual liberty. But we appreciate those things, in large part, *because* of the way they contribute to important human goods—and especially the way in which they allow some of society's most vulnerable members to realize those goods."[100]

Over the next decade, the BHL blog served as the focal point for libertarians (and critics) to explore "progressive" possibilities within the traditional libertarian view. A universal basic income requires (coercive) taxation but also seems to be a liberty-friendly way of providing help to the least fortunate members of society. Should libertarians who care about social justice support a basic income?[101] Libertarians have traditionally defended the right of people to create, publish, and view pornography (as long as it is produced voluntarily by adults). But BHL bloggers discussed whether libertarians should take more seriously feminist ideas about pornography as creating harm, and whether libertarians should recognize psychological harms as violations of rights.[102] Libertarians, following their classical liberal forebears, historically have been among the strongest advocates of strictly separating church and state. BHL bloggers asked whether there might sometimes be libertarian grounds for exempting religious groups from general laws and regulations, and whether elected officials might sometimes appropriately appeal to religion in public speech.[103] Writers also took to the blog to debate whether libertarians ought to recognize the dispersed harms of environmental damage, or the harms created by people who refuse to take vaccinations.[104]

While these progressive BHL proposals drew plenty of attention from nonlibertarians, much of the heaviest fire came from within the libertarian camp itself. More orthodox libertarians, working roughly from Cold War libertarian premises, critiqued the Bleeding Hearts' ideas. Tom Palmer, for example, objected to the affirmation of positive liberty as both a strategic mistake and conceptual error. It is a mistake, Palmer argued, to refer to the many social benefits produced by the conditions of (negative) liberty as being themselves forms of "liberty." As Palmer memorably put it: "That's just a confusion, like confusing health and medicine (I take the medicine to become healthy, but I don't call medicine 'health')."[105]

The BHLers were also challenged by left-anarchist libertarians such as Roderick Long, Kevin Carson, Charles Johnson, and Gary Chartier. Carson declared: "We repudiate mainstream libertarianism's role in defense of corporate capitalism in the 20th century, and its alliance with conservativism." According to Carson, the aim of his colleagues at the Center for a Stateless Society (C4SS) was "to take back free market principles from the hirelings of big business and the plutocracy, and put them back to their original use: an all-out assault on the entrenched economic interests and privileged classes of our day."[106] More gently, BHL blogger Roderick Long rejected "the somewhat more tepid statism of the minimum basic income offered by some of my fellow BHL bloggers." Instead, Long asserted, "the solution is to smash the structures of government-imposed privilege that put workers into a position of dependency on employers in the first place."[107]

Intellectual heirs to the anti-capitalist American individualists of the nineteenth century, this branch of the Third Wave libertarianism focused on structures of power as the key to eliminating poverty. Conventional capitalism must be abandoned. Chartier writes: "Being a libertarian means opposing the use of force to restrain peaceful, voluntary exchange. That doesn't mean it should be understood as involving support for capitalism."[108] Johnson fills out this idea: "the features conventionally associated with American capitalism—large-scale, top-down firms, the predominance of wage

labor, corporate domination of economic and social life, the com-
mercialization of social space, etc.—are as often as not the products of state intervention, not of market dynamics."[109] Instead of
advocating "free markets," libertarians should ask whether and how
existing markets might be "freed." From this perspective, the state
limits workers' freedom—as always, to the benefit of entrenched
elites—chiefly by denying workers access to the means of production. By separating labor from capital and capital products (land,
housing, factories), the state forces laborers to become tenants and
hirelings to others, rather than being independent, creative producers in their own right.[110] Most libertarians (including most BHL
bloggers) argue that wage labor is just—even under "sweatshop"
conditions—so long as workers freely choose those working terms
in light of their other options. The anti-capitalist libertarians point
out, however, that this view takes the structural factors resulting in
those work options as a given. This is unjust to workers and "tends
to reinforce the pernicious idea, not only among libertarianism's
critics but among libertarians as well, that exploitation is not a libertarian concern."[111]

Channeling Benjamin Tucker—and other nineteenth-century
radicals such as Thomas Hodgskin and Gustave de Molinari—these
Third Wave mutualist libertarians call for an end to the state and
to the coercive political economy that the state supports. Carson
writes:

> All tenants paying rent on apartments, urban tenements, public hous-
> ing, etc., should stop. Those of us working for manufacturers and other
> large employers should "fire the boss," as the Wobblies put it, and keep
> the fruits of our own labor. Agricultural wage laborers should dispos-
> sess the agribusiness companies and rich landlords whose plantations
> they work. Possession, for groups and individuals, should be the basis
> of ownership. The land to the cultivator, the shop to the worker, free
> and equitable exchange.[112]

From the nearly opposite direction, BHLers were also challenged
by Tyler Cowen's 2020 proposal for "state-capacity libertarianism."
Claiming that traditional forms of (Cold War) libertarianism have
been "hollowed out," Cowen urges libertarians to begin thinking
about how improved government programs might better support

the free markets that libertarians prize. State capacity refers to the ability of government to enact policies and to execute them effectively. Cowen believes that many problems traced by libertarians to excess government are actually due to the inability of governments to act effectively: "Our governments cannot address climate change much less improve K–12 education, fix traffic congestion, or improve the quality of discretionary [that is, nonentitlement program] spending. Much of our infrastructure is stagnant or declining in quality." By improving state capacity in areas like infrastructure, science subsidies, nuclear power, and space programs we can boost markets. State capacity, when viewed as an investment in long-term economic growth, provides a better approach to poverty than transfer programs. Cowen writes: "The liberaltarian starts by assuring 'the left' that they favor lots of government transfer programs"—for example, basic income or direct-cash payment programs. By contrast, "the State Capacity Libertarian recognizes that demands of mercy are never ending, that economic growth can benefit people more than transfers, and, within the governmental sphere, it is willing to emphasize an analytical, 'cold-hearted' comparison between discretionary spending and transfer spending." Indeed, if our concern is to improve people's lives over the long term, "discretionary spending might well win out at many margins."[113]

In a related piece, Cowen describes the inadequacy of traditional libertarian formulas like "big government is bad" and "liberty is good." He notes that the second of these two is actually the more important, especially if we think of liberty in the positive sense of individuals experiencing richer life opportunities. The libertarian movement has achieved many victories since its heyday in the 1970s and 1980s: marginal tax rates fell from 70 percent to below 40 percent, private capital markets became more liquid and geared toward funding new ideas, high tech grew dramatically without any serious calls to nationalize those industries, and the fall of communism spread market-based principles around the globe. Along with all these gains, however, came bigger government. Greater wealth makes bigger government more affordable. As a point of historical fact, Cowen claims, the old formula of "big government crushes liberty" is being replaced by a new formula: "advances in liberty bring bigger government." Paradoxically, greater liberty and bigger government arrive together. These ideas provide the background to state capacity libertarianism. Cowen writes, "We should embrace a world with growing wealth, growing positive liberty, and yes, growing government." To his libertarian friends, Cowen concludes: "We don't have to favor the growth in government per se, but we do need to recognize that sometimes it's a package deal."[114] To fight poverty, on this libertarian view, the state should spend on infrastructure, not welfare.

This chapter began by examining the charge that libertarians are Social Darwinists. That idea has long been used as a stick to beat libertarians, in part because of the perception that Darwin's theory is that evolutionary change is driven by an amoral and sometimes ruthless competition. As we close this chapter, it may be worth noting that, strictly speaking, not even Charles Darwin was a Darwinist in this sense. True, Darwin viewed animal species as being in a metaphorical "competition" with each other. But Darwin also observed that the most successful species were often the ones whose members were best at *cooperating* with each other. As Darwin notes in *The Origin of Species* (1859), "Those communities which included the greatest number of the most sympathetic members would flourish best, and rear the greatest number of offspring." Systems of sympathetic cooperation—indirectly through market rules that enable positive-sum interactions between strangers, and more directly through voluntary structures of mutual aid—have long been the heart of the libertarian response to hunger and need. In this sense, we might say, libertarians are "True Darwinists" in their fight against poverty.

CHAPTER SEVEN

Racial Justice and Individualism

ANOTHER VIDEO OF police brutality against an unarmed Black citizen. The camera captures the gut-wrenching violence while officers hold back onlookers. The images spread. Black civic leaders call for protests. In cities across the country, rallies fill the streets. Initial calls for police reform grow into a wider demand for racial justice and institutional change. At nightfall the anger boils over. Rocks sail through windows. Statues fall. Shops, banks, and even police stations are looted and burned. Family members of the victim make impassioned appeals for peace, and justice. New voices demand "law and order." As the violence spreads, the government response escalates: first street cops, then riot gear, and then the National Guard. The protests become riots, police brutality floods the evening news, protesters are beaten and killed. Parents weep. America is convulsed by race yet again.

In these moments, two different libertarian voices can be heard. One stands firmly with the protestors and against the police. This libertarian thinks Black Americans live under an oppressive white power structure and that the police are merely the most visible, and brutal, arm of a system of surveillance and oppression. Indeed, for this kind of libertarian, the oppression endured by African Americans at the hands of the police symbolizes the oppression endured by all Americans at the hands of the state. This voice wants to see the state dismantled, beginning with its enforcers: the police. This voice expresses sympathy with Black Nationalists and sees analogies between white imperialist policies at home and abroad. This libertarian argues that, at the limit, it is perfectly appropriate for an oppressed people to respond with violence to the violence of their oppressors. This libertarian admires the uncompromising, muscular immediacy of Malcolm X, not the moral gradualism of Martin Luther King.

The other voice assesses such situations differently. This other libertarian stands with the police against the protestors. Private property must be protected from looters and rioters. This libertarian calls on the police to be reinforced to whatever degree necessary to protect businesses, automobiles, and homes from would-be transgressors, and as for the "victims" of police violence, this voice has little sympathy: criminals who threaten or violate the rights of others belong behind bars, period. Indeed, this libertarian bemoans recent reforms—such as the banning of police chokeholds—and suggests that cameras, which make police actions publicly known, are part of the problem. This libertarian voice pines for an earlier era when "good neighborhoods" were safer thanks to white vigilantes and white police officers who could administer "rough justice" on the spot.

Occasionally—as was the case with Mr. Libertarian himself, Murray Rothbard—these two voices pass through the same lips. As we will see, Rothbard held both of these positions about racial justice and police violence scarcely thirty years apart. Each position was extreme, and for Rothbard, perhaps, the extremity was predictable. But the split in Rothbard's thinking reflects a deeper division within libertarian thought on issues of identity.

On issues of race, gender, and sexual orientation, is libertarianism a doctrine that speaks on behalf of the weak, the marginalized, and the historically oppressed? Or is libertarianism a doctrine that, wittingly or not, props up the premises and policies of inherited structures of power?

As with so many issues, race makes this problem vivid. For the division between progressive and regressive libertarian attitudes toward race arises directly from libertarians' commitment to individualism. Historically this individualism drove opposition to racism and collectivism in every form. Libertarians believe that individuals have rights, and these rights are universal, with no regard for distinctions of race, class, sex, or creed. Yet this same individualism obscures for libertarians the harms that racism and sexism impose on individuals as members of *groups*. Their concern for individual liberty makes libertarians highly critical of government. But racism, like sexism, often constrains our liberty through *private* activity, not just through government action. And the harms born of racism do not always take the form of explicit violations of rights. Identity-based threats to liberty often come from the *social context* in which parties interact, and those threats are not always visible (or even present) in the motives and intentions of the various parties. Racism can operate as a *structure* of oppression.

No wonder that libertarians, with their uncompromising focus on the rights and responsibilities of individuals, sometimes struggle to see the threats to liberty in racism. Jonathan Blanks, a Black libertarian, writes: "I would venture that many, if not most libertarians—like the general American public—haven't come to terms with the widespread, systemic subversion of markets and democracy American racism wreaked on its most marginalized citizens."[1]

In this chapter, we explore the history of the libertarian response to identity-based oppression, with special attention to race. We show how an individualism that was radically progressive in the nineteenth-century fight to end slavery became less so—and arguably even became regressive—during the civil rights era. We also examine the work of contemporary, Third Wave libertarians and consider how American libertarians today are coming to terms with racism in the history of their country and in the history of the libertarian movement itself.

The Dismal Science

A nineteenth-century libertarian might be surprised at the movement's subsequent course. After all, first wave libertarians were known for radicalizing an already egalitarian and racially progressive doctrine: classical liberalism. In the nineteenth century, libertarians were criticized for being *too* idealistic, *too* revolutionary in their demands for racial justice. Here as elsewhere, to understand the racial radicalism of early libertarians we must first examine the classical liberal context from which it emerged.

In 1849, Thomas Carlyle (1795–1881), the conservative Scottish philosopher and essayist, wrote a scathing essay for *Fraser's Magazine* titled "Occasional Discourse on the Negro Question." Carlyle decried the state of affairs in the recently emancipated West Indies.[2] Under the previous system of slavery, plantations in Jamaica and the surrounding colonies had furnished English homes with abundant luxury goods such as pepper, sugar, coffee, and cinnamon. After emancipation the plantations had mostly been split into small, privately owned plots, on which—to Carlyle's outrage—the natives planted subsistence crops for their own consumption, most notably pumpkins, which grew easily and plentifully in that climate.

To Carlyle, this was damning evidence that the Black West Indians were unfit for political self-governance. Indeed, they were unfit even to make their own decisions about work and leisure. "The gods wish," wrote Carlyle, "besides pumpkins, that spices and valuable products be grown in their West Indies; thus much they have declared in so making the West Indies; infinitely more they wish—that manful, industrious men occupy their West Indies, not indolent, two-legged cattle, however 'happy' over their abundant pumpkins!" And what if the natives chose not to work on the tasks that Carlyle thought they should? "Quashee, if he will not help in this bringing out the spices, will get himself made a slave again (which state will not be a little less ugly than his present one), and with beneficent whip, since other methods avail not, will be compelled to work."[3]

Carlyle was, of course, a blatant racist. But his racism drew from a deeper and more pernicious ideology. Carlyle was an authoritarian, and that authoritarianism led him to despise not only the freedom of the emancipated Jamaicans but freedom *in general*, especially the freedoms of trade, occupation, and democracy championed by the classical liberal economists.[4] With respect to the poor white people of Britain and Ireland, for instance, he wrote that "all this that has been sung and spoken, for a long while, about enfranchisement, emancipation, freedom, suffrage, civil and religious liberty over the world, is little other than sad and temporary jargon, brought upon us by a stern necessity,—but now ordered by a sterner to take itself away again a little."[5] What such people need, Carlyle argued, was not freedom but *command*.[6]

> To each of you I will then say: Here is work for you; strike into it with manlike, soldier-like obedience and heartiness. . . . Refuse to strike into it; shirk heavy labor, disobey the rules,—I will admonish and endeavor to incite you; if in vain, I will flog you; if still in vain, I will at last shoot you,—and make God's Earth, and the forlorn-hope in God's Battle, free of you.[7]

Where Carlyle saw conflict between liberty and social order, however, the classical economists saw harmony. Shortly after Carlyle's tirade on the "Negro Question," *Fraser's* published a sharp reply by John Stuart Mill.[8] Due to the fortunate circumstances of the West Indian climate, Mill noted, freed Black people could choose how much or how little time they would devote to productive labor. Mill castigated Carlyle's view that the natives should be compelled to work so as to supply sugar and spices for English tables. Such a position could only rest on a theory of the world built on two great and unequal classes: one fit to rule, the other to be ordered about. Mill saw Carlyle's proposal as a species of the dying view that might makes right. Instead, Mill argued that people should interact voluntarily, and thus peacefully, in pursuit of interests and values of their own. Regarding the plantation owners, Mill wrote: "if they cannot continue to realize their large incomes without more labourers, let them find them, and bring them from where they can best be procured, only not by force." If Black West Indians chose not to work for the wages being offered, that was entirely their choice. As Mill put it: "To work voluntarily for a worthy object is laudable; but what constitutes a worthy object?"[9] That was a matter for each individual to decide, since only individuals know their own interests.

This individualist worldview—shared by all the classical liberals—was fundamentally egalitarian. Differing experiences and circumstances, not differences in nature, best explained the variations in behavior and aptitude observed in society. As Adam Smith had put it a half century before: "The difference between the most dissimilar characters, between the philosopher and a common street porter, for example, seems to arise not so much from nature as from habit, custom, and education."[10] People are owed an equal sphere of liberty because of their equal capacity to form interests and to act on them.

Because this stream of economic thought ran across an egalitarian and individualist bedrock, it was able, at a key historical moment, to join with another reformist stream of thought: the Christian tradition of religious belief. In England, Quakers and Methodist ministers such as John Wesley insisted that all humans, regardless of their race, were fellow children of God. As such, each human life demanded our respect. By the early 1800s, these two streams, one religious, one economistic, merged. Together they formed a powerful current behind the ideal of the natural unity of humanity and against the racist institutions of the day. As we will see in a moment, the early libertarians seized upon and radicalized ideas from both of these streams of thought. On the level of practical policy, this led the libertarians to uncompromising, immediatist forms of racial progressivism— especially regarding the emancipation of American slaves. The contrast with the more pragmatic, racial gradualism of the classical liberals is stark.

In England during the late 1820s, when it was becoming clear that slavery would soon be abolished across the British holdings, the question of how to achieve an effective transition loomed. Regarding Jamaican slavery, the historian Jim Powell captures the pragmatic perspective of the classical liberals: "After abolition, former slaveholders and former slaves were probably going to exist in the same society together, and the former slaveholders would still have more money and power. Consequently, the former slaves would be safer if the former slaveholders had the fewest incentives to abuse the former slaves."[11] So the classical economists and their religious allies focused on a practical problem: given the realities of human nature, how best to achieve a lasting and peaceful brotherhood between whites and Blacks as equal citizens?

Eventually (in part because of the threat of immediate abolishment without compensation) a deal was struck that included a number of financial incentives. As part of the plan to liberate the 800,000 slaves held in the British Caribbean colonies, a system of high tariffs was imposed on sugar imported to Britain from non-colonial competitors such as Cuba and Brazil—thus boosting the value of sugar from the (formerly slaveholding) British colonies.[12] These tariffs were in effect subsidies to the former slaveholders that would be paid for by the British public. To further ease the burden on the former slaveholders, slaves would be required to continue working as "apprentices" for a time before they would become wholly free citizens of Britain—four years of additional servitude for house slaves, six years for field slaves (though later these periods were reduced). Many, such as the English abolitionist Edward Stanley, hailed this gradualist approach, declaring that Britain had conducted a "mighty experiment": the peaceful transition from a slave society to a free one.

The Radical Abolitionists

American abolitionists radicalized the views inherited from their classical liberal forebears. Here the story begins with William Lloyd Garrison, the individualist anarchist who in 1831 began publishing the *Liberator*, his widely circulated abolitionist newspaper. The *Liberator* was largely funded by James Forten (1766–1842), a freed Black who, after fighting in the Revolutionary War, built a sail-making empire that made him one of the wealthiest business owners in Philadelphia. Garrison's religious faith informed his opposition to both slavery and government. He believed that all humans properly lived under a "government of god," which was the only true moral government. The moral disorder of contemporary society was, perhaps paradoxically, a *product* of government actions, which are by their very nature coercive. The government of God, by contrast, was an ideal of wholly peaceful interactions between individuals, in which equal freedom was the birthright of each individual—white or Black, male or female (see below). Rejecting even the hierarchies of organized religions, Garrison embraced the "come-outerism" of his day: "the old belief that true Christians ought to be religious individuals without organized churches."[13] Garrison describes the political implications of his embrace of the government of God:

> As every human government is upheld by physical force and its laws are enforced virtually at the point of a bayonet, we cannot hold any office which imposes upon its incumbent the obligation to compel men to do right on pain of imprisonment and death. We therefore voluntarily exclude ourselves from every legislative and judicial body and repudiate all human politics, worldly honor, and stations of authority. If we cannot occupy a seat in the legislature, or on the bench, neither can we elect others to act as our substitutes in such capacity.[14]

Garrison's abolitionism arose from the uncompromising primacy of God-given law over government-given law.

In an 1833 address in Philadelphia, Garrison argued that every individual has a God-given, inalienable right to liberty. "To invade [that liberty] is to usurp the prerogative of Jehovah." Why? Because God created us as self-owners: "Every man has a right to his own body—to the products of his own labor—to the protection of law— and to the common advantages of society."[15] As Garrison explained elsewhere, slavery was a sin precisely because it rebelled against God: the institutions of slavery destroyed the God-given agency of the enslaved. God meant every individual to live and love freely, and to fully enjoy the fruits of their own labor. Lewis Perry describes the Garrisonian outlook: "When a man presumed to claim he owned another man, he competed with God for control and government over mankind. He tried to make his slave accountable to himself instead of to God."[16] Since it was wrong for anyone to financially benefit from slavery, it would be doubly wrong for a slaveholder to receive financial compensation as part of a settlement to end that unjust arrangement. According to Garrison, "freeing the slave is not depriving them of their property, but of restoring it to its rightful owner; it is not wronging the master, but righting the slave—restoring him to himself." As a result: "if compensation is to be given at all, it should be given to the outraged and guiltless slaves, and not to those who have plundered and abused them."[17] As Perry summarizes Garrison's position: "Slavery, government, and violence were considered identical in principle. All were sinful invasions of God's prerogatives; all tried to set one man between another man and his rightful ruler."[18]

In 1833, Garrison joined with Arthur Tappan and Frederick Douglass to found the American Anti-Slavery Society. But differences of opinion soon emerged. Garrison's idea of the Government of God, for reasons just sketched, led him to a position of extreme "nonresistance." Believing that Christians must renounce all use of force, Garrison rejected politics (read: coercion) as a means of abolishing slavery, even to the point of refusing to vote for anti-slavery candidates. The only properly Christian approach was moral persuasion. Garrison rejected the idea of seeking abolition within the existing political order and insisted that the U.S. Constitution was an irredeemably racist document. At a meeting in Framingham, Massachusetts, in 1854, Garrison and a group of abolitionists gathered to protest the return of a runaway slave named Anthony Burns. When it was his turn to speak, Garrison held aloft a copy of the Constitution, decrying it as "a covenant with death and an agreement from hell." Then Garrison set the Constitution afire, declaring, "So perish all compromises with tyranny!"[19]

Other abolitionists embraced Garrison's Government of God and the strict anti-governmentalism it implied. Closely affiliated with England's nascent Manchester School and Richard Cobden's Anti-Corn Law League, Henry C. Wright was an extreme individualist and voluntaryist who denied the legitimacy of government:

> States and nations are to be regarded as we regard combinations of men to pick pockets, to steal sheep, to rob on the road, to steal men, to range over the sea as pirates—only on a larger and more imposing scale. When men steal, rob and murder as states and nations, it gives respectability to crime—the enormity of their crimes is lost sight of, amid the imposing number that commit them, and amid the glitter and pomp of equipage. The little band of thieves is scorned and hunted down as a felon; the great, or governmental band of thieves, is made respectable by numbers, and their crimes cease to be criminal and hateful in proportion to the number combined to do them.[20]

Also like Garrison, Henry Wright's faith-based libertarianism led him to put women's equality on a par with racial equality (alongside equality for the laboring poor as well). In 1840, a number of more conservative abolitionists left the Anti-Slavery Society to protest the appointment of a woman, Abby Kelly, to a governing

committee. Wright, standing with Garrison, defended the appointment, stating that "every human being, without regard to complex-
ion, sex, or condition, is a being in the image and representative of
God on earth."[21]

Wright was what we might call an "immediatist" regarding
slavery. He rejected appeals to gradualism in the pursuit of justice.
He fiercely criticized the Republican Party on these grounds, saying: "You cannot be true to liberty, without being an irreconcilable
enemy to all slaveholders, as such, and to all slaveholding States
and institutions. The Republican party cannot be a true embodiment and exponent of liberty, without seeking to annihilate all
institutions that embody slavery."[22] Like Garrison, Wright rejected
the U.S. Constitution and political activity generally, and was an
early advocate of Disunionism. In October 1835, Wright applauded
the Southern threat of secession: "Quicker the better; the sooner
will slavery die. Let the free States cut loose from the slave States,
and their system of piracy cannot be maintained. I wish the Union
was dissolved tomorrow; it would be a great blessing."[23]

Wright's radical libertarianism often put him at odds with other
abolitionists. In 1837, the American Anti-Slavery Society effectively
terminated his membership, on the grounds that Wright refused to
"cease . . . interweaving his 'no government' views with abolitionism."[24] Perhaps because of the urgency of emancipation, Wright
eventually narrowed his advocacy of nonviolence, apparently seeing his personal commitment to nonviolence as compatible with
his defending the use of violence on the part of others. Natural law
gives men a right of rebellion; no means is out of bounds in the
fight against injustice. Wright publicly defended the slaves who
revolted with Nat Turner merely as attempting what George Washington and the American Revolutionaries had righteously done.[25]
Writing in the *Liberator* in 1857, Wright ominously declared: "A
baptism of blood awaits the slaveholder and his abettors. So be it.
The retribution is just."[26]

Garrison and Wright fused anarchism and abolitionism
through their religious vision of godly government. Other libertarians reached similar conclusions by way of natural rights.
Lysander Spooner, whom we met in chapter 3, was foremost among
these. Spooner's 1846 canonical formulation of natural rights

libertarianism influenced a host of libertarians in the twentieth century, most notably Murray Rothbard. Spooner wrote:

> Each man has a natural right to acquire all he honestly can, and to enjoy and dispose of all that he honestly acquires; and the protection of these rights is all that any one has a right to ask of government in relation to them. It is all that he can have, consistently with the rights of others. If government gives any individual more than this, it can do so only by taking it from others. . . . To do this, is of the very essence of tyranny. And whether it be done by majorities, or minorities, by the sword, the statute, or the judicial decision, it is equally and purely usurpation, despotism, and oppression.[27]

Rejecting Garrison's Government of God, Spooner focused on legal and constitutional issues—with natural rights as his guide. (Spooner was trained as a lawyer but never met the requirements of the Bar Association, which he regarded as an unjust monopoly.) Natural law showed the illegitimacy of the U.S. Constitution. Since individuals have ownership rights over their persons and possessions, Spooner objected to taxation without the consent of each citizen. He likewise objected to political participation, including voting, since this treats "law" as mere majority rule. But, for the cause of abolition, while personally disavowing the Constitution, Spooner thought it tactically vital to make the case to the public that the Constitution was anti-slavery.

In "The Unconstitutionality of Slavery" (1860), Spooner argues that, whenever written law is ambiguous, it must be read as siding with natural law. Just as the U.S. Constitution does not grant the government exclusive monopoly powers (for example, in establishing a postal service), so the Constitution does not positively establish slavery. It therefore cannot be read as supporting slavery. Further, the Declaration of Independence describes life, liberty, and the pursuit of happiness as natural rights. Though slavery had been an established practice in the colonies (since at least 1619, as we all are now aware), the Declaration effectively deemed the practice illegal, since self-evident truths cannot be rescinded by social custom or legal practice. For all these reasons, Spooner declared: "Slavery neither has, nor ever had any constitutional existence in this country; that it has always been a mere abuse, sustained, in the first instance, merely by the common consent of the strongest party, without any law on the subject, and, in the second place, by a few unconstitutional enactments, made in defiance of the plainest provisions of the fundamental law."[28]

Spooner thought that abolition should not come through the federal government—which in any case was dominated by the South—but directly through nongovernmental force. To this end, in 1858 Spooner published a pamphlet titled "A Plan for the Abolition of Slavery, and to the Non-Slaveholders of the South." In it, Spooner laid out four natural law principles that justified, indeed required, the ending of slavery through a slave revolt:

> 1. That the Slaves have a natural right to their liberty. 2. That they have a natural right to compensation . . . for the wrong they have suffered. 3. That so long as governments, under which they live, refuse to give them liberty or compensation, they have the right to take it by stratagem or force. 4. That it is the duty of all, who can, to assist them in such enterprise.[29]

Like some libertarians of the twentieth century, Spooner saw the Second Amendment as a key guarantor of liberty for Blacks. The right "to keep and bear arms" was incompatible with some people being held as slaves. For Spooner, the Second Amendment was intrinsically emancipatory:

> Under this provision any man has a right either to give or sell arms to those persons whom the States call slaves; and there is no constitutional power, either in the national or State governments, that can punish him for doing so; or that can take those arms from the slaves; or that can make it criminal for the slaves to use them, if, from the inefficiency of the laws, it should become necessary for them to do so, in defense of their own lives and liberties.[30]

Spooner also understood the psychological impact of a slave revolt: "A band of ten or twenty determined negroes, well armed, having their rendezvous in the forests, coming out upon the plantations by day or night, seizing individual Slaveholders, stripping them, and flogging them soundly, in the presence of their own Slaves would soon abolish slavery over a large district."[31]

In the spring of 1859, barely a year after his manifesto appeared, Spooner met the radical abolitionist John Brown in Boston. Brown reportedly asked Spooner to cease publishing the essay, worrying that it might put Southern authorities on alert. The extent of Spooner's involvement in John Brown's subsequent raid on the armory at Harpers Ferry remains unclear, in part because Spooner burned his papers in its aftermath. In later letters, Spooner suggested that he had not given Brown the idea but rather that the two had arrived at the same plan independently.[32]

Other libertarians were involved in Brown's plot. One was Gerrit Smith. While rejecting the extreme anarchism of Garrison and Spooner, Smith developed libertarian arguments for progressive ideals. Smith advocated free international trade; championed equal rights for women and Blacks (including private economic liberty and political suffrage for both); protested war and capital punishment; argued for legalizing interracial marriage; and insisted that homesteading be recognized as a natural right. In his 1851 address "The True Office of Civil Government," Smith set out his theory of formal equality and limited government: "Government owes nothing to its subjects but protection. And this is protection not from competition, but from crimes. It owes them no protection from the foreign farmer, or foreign manufacturer, or foreign navigator." Smith continued, "To call on government to increase the wealth of its subjects, or to help promote the progress of religion among them, or, in short, to promote any of their interests, is to call on it to do what it has no right to do, and which, it is safe to add, it has no power to do."[33]

Prior to the raid on Harpers Ferry, rumors of John Brown's plan began circulating among the radical abolitionists. Gerrit Smith and Spooner exchanged letters, expressing concern about whether the attempt had sufficient men and arms to succeed. They also debated whether the raid should be delayed until Spooner's call to arms, "To the Non-Slaveholders of the South," could be distributed more widely in neighboring states. In the aftermath of the failed raid, Smith was eventually identified as one of the infamous "Secret Six" who had supported it. No action was taken against him. With Brown in captivity and awaiting trial, Spooner began devising schemes to free Brown (one of which involved kidnapping the governor of Virginia).

Frederick Douglass was another individualist connected to John Brown. In 1838, Douglass escaped from slavery by impersonating a free Black sailor. Reaching safety in New Bedford, Douglass was dumbstruck by the manner in which free people labored: "almost everybody seemed to be at work, but noiselessly so, compared to what I had become accustomed to in Baltimore. . . . I heard no deep oaths or horrid curses on the laborer. I saw no whipping of men; but all seemed to go smoothly on. Every man appeared to understand his work, and went at it with a sober, yet cheerful earnestness, which betokened the deep interest which he felt in what he was doing, as well as a sense of his own dignity as a man."[34] On his third day in town, Douglass found work loading casks of oil onto a sloop. It was a transformative moment: "I was now my own master. It was a happy moment, the rapture of which can be understood only by those who have been slaves. It was the first work, the reward of which was to be entirely my own. . . . It was to me the starting point of a new existence."[35]

Douglass was not immune to racism in the North. Seeking work as a carpenter on the docks, he writes, "such was the strength of prejudice against color, among the white calkers [sic], that they refused to work with me, and of course I could get no employment." Finding his trade of no use, Douglass threw aside his caulking equipment and took up any menial work he could find. For three years, he swept floors, sawed wood, shoveled coal, and rolled oil casks, until a visit to Nantucket made him known to the world of anti-slavery activists.

Shortly after arriving in New Bedford, Douglass took out a subscription to *The Liberator* and soon attended a meeting where he heard Garrison denounce slavery. A brilliant orator himself, Douglass began giving public talks about his experiences as a slave. In 1841, Garrison heard Douglass speak at a convention in Nantucket. Mesmerized, Garrison invited Douglass to join the abolitionist campaign. Initially adopting Garrisonian themes and anti-Constitutionalism, Douglass launched himself upon a life as one of the leading public intellectuals and social activists of his day.

Though his political views are a complex mix, it is no surprise that Douglass has long been a hero to libertarians. As a former slave, Douglass described liberty with a freshness and immediacy few can match. The desire for freedom, he wrote, "is the deepest and stron-gest of all the powers of the human soul."[36] He saw liberty as a natu-ral right held equally by everyone, regardless of race or gender: "It existed in the very nature of man's creation. It was his even before he comprehended it. He was created in it, endowed with it, and it can never be taken from him."[37] Like Locke and the Spanish Scholastics before him, Douglass saw individuals as self-owners, each with a natural right to the product of his own labor.

Like other individualists, including homesteaders such as Gerrit Smith, Douglass gave an egalitarian twist to the concept of legiti-mate acquisition: "The theory of property in the soil, runs thus: that man has a right to as much soil as necessary for his existence."[38] When a person commits his labor to the soil, the fruits of that labor are rightfully his. Once each person's claims to those fruits are secured, Douglass declared, there was "very little left for society and government to do."[39] Though less extreme than the individualist anarchists of his circle, Douglass believed that the system of natural liberty provided the main resources needed to remedy social prob-lems. Foreshadowing the perspective of twentieth-century libertar-ians, Douglass declared in 1893: "Give the Negro fair play and let him alone."[40]

A passionate individualist, Douglass signed a petition in 1855 opposing capital punishment. An advocate of equal rights for women, Douglass drew on the work of the individualist feminist Sarah Grimke to analogize slavery and the laws used to oppress women.[41] Douglass was the only man given a prominent speaking role in the women's rights conference at Seneca Falls, New York, in July 1848. He defended the rights of the oppressed Chinese immi-grants who were arriving in large numbers. Douglass advocated reli-gious toleration, insisting that Mormons, a particular target of abuse, had equal rights to practice their religion. He even argued that every lover of liberty had a positive obligation to speak out against intoler-ance that others might endure—whether female, Mormon, Chinese, or Black.[42] This leads us back to Harpers Ferry.

Douglass's relationship with John Brown was long and com-plicated. The two first met in 1847 or 1848. Impressed by Brown's passion but initially appalled at his advocacy of violence, Douglass edged closer to Brown's perspective in the decade prior to Harpers

Ferry.[43] In fact, Douglass and Brown eventually became so close that Brown did much of the planning and fundraising for the raid in Douglass's home.[44] Immediately after Brown's capture, newspapers across the country identified Douglass as a co-conspirator,[45] and though he denied direct involvement, Douglass was forced to flee to Canada.

Brown's raid on Harpers Ferry and subsequent execution for treason marked a turning point for libertarians. Most still eschewed the use of state power to liberate the slaves (in part because military conscription was yet another type of slavery). Still, even the most pacific among them grew frustrated by Southern obstinacy. As Lewis Perry puts it: "By the end of 1859 almost no nonresistant voice remained to be raised against force and violence."[46] With the outbreak of the Civil War, the remaining ideas of the radical individualist libertarians were scattered.

Late in Douglass's life, a young man asked him for advice on how to fight injustice. Douglass reportedly answered: "Agitate! Agitate! Agitate!" Experience had also impressed upon him the importance of personal agency. The public address Douglass delivered more than any other was titled "Self-Made Men." In it, Douglass said: "[We] may explain success mainly by one word and that word is WORK! WORK!! WORK!!! WORK!!!!"[47] This tension, between individual and collective responsibility, would foreshadow coming debates about racial justice in America.

Libertarians and Civil Rights

Rachel Maddow, host of the eponymous left-liberal news program, looked at her guest with surprise.[48] She smiled. It was 2010 and Maddow was interviewing Rand Paul, Tea Party darling and the son of legendary libertarian physician-turned-politician Ron Paul. The younger Paul had recently shocked pundits by defeating his establishment-backed opponent in Kentucky's Republican primary. A libertarian was now the front-runner for a seat in the United States Senate. But that's not why Maddow was smiling.

Maddow had asked Paul whether he supported the Civil Rights Act of 1964. Paul replied that he personally opposed racial discrimination in all its forms. As a libertarian, however, Paul objected to key parts of the act, including provisions such as Title II that made it a crime for owners of lunch counters, hotels, gasoline stations, and other "public accommodations" to discriminate on the basis of race. After all, Rand reasoned, that provision limits the liberty of people to run their businesses on their own terms, a fundamental libertarian freedom. "Had I been around, I would have tried to modify that," Paul said. Maddow was quick to pin the tail on the libertarian donkey: so "there is nothing under your worldview to stop the country from resegregating."[49] Paul had nothing to say in response.[50]

The next morning, the Republican leadership distanced itself from Paul's position, and Paul himself soon apologized and reversed his position.[51] Not so the libertarians. Prominent libertarian scholars, such as African American economist Walter Williams, insisted that Paul was right the first time: to be consistent, libertarians must object to the Civil Rights Act.[52] On Fox News, John Stossel brought the libertarian position to a mass audience. One cost of liberty is that people have a right to do bad things, Stossel explained. The government has no more authority to prohibit discrimination in the private economic sector than it had to require it. Stossel looked straight into the camera and called for the repeal of Title II. In a free society, white-owned restaurants, hotels, and banks should be able to post signs reading "No Blacks." (Of course, Black business owners should be free to do the same.) As a matter of libertarian principle, it seemed, Maddow was right.[53]

How did libertarianism, a doctrine at the radical edge of the abolitionist movement, not merely lose but apparently *reverse* its progressive orientation on race by the late twentieth century?

We begin with the individualist philosophy of Rand Paul's namesake, Ayn Rand. For Rand, "Racism is a doctrine of, by and for brutes."[54] Racism says that people are to be judged not according to their own character and actions but by the (supposed) character and actions of some collective of ancestors. Some use this affiliation to claim superiority. But doing so mistakes what distinguishes man from all other species: "Racism negates two aspects of man's life: reason and choice, or mind and morality, replacing them with chemical predestination."[55] Even if we were to discover evidence that some "race" tends to have superior attributes (say, intelligence), this would tell us nothing of social relevance. Each person must be judged as an individual.

Racism, according to Rand, is not merely exacerbated by statism (though she felt this to be historical fact). Racism and statism are conceptually connected because statism is the political form of collectivism. This revealed for Rand a contradiction within the civil rights movement. Its central claim—racism is wrong—is predicated on individualism. Yet the Civil Rights Act offered only collectivism as a remedy, most notably by violating the property rights of white business owners as a group.[56] "There is only one antidote to racism: the philosophy of individualism and its politico-economic corollary, laissez-faire capitalism."[57]

How can capitalism fix racism? As sketched above, Rand runs the argument theoretically and rooted in her theory of objectivism (Mises's argument against racism worked on a similarly high level of abstraction).[58] Other libertarians of the era—most notably Milton Friedman—joined Rand in offering capitalism as the best cure for racism. Unlike Mises and Rand, however, Friedman framed his argument using the more ecumenical approach of economic incentives.[59]

Like most libertarians who opposed the Civil Rights Act, Friedman personally decried racism:

> I strongly believe that the color of a man's skin or the religion of his parents is, by itself, no reason to treat him differently; that a man should be judged by what he is and what he does and not by these external characteristics. I deplore what seem to me the prejudice and narrowness of outlook of those whose tastes differ from mine in this respect.[60]

However, Friedman observed, while racism becomes entrenched in hierarchical societies by the state agents who control the flow of goods and opportunities, market societies work against such prejudices. The "free market separates economic efficiency from irrelevant characteristics."[61] In market society, racial prejudices impose costs upon economic actors. "The man who objects to buying or working alongside a Negro, for example, thereby limits his range of choice."[62] So too with owners of banks and hotels and lunch counters. Anyone who refuses to exchange with people based on race reduces his pool of customers. In a competitive market, this strategy will work against him, allowing his competitors to build market share and, very possibly, drive the racist out of business.[63]

To their credit, midcentury libertarians applied the same individualist logic to the laws that perpetuated racism. They thought Jim Crow–era laws that forced business owners to treat white and Black customers differently were manifestly unjust. As Rand put this point: "The policy of the Southern states towards Negroes was and is a shameful contradiction of this country's basic principles. Racial discrimination, imposed and enforced by law, is so blatantly inexcusable an infringement of individual rights that the racist statutes of the South should have been declared unconstitutional long ago."[64] For Rand, "states' rights" did not include the right to violate the rights of individuals.[65] Insofar as the civil rights movement opposed such laws, libertarians such as Rand and Friedman strongly approved.

Still, for reasons just described, Friedman generally advocated market-based solutions to racism and opposed coercive government-based ones. Like many libertarians of the time, he opposed fair employment legislation such as Title VII of the Civil Rights Act. Friedman said the approach "involves interference with the freedom of individuals to enter into voluntary contracts with each other."[66] Friedman thought racist attitudes were merely personal "tastes." He even once argued that the harm imposed on a Black worker not hired for racist reasons is similar to that experienced by a white opera singer who is not hired because the community prefers the blues.[67]

A distinction between fairness and freedom underlay Friedman's view: the proper role of government is protecting individual freedom, not imposing any particular conception of fairness. Friedman seemed to think the definition of fairness was also merely a matter of taste. Allowing government agents to impose their conception of "fairness" (even when backed by majorities) would curtail the freedom of some in service to the tastes of others. Friedman compared the distinction between free speech and fair speech to the distinction between free employment practices and (so-called) fair ones: "It is any more desirable that momentary majorities decide which characteristics are relevant to employment than what speech is appropriate? Indeed, can a free market in ideas be long maintained if a free market in goods and services is destroyed?"[68]

For Friedman, the market contains internal correctives that work against racist attitudes. In the end, he believed that progress in race relations can only be made if we change attitudes: "The appropriate recourse of those of us who believe that a particular criterion such as color is irrelevant is to persuade our fellows to be of like mind, not to use the coercive power of the state to force them to act in accordance with our principles."[69] Friedman advocated active conversations about the evils of racism. Using state power to end racism would not work and, like many coercive rules and programs, might have the opposite effect.[70]

Similar positions were taken by most of the major libertarian thinkers of the civil rights era. Mises's critique of the conceptual errors of racism was every bit as adamant as Rand's. Nozick never wrote specifically about the Civil Rights Act, but he once stated that hotel owners and other businesspeople should have the right to serve, and refuse to serve, whomever they wanted.[71] On the political front, Barry Goldwater, the most libertarian politician of the era, voted against the Civil Rights Act (reluctantly, he said) because of Articles II and VII.[72]

The views of leading Black libertarians are particularly interesting here. Thomas Sowell initially supported the Civil Rights Act in its full form—but not because he thought it was just or likely to be effective. Rather, Sowell predicted that the act's passage would be followed by a "bitter anti-climax" that might lead to more productive conversations about racism and its remedies. But that moment of positive rethinking did not occur. Instead, writing in 1975 about the way the law was being implemented, Sowell wrote: "The burden of proof has been put on the employer whose work force does not reflect the racial or sex proportions deemed appropriate by the federal agencies administering the law."[73] Reflecting on the actual effects of the act decades later, Sowell said: "Judging everybody by the same standard came to be regarded in some quarters as 'racist' because it precluded preferences and quotas. There are people today who talk about 'justice' when they really mean payback—including payback against people who were not even born when historic injustices were committed."[74]

While generally hewing to an individualist line, Sowell sometimes pointed to cultural histories as posing barriers to racial
equality, where protection for negative liberties might be inadequate to protect people's economic liberty interests: "Racial discrimination is another obvious area where merely to 'cease and
desist' is not enough. If a firm has engaged in racial discrimination
for years and has an all-white work force as a result, then simply to
stop discrimination will mean little as long as the firm continues
to hire its current employees' friends and relatives through word-
of-mouth referral. . . . Clearly the area of racial discrimination is
one in which positive or affirmative steps of some kind seem reasonable, which is not to say that the particular policies actually
followed make sense."[75]

That last caveat is a big one. Sowell is tracking libertarian
principles, with an awareness of the very different ways laws actually function in the world. When you blend all this with the lived
experience of a Black man entering the academic profession in
the 1960s, the result is a morally striking mélange. Sowell writes:
"When James Perkins became president of Cornell in 1963, it had
an almost totally white faculty and student body. When I joined
the faculty two years later, I did not see another Black professor
anywhere on this vast campus. Perkins, like other presidents of elite
colleges and universities sought to increase student enrollment—
and to do so by admitting students who would not meet the existing
standards at Cornell. The emphasis was on getting militant Black
ghetto kids, some of whom turned out to be hoodlums who terror-
ized other Black students, in addition to provoking a racial back-
lash among whites."[76]

Walter Williams, another leading Black libertarian, opposed the
Civil Rights Act on what will now be familiar libertarian lines: while
personally objecting to discrimination on the basis of race, sex, or
religion, Williams says that employers, as much as individuals and
clubs, have the right to make such discriminations if they choose:
in a free society, freedom of association should be our overriding
value. Strikingly, though, Williams consistently highlights the role
of the *state* in creating and enforcing racial hierarchies in society,
a point with applications well beyond the principled libertarian
objection to Jim Crow. While allowing for private discrimination,

Williams argues that discrimination may properly be outlawed in "government-financed services such as schools and libraries."[77] As Williams writes elsewhere: "There are numerous government acts that subsidize racial preference. One is price-fixing, such as minimum-wage laws. When the government dictates that an employer must pay a minimum of five dollars an hour to anyone he hires, that law reduces the cost of, and hence subsidizes, racial preference . . . the reason is simple: the cost of indulging one's preferences goes to zero."[78] Welfare is another government system that disproportionately harms Black people: "Like some giant drug pusher, their government has lured them into dependency on a system that will maintain them in permanent poverty."[79] According to Williams, many state programs have the practical effect of empowering whites at the expense of Blacks and other minorities. Thus: "Government licensing closes the door for economic opportunity. . . . All those licensing laws do just one thing: Keep outsiders out. Those outsiders are often members of minority groups."[80]

So, libertarians had an ambivalent relationship with the civil rights pioneers—aligning with them on some issues (such as dismantling Jim Crow) while diverging on others.[81] This can be explained, in part, by the divisions within the civil rights movement itself, with some factions seeking reform within the liberal, free-market system and others seemingly rejecting that whole system in favor of socialist or communist alternatives that were anathema to libertarians. But other divisions within the libertarian movement soon began opening, and these divisions have done the most damage to libertarianism's reputation on racial liberation.

The Paleo-Libertarians

In a 1990 manifesto, Llewelyn Rockwell made the case for a novel form of libertarianism that he dubbed "paleo-libertarianism."[82] The fall of the Soviet Union had divided conservatives. While statist neo-conservatives such as Jeane Kirkpatrick continued to push an aggressive international role for the United States, paleoconservatives led by Patrick Buchanan argued for a return to an isolationist, America First conservatism. Rockwell believed that this split had opened an opportunity for the (still tiny) libertarian movement of his day: an alliance between libertarians and the resurgent old right: "The Cold War ruptured the Right; now the healing can begin, for Lord Acton's axiom that 'liberty is the highest political end of man' is at the heart of the old conservatism as well."[83] The real obstacles preventing libertarians from joining forces with the limited-government advocates of the old right, according to Rockwell, were not political issues but cultural ones.

During the 1960s and 1970s, Rockwell opined, the libertarian movement had allowed itself to be infected with a libertine, Woodstockian orientation. This was especially true of the Libertarian Party, which Rockwell describes as a debating club for former hippies. ("*Hair* may have left Broadway long ago, but the Age of Aquarius survives in the LP.")[84] Too many libertarians saw the protection of individual freedom as not only necessary but *sufficient* for the creation and maintenance of a good society: "Worse, they equate freedom from State oppression with freedom from cultural norms, religion, bourgeois morality, and social authority."[85] Most Americans affirm individual freedom *within the context of* traditional values, and they see libertarians as rejecting those values. The libertarian affinity for moral relativism, Rockwell claimed, undercut its political appeal. Libertarian arguments against the war on drugs, however valid, are less persuasive when they come from "the party of the stoned."[86] And when libertarians, correctly, advocate the decriminalization of prostitution, it's no wonder that ordinary Americans hear them lauding the morality of prostitution too.

Rockwell's libertarianism would free itself from this "libertine muck." It would ally libertarians with the cultural conservatives of the old right. Along with familiar libertarian themes—the defenses of private property and the free market, attacks on the state as the primary institutional source of evil throughout history—Rockwell's manifesto added a variety of cultural principles. Specifically, Rockwell recognized (1) "social authority," embodied in family, church, and community, as vital intermediate institutions for the practice and defense of liberty; (2) "Western culture" as worthy of our honor and defense; and (3) "objective standards of morality, especially as found in the Judeo-Christian tradition, as essential to the free and civilized social order."[87]

In his defense of Western culture, however, Rockwell's paleo-libertarianism edged into racial terrain. Civil rights once referred to protection from state intrusion; now, for many Americans, Rockwell thought it denoted favored treatment for Black people and other minorities such as affirmative action and set-asides in government contracting: "Most Americans despise civil rights and rightly so."[88] Like the mainstream libertarians just discussed, Rockwell objected to the Civil Rights Act of 1964 because it violated property rights. But paleo-libertarianism goes further. Racial segregation is morally problematic only insofar as it is compelled by the state: "Wishing to associate with members of one's own race, nationality, religion, class, sex, or even political party is a natural and normal human impulse."[89] Along with political parties, neighborhood associations, and ethnic clubs, a paleo-libertarian society would also make room for "Black churches, Jewish country clubs, and white fraternities."[90]

Rockwell noted that leftists are often soft on crime (and hard on the police) because they see crime as a result of "white racism" pervading society. Paleo-libertarians have no such illusions. Crime is a moral evil, a result of free choices made by bad individuals. Individuals have a right, and possibly a duty, to prevent criminals from violating other people's rights. Rockwell tells a story of a woman living in an Italian neighborhood "surrounded by Cleveland's slums." While crime was rampant all around the neighborhood, Rockwell recounts, the woman was perfectly safe in her home or on the street. This was because "anyone who crossed into the Italian area" would be noticed and carefully watched. If the intruder committed a crime, he would not be turned over to the police to be released soon after. Instead, neighborhood watch groups would punish the person on the spot. Rockwell applauds this approach: "While hardly an ideal system, it was rough justice and eminently libertarian." Noting that other libertarians might object to this simply because the intruders often were Black, paleo-libertarians have no such scruples: "There should be equal opportunity punishment."[91]

A year after Rockwell published his paleo-libertarian manifesto, the brutal police beating of Rodney King was caught on video, sparking race riots in Los Angeles and across the country. In an infamous letter to the *Los Angeles Times*, however, Rockwell repeated his call for "rough justice" delivered on the spot. However, Rockwell now advocated "rough justice" not when dealt out by private neighborhood groups (that "eminently libertarian solution") but by the police themselves. For now, in the wake of the Rodney King affair, Rockwell offered a libertarian defense of police brutality—calling upon the *agents of the state* to administer "rough justice." In America of the 1950s, Rockwell continued, the police acted on an effective principle: whatever recourse the legal system might eventually afford, rapists and muggers knew for sure they faced a serious beating whenever they were caught by the police. Streets were safe because police were feared. Rockwell expresses regret that, because of cameras, incidents of extrajudicial police brutality were increasingly brought to light. He concludes his letter: "Liberals talk about banning guns. As a libertarian, I can't agree. I am, however, beginning to wonder about video cameras."[92]

The next year, Murray Rothbard (Rockwell's colleague at the Mises Institute) published a similar paleo-libertarian manifesto, a proposal for what Rothbard described as "right-wing populism."[93] Some of these principles were predictable: slashing taxes, abolishing the Federal Reserve, and so on. But like Rockwell, Rothbard's list soon shaded into less recognizably libertarian terrain. "Defend Family Values," we are told, is a matter not only of getting the state out of the family but of reestablishing "parental control." "America First" is a matter not only of bringing the troops home but of checking international trade and "export industries." Rothbard, too, rails against the Civil Rights Act and other governmental efforts at forced desegregation. He finds that *Brown vs. Board of Education* produced "all the horrors of compulsory integration, forced busing, and white depopulation and decay of the inner cities."[94] Other familiar libertarian positions are now justified on grounds of race. Rothbard attacks the welfare state not just for its property rights violations but as a form of political inversion: welfare is "underclass rule." Issues of law and order take on a surprisingly central role in the essay, without much fussing over the rights of individuals against the state. For example, "Take Back the Streets" entails "unleashing the cops to clear the streets of bums and vagrants." (Rothbard quips: "Where will they go? Who cares?") By "Crush Criminals," Rothbard elaborates, "I mean, of course, not 'white collar criminals' or 'insider traders' but violent street criminals—robbers, muggers, rapists, murders." Rothbard too wants the police to administer rough justice on the spot (subject to "liability when they are in error"—whatever that might mean).

As we will see in more detail in the next chapter, paleo-libertarians such as Rothbard and Hans-Hermann Hoppe also depart from libertarians' traditional defense of immigration. As individualists, libertarians understand "immigration" as individual freedom of movement, and thus among the most basic of human rights. Paleo-libertarians, in contrast, see immigration restrictions as justifiable—and perhaps necessary—as an exercise of, and mechanism for defending, libertarian rights of private property.

Finally, Rothbard adopts a nomenclature that removes all doubts about paleo-libertarianism's racial valence. He says that libertarians of his day usually fall into two main sociological groups: there are the "hippies," with their 1970s anything-goes lifestyles, and there are the equally ineffectual "yuppies" (many of them associated with the libertarian billionaire Charles Koch) who seek what Rothbard decried as mere incremental social change, typically through corridors-of-power strategies (e.g., through DC-based think tanks such as the Cato Institute). By contrast, paleo-libertarianism appeals to a third, potentially much larger and more powerful group: the "rednecks." While the libertarian hippies and yuppies are elites, in America the rednecks are "the real people." Paleo-libertarianism is explicitly "a strategy of Outreach to the Rednecks."[95]

Rothbard's relish for police brutality against Black people is all the more surprising—and egregious—given the *sympathy* he had expressed for the plight of Black Americans earlier in his career. The young Rothbard had described the inner cities, with their thick networks of government intervention and control, as the central locus of America's anti-Black "power structure."[96] Urban public schools, beloved by liberals and overwhelmingly staffed by whites, were based on compulsory attendance laws that had no regard for differences in talents and inclination among Black children. Such schools amounted to "a vast prison-house and chain-gang for the nation's youth."[97] It is no accident, Rothbard observed, that welfare workers were almost always white. He wrote: "Not only are these workers engaged in setting up unmanly dependence among the Negro 'clients' and are resented therefore, they also organize Gestapo-like raids on their clients in the middle of the night—without a search warrant, by the way—to make sure there are no men in or under the female client's bed, who could serve her as a private means of support."[98] Just as bad as (or worse than) the welfare agents were the urban renewal planners, who again were almost always white. In addition to generating a massive (unjust) subsidy to white real estate interests, these programs systematically displaced Blacks from their neighborhoods and artificially increased Black density elsewhere. The police were merely the most visible agents supporting white power in America: "It is overwhelmingly white police who are the enforcers of racial law and who express the basic racism of their own community by systematically brutalizing the subject population."[99]

Rights-Respecting Racism: A Libertarian Blind Spot?

If racism were always violent, all libertarians would be anti-racists. But the problem is not so easy. Racism can set back basic interests even *without violating negative liberty*, one's right to be left alone. If white shipowners refuse to hire Black caulkers, or if hotel and lunch-counter operators refuse to serve Black customers, such people do not, by their refusal, aggress against the personal or property rights of any individual in the targeted group. Refusal could only count as an act of aggression if the would-be employee or customer had some sort of preexisting claim on the property of the business owner, such that the proprietor had a duty to transfer their property through financial exchange. But this libertarians deny. Rights, for most libertarians, are negative liberties. Free society is peaceful and just precisely because it is *voluntarily*. Indeed, for libertarians, the only form of cooperation worthy of the name is voluntary cooperation. During the civil rights era, libertarians such as Milton Friedman consistently presented their anti-racist credentials in those terms.

Here, history should be our guide. As Jonathan Blanks notes, "The dominant libertarian assumption that rational economic self-interest would trump racism if government only got out of the way fails to reckon with more than 200 years of evidence to the contrary."[100] The U.S. Civil Rights Act of 1875 contained many of the same provisions of the more famous act of 1964, including a provision outlawing discrimination in public accommodations.[101] That earlier civil rights act was ruled unconstitutional by the Supreme Court in 1883, the start of a period that is widely regarded as the Court's most libertarian. But throughout that whole run of "libertarian" decades, roughly from 1880 to 1940, Blacks continued to suffer from structural racism.[102] The economic logic is obvious: business owners who started serving Black customers might well expect to lose many, and maybe all, white customers. White business owners who hired Blacks, or who promoted Blacks to positions of authority over whites, might struggle to retain talent given the racism among the labor pool. Frederick Douglass, as we have seen, was forced to abandon his profession due to racism of precisely this sort—with no violation of the non-aggression axiom whatsoever.

External critics of libertarianism, like Rachel Maddow, and internal ones, like Blanks, highlight a legitimate worry about the orthodox libertarian theory of civil liberty. Even if the nonaggression principle could ground an ahistorical utopia, it gives poor guidance for a community in which injustice has *already* been perpetuated on a massive scale. "No discrimination . . . starting now!" rings hollow when one side has greatly benefited from hundreds of years of prior discrimination.[103] The harms of historical racism might well persist even if, through some magical process, we could precisely mete out rectificatory justice to all those affected. Like radioactive waste, historical injustices against groups have a long, diffuse, and toxic half-life. The harms caused by cultural racism are insidious partly because they are so difficult to detect by onlookers.

The harms of what we might call "rights-respecting racism" emerge from seemingly coercion-free acts. Yet libertarians see only individuals and individual acts. This impasse leads many to find the Cold War libertarian vision defective when confronting racism in the real world, and in response, libertarians have begun rethinking their familiar anti-anti-discrimination posture. Specifically, libertarians have begun rethinking the traditional opposition to the Civil Rights Act. An awareness of libertarianism's history helps inform, and demonstrate the pedigree of, these reformist libertarian positions.

As we have seen in earlier chapters, libertarians have long been suspicious of monopolies, especially those created or sustained by state action. David Bernstein uses this point to reformulate the libertarian response to the Civil Rights Act.[104] Viewed as justice-restoring responses to state-granted monopolies, libertarian principles would allow and perhaps require anti-discrimination laws of various sorts. Bernstein offers an example from labor law: "if the government grants labor unions the exclusive power to represent workers, there is nothing 'unlibertarian' about insisting that unions represent all workers without discrimination."[105] Back in 1964, Bernstein argues, a similar situation obtained in many southern states. Jim Crow segregation was in effect a government-granted monopoly, or what Bernstein calls "a white supremacist cartel." That cartel was enforced not only by racist government regulations but by the implicit threat of extralegal violence. Local officials not only permitted such threats but often helped carry them out (thus the old saw of civil rights activists in the South: "No need to call the police; they're already there"). Because southern businesses operated within this cartel, Bernstein suggests, those businesses were "private" only in name. Southern businesses were embedded in a wider, coercively backed system by which their "private" practices were directed and controlled.

The state-backed cartel of the 1960s South flatly violated libertarian principles. How could that cartel be broken? One option would have been a federal law invalidating state-based segregationist laws, along with a massive federal takeover of local law enforcement (and other branches of government, such as tax and permit offices) to prevent the extralegal threats of violence and other forms of harassment. As a purely theoretical matter, Bernstein notes, libertarian principles might well support such an approach. But in America in the 1950s and 1960s, such an approach was utterly impractical. The other option was the one actually pursued: a federal law banning discrimination by private businesses. As a practical matter, this law had the effect "that threats of violence and harassment would generally be met with an appeal to the potential victim's obligation to obey federal law."[106] Facing a government-backed racist cartel, Bernstein concludes, there were good libertarian grounds in 1964 for supporting the parts of the Civil Rights Act (specifically, Titles II and VII) that libertarians of that era rejected.

What about the contemporary setting? The old racist cartel of the South no longer exists. Still, Bernstein suggests that anti-discrimination laws could be acceptable to libertarians even today. Such laws might function as default rules around which parties could contract. Bernstein explains: "an antidiscrimination law could replace the common law 'at will' employment with a default rule that no employer may discriminate based on a variety of criteria. If an employer nevertheless wished to retain the right to discriminate on one of the prohibited bases, it would have to acknowledge that desire to potential employees, and therefore, inevitably to the public at large."[107] On Bernstein's scheme, racist restaurant and hotel owners might have the formal right to not hire Black employees or serve Black customers. But business owners would be required to make that policy public. In today's very different social and cultural environment, the economic consequences of adopting such a policy would be grim.

On Bernstein's approach, then, faithful adherence to libertarian principles looks different as the cultural contexts change. In a context where racist ideas are widely and openly endorsed and the economy is organized around a white supremacist cartel, libertarian principles support limiting the economic liberties of business owners. In a different context—say, with a more open economy and an actively anti-racist wider culture—they might support a less intrusive system of default rules. To us, this tack offers an attractive alternative to the libertarian theory of civil rights defended by twentieth-century icons such as Mises, Friedman, Nozick, and Rand.

The radical libertarian Sheldon Richman agrees with Bernstein: white-owned southern businesses in the 1960s benefited from the race-based cartel, and there were sound libertarian reasons to support governmental efforts to break up that cartel.[108] However, Richman goes on to ask, why should any libertarian treat a massively coercive state intervention (i.e., complete takeover of local government) as the only alternative to a smaller but equally coercive state intervention? Instead, Richman suggests, libertarians should look first to a noncoercive but *systemic* solution: namely, networked and nonviolent social action by the targets of the discrimination, joined and supported by fellow citizens (of all races) who are committed to the anti-racist ideal of individualism.

Even during Jim Crow this strategy scored some impressive wins. In the 1950s, T.R.M. Howard, the gun-carrying Black physician and entrepreneur, organized a boycott of national gasoline companies that eventually forced many franchises to open bathrooms to Black customers.[109] Beginning in 1960, sit-ins and other acts of public shaming by private activists had already begun desegregating lunch counters and bus companies throughout the South. As Richman admits, we cannot know the path this emancipatory movement might have taken had it been allowed to unfold without the drama of political intervention in the form of the passage of the Civil Rights Act. But a change in white people's racial attitudes was well underway in America by the mid-1960s. Through their campaigns of direct nonviolent action, private citizens called attention to the ugly facts of American racism, just as writers such as Frederick Douglass had brought the reality of slavery to public consciousness a century before.

Richman goes on to argue that the domain of social life under the scope of the Title II provision has a delicacy that should give libertarians pause before calling in the state. First, the sweeping anti-discrimination law born from the Title II provision, in its underlying logic, put the federal government on a collision course with other basic civil liberties, including religious liberty. But Richman suggests a broader reason for libertarians to pause: "the social campaign for equality that was desegregating the South was transmogrified when it was diverted to Washington."[110] Instead of grassroots organizing and the building of progressive, mutual aid institutions (such as the petrol boycott organized by T.R.M. Howard), the focus shifted "to a patronizing white political elite in Washington that had scurried to the front of the march and claimed leadership."[111] As a result, racial justice lost its passionate, personal character. When the federal government took over the problem of race, many citizens became passive rather than active in their commitment to racial equality. The sense of personal responsibility that enflamed the early activists was dissipated and lost.

Faced with the question of whether white business owners should have been allowed to exclude Blacks from their lunch counters, Richman says, libertarians *as libertarians* should answer proudly that "they should have been stopped—not by the State, which can't be trusted, but by non-violent social action on behalf of equality."[112] The most organic libertarian response to structural oppression, Richman suggests, is community organizing.

Black Liberty Matters

Fairly or not, libertarianism has the reputation of appealing primarily to white males.[113] One reason for this may be innocuous. Jonathan Blanks observes that as a relatively obscure and esoteric ideology, perhaps African Americans (who are disproportionately economically disadvantaged) are simply more concerned with day-to-day realities than with the abstract debates that have featured so prominently in the libertarian tradition. But Blanks also points to a more ominous concern. While claiming to care about liberty generally, it seems to many outsiders that libertarians in fact care about just one kind: *white liberty*.[114]

American libertarians frequently invoke the Founding Era as a halcyon moment when government was limited and America had not yet started down the road to serfdom. But for Black people, that libertarian golden era brought suffering and repression and death. David Boaz, executive vice president of the Cato Institute, offers a telling anecdote. For years, the Cato Institute's mission statement included the following: "Since [the American] revolution, civil and political liberties have been eroded." Cato changed that statement only after Clarence Thomas, then chairman of the Equal Opportunity Employment Commission, gave a talk at Cato pointing out that things did not look that way to Black Americans. The point is generalizable. According to Boaz, libertarians "tend to say 'Americans used to be free, but now we are not'—which is a claim that doesn't ring true to a lot of Jewish, Black, female and gay Americans."[115]

Even the libertarian commitment to principle has been called out as racially suspect. Blanks says their hold-to-premises-wherever-they-lead tendency has often blinded libertarians to the freedom of Black people. Regarding the traditional libertarian opposition to the Civil Rights Act, Blanks writes: "This sort of adherence to principle at the expense of the tangible freedom of millions of African Americans sent a clear message of whose liberty received priority."[116]

In 2017, Jacob Levy posted a brief but provocative essay titled "Black Liberty Matters." Opening with a quotation from Samuel Johnson—"'How is it that we hear the loudest yelps for liberty among the drivers of negroes?'"—Levy goes on to urge libertarians to confront an ugly fact: "The language of freedom in American political discourse has very often been appropriated for the defense of white supremacy."[117] Libertarian strategies for limiting the power of government—economic liberty, freedom of religion and association, federalism, bicameralism, and so forth—have historically *also* been deployed by racists in defense of white supremacy, as tools to hinder attempts by the federal government to break the institutions of white rule. According to Levy, the problem goes well beyond the outliers, as with Lew Rockwell's defense of Rodney King's beating. The (comparative) invisibility of Black liberty to libertarians is obvious: a fascination with the liberty-related *flaws* rather than successes of Abraham Lincoln; a too-ready impulse to defend freedom of expression by defending racially charged "political incorrectness"; the tendency to use paternalistic talk about "dependency" and "moral harm" when opposing urban welfare programs (moralized language that, curiously, gets dropped when libertarians oppose subsidies to white farmers in the Midwest); and so on. According to Levy, "The capture of the language of freedom by the defenders of white supremacy and the Confederacy is a *major* fact about American political language and its history."[118] Libertarianism may be logically and morally incompatible with white supremacist structures and tactics—but it does not always *seem* that way. Especially in America, the language of liberty gets entangled with the supremacist's cause, and this means that, like it or not, libertarianism gets entangled with white supremacy too.

What is to be done? Levy can be read as calling upon contemporary libertarians to join him in a new Black Liberty Matters movement (what we might call "libertarian BLM"). This would mean developing libertarianism in explicitly race-conscious and anti-racist directions. The work is already underway. A race-conscious libertarianism might shift from a traditional (and narrow) focus on noncoercion to a new (and broader) focus on issues of human *well-being*. Third Wave libertarian Fabio Rojas advocates a "thick" approach to libertarianism: "Libertarian writers depict dynamic societies where people's lives just get better over time. They don't advocate freedom because it gives you the power to make the lives of others miserable." A society of universal freedom with a permanent racial underclass could never qualify as a good society by libertarianism's standards.[119]

But can anti-racist libertarians go further? Can libertarian principles be used to address the challenge of structural racism itself? For our purposes, let's think of structural racism as a set of identity-based threats to liberty that arise not so much from the racist attitudes and actions of individuals (as with the white supremacist cartel of the South discussed by Bernstein) but from the operation of social institutions themselves.[120] Social structures can limit liberty even if none of the individuals living and operating within those structures *intends* to be racist all.

In a famous 1971 article, Thomas Schelling demonstrated how white flight could be understood as a spontaneous order, since the resulting patterns of segregated housing were not intended by the individual (white) homeowners who moved. Schelling's finding sometimes gets presented as exculpatory: white homeowners who left when Black neighbors arrived were merely following their economic self-interest. However, as Jacob Levy has recently observed, "if we are interested in social analysis rather than in treating racism as an individual sin and providing white people with a defense against this charge, this is very strange." As libertarians, Levy suggests, "our interest should be less in the souls of individual actors than in the shape of the world they create."[121] In the case of white flight, that world looks like one in which quality housing and the public goods attached thereto constantly recede from the reach of Black Americans. If libertarians want to recognize and promote Black liberty, they should be especially sensitive to oppressive structures that arise from human action but not human design.[122]

The influence of the nascent Black Liberty Matters movement can already be felt. Charles Koch and his network spearheaded an important effort at criminal justice reform, with an explicit concern

about racial justice.[123] In the wake of Ferguson and the police killing of George Floyd, it was the libertarian congressman Justin
Amash who introduced a congressional bill to end qualified immu-
nity for police (a major goal of the Black Lives Matter movement).
When reparations-for-slavery regained prominence (another key
goal of Black Lives Matter), libertarians such as Jessica Flanigan
offered strong pro-reparations arguments (though, in a typical libertarian twist, Flanigan proposed reparations for victims of America's [racist] criminal justice system). When the *New York Times*
launched its controversial 1619 Project and it became the target
of strong criticism from the right (as well as from leading historians), the Cato Institute published a series of articles *praising* that
initiative, despite its flaws.[124] When on Martin Luther King Day
in 2020 the civil rights leader and big government stalwart Representative John Lewis announced that he had pancreatic cancer,
Michael F. Cannon wrote a remarkable essay affirming Lewis as a
hero of the liberty movement: "Few in the libertarian movement
have suffered as much as Lewis for the cause of freedom. Lewis
offered his voice and his body—and sacrificed his right to self-
defense—to make Americans confront the violence inherent in the
Southern system of government-imposed white-supremacy." Noting that, as a libertarian, Cannon opposed many of the proposals
for expanded government that Lewis, a Democrat, had promoted,
Cannon urged caution in dismissing Lewis as a libertarian champion: "If libertarians can honor Founding Fathers who participated
in 'the most oppressive dominion ever exercised by man over man,'
we can honor John Lewis even though he supports single-payer
health care." Cannon concluded by recommending that the Cato
Institute present that year's Milton Friedman Prize for Advancing
Liberty to John Lewis.[125]

Of course, libertarians being libertarians, controversies abound.
Cato recently hosted a forum on intersectionality theory, an analytical approach introduced by Kimberlé Crenshaw that considers
how different dimensions of oppression interact (e.g., racism and
sexism).[126] Some participants (notably, Jacob Levy) argued that
libertarians should welcome intersectionality theory for insights
it might give about hidden forms of liberty suppression. Others
insisted that intersectionality theory, with its deep connections to

Marxism, was so prescriptively anti-individualist and anti-market that it should be anathema to libertarians.

However the libertarian debate about intersectionality shakes out, the very *existence* of such debates heartens us. Perhaps today's discussions say something about the future direction of the modern liberty movement: a future libertarianism, like its past, where the liberty of everyone matters.

CHAPTER EIGHT

Global Justice and Nonintervention

IN THE WINTER of 1909, a play called *A Message from the Forties*
opened in London. The play spoofed Charles Dickens's classic *A
Christmas Carol* from 1843, in a decade remembered as "the hungry Forties." In 1804, England had imposed a series of tariffs on
foreign-grown grains: wheat, oats, barley, and other ground food-
stuffs (generically called "corn"). Intended to keep grain prices high
in order to favor domestic producers, the Corn Laws also had the
effect of raising the price of bread, creating hardship.[1] Between
1838 and 1846, a group of free traders led by Richard Cobden successfully campaigned to remove the tariffs. By 1909, however, some
Britons had begun demanding an end to free trade and a return
to protectionism. The new play—sponsored by advocates of free
trade—was as politically charged as it was popular.

As with Dickens's original, *A Message from the Forties* opens on
Christmas Eve. But instead of gloom and despair, we find a cheery
scene. Standing in for Bob Cratchit is a well-paid clerk named
Hatchet, whom we find relaxing with his children and delighting
in goods available through international trade: Australian beef
for dinner, a pat of sweet butter from Canada, table flowers from
France, and a box of toy soldiers "none the worse for having been
made in Switzerland."

Mr. Scrooge stomps onto the stage. But where Dickens had
portrayed Scrooge as an evil capitalist, *A Message from the Forties*

casts Scrooge as a pitiless *opponent* of free trade. He announces that he has decided to support protectionism. Alarmed, Hatchet recalls the days when workers groaned under the tariffs on corn. If the new generation of protectionists have their way, the price of staples will rise and he might have his wages docked or even lose his job. Hatchet frets, "Tiny Tim won't get that wooden horse he's fancied for so long." Scrooge is unmoved: "You're all too rich and lazy now. . . . Why, in the old Protectionist days clerks didn't come around yapping for holidays, and more wages, and Christmas dinners, and things that ought to be left to their betters."

Alone in his room that night, Scrooge pulls on his nightshirt and climbs into bed. He mutters protectionist slogans as he drifts into uneasy sleep. Claps of thunder. A clanking of chains. A towering dream-like figure appears before Mr. Scrooge: it is the ghost of Richard Cobden, legendary leader of the Anti-Corn Law League. Scrooge beholds the apparition with a mixture of horror and awe:

> SCROOGE: What do you want with me? I thought your voice was silenced forever, and you and your work long since forgotten.
>
> COBDEN'S GHOST: No, my spirit walks abroad among my fellow-men, and travels far and wide, for those who have forgotten must learn again the bitter lesson of the past.
>
> SCROOGE: What are those chains?
>
> COBDEN'S GHOST: These are the chains that were forged by the Bread Tax, link by link and yard by yard girded round the people of England, and which I, after years of toil, yea, even of persecution, struck from the fettered limbs of the poor.
>
> SCROOGE: What business have you with me?
>
> COBDEN'S GHOST: Mankind is my business; the common welfare is my business; charity, mercy, forbearance, and benevolence are my business; and, therefore, Free Trade is my business.

By play's end, Scrooge has been convinced. Throwing open his windows as children march past singing "Tramp, tramp, tramp upon Protection," Scrooge exclaims: "A Merry Christmas—a Merry Christmas, children. Go home to your untaxed dinners, and Thank God England is still Free Trade."

The libertarian ideal of global order rests on three legs. The play references two: first, libertarians want trade to be free;

second, as Richard Cobden and many others have argued, the nations of the world should be at peace, and peace is made easier by trade. Libertarians see those two legs supported a third: if trade is truly to be free, and if we hope for lasting peace between peoples, then those people also must be free to move—to seek work and to build lives for themselves and their families, in places of their own choice. Libertarians think freedom of movement a basic human right. The libertarian position on international relations is frequently summed up in the mantra: free trade, free migration, and peace.

Tellingly, this slogan sums up the libertarian position on *intra*-national relations as well. After all, as individualists, libertarians insist that the rights and liberties of every person ought to be respected, no matter where they happen to reside. Just as individuals ought to be free to trade, to move, and to live peacefully *within* states, so too should they be able to do so *between* states. The libertarian vision is cosmopolitan, insisting that basic human rights—including economic rights—apply to all persons everywhere, regardless of boundaries.

Indeed, at the extreme, some strict libertarians insist that all we need is a theory of justice based on the rights of individuals. At a stretch, libertarians can allow talk about *global justice*, but merely as a way to denote the application of individual rights doctrine at a global scale (in the same way that Nozick allows talk of "social justice," which is merely the application of individual rights theory on a societal scale).[2]

At the start of this book, we identified a commitment to *negative liberty* as one marker of membership in the libertarian family. This conception of liberty sees freedom as the absence of interference. In the post-Westphalian world of nation-states in which we find ourselves, the libertarian commitment to negative liberty presents itself as a principle of *nonintervention*. A state-launched war of aggression may be the ultimate violation of the principle of nonintervention. But state restrictions on the movement of goods and persons are also acts of interventionism—violations of our negative liberties. As Loren Lomasky and Fernando Tesón have recently summarized the libertarian position on global justice: "What is primarily owed to others is to *leave them alone*."[3]

This commitment to nonintervention remains constant across our three eras of libertarian thinking. Yet as the world changed around them, libertarians came to understand and express that commitment in different ways—and with different allies. Nineteenth-century libertarians opposed war, supported free trade, and defended the rights of embattled immigrants and people held as slaves. Visionaries of a radical new world based on free trade and universal individual liberty, the first libertarians saw conservative defenders of the old order as implacable foes. But in the twentieth century, the rise of the Soviet Union and emergent statism in liberal Western societies restructured libertarian alliances. Opposition to central planning brought libertarians and conservatives together for the first time. Both groups opposed the New Deal not just for its unprecedented interventions into the domestic economy but because, inspired by the Soviet model, it put the United States on what they believed to be a path to communism. *Opposition to socialism* became a defining feature of the libertarian worldview, and as we have seen in previous chapters, this made the twentieth-century expression of libertarian principles distinct from nineteenth-century antecedents—notably (but not only) on issues of labor and race.

We begin our story in nineteenth-century England with Richard Cobden—not the ghostly image of Cobden from our West End stage but the historical Cobden who, more than any other figure of the time, embodies the radical and inspirational elements of the libertarian global creed.

The International Man

In 1837, a small group of activists in London established the Anti-Corn Law Association. Richard Cobden helped form a branch of this organization the following year in Manchester, where he was in business as a calico printer. By 1839 Cobden had helped reorganize the association into the more ambitious Anti-Corn Law League. Its mission: the immediate and total repeal of the Corn Laws.

One of Cobden's first moves was to recruit his Quaker friend and brilliant orator John Bright. Bright became known as the "heart" of the Anti-Corn Law movement while the more measured Cobden, its "brain." Leaders of the League traveled across the country, mixing economic and moral arguments against the Corn Laws (or the "Bread Tax," as Cobden called the tariffs). The group published several papers such as "The Anti-Bread-Tax Circular," and *The Economist* magazine was founded in August 1842 to support the repeal of the Corn Laws. The League reached millions with its message of free trade.[4]

The emergent class of manufacturers helped fund the anti–Corn Law campaign from the beginning, so much so that the movement became known by the hometown of prominent industrial supporters: the Manchester School. Some business leaders joined the campaign because they shared Cobden's almost messianic belief in the transformative power of free trade; others believed that the Corn Laws raised the price of labor and thus hurt their bottom line. Support from the manufacturers gave Cobden and his fellow reformers deep pockets, but it also opened them to the charge of being shills for "big business" interests of their day—a line of attack against libertarians with a long pedigree, as we have seen.[5] The League's accusers were both the aristocratic landholders who favored the status quo and the Chartists who demanded more radical change. But the League also relied on "penny campaigns" through which tens of thousands of middle-class people contributed to the cause. Rarely in history has a single issue of political economy gained such popular appeal.

The League mustered a range of economic, political, and moral arguments against the laws. Citing principles from classical economics, they argued that the Corn Laws raised the price of bread and lowered real wages. The tariffs restricted the export of manufactured goods, creating unemployment in manufacturing while making domestic agriculture inefficient. Politically the laws perpetuated the domination of the landed aristocracy, a group Bright called "the lords and great proprietors of the soil." Cobden and Bright argued that the agricultural "monopolists" were also imperialists: they saw Prime Minister Palmerston's military adventures abroad as an attempt to divert attention from domestic harms of the Corn Laws. They claimed that Palmerston's imperialist policies—which the League claimed were inextricably tied to the Corn Laws—antagonized foreign powers and threatened Britain's long-term security.

But it was the League's moral argument, built from economic premises, that proved most powerful. For Cobden, the central injustice was the high cost of bread for the poor and middle classes. This also ran counter to distinctively Victorian values, such as the idea that prosperity was the natural reward for hard work. With the economy strangled by the import tariffs on food, the "bourgeois virtues" of hard work and personal responsibility could not produce the favorable outcomes God intended. Even honest, hardworking people went hungry. Cobden and Bright often said that they were simply applying Christianity to the business of public life.[6]

Cobden's objections to the Corn Laws were born of a philosophical commitment to liberty that applied as much to the internal relations of British citizens as to (would-be) trading partners abroad. Free trade is mutually beneficial. Cobden saw this as an eternal truth, comparable to physical truths such as the law of gravity. Indeed, according to the biographer J. A. Hobson, Cobden believed "that a secular salvation lay open to any man through a proper understanding of economic law." Economic liberty unlocks the natural bounty of our world. Cobden's concern for individual liberty would also lead him to oppose restrictions on the transfer of land (such as the feudal principle requiring entailment of estates) and restrictions on the free movement and settlement of labor (in that era, movement was often restricted even within states, another feudal relic). He also called for freedom of conscience and the separation of church and state, and opposed religious tests for public offices and university posts.[7] Progressive social change, across every domain, would flow from a commitment to liberty.

Cobden had no illusions about the power of the entrenched elites set against the League. He wrote: "The citadel of privilege in this country is so terribly strong, owing to the concentrated masses of property in the hands of the comparatively few, that we cannot hope to assail it with success unless with the help of the propertied classes in the middle ranks of society, and by raising up a portion of the working classes to become members of the propertied order."[8] This worry about concentrated power became a steady theme in Cobden's work, always pushed from the fulcrum point of individual liberty.

Cobden and Bright styled themselves as the intellectual heirs of Adam Smith and the other classical economists, but there were tensions between Cobden's radical libertarian position and the more measured approach of the classical liberals.[9] While a staunch advocate for free trade in principle, Smith also thought that real-life politics required compromise. Smith argued that if, for example, a domestically produced good was taxed by the home government it might be appropriate to impose a matching tax on imported goods, to prevent home producers from working under a disadvantage.[10] Since domestic agriculture was indeed taxed in Britain, Smith's position appeared to favor taxing imported grain too.

David Ricardo also had argued that tariff reforms must consider the effects on domestic agriculture.[11] If import tariffs were repealed while domestic taxes remained, Ricardo predicted an exodus of domestic labor from agriculture toward manufacturing, which was taxed less. The most efficient policy would first level domestic taxes on agriculture and manufacture and then gradually reduce import tariffs. As Ricardo put it:

> We cannot now help living under a system of heavy taxation, but to make our industry as productive as possible, we should offer no temptations to capitalists to employ their funds and their skill in any other way than they would have employed them, if we had had the good fortune to be untaxed, and had been permitted to give the greatest development to our talents and industry.[12]

Cobden's main economic argument against the Corn Laws claimed that they artificially raised the price of bread and simultaneously drove down manufacturing wages (since capital that would have been available to that industry was, through the tariffs, being captured by agriculture). Here, too, he broke ranks with Ricardo. In his Corn Laws pamphlet of 1815, Ricardo had examined the effect of corn tariffs on wages. Ricardo argued that when the price of corn falls, money wages fall too. After all, Ricardo reasoned, the repeal of the Corn Laws would lead to an increase in grain imports. This would lead to a fall in the cost of grain and a *decrease* in money wages—quite against the claims later made by Cobden and his followers.[13] Ricardo's "iron law of wages" thus played into the hands of Cobden's opponents, who sought to portray Cobden as not the honest spokesman for the poor but a man in the pocket of manufacturers (who, with repeal, would benefit from lower wages).

Of course, Cobden and Bright were correct to think of Smith, Ricardo, and David Hume as allies in the broader movement for free international trade.[14] But there were deeper divisions between the idealistic, rationalistic views of Bright and Cobden and the more skeptical, empirical works of Hume and Smith. One difference concerned the plasticity or fixedness of human nature. Through his study of English history, Hume saw a limited capacity for sympathy as a fixed feature of human nature: "we sympathise more with persons contiguous to us than with persons remote; with our acquaintances, than with strangers; with our countrymen than with foreigners."[15] Smith had similarly observed that an ordinary person would feel the loss of his little finger more deeply than he would receive the news of a calamity that took the lives of thousands of people in China.[16] Limited sympathy gives the *nation-state* a more central place in the classical liberalism of Hume and Smith than in the more libertarian writings of Cobden and Bright.[17] According to Smith, "we do not love our country merely as part of the great society of mankind: we love it for its own sake, and independently of any such consideration." Therefore, "the interest of the great society of mankind would best be promoted by directing the principal attention of each individual to that particular portion of it, which was most within the sphere both of his abilities and of his understanding."[18] Given the fixed features of human nature, neither Smith nor Hume called for any great cosmopolitan transformation of the international system of states.

The classical economists were also more cautious than Cobden about the pacific possibilities of trade. International conflict has many causes: territorial disputes, expansionist religions, historic resentment, national pride, and so on. From this more cautious classical liberal perspective, we should not expect a bourgeois concern for economic self-interest to wash away all sources of strife. Rather than a perpetual peace achieved through a world focused upon free commercial relations, the benefits of trade must be considered in the context of a world in which states have an enduring and beneficial role. Hume writes: "There is nothing more favorable to the rise of politeness and learning than a number of neighboring and independent states, connected together by commerce and policy."[19] (As Razeen Sally wryly observes, Smith did not call his great book the wealth of the *world* but the wealth of *nations*.)[20]

The emerging libertarians of Cobden's generation were more willing to accept his radical vision. The epigram "When goods don't cross borders, soldiers will" often gets attributed to Frédéric Bastiat, and although the attribution is likely apocryphal, the sentiment is *Bastiatian* to the core.[21] In *Economic Sophisms*, Bastiat frequently claims that international trade produces international peace. He punctures the popular illusion that the importation of foreign goods amounts to some type of invasion: "What possible similarity can there be between a warship that comes to vomit missiles, fire, and devastation on our cities, and a merchant vessel that comes to offer us a voluntary exchange of goods for goods?"[22] In the closing paragraph of "Our Products Are Burdened by Taxes," Bastiat firmly links trade with peace: "Finally, with respect to these heavy taxes that you are using as a justification for the protectionist system, have you ever asked yourself whether it is not the system itself that produces them? I do wish someone would tell me what would be the use of large standing armies and powerful navies if trade were free."[23]

Gustave de Molinari saw war as anachronistic in the modern age of trade. Where wars were once waged to ensure security, they now benefit only the ruling class on the backs of the working class: "War has ceased to be productive of security, but the masses, whose existence depends upon the industries of production, are compelled to pay its costs and suffer its losses."[24] Rather than allowing a market for security services, governments had illegitimately monopolized production. Breaking with the classical liberals, Molinari decries the state system as a whole, arguing that the boundaries between nation-states are products of political interests rather than economic ones: "Is it not the height of absurdity to transform these frontiers, which chance events alone have determined, and which it may enlarge or contract to-morrow, into formal boundaries which limit trade? Is not an economic system which is founded on a political basis and which is politically modifiable, a monstrosity to which good sense objects?"[25] The unjust monopolization of security itself leads to war: "Just as war is the natural consequence of monopoly, peace is the natural consequence of liberty."[26]

Under the leadership of Cobden and Bright, the Anti-Corn Law League grew into a mass movement. Cobden was elected to Parliament in 1841 and was joined there by Bright in 1843. As Members of Parliament, Cobden and Bright relentlessly pressured the prime minister, Sir Robert Peel, on this issue. (Peel was a famed debater; Cobden is recognized as the only man who defeated him in a parliamentary debate.) By 1844, Peel's ineffectiveness against the political strategies of the League made him increasingly unpopular even among his own backbenchers. Poor wheat harvests in England, combined with the Irish Potato Famine that began in 1845, made Peel's defense of the "Bread Tax" increasingly untenable. To the dismay of his supporters, in January 1845, Peel publicly accepted the need for reform. On May 15, 1846, a coalition of Whigs, Conservatives, and free traders came together and the Corn Laws were repealed. Its mission accomplished, the Anti-Corn Law League was disbanded.

The Corn Laws' repeal signaled a decisive shift in British ideological self-understanding. In rejecting import tariffs Britain embraced a new form of political economy. It was not by accident or stealth, but with conviction and pride, that Victorian Britain came to embrace the sobriquet of Free Trade Nation.[27] After repeal, Britain's economy quickly improved and Cobden and Bright became national heroes. In 1846, Cobden embarked on a triumphant tour of the capitals of Europe, pitching free and peaceful commerce to leaders and finance ministers across the continent. (Before the Corn Laws campaign, Cobden had made various private journeys to the United States and Canada, as well as to Turkey and Egypt, making him perhaps the most well-traveled member of Parliament.) Capturing the enthusiasm of the moment, a businessman from Bolton described Cobden as "the greatest benefactor of mankind since the inventor of the printing press."[28]

Cobden's sainthood was short-lived. In October 1853, the Ottoman Empire declared war on Russia and soon suffered a crushing defeat in which Russia seized control of the strategic Crimean peninsula. War fever swept England. England and France entered the conflict against Russia in 1854, signaling the start of the Crimean War. To the surprise of many constituents, Cobden argued that the British tradition of militarism, and its Victorian policies of

empire-building, had led Britain into this conflict—all in violation of his sacred principle of noninterventionism. Cobden's once-
adoring public deserted him.[29] His old enemies in Parliament piled
on, some even accusing Cobden of treacherously supporting the
Russians. Cobden's great weapon, the mass public meeting, slipped
from his hand. We get a sense of Cobden's defiance—and despair—
in a letter to Bright from October 1854:

> I am willing to incur any obloquy in telling the whole truth to the pub-
> lic as to the share they have had in this war, and it is better to face any
> neglect or hostility than allow them to persuade themselves that any-
> body but themselves is responsible for the war.[30]

Why did Cobden take this path? The answer takes us to the heart
of his thinking. Despite his association with laissez-faire, Cobden's
guiding principle was not economic. Instead, Cobden supported
free trade because he believed it would lead to peace.[31] In Cobden's
personal library, there is a copy of *The Wealth of Nations* that he
studied as a young man. The margins of the passages where Smith
condemns Britain's colonial policies are filled with his enthusiastic
notes. The passages about the invisible hand, intriguingly, were left
blank.[32]

Cobden stated his basic commitment to peace during the lead-
up to the Crimean conflict in 1850:

> But when I advocated Free Trade, do you suppose I did not see its rela-
> tion to the present question [of peace], or that I advocated Free Trade
> merely because it would give us a little more occupation in this or that
> pursuit? No; I believed Free Trade would have the tendency to unite
> mankind in the bonds of peace, and it was that, more than any pecu-
> niary consideration, which sustained and actuated me, as my friends
> know, in that struggle.[33]

Indeed we find just these cosmopolitan sentiments in speeches
delivered by Cobden and Bright at Covent Garden Theatre in 1842,
at the height of the Corn Laws campaign. Cobden said:

> Free Trade—what is it? Why, breaking down the barriers that sepa-
> rate nations; those barriers behind which nestle the feelings of pride,
> revenge, hatred and jealousy, which every now and then break their

bonds and deluge whole countries with blood; those feelings which nourish the poison of war and conquest, which assert that without conquest we can have no trade, which foster that lust for conquest and dominion, which send forth your warrior chiefs to sanction devastation through other lands, and then calls them back that they may be enthroned securely in your passions, but only to harass and oppress you at home.

At that same rally, Bright likewise explained that the Free Trade campaign grew from deeper longings, longings for a new world in which patriotic boundaries would be overcome and humanity might be united at last. Speaking about the workers who first joined the Free Trade campaign, Bright said: "They wanted to have the question settled for the world as well as for England. They were tired of what was called the natural division of empires. They wanted not that the Channel should separate this country from France—they hoped and wished that Frenchmen and Englishmen should no longer consider each other as naturally hostile nations."[34]

Like Bright, Cobden was a fierce critic of Palmerston's idea of a "balance of power"—the notion that peace is best achieved within a system of heavily, but equally armed, powers. Bright referred to the balance-of-power concept as a "filthy idol."[35] At base, noninterventionism was a policy of *humility*: peace is best achieved by seeking conditions in which nations disarm and allow their citizens to become friends. By contrast, militarism was a form of hubris, tempting strong nations to take up ever-expanding military obligations. As Cobden wrote in a letter of 1854, "If we are to assume responsibility of keeping the peace and 'doing justice' to the whole world, then we can never with consistency or security reduce our military establishments."[36] A mighty England should resist the temptation to act as the policeman (or overlord) of the world.

Cobden was also open to the idea of international organizations pursuing peace. In typical libertarian fashion, however, he insisted that such organizations be voluntary, with disputes decided by judges agreed upon by the conflicting parties themselves. For example, Cobden proposed a system of voluntary arbitration under which disputes between nations would be settled by "the absolute decision of arbitrators mutually appointed."[37] Faced with Russian aggression in Crimea and challenged to propose some alternative to war, Cobden even floated the idea of a "federation of the States of Europe." He wrote: "I should appeal not only to Germany, but to all the States, small as well as great, of the Continent, for such a union as would prevent the possibility of any act of hostility from the common enemy. This is the work of peace."[38]

Cobden remained true to these principles to the end. Shortly after the war the commercial ship *Arrow*, owned by Englishmen but manned by a Chinese crew and docked in Canton, allowed its registration to lapse. When the Chinese government ordered the *Arrow* to haul down its British flag, a dispute broke out. A chain of tragic events eventually led to the British bombardment of Canton and the opening of the Second Opium War. In Parliament, Cobden spoke out against this military campaign, arguing that Britain should instead turn the dispute over to international arbitrators. Outraged, Palmerston's allies proposed censuring Cobden in the House of Commons. Cobden managed to fend off this formal motion, but the damage was done. Facing an angry electorate, Cobden lost his seat in Parliament in March 1857. Bright and other allies of Cobden lost their seats soon after, completing Palmerston's victory and marking the end of the Manchester School as a political force.[39]

Liberty against Empire

For libertarians in the United States at the end of the nineteenth century, the Spanish-American War (1898) represented the spirit of plunder in its worst form. The war was presented to the American public as a patriotic effort to liberate the Cuban people from the tyrannical Spanish Empire. But less reputable motives were at work. Partly, the U.S. government wanted to protect the economic interests of certain American businesses that had made large investments in Cuban sugar and other industries; partly it hoped to bolster its naval power with a strong Caribbean presence and a canal across the Isthmus of Panama; partly it drew on a racist paternalism that saw the coercive civilization of "backward" peoples as a moral imperative of the state. By war's end, the United States had taken control of former Spanish possessions in Guam, the Marianas, Cuba, Puerto Rico, and the Philippines. Control of many of these territories was transferred peacefully after the Treaty of Paris; the Philippine people resisted. Subduing the Philippines took another three years of war and the death of over two hundred thousand Philippine civilians.

The American imperialist adventurism of this time is sometimes blamed on a belief in an international version of "Social Darwinism" that would countenance the conquest and subjugation of "inferior" peoples by "superior" ones. Ironically, Herbert Spencer and William Graham Sumner—the two libertarians routinely vilified for Social Darwinism—were, as we have seen, among the most vociferous and unrelenting critics of imperialism, which they saw as a kind of piracy writ large. According to Spencer, imperialism largely benefited the "rich owners of colonial property" and involved "deeds of blood and rapine" and the exploitation of "the poor, starved, overburdened people."[40] In an early version of the libertarian moral parity thesis, Spencer expressed contempt even for individual soldiers who joined imperialist militaries: "When men hire themselves out to shoot other men to order, asking nothing about the justice of their cause, I don't care if they are shot themselves."[41]

Sumner likewise spoke out against imperialism and especially against the Spanish-American War. In "The Conquest of the United States by Spain," Sumner argued that America was winning the military conflict but losing its position as a leader for liberty. He described the American military involvement in the Philippines as an affront to liberty that was "combating the grand efforts of science and art to ameliorate the struggle for existence." Sumner recoiled at imperialists' rejection of basic moral equality and their insistence that other peoples were so inferior as to be unfit for the freedoms that Americans cherished. He wrote:

> It is this disposition to decide off-hand that some people are not fit for liberty and self-government which gives relative truth to the doctrine that all men are equal, and inasmuch as the history of mankind has been one long story of the abuse of some by others, who, of course, smoothed over their tyranny by some beautiful doctrines of religion, or ethics, or political philosophy, which proved that it was all for the best

good of the oppressed, therefore the doctrine that all men are equal has come to stand as one of the corner-stones of the temple of justice and truth. It was set up as a bar to just this notion that we are so much better than others that it is liberty for them to be governed by us.[42]

Sumner's opposition to the Spanish-American War led him to become an active member of the Anti-Imperialist League, an organization that included among its prominent members labor organizer Samuel Gompers, industrialist Andrew Carnegie, and the writer and humorist Samuel Langhorne Clemens, better known as Mark Twain.[43] The platform of the Anti-Imperialist League was unequivocal:

> We hold that the policy known as imperialism is hostile to liberty and tends toward militarism, an evil from which it has been our glory to be free. We regret that it has become necessary in the land of Washington and Lincoln to reaffirm that all men, of whatever race or color, are entitled to life, liberty and the pursuit of happiness. We maintain that governments derive their just powers from the consent of the governed. We insist that the subjugation of any people is criminal aggression and open disloyalty to the distinctive principles of our Government.

As the membership list suggests, the League was not exclusively libertarian. But its leadership included several prominent libertarians along with Sumner, including civil rights leader Moorfield Storey and a colorful economist-turned-activist named Edward Atkinson.

Atkinson—who helped found the League in 1898—had been a passionate abolitionist, an active member of the Free Soil Party, and a major fundraiser for John Brown's raid on Harpers Ferry.[44] Atkinson went on to become a leading member of the "Cobden Club" of London, an organization dedicated to promoting the ideal of trade-based noninterventionism. Atkinson brought the same radicalism he exhibited as an abolitionist to his anti-imperialism. Convinced that the Spanish-American War was both imprudent and unjust, in 1899 he tried to mail a series of pamphlets directly to American soldiers and officers serving in the Philippines. Atkinson's pamphlets had incendiary titles such as "The Cost of a National

Crime," "The Hell of War and Its Penalties," and "Criminal Aggression: By Whom Committed." They argued that American military involvement in the Philippines was financially disastrous, illegal, and a crime against the human race. Unfortunately for Atkinson's plan, the U.S. Department of War refused to divulge the names of soldiers serving in the Philippines. Atkinson's backup plan involved sending the pamphlets to a smaller number of key personnel, but several test mailings were seized by the Postmaster General and condemned as "seditious." Only Atkinson's advanced age (he was seventy-two at the time) saved him from being prosecuted—and possibly executed—for treason.[45]

The Anti-Imperialist League was short-lived, officially dissolving in 1920 as its influence waned. By the second decade of the twentieth century, America was becoming ever more enmeshed in international conflicts. The idealist noninterventionism of Cobden's era had passed. As statist principles grew around the world, the principled libertarian opposition to war was ridiculed as a naïve "isolationism." Many libertarians harbored a growing sense of hopelessness as the twentieth century dawned. In 1898, Herbert Spencer wrote to an American friend that it seemed "useless to resist the wave of barbarism" that was washing over the world. Spencer saw the world as having entered "an era of social cannibalism in which the strong nations are devouring the weaker," with the likely outcome being the rise of "military despotism."[46] William Graham Sumner despaired that the nineteenth-century era of peace and prosperity in America was a brief historical exception that was coming to an end and that the twentieth century would be "as full of war" as the eighteenth.[47] So profound was Sumner's despair that he suffered an emotional collapse in 1890 that required him to take his first academic leave. As statist ideologies continued to rise, the first wave of libertarian thinking receded in defeat. The anarchist Benjamin Tucker despaired that civilization was entering its "death throes."[48] In France, Gustave de Molinari spent the last two decades of his life warning that the dawning century would be dominated by militarism, imperialism, protectionism, and socialism.[49] The optimism and energy of the Richard Cobden era were over.

The "Old Right" and the First
Libertarian-Conservative Alliance

In the period leading up to World War II, libertarians began to forge the ideological alliance with conservatives that would persist, despite many strains, throughout most of the twentieth century. The most prominent members of the "Old Right" with whom libertarians forged their earliest alliances were the staunchly anti-Roosevelt journalists John Flynn and Garet Garrett. Meanwhile, on the libertarian side of the marriage were two of the most important women in the twentieth-century libertarian movement: Isabel Paterson, whose book, *The God of the Machine*, was a celebration of the creative powers of a free economy, and Rose Wilder Lane, daughter of *Little House on the Prairie* author Laura Ingalls Wilder and author of the libertarian classic, *The Discovery of Freedom*.[50] The social critic Albert Jay Nock also played an important role in this movement, straddling the boundary between old right conservativism and a more radical libertarianism.

What brought these two ideological groups together was their opposition to both the New Deal and American entry into World War II. Roosevelt's domestic policies constituted a dangerous usurpation of power by the federal government; America had no business involving itself in what they regarded as a purely intra-European military conflict. On these two points, at least, all these disparate individualists found common cause.

Although they agreed on these policy goals, there were important differences in both the underlying *rationale* and the *strength* of their commitment to economic freedom and their opposition to war that would become more and more apparent as time went on. Libertarians such Paterson and Lane were generally cosmopolitans who favored peaceful interaction and engagement with other countries. By contrast, the more conservative members of the old right really *did* appear to fit the label of "isolationist" that was sometimes unfairly applied to all opponents of American involvement in World War II. Garet Garrett, for instance, argued for a policy of economic and cultural "self-containment," believing that too great a dependence on foreign trade made a country vulnerable to exploitation, and that unchecked immigration could lead to growing resentment and political instability.[51] For Garrett, the liberal idea of a universal harmony of interests realized under a regime of free trade and free migration was a myth, or at best only a partial truth. In his novel *The Blue Wound*, Garrett uses the voice of a group of Japanese elders to explain his own ambivalence about free trade:

> There are two interests among us. On one hand lies the interest of the individual, whose advantage is served by the present cheapness of things; on the other hand lies the interest of the people, whose future is at stake. These two interests we find to be antagonistic.[52]

For Garrett, trade was not harmony but conflict. It was, moreover, a conflict that, contra Cobden, tended to benefit the privileged at the expense of the vulnerable.

> What you call international trade is a dangerous and turbulent relation between, on the one side, that eight or ten per cent of the human race which is efficient and skilled and has reserved to itself the preferred labor, and, on the other side, the inert and unskilled people, fit only to perform the drudgery.[53]

There is a deep rift here between conservatives such as Garrett and libertarians on issues of policy. But Garrett's remarks on the conflict between "skilled" and "unskilled" laborers points in the direction of an even more interesting and more fundamental tension on the issue of human equality. One strand in libertarian thought, which we have already seen in chapter 5, holds that inequalities in talents and ability are largely or almost entirely a product of the environment. For these libertarians, bad economic and political institutions play an especially large role in generating and exacerbating these inequalities. There is, however, another strand of libertarianism—exemplified by figures such as Nock, Rand, and (sometimes) Murray Rothbard—according to which inequality is a deep and ineradicable fact of the human condition. Both groups of libertarians converge on the idea—and diverge from the old right—that the proper response to inequality is freedom. And both groups hold that there is generally a harmony of interest among individuals regardless of their degree of natural talent. Nevertheless, for the former group, freedom is seen as a progressive and leveling force that will gradually but inevitably reduce inequality. For the latter, freedom is necessary primarily so that those few "men of ability" on whom progress and civilization depend will have the fullest scope for their creative activity.[54]

We find a commitment to the harmony of interests central to the approach taken by the two most prominent libertarian economists of the twentieth century: Ludwig von Mises and Friedrich Hayek. But even here, differences emerge, differences that illuminate the tensions between the rationalistic absolutism of strict libertarianism and the pluralist empiricism of classical liberalism.

Federalism or Cosmopolitanism? Hayek and Mises

Hayek had burst onto the public stage with the publication of *The Road to Serfdom* in 1944. It had become popular among the intellectual class of that era to affirm socialism as a moral ideal and to decry the fascist dictatorships of Hitler and Mussolini as capitalist reactions against that ideal. The military alignment of the New Deal–era United States and the Soviet Union against Germany and Italy encouraged this view. But, to the delight of conservatives, Hayek argued that fascism, socialism, and New Deal thinking alike spring from a common principle: the valorization of central decision making over individual liberty. The imperatives of planning necessarily conflict with the liberties of individuals, civil as well as economic. Hayek warned of "the danger of tyranny that inevitably results from government control of economic decision-making through central planning."[55] Shockingly to his fellow intellectuals, Hayek claimed there was a deep conceptual connection not only between socialism and fascism but also between the New Deal and fascism. Central authority *or* individual liberty: every society has to choose.

Like the libertarians of the nineteenth century, Hayek believed that a commitment to individual freedom led naturally toward a moralized form of internationalism, though Hayek's more cautious, empirically based approach held him back from endorsing outright cosmopolitanism. Hayek writes: "It is neither necessary nor desirable that national boundaries should mark sharp differences in standards of living, that membership of a national group should entitle one to a share in a cake altogether different from that in which members of other groups share."[56] Peace too requires moving away from nationalism toward individualism: "If international economic relations, instead of being relations between individuals, become increasingly relations between whole nations organized as trading bodies, they inevitably become the source of friction and envy between whole nations."[57] To preserve domestic freedoms and to promote international peace, power must be stripped from sovereign states.

However, like Smith and Hume, Hayek allowed a more enduring role for states in a globally just world. Indeed, in response to the bloodbaths of early twentieth-century Europe, Hayek suggested a system of interstate federalism. He was sharply critical of previous attempts at federation such as the League of Nations, which, due to its global scope, was too weak to be effective: "a smaller and at the same time more powerful League might have been a better instrument to preserve peace."[58] As an alternative, Hayek proposed a network of local federations that might begin by connecting culturally similar nations. Such a network might in turn be nested within some larger, looser confederation. Federations would preserve individual liberty by restraining member countries from harming their neighbors—through restrictions on international trade, for example. (Gustave de Molinari had proposed something similar a century before.)[59] The federations must be powerful enough to prevent states from erecting economic barriers but limited enough to prevent federations from imposing any economic plan upon member states. Nonintervention, at home and abroad, would be the guiding principle. As Hayek put it: "the federation will have to possess the negative power of preventing individual states from interfering with economic activity in certain ways, although it may not have the positive power of acting in their stead."[60] Once again, the protection of negative liberty—in this case, the right to trade freely—is the key.

Hayek's interstate federalism aimed to weaken existing state structures, with power being either transferred up to the federation or transferred down to more localized institutional forms. Hayek's advocacy of local planning springs from his theory of information: whenever possible, decision points should be delegated to agents

with the best understanding of "the particulars of time and place."
In this way, localizing authority would be a democratic improvement: "the desirable forms of planning that can be affected locally
and without the need for restrictive measures are left free and in
the hands of those best qualified to undertake it."[61] On Hayek's
vision, an interstate federation "would do away with the impediments as to the movement of men, goods, and capital between the
states and . . . would render possible the creation of common rules
of law, a uniform monetary system, and common control of com-
munications."[62] Hayek's plan for interstate federalism is one way
to institutionalize the libertarian ideal of free trade, free migration,
and peace. This state-weakening approach flows from Hayek's commitment to liberty. As Hayek wrote: "the abrogation of national
sovereignties and the creation of an effective international order
of law is a necessary complement and the logical consummation
of the liberal program."[63] Libertarianism is not merely a domestic
policy: it is an internationalist, indeed global, doctrine.

Hayek's ideas here were influenced by the more cosmopolitan
view that Mises had laid out in his 1927 work, *Liberalism*. According to Mises, "The goal of the domestic policy of liberalism is the
same as that of its foreign policy: peace. It aims at peaceful cooperation just as much between nations as within each nation."[64]
Aspiring to protect negative liberty everywhere, Mises sees liberalism as a universalizing doctrine: "Its thinking is cosmopolitan and
ecumenical: it takes in all men and the whole world. Liberalism
is, in this sense, humanism; and the liberal citizen, a citizen of the
world."[65] Like the radical individualists of the nineteenth century,
Mises saw the protection of private property, including the right of
individuals to trade freely across national boundaries, as essential
to peace: "A capitalist world organized on liberal principles knows
no separate 'economic' zones. In such a world the whole earth's
surface forms a single economic territory."[66] The disaster of World
War I was a predictable outcome of the growing protectionist and
anti-liberal sentiments of that era. "When private property must
be respected even in time of war, when the victor is not entitled
to appropriate to himself the property of private persons, and the
appropriation of public property has no great significance because
private ownership of the means of production prevails everywhere,

an important motive for waging war has already been excluded."[67] Private property promotes peace.

While a cosmopolitan in principle, Mises was sensitive to the importance of linguistic and cultural differences, especially among minority groups. Mises developed a form of libertarian multiculturalism on this basis. Political issues, he believed, are necessarily mediated through cultural and—especially—linguistic differences: "To be a member of a national minority always means that one is a second-class citizen."[68] Even within a properly liberal order, Mises recognized that cultural difference can cause tension, and even hatred, between peoples. But the centralization of economic power can enflame tribal feelings: "Because people are prepared to resort to violent means in order to create favorable conditions for the political future of their own [linguistic] nation, they have established a system of oppression in the polyglot areas that imperils the peace of the world."[69] The history of colonialism makes this vivid. According to Mises, "The basic idea of colonial policy was to take advantage of the military superiority of the white race over members of other races."[70] While some earlier liberals, including John Stuart Mill, had justified colonialism on "civilizing" grounds, Mises rejects this absolutely. If European culture is not freely accepted but must be imposed by force, how can it be superior? The only justification for European involvement in the affairs of developing countries is to ensure the protection of individual property rights, thus ensuring that all people can enjoy voluntary, mutually beneficial international trade. Colonial powers egregiously violated this principle. Instead of extending open markets, the colonial powers pursued the mercantilist policies of "economic nationalism," which typically amounted to outright theft. But capitalism and colonialism are intrinsically incompatible. "No chapter of history is steeped further in blood than the history of colonialism. Blood was shed uselessly and needlessly. Flourishing lands were laid waste; whole peoples destroyed and exterminated. All this can in no way be extenuated or justified."[71]

Mises's multiculturalism made him a strong advocate of political self-determination. But the libertarian approach to self-determination has a special concern for members of cultural and national minority groups. Specifically, Mises saw the political secession as something like a universal human right. He writes: "whenever the inhabitants of a particular territory, whether it be a single village, a whole district, or a series of adjacent districts, makes it known, by a freely conducted plebiscite, that they no longer wish to remain united to the state to which they belong at the time, but wish either to form or attach themselves to some other state, their wishes are to be respected and complied with." Of course, this right of self-determination only has force within a background of economic liberalism. For Mises, the right of secession is so fundamental to freedom that, were it practical, it could be exercised not only by groups but even by individual persons.[72]

This libertarian principle of self-determination also justifies freedom of movement. According to Mises, every person and every family have the right to live and to seek work wherever they choose. Of this right to free movement, Mises states: "It belongs to the very essence of a society based on private ownership of the means of production that every man may work and dispose of his earnings where he thinks best."[73] As Mises is aware, most people recoil at the idea of open borders. But, in large part, this is simply because people in wealthier countries have come to expect the (unjust) benefits of artificially limited labor competition. However, according to Mises, it is also because, under prevailing systems of economic nationalism, majorities (or voting blocs) are allowed to wield the power of the state to their own benefit and against the interests of others. With the large welfare states that result, it is understandable that people fear large influxes of foreigners. But under economic liberalism, these powers would be removed from the state. Individuals who choose to migrate would do so only because they see an opportunity to make economic contributions, contributions that, in a free market, benefit everyone. Thus: "Only the adoption of the liberal program could make the problem of immigration, which today seems insoluble, completely disappear."[74]

Like Hayek, Mises opposed the League of Nations. Mises thought that experiment failed not just because the United States refused to join or because it granted unequal power to member nations. The real problem was that the League sought to maintain the status quo: it accepted historically determined state boundaries as inalterably fixed.[75] By contrast, Mises worked from a commitment to economic cosmopolitanism. This approach sees "the law of each nation as subordinate to international law . . . and demands supranational tribunals and administrative authorities to assure peace among nations in the same way that the judicial and executive organs of each country are charged with the maintenance of peace within its own territory."[76] All told, Mises advocates a form of *libertarian internationalism*. Liberal thinking must pervade all nations, just as liberal principles must pervade all institutions, if the optimum conditions for global prosperity and peace are to be achieved. Indeed, political organizations should be extended until, at the limit, the liberty of all is protected equally by a kind of world state.[77]

Fusionism and the Second Libertarian-Conservative Alliance

In 1934, Frank Meyer was expelled from the doctoral program at the London School of Economics and deported from England to the United States. Since his undergraduate studies at Oxford, Meyer had been a leader in the student communist movement, operating under instructions from his official Communist Party handlers and earning a record in the files of Britain's MI5.[78] Barely ten years later, while serving in the U.S. Army during World War II, Meyer experienced a moment of conversion while reading Hayek's *The Road to Serfdom*. From that moment Meyer was a free-market conservative, becoming an influential contributor to such periodicals as Frank Chodorov's *The Freeman* and William F. Buckley's *National Review* and the leading proponent of what would come to be described as a conservative/libertarian "fusionism."[79] Meyer claimed that the conservative concern for virtue could not be realized without the individual freedom prized by libertarians. Virtue is not virtue unless it is freely chosen, he argued, and conservative attempts to promote it by means of state compulsion were doomed to fail. On the other hand, without the conservative faith in an objective, absolute source of moral value, the libertarian commitment to freedom was baseless.[80] Meyer claimed that, philosophically, a synthesis was needed. But there were more practical reasons as well. With the decline of Cobdenite idealism and the passing of the first generation of libertarians, what libertarians remained were adrift and looking for a new home. A rallying point was found in the shared libertarian and conservative opposition to Roosevelt's New Deal and, for many on the conservative side, the American entry into World War II. Fusionism marked the start of the second wave of libertarian thinking that would rise to prominence in the twentieth century.

As an abstract philosophical argument, Meyer's fusionism had considerable power. And for a while, the idea seemed to gain some real political traction. Throughout the 1960s, chapters of Young Americans for Freedom grew on college campuses across the United States by focusing on issues that seemed to unite both conservative and libertarian activists: commitment to free-market economics and opposition to international communism.

From the beginning, however, there were tensions within this fusionist movement. Frank Chodorov, a follower of Albert Jay Nock and of Henry George, had joined with the old right in opposing American entry into World War II. So outspoken (and controversial) was his opposition, continuing even after the Japanese attack on Pearl Harbor, that in March 1942 Chodorov was stripped of his editorship of *The Freeman*, the once defunct newsletter he had inherited from Nock and began republishing as the school paper of the Henry George School of Social Science. Chodorov did not shrink from the label of "isolationist": in military matters, the "negative liberty" approach of the libertarian pioneers was fine by him.

However, unlike earlier figures in the old right such as Garet Garrett, Chodorov drew a sharp distinction between *political* and *economic* isolationism. Properly understood, isolationism was a matter of keeping the state out of individuals' lives. But economic isolationism, as manifested in protectionist tariffs and immigration quotas, *increased* the power of the state over the individual rather than limiting it. The only defensible form of isolationism keeps politics out of individuals' lives so that they can make their *own* decisions about with whom and under what conditions they will trade or otherwise associate. Free trade and isolationism were complements, not opposites.

Chodorov was troubled by conservatives' apparent willingness to make peace with statism in order to more effectively wage war against the Soviet menace. It was one thing to hate communism—and Chodorov was as committed an anti-communist as anybody on the editorial board at *National Review*. But communism was an *idea*, and one could not, and should not, kill an idea by killing the people who hold it, especially when those people were often guilty of nothing worse than accepting an unworkable ideology.[81] Moreover, the means by which conservatives sought to defeat communism—higher taxes, military conscription, and more power for the military-industrial complex—would diminish individual liberty in ways that could not be undone. Powers granted to governments for the relief of a temporary emergency, Chodorov noted, are almost never given up once the crisis has passed.[82]

By the late 1950s, Murray Rothbard was beginning to rise to prominence in the libertarian movement. Rothbard, too, was uneasy about the prospects for fusionism. In 1959, Rothbard submitted an essay to *National Review* titled "For a New Isolationism." In it, he wrote of his opposition to "the tough anti-Soviet foreign policy" of the right and argued for a strict policy of non-interventionism based on American national interests. The piece was rejected ("in a friendly fashion") by Buckley. But Rothbard was undeterred. In a letter to a colleague, he wrote:

> I am getting more and more convinced that the war-peace question is *the* key to the whole libertarian business, and that we will never get anywhere in this great intellectual counter-revolution (or revolution) unless we can end this Verdamte cold war—a war for which I believe our "tough" policy is largely responsible.[83]

As we will see in the next section, Rothbard's opposition to militarism became increasingly radical as the Cold War progressed. Tensions between libertarians and conservatives increased. Rothbard wrote his final piece for *National Review* in March 1961. In 1962, *National Review* published a strongly worded critique of Rothbardian libertarianism (though it never mentioned Rothbard by name). The critique, titled "The Twisted Tree of Liberty," was written by none other than the erstwhile-fusionist Frank Meyer. In it, Meyer lamented the inability of libertarians to recognize the danger posed by international communism to human freedom. In the end, he described the radical libertarian worldview as "patently distorted," "absurd," and suffering from a "monstrous misapprehension of reality."[84]

Young Americans for Freedom (YAF) held their national convention in St. Louis in 1969. Prior to the meeting, Rothbard wrote his followers, urging them "to go, to split, to leave the conservative movement where it belongs." Despite earlier talk of fusionism, Rothbard held, the conservative movement was dominated by authoritarian sentiments. This is why the conservatives, unlike the libertarians, supported the use of state force to prohibit recreational drugs like marijuana, supported police even in cases like the incident at People's Park where unarmed demonstrators were gassed and beaten, and supported the Vietnam War, which involved "the slaughter of tens of thousands of American soldiers, [and] of hundreds of thousands of Vietnamese peasants."[85]

Many libertarians took Rothbard's advice, and showed up to the meeting, ready to fight. There, tensions between libertarian and conservative members erupted. Some libertarians publicly burned their draft cards in protest of the U.S. war in Vietnam. Conservatives heckled the libertarians, deriding them as "laissez-fairies." Finally, the libertarians left, and were led by former Goldwater speechwriter-turned-libertarian-radical Karl Hess on a march to the St. Louis arch where Hess delivered a speech calling on libertarians to embrace freedom and leave the YAF behind.[86]

The "fusion" between libertarians and conservatives was finished. At least for the moment.

Rothbard and Rand: Tensions within Cold War Libertarianism

As an anarchist, Rothbard opposed the entire state-based global order. In a perfectly libertarian world, Rothbard observes, there would be no "foreign policy" because there would be no *states*. In the state-based world in which we find ourselves, Rothbard gives libertarian international policy two goals: "to reduce the degree of coercion by States over individual persons as much as possible"[87] and "to keep each of these States from extending their violence to other countries, so that each State's tyranny is at least confined to its own bailiwick."[88] Like Chodorov before him, Rothbard's opposition to state interventionism led to a distinctively libertarian hybrid of what we shall call *isolationist internationalism*: "political nonintervention in the affairs of other countries, coupled with economic and cultural internationalism in the sense of peaceful freedom of trade, investment, and interchange between the citizens of all countries."[89]

For Rothbard, as for other strict libertarians who embrace the moral parity thesis, state violence is no more just than private violence. War, despite its trappings of nationalism and protocol, is nothing more than "mass murder" and "the ultimate crime."[90] Echoing the early twentieth-century American dissident Randolph Bourne, Rothbard held that "war is the health of the state."

> It is in war that the State really comes into its own: swelling in power, in number, in pride, in absolute dominion over the economy and the society. Society becomes a herd, seeking to kill its alleged enemies, rooting out and suppressing all dissent from the official war effort, happily betraying truth for the supposed public interest.[91]

Wars are commonly presented as events in which a state seeks to protect its citizens from some external danger. According to Rothbard, the opposite is true. Since a state can "die" as the result of warfare, "the State frantically mobilizes the people to fight for *it* against another State, under the pretext that *it* is fighting for them." In fact, the prime threat to citizens is their state.

Such anti-war views do not make libertarians pacifists: individuals have a right to defend themselves and their property and may use violence in doing so. But libertarianism does generate a distinctive just war theory. According to Rothbard, within the existing world of states, there are three criteria for just war: "(a) weapons limited so that no civilians were injured in their persons or property; (b) volunteer rather than conscript armies; and also (c) financing by voluntary methods instead of taxation."[92] As Rothbard observes, revolutionary guerrilla warfare is generally more compatible with libertarian just war theory than traditional interstate war since "by the very nature of their activities, guerrillas defend the civilian population against the depredations of a State."[93] On these criteria, Rothbard believes that there have only been two just wars in American history: the American Revolution and the "War for

Southern Independence." This is because, in the existing world of states, libertarian just war theory seems particularly well-suited to justify wars for political secession. As Rothbard puts it in another formulation of his theory: "a just war exists when a people tries to ward off the threat of coercive domination by another people, or *to overthrow an already existing domination.*"[94]

That the American Revolution satisfies the libertarian test for a just war may be unsurprising. But Rothbard insists that the military cause of the Confederacy also was just: "In 1861, the Southern states, believing correctly that their cherished institutions were under grave threat and assault from the federal government, decided to exercise their natural, contractual, and constitutional right to withdraw, to 'secede' from that Union."[95] Among the main grievances of the South, Rothbard says, was overtaxation from the North. He concludes: "If the American Revolutionary war was just, then it follows as the night the day that the Southern cause, the War for Southern Independence, was just, and for the same reason: casting off the 'political bonds' that connected the two peoples."[96]

In our chapter on race, we asked if libertarians of Rothbard's era had a blind spot about the importance of Black liberty. Rothbard's tax-based defense of the South raises that question again. Still, it is worth noting that whatever its merits, Rothbard's defense of the Southern states' right to secede is not unique among libertarians, nor necessarily incompatible with a principled commitment to abolitionism. Lysander Spooner, as we have seen, dedicated a significant portion of his life to both legal and more radical anti-slavery activity. But Spooner, too, opposed the Civil War as an illegal and unjust method for remedying the injustice of slavery.[97]

We do know that Rothbard had a principled opposition to "humanitarian" and "human rights" justifications for wars of aggression. He claimed that such justifications for war sprang from a paternalistic, "government of god" attitude toward other peoples, in which nations convinced of their own righteousness unleash their military forces to plunder, terrorize, and commit mass murder on the members of weaker states, all in the name of "high principle" and "the birth of a perfect world."[98] In part for this reason, Rothbard was sharply critical of American foreign policy during the twentieth century. Writing in the 1970s, he proclaimed: "the single most warlike, most interventionist, most imperialist government has been the United States."[99] He criticized Woodrow Wilson—along with Hoover, Roosevelt, and Nixon—for setting America on a course of world domination and for suppressing rebellions against the status quo all around the world: "In the name of combating 'aggression' everywhere—and being the world's 'policeman'—it has itself become a great and continuing aggressor."[100] Rothbard thought Vietnam a doomed attempt to suppress the wishes of the mass of the Vietnamese population and to cynically prop up dictators willing to accede to America's imperial hegemony in the region—even by genocide if necessary.[101]

Rothbard proposed two planks for a libertarian American foreign policy. First, America should abandon its policy of global interventionism and adopt political isolationism and strict neutrality: "The United States should dismantle its bases, withdraw its troops, stop its incessant political meddling, and abolish the CIA. It should also end all foreign aid."[102] The second plank is disarmament. Rothbard adamantly opposed nuclear weapons, and indeed any weapon that cannot be precisely aimed at aggressing individuals or groups. "Not only should there be joint disarmament of nuclear weapons, but also of all weapons capable of being fired massively across national borders, in particular bombers."[103] Regarding conservatives' anti-Soviet foreign policy, Rothbard quips: "anyone who wishes is entitled to make the personal decision of 'better dead than red' or 'give me liberty or give me death.' What he is not entitled to do is to make those decisions for others."[104]

Ayn Rand shared Rothbard's commitment to nonintervention, at least for the most part. According to Rand, the true cause of war is statism, which always posits some collective "good" that justifies restricting individual liberties. As such, statism is "the tribal premise of primordial savages who, unable to conceive of individual rights, believed that the tribe is a supreme, omnipotent ruler."[105] Statism is simply gang rule—"a system of institutionalized violence and perpetual civil war." So long as we accept the principle of gang rule in our own countries, we will acquiesce to war waged against other countries too. Rand writes: "If men want to oppose war, it is *statism* that they must oppose. So long as they hold the tribal notion that the individual is sacrificial fodder for the collective, that some men have the right to rule others by force, and that some (any) alleged 'good' can justify it—there can be no peace within a nation and no peace among nations."[106]

Rand thought that the essence of capitalism's foreign policy is free trade: the abolition of trade barriers, protective tariffs, and subsidies to domestic producers.[107] All humans need to acquire goods in order to live, but there are only two ways to acquire goods from others: by trading or by looting. In societies based on private property and free trade, people have incentives to acquire goods peacefully; by contrast, in societies based on collective principles of force, there are incentives to use force. For this reason, Rand says that, in every society, the "trader" and the "warrior" historically have been the fundamental rivals.[108] Statism, which survives by looting, *needs* war; capitalism does not. According to Rand: "Laissez-faire capitalism is the only social system based on the recognition of individual rights and, therefore, the only system that bans force from social relationships. By the nature of its basic principles and interests, it is the only system fundamentally opposed to war."[109] We might call this the libertarian peace hypothesis: the only hope for peace around the world is the spread of free-market institutions and ideas.

Despite working from many common premises, the question of Israel was a flashpoint among Cold War libertarians (many of whom were themselves Jewish). On one side, Milton Friedman was a quiet but steadfast supporter of Israel throughout his life. He visited Israel several times to lecture, and received an honorary degree from Hebrew University. In addition to intellectual and financial support, Friedman was known to have written frequently to U.S. policymakers, encouraging them to support Israel.[110] Friedman described Israel as a small island in a sea of enemies, making its survival a miracle. The presence of so many enemies required a large military which, Friedman explained, required a large role for government in Israel's economy (what Friedman described as "a sizable socialist sector"). Still, he was optimistic. In an echo of the libertarian peace hypothesis, Friedman wrote: "The true hope of Israel—and of freedom everywhere—is the enterprise, initiative, ingenuity, drive, and courage of the individual citizens, cooperating voluntarily with each other, producing the incredible progress in every sphere that comes only from the activities of the individual."[111]

Rand too supported Israel, and did so in characteristically pyrotechnic language. At a lecture she gave in October 1973, during the height of the Yom Kippur War (also known as the Ramadan War), Rand was asked what she thought of that conflict. Without hesitation, she told the audience that they should support Israel. First, she noted, Israel is fighting not only the Arabs states but the Soviet Union, who was using the war as part of its larger attack on capitalism. But Rand emphasized that the main reason she supported Israel was not strategic but moral. The real conflict in the Middle East, Rand declared, was one between a civilized society committed to science and reason and a group of backward, collectivist societies she described as being "practically nomads." She said: "When you have civilized men fighting savages, you support the civilized men, no matter who they are." Of course, Rand said, it is wrong to send men to die fighting for another country, no matter the cause. But what Israel most needs is financial support for military arms. Declaring that there is no need to wait for the government to provide such support, Rand urged her audience to make donations to Israel themselves, noting that she herself had done so: "Give whatever you can. This is the first time I've contributed to a public cause: helping Israel in an emergency."[112]

Rothbard was incensed by this exchange and penned an essay in response. The Palestinians and other Arab peoples are not "nomads" or "savages," but it would not matter to libertarians if they were. Even nomads and savages are humans, with inalienable rights to their own persons and property. Rothbard asks: "Whatever happened to the great libertarian principle, to which Miss Rand presumably adheres, of no initiation of force against another person?" Rothbard noted that Soviet Russia (which Rand opposed) was arguably more scientifically and technically advanced than some neighboring states, such as Mongolia. "Does that mean that if Russia were to attack and sweep into Mongolia that we would all be honor bound to cheer for the Russians, and even to kick in our dollars for the great cause? If not, why not?"[113]

For Rothbard, the legitimacy of the modern Israeli state is itself problematic. The British promise to the Zionists after World War

II was morally wrong, as was the Zionist demand for that land: "The fact that Palestine was not a virgin land, but already occupied by an Arab peasantry, meant nothing to the ideologues of Zionism."[114] Rothbard claims that Israel was the aggressor in the Six-Day War and condemns America for its support. "One of the most repellent aspects of the 1967 slaughter is the outspoken admiration for the Israeli conquest by almost all Americans, Jew and non-Jew alike. There seems to be a sickness deep in the American soul that causes it to identify with aggression and mass murder—the swifter and more brutal the better."[115] Rothbard saw America and Israel as equally imperialist states, differing only in the scope of their wrongdoing.[116]

Postscript: What Happened to Free Migration?

We opened this chapter by summarizing the libertarian theory of international relations with the slogan "Free trade, free migration, and peace." But while we have devoted substantial attention to the first and third items on that list, we have said relatively little about the second. Why have we paid so little attention to the issue of free migration in our survey on the history of libertarian ideas?

The answer—surprisingly to us!—is that there isn't much libertarian intellectual history on the topic of free migration to report. The issue is certainly a hot topic among libertarians *now*, and one can find defenses of free migration by various libertarians scattered throughout the twentieth century. But there is almost no discussion of the topic by the great libertarians of the nineteenth century. Not in Spencer, not in Bastiat, and not even in that great prophet of libertarian cosmopolitanism, Richard Cobden.

What explains the silence of nineteenth-century libertarians on this issue? The answer, most likely, is that international migration simply wasn't much of an issue prior to the dawn of the twentieth century. The absence of safe, affordable transportation options like railroads meant that international migration was difficult, dangerous, and expensive. And, perhaps partly because the demand for migration was so low, there were few legal barriers to international migration for libertarians to complain about. *Within* European countries there were often legal barriers preventing individuals—especially the poor—from moving from place to place. But international migration was much less regulated—if it was regulated at all. Thus, for example, we find the following remarkable language in the Burlingame Treaty of 1868 between the United States and China:

> The United States of America and the Emperor of China cordially recognize the inherent and inalienable right of man to change his home and allegiance, and also the mutual advantage of the free migration and emigration of their citizens and subjects respectively from the one country to the other, for purposes of curiosity, of trade, or as permanent residents.

That such radical and, dare we say, *libertarian* language should find its way into a major international treaty with almost nothing in the way of controversy is a testament to how great a change has occurred in social attitudes toward immigration in the time since its ratification.

That change did not take long to occur. By 1875, the United States had passed the Page Act, which prohibited the entry of "undesirable" immigrants from Asia; by 1882 it had passed the notorious Chinese Exclusion Act; and by 1924, the National Origins Quota Act. In part, these restrictions were based in racism and cultural fears; in part they were based on the expanding power of trade unions and the desire to protect domestic laborers from foreign competition; and in part they were based on fears created by the growing nationalism and militarism of the late nineteenth and early twentieth centuries.

In the face of such changes, the libertarian position was clear and uncompromising: free migration is a basic human right, and a blessing both for immigrants and for the countries that receive them. This "main line" libertarian view of immigration received one of its clearest expressions in Ludwig von Mises's 1927 book *Liberalism*, where he wrote:

> The liberal demands that every person have the right to live wherever he wants. . . . It belongs to the very essence of a society of private ownership in the means of production that every man may work and dispose of his earnings where he thinks best. . . . The issue is of the

most momentous significance for the future of the world. Indeed, the fate of civilization depends on its satisfactory resolution.[117]

Mises was not the first person in the libertarian intellectual tradition to articulate this position. During the controversy over Chinese immigration, Frederick Douglass spoke eloquently in defense of the "eternal, universal and indestructible" human right of migration.[118] Earlier in the nineteenth century, William Leggett had decried attempts to limit the immigration of "paupers" into the United States, arguing instead that we should "open our arms to them, and embrace them as brothers."

> For are they not a part of the great family of man? It is a violation of the plainest principles of morals, it is a sin against the most universal precepts of religion, to harden our hearts against these men, and seek to expel them from a land, which they have as much right to tread as we who assume such a lofty port. The earth is the heritage of man, and these are a portion of the heritors. We are not bound to support them; they must support themselves. If they are idle, let them starve; if they are vicious, let them be punished; but, in God's name, as they bear God's image, let us not turn them away from a portion of that earth, which was given by its maker to all mankind, with no natural marks to designate the limits beyond which they may not freely pass.[119]

By and large, however, the full libertarian position did not come into its own until it had something to push against. The importance of free migration, its relation to self-ownership and the justification of free trade, would not become entirely clear to libertarians until shifting intellectual and political tides revealed what the *denial* of those claims entailed. On this issue, as on others, the presence of a clear and imminent alternative to libertarianism both sharpened and radicalized the libertarian position itself.

Of course, the libertarian support of free migration is no more unanimous than any other element in the libertarian intellectual tradition: it is a quarrelsome family. In 1999, Milton Friedman, for example, famously claimed that while free migration might be a proper libertarian *ideal*, nevertheless "you cannot simultaneously have free immigration and a welfare state."[120] Immigrants who must support themselves by their own labor will be a net benefit to the country that receives them, since whatever they earn to support themselves will necessarily be gained as part of a mutually beneficial trade. But the welfare state, by forcing transfers between the well-off and the poor, undermines the positive-sum nature of immigration. Friedman has sometimes been interpreted, on the basis of this claim, as being opposed to immigration. In fact, the conclusion he explicitly draws from the incompatibility of the welfare state and free migration is that we should celebrate and encourage *illegal* immigration.[121]

Other libertarians, especially those associated with the paleo-libertarian movement, argue that immigration restrictions could be regarded as legitimate expressions of private property rights. Of course, libertarians deny that the *government* has a legitimate property title in its territory. But, these libertarians suggest, in the absence of a legitimate claim by government, property rights over nonprivately held portions of a nation's territory ought to be construed as belonging to the communities who inhabit and/or use them, and with the power such a right gives them, those communities might legitimately decide to restrict access to outsiders.[122]

Hans-Hermann Hoppe has, for several decades, been one of the most prominent and notorious libertarian supporters of immigration restrictions. And his writings and activism on the topic have, over time, helped forge connections between libertarianism and what is now called the "alt-right." Hoppe's Property and Freedom Society has run yearly symposia featuring talks by the white supremacists Richard Spencer and Jared Taylor, as well as Peter Brimelow, the founder of VDARE, an organization the Southern Poverty Law Center describes as an "anti-immigration hate website." His claim that Democrats, communists, and advocates of homosexuality will have to be "physically removed from [a libertarian] society" has spawned a series of internet memes depicting this physical removal taking place by throwing or hanging members of these undesirable groups from helicopters.[123]

Christopher Cantwell, a neo-Nazi who achieved notoriety in the wake of the Charlottesville "Unite the Right" march of 2017, described Hoppe's role in his own conversion process:[124]

As immigration became a leading news story in America and Europe, Lew Rockwell gave a talk titled "Open Borders Are an Assault on

Private Property."[125] From here, I decided to read Hans Hermann Hoppe's "Democracy: The God That Failed." From these, I realized that the libertine vision of a free society was quite distorted. The society we sought actually would provide far more order and control than [would] modern democratic governments. It would encourage more socially conservative behavior and less compulsory association. Just when I thought I had everything figured out, I was once again reminded of my naivety. . . .

People should be free to exercise complete control over their own person and property. If blacks are committing crimes, or Jews are spreading communism, discriminating against them is the right of any property owner. The fact that he may or may not miss out on good blacks or Jews is a risk he takes, and the merit of his decisions will be proven out by the market. Since a libertarian society would permit this, it seemed foolish that I should be compelled to support a democratic government policy which did not. . . . It was only after all this that Donald Trump seemed worth taking seriously.

These relatively isolated paleo-libertarian stances noted, the standard libertarian position on immigration traditionally has been somewhere between moderately and radically open borders. That position is represented today by philosophers such as Chandran Kukathas and Michael Huemer, who decry the coercion and injustice inherent in immigration restrictions.[126] It is supported by economists such as Bryan Caplan who note that even if there are legitimate concerns with increased immigrations, it is almost always possible to address those restrictions directly in a way that is cheaper, less coercive, and more humane than mass restrictions on freedom of movement.[127] And it is supported by libertarian scholars such as Alex Nowrasteh and Benjamin Powell, who argue that anti-immigration narratives such as those put forward by Hoppe and Cantwell rely on discredited empirical claims regarding the effect of immigration on culture, institutions, and economic productivity.[128] Free migration, like free trade and like peace, might not be an exceptionless absolute for libertarians. But it is certainly the rule, exceptions to which must be justified after undergoing the highest level of scrutiny.

Conclusion

ON MAY 28, 2022, the Mises Caucus took over the Libertarian Party of the United States.[1]

The organization had been formed a few years earlier in 2017 out of dissatisfaction with the ideological trajectory of the party. At the time, the main source of dissatisfaction was the 2016 presidential campaign of Gary Johnson and Bill Weld. The ticket had done well, bringing in 3.3 percent of the vote in the national election, the highest ever in party history. But some felt that the campaign succeeded only by soft-pedaling libertarian principles. Johnson and Weld, it was argued, made libertarianism palatable only by downplaying its radicalism in an appeal to the political center.

By 2020, the rift had widened. Not only did Libertarian Party leadership refuse to take a firm stance against government lockdowns and vaccine mandates during the Covid-19 pandemic, but its presidential candidate now seemed to be pandering not merely to the center but to the woke political *left*.[2] Enough was enough. Why was the Libertarian Party pretending to be something it wasn't? Why couldn't it just be *libertarian*?

Not everyone agreed with this diagnosis. To some, the Mises Caucus seemed more concerned with moving the Libertarian Party toward the *right* than realizing some Platonic ideal of libertarian purity.

Shortly after taking control of the party, for example, the caucus deleted a sentence from the platform that condemned bigotry as "irrational and repugnant." It reversed the party's long-standing support of abortion rights. Drawing on the ideas of Hans-Hermann

Hoppe, members of the Mises Caucus condemned the Libertarian Party's unequivocal support of free migration and open borders, claiming that such a stance is incompatible with the libertarian commitment to property rights. And while the Mises Caucus was quick to distance itself from the woke left, it seemed to many to be a bit too comfortable associating with members of the explicitly racist right like the white supremacist and Holocaust denier Nick Fuentes and neo-Nazi Christopher Cantwell.[3]

We cannot predict how this struggle within the Libertarian Party will play out, even in the short term. But the history we have presented in this book can help us better understand it and recognize that the tensions and disagreements that gave rise to it are nothing new. Since its very beginning in the mid-nineteenth century, what it means to be a libertarian—its key philosophical commitments, its policy implications, its natural political alliances—has been the subject of vigorous and persistent contestation.

The notion that libertarianism is self-interpreting—that its political conclusions can be discovered through a simple, unilinear deduction from first principles—has long been part of the lure of libertarianism. But this notion falters when we widen our historical lens. Understanding libertarianism as a cluster concept, with each set of ideas subject to a range of interpretations, one can see why so many "libertarianisms" have evolved. How libertarians understand ideas like "freedom" and "property" depends not only on their prior ideological commitments but also on their social and historical context. Libertarian conclusions are not derived from cold logic alone: they are reached through warmer, more idiosyncratic processes. The sound of libertarian thinking is not digital, but vinyl.

The flexibility of libertarianism was apparent from its birth. True, the first generation of libertarians in nineteenth-century England and France were united in their opposition to state socialism. Yet even here, differences were immediately visible. Were socialists right that there was *something* fundamentally wrong with society, even if they were wrong about what it was and how to fix it? Libertarians such as Thomas Hodgskin and (at times) Herbert Spencer were sympathetic to such radical ideas. Others of the first generation, such as the members of the Liberty and Property Defense League, were just as convinced that libertarian principles led to conservative conclusions. Existing society was basically just, they believed, so the appropriately libertarian attitude was to defend existing institutions against emerging threats.

In the nineteenth-century United States, as we have seen, the threat of state socialism was almost entirely absent. In this different social context, it was not socialism but slavery that captured the attention of the first American libertarians. As a result, status quo-preserving issues of private property in land and economic liberty—so central to the first expositions of libertarianism in England and France—drifted into the background. For the American libertarians, confronted with the moral outrage of slavery, the imperative of *self-ownership*, and thus ownership of the product of one's own labor, took center stage.

It was not until the mid-twentieth century that American libertarians came to resemble their cousins in Britain and France. As state socialism grew, issues of economic liberty became increasingly salient. Essays by Bastiat and Spencer found a new audience among American libertarians such as Leonard Read and Albert Jay Nock. Meanwhile, the economic mutualism of early American libertarians such as Benjamin Tucker faded into obscurity.

Our history has traced a broad narrative arc, from the primordial libertarians of the nineteenth century to the better-known Cold War band. Libertarianism was largely progressive and radical in the nineteenth century, then took a conservative turn in the twentieth. But at every point along that arc, contestation and division were the great constants. Whether libertarians took their doctrine in more radical or more reactionary directions depended on the topic, the social context, and the temperament of the thinker in question.

Thus, as we saw in chapter 3, the question of historical injustice has long vexed the libertarian treatment of property rights. Libertarian principles counsel an absolute respect for justly acquired property. But what should a good libertarian say about cases where the chain of title is tainted with violence, fraud, and theft? Some, like Lysander Spooner, took a radical stance, arguing that unjustly acquired property must be relinquished, no matter how many generations have gone by. Others, like Auberon Herbert, more concerned with preserving existing rights and freedoms, responded that nothing could, or should, be done to fix a broken past.

Similarly, as we saw in chapters 5 and 8, libertarian views of their place on the political spectrum—which groups they call allies, which enemies—have been in constant flux. In the early twentieth century, when issues of war and imperialism loomed large, many libertarians aligned themselves with the left-leaning Anti-Imperialist League. Later, when the New Deal captured their attention, the center of gravity shifted to the right, as alliances were formed with business interests opposed to rising taxation and regulation. In the 1960s, with issues of race and war central, libertarians such as Murray Rothbard allied themselves with radical leftist groups such the Black Panthers and Students for a Democratic Society—until, as the social context changed, Rothbard's libertarian thinking took a populist, conservative turn.

And what now? The collapse of international socialism in the late twentieth century was like the lifting of a sea anchor that had held libertarian boats together. Libertarianism in the early twenty-first century finds itself in a place where its priorities and alliances are more contested than in any period in its long history.

In its primordial era, libertarians defined themselves in reaction to clear and obvious threats to liberty: socialism in Europe, slavery in America. Similarly, twentieth-century libertarianism was best understood by what it was against: socialism, war, or the welfare state. But what does libertarianism stand for—and against which threat to liberty should it set itself—today?

In chapter 2, we distinguished three strands of twenty-first-century libertarianism: bleeding-heart libertarianism, left-libertarianism, and paleo-libertarianism. One way to understand these different approaches is to ask what each identifies as the primary threat to liberty.

Bleeding-heart libertarians, as we have seen, are distinctive in taking social justice seriously. Sometimes that concern takes the form of an embrace of a positive, as opposed to merely negative, understanding of freedom. This understanding of freedom underlies their relative openness to redistribution (see chapter 6). But bleeding-heart libertarians are also more sensitive to issues of *structural*, as opposed to merely individual, injustice, a feature that leads them to take a different view on questions of race than traditional libertarians. A free society, for bleeding hearts, would be a

society in which each individual citizen, while recognizing themselves as authors of their own lives, also recognizes each of their
fellow citizens as a life-author. Seeing this, they seek social arrangements that enable citizens to realize their own values in ways that
empower their fellow citizens to realize their (different) values too.
Individual freedom is an ideal to be pursued *together*.

Left-libertarians, by contrast, are primarily driven by wor-
ries about concentrated and monopolistic power. It is partly this
opposition to monopoly that leads left-libertarians to embrace
anarchism, and to hold that the creation and enforcement of law
is best undertaken by decentralized and competing firms. But left-
libertarians are also severe critics of "crony capitalism," which they
see as the product of collusion between private actors and the state.
A free society, left-libertarians believe, would be one swept clean of
coercive privilege and the hierarchies and inequalities such privileges support. Liberty is about solidarity—without the state.

Which brings us back to the paleo-libertarians and their heirs in
the Mises Caucus, who take a distinctly conservative approach to
libertarianism. What perhaps distinguishes this group most fundamentally from other sects of libertarianism is its focus on the link
between freedom and culture. Their opposition to open borders, for
instance, is based not merely on a commitment to property rights
but on the belief that property rights should be exercised to preserve native ideas of virtue, freedom, and the rule of law from the
perceived threat of outside corruption. Their opposition to "woke-
ism," similarly, is motivated by the belief that "virtue signaling"
leads down a road where freedoms of association and expression,
and the cultural forms they support, are lost. A free society, for the
paleo-libertarians, would be one with a deep popular *commitment*
to freedom and to the moral and cultural factors that freedom presupposes. Freedom is the absence of coercion, but such freedom
does not entail and is in fact incompatible with the absence of traditional moral and cultural restraints.

It is tempting, at the close of this book, to make a prediction
about which of these three rival versions of libertarianism will
emerge triumphant—say in ten, or twenty, or fifty years. But our
historical study suggests a different way of peering into the future.
Libertarianism is not accidentally but intrinsically a diverse

ideology. Rather than a timeless Euclidian proof, each version of libertarianism is a product of individual judgment and choice—judgments shaped by the social context (and personality) of individual thinkers. In the same way, the tension between radical and reactionary elements is not accidental but intrinsic to libertarian thinking. For all these reasons, the struggle between libertarianism's progressive and conservative tendencies, a struggle for the soul of libertarianism, is likely to go on.

NOTES

Introduction

1. Brian Doherty's *Radicals for Capitalism: A Freewheeling History of the Modern American Libertarian Movement* (New York: Public Affairs, 2007) remains the definite treatment of the libertarian movement.

2. For recent discussions of neoliberalism, see Angus Burgin, *The Great Persuasion: Reinventing Free Markets since the Depression* (Cambridge, MA: Harvard University Press, 2012); Quinn Slobodian, *Globalists: The End of Empire and the Birth of Neoliberalism* (Cambridge, MA: Harvard University Press, 2018); and Kevin Vallier, "Neoliberalism," *Stanford Encyclopedia of Philosophy* (Summer 2021 ed.), ed. Edward N. Zalta, https://plato.stanford.edu/archives/sum2021/entries/neoliberalism/. On the Austrian school of economics, see Karen Iversen Vaughn, *Austrian Economics in America: The Migration of a Tradition*, Historical Perspectives on Modern Economics (New York: Cambridge University Press, 1994); Janek Wasserman, *The Marginal Revolutionaries* (New Haven: Yale University Press, 2019); and Peter J. Boettke, "Libertarianism and the Austrian School of Economics," in *The Routledge Companion to Libertarianism*, ed. Matt Zwolinski and Benjamin Ferguson (New York: Routledge, 2022). On the Chicago school, see Johan Van Overtveldt, *The Chicago School: How the University of Chicago Assembled the Thinkers Who Revolutionized Economics and Business* (Evanston, IL: Agate Publishing, 2009); Ross B. Emmett, *The Elgar Companion to the Chicago School of Economics* (Cheltenham: Edward Elgar, 2010); Ross B. Emmett, "Libertarianism and the Chicago School of Economics," in *The Routledge Companion to Libertarianism*, ed. Matt Zwolinski and Ben Ferguson (New York: Routledge, 2022); and Rob Van Horn and Philip Mirowski, "4. The Rise of the Chicago School of Economics and the Birth of Neoliberalism," in *The Road from Mont Pèlerin*, ed. Philip Mirowski and Dieter Plehwe (Cambridge, MA: Harvard University Press, 2015), 139–78, https://doi.org/10.4159/9780674054264-005.

3. Lysander Spooner exemplifies the first approach; see chapter 4. William F. Buckley, who was tutored by the libertarian Albert Jay Nock and who described himself as an "individualist," exemplifies the second. See his notorious editorial, "Why the South Must Prevail," *National Review*, August 24, 1957. For context, see Carl T. Bogus, *Buckley: William F. Buckley Jr. and the Rise of American Conservatism* (New York: Bloomsbury, 2011).

Chapter 1. What Is Libertarianism?

1. The *Oxford English Dictionary* (3rd ed., November 2010) attributes the first usage of the word "libertarian" to William Belsham in 1789, who asked in his *Essays, Philosophical, Historical, and Literary*, "What is the difference between the Libertarian . . . and the Necessarian?"

2. "Lately marched out of the Prison at Bristol, 450 of the French Libertarians," *London Packet*, February 12, 1796 (*Oxford English Dictionary*, 3rd ed., November 2010).

3. Stephan Kinsella reports the following 1802 usage in *The British Critic*: "The author's Latin verses . . . mark him for a furious *Libertarian* (if we may coin such a term) and a zealous admirer of France, and her liberty, under Bonaparte, such Liberty!" See *The British Critic*, vol. 20 (London, 1802), 432. From the authors' own search, this appears to be the earliest use of the term in this sense recorded in Google Books.

4. Montesquieu, *The Complete Works of M. de Montesquieu*, vol. 2, *The Spirit of the Laws* (T. Evans, 1748), 149. Lord Acton wrote similarly that liberty "is an idea of which there are two hundred definitions, and [this] wealth of interpretation has caused more bloodshed than anything, except theology." Baron John Emerich Edward Dalberg Acton, "Inaugural Lecture on the Study of History," in *Lectures on Modern History* (London: Macmillan, 1906), 12.

5. Joseph Déjacque coined the term "libertaire" in an 1857 letter to the French mutualist anarchist Pierre-Joseph Proudhon, in which he criticized what he regarded as the latter's refusal to support the freedom and rights of women. See his "De l'être-humain mâle et femelle," May 1857, http://joseph.dejacque.free.fr/ecrits /lettreapjp.htm.

6. The etymological discussion here and in the remainder of this section was improved through conversations with Charles Johnson.

7. Déjacque stands out from later libertarians not only in virtue of his communism but also in virtue of his enthusiastic advocacy of violence as a revolutionary tool, which was, according to the historian of anarchism George Woodcock, "so extreme as to embarrass even the anarchists in a later generation." George Woodcock, *Anarchism: A History of Libertarian Ideas and Movements* (Toronto: University of Toronto Press, 2009), 235.

8. Tucker uses the term in several of the essays collected in Benjamin Tucker, *Instead of a Book: By a Man Too Busy to Write One* (New York: Elibron Classics, 2005), always with this broad meaning. See, for instance, "State Socialism and Anarchism: How Far They Agree, and Wherein They Differ" (*Liberty* 5, no. 16 [March 10, 1888]: 2–3, 6: "There are two socialisms . . . one is dictatorial, the other libertarian"), "A Libertarian's Pet Despotisms" (1887), and "Liberty and the George Theory" (1887: "But the divorce laws, instead of being libertarian, are an express recognition of the rightfulness of authority over the sexual relations"). Peter Kropotkin used the term in a similarly broad way, writing in 1901 that "throughout the whole history of our civilization, two traditions, two opposed tendencies, have been

in conflict: The Roman tradition and the popular tradition; the imperialist tradition and the federalist tradition; the authoritarian one and the libertarian one." Quoted in *The Public*, April 27, 1901, ed. Louis Post.

9. In 1878, for instance, Sir John Robert Seeley described a libertarian as one "who can properly be said to defend liberty" by opposing tyranny and "resist[ing] the established Government." *Life and Times of Stein, or, Germany and Russia in the Napoleonic Age*, vol. 3 (Cambridge: Cambridge University Press, 1878), 355.

10. In 1901, Frederick William Maitland characterized the English as "individualists and libertarians" for their dislike of the thought of "an editor [having to defend] his proof sheets sentence by sentence before an official board of critics." From "William Stubbs, Bishop of Oxford," *English Historical Review* 16, no. 63 (July 1901): 419.

11. Charles T. Sprading, *Liberty and the Great Libertarians* (Los Angeles: Golden Press, 1913).

12. Ibid., 5.

13. Ibid., 6.

14. On Mencken, see H. L. Mencken, *Letters of H. L. Mencken*, ed. Guy Forge (New York: Knopf, 1961), xiii, 189. On Nock, see Albert Jay Nock, *Letters from Albert Jay Nock, 1924–1945 to Edmund C. Evans, Mrs. Edmund C. Evans and Ellen Winsor*, ed. Frank Garrison (Caldwell, ID: Caxton Printers, 1949), 40, cited in Jennifer Burns, *Goddess of the Market: Ayn Rand and the American Right* (New York: Oxford University Press, 2009), 306.

15. Not to be confused with an earlier publication of the same name published by Albert Jay Nock. See, for a discussion of Read and the Foundation for Economic Education, Doherty, *Radicals for Capitalism*, chap. 4.

16. Leonard E. Read, *Talking to Myself* (Irvington-on-Hudson, NY: Foundation for Economic Education, 1970), 120–21. See also Read's 1975 interview with *Reason* magazine in which he says, "I'm the one who brought about and popularized the word 'libertarian.'" Tibor R. Machan, "Educating for Freedom: An Interview with Leonard Read," *Reason*, April 1975, https://reason.com/1975/04/01/educating-for-freedom/. Ironically, given the term's nineteenth-century origins, Read goes on to complain that the word has now been "taken over" by "anarchists [and] out-and-out socialists." We are indebted to Stephan Kinsella for the references. See his "The Origin of 'Libertarianism,'" *Mises Wire* (blog), September 10, 2011, https://mises.org/wire/origin-libertarianism.

17. Dean Russell, "Who Is a Libertarian?" *The Freeman*, May 1, 1950, http://www.fee.org/the_freeman/detail/who-is-a-libertarian#axzz2d1BZd095.

18. Ayn Rand famously refused to identify herself as a libertarian and dismissed anarchist libertarians in particular as "hippies of the right." See her "Brief Summary," *The Objectivist* 10, no. 9 (September 1971): 1. Rand's issue seems to have been with both what she perceived to be the political commitments of libertarianism (she rejected anarchism) and libertarianism's lack of what she thought were the correct philosophical foundations (Objectivism). Still, despite her refusal to self-identify as such, Rand counts as a libertarian according to the definition adopted in this book and most other common definitions in the scholarly and popular literature. For more

on the connection between Objectivism and libertarianism, see Gregory Salmieri, "Objectivism," in *The Routledge Companion to Libertarianism*, ed. Matt Zwolinski and Benjamin Ferguson (New York: Routledge, 2022).

19. See, for discussion, George H. Smith, *The System of Liberty: Themes in the History of Classical Liberalism* (New York: Cambridge University Press, 2013), chaps. 1–2.

20. Adam Smith, *The Wealth of Nations* (Indianapolis: Liberty Fund, 1982), 1:324, 539.

21. Hayek's comment on laissez-faire can be found in *The Road to Serfdom: Definitive Edition* (Chicago: University of Chicago Press, 2007), 71. His endorsement of a minimum income can be found in *Law, Legislation, and Liberty*, vol. 1, *Rules and Order* (London: Routledge, 1973), 55.

22. See, for example, Richard A. Epstein, *Principles for a Free Society: Reconciling Individual Liberty with the Common Good* (New York: Basic Books, 1998).

23. John Stuart Mill, *Principles of Political Economy (Ashley ed.)* (London: Longmans, Green, 1848), 2:444.

24. See Herbert Spencer, *Social Statics* (1851; New York: Robert Schalkenbach Foundation, 1995); and Murray N. Rothbard, *The Ethics of Liberty* (Atlantic Highlands, NJ: Humanities Press, 1982).

25. Though, as we will see, not all approaches to libertarianism fit neatly within this dichotomy. For an overview of alternative approaches, see part 1 of Matt Zwolinski and Benjamin Ferguson, eds., *The Routledge Companion to Libertarianism* (New York: Routledge, 2022).

26. We will discuss libertarians' views on the right to property extensively in chapter 3.

27. See, for example, Smith, *The System of Liberty*, chap. 8.

28. See, for a discussion, David Weinstein, *Equal Freedom and Utility: Herbert Spencer's Liberal Utilitarianism* (New York: Cambridge University Press, 1998).

29. See Ludwig von Mises, *Human Action: A Treatise on Economics*, 4th rev. ed. (Indianapolis: Liberty Fund, 1996); and Hayek, *Law, Legislation, and Liberty*, chap. 3. Hayek seems to have been of two minds about this matter. It is difficult to reconcile his insistence upon principle in *Law, Legislation, and Liberty* with his criticism of the "wooden insistence" on laissez-faire in *Road to Serfdom* and the many exceptions to the general principle of liberty he seemed willing to countenance throughout his writings.

30. For helpful discussions, see Norman P. Barry, *On Classical Liberalism and Libertarianism* (London: Macmillan, 1986); and Eric Mack and Gerald Gaus, "Classical Liberalism and Libertarianism: The Liberty Tradition," in *Handbook of Political Theory*, ed. Gerald Gaus and Chandran Kukathas (London: Sage, 2004), 115–30.

31. Burgin, *The Great Persuasion*; Slobodian, *Globalists*; Kevin Vallier, "Neoliberalism," *Stanford Encyclopedia of Philosophy* (Summer 2021 ed.), ed. Edward N. Zalta, https://plato.stanford.edu/archives/sum2021/entries/neoliberalism/.

32. Slobodian, *Globalists*.

33. Neoliberalism is a broad and diverse political movement, and some of its members bear a closer connection with and resemblance to the libertarian family

than others. Figures like Hayek, Friedman, and Buchanan have enough in common with libertarians in terms of both their sociological networks and their substantive philosophical commitments to warrant inclusion in this book. Others, such as Röpke and Knight, are connected only more tangentially.

34. Ayn Rand, "The Nature of Government," in *The Virtue of Selfishness* (New York: Signet, 1964), 109; Robert Nozick, *Anarchy, State, and Utopia* (New York: Basic Books, 1974), chap. 7. Minimal-state libertarians are a relatively rare breed compared to classical liberals and market anarchists. This may be due to the fact that their position seems to occupy a precarious middle ground between those other two positions. Anarchists will ask why, if government is so immoral or inefficient as to rule out the provision of public goods, should it nevertheless be entrusted with a monopoly on protective and legal services. And classical liberals will ask why, if *those* public goods (and the coercive taxation they require) are allowed, others might not be as well. For one of the earliest statements of a minimal-state libertarian self-consciously contrasting his position with both socialism *and* anarchism, see J. H. Levy, *The Outcome of Individualism* (London: P. S. King and Son, 1892).

35. Rothbard was probably the most well-known market anarchist of the twentieth century. His position is developed in *The Ethics of Liberty*; *For a New Liberty* (New York: Collier, 1973); *Man, Economy and State* (Los Angeles: Nash, 1970); and *Power and Market* (Kansas City, MO: Sheed Andrews & McMeel, 1970). Other contemporary proponents of the doctrine include Randy E. Barnett, *The Structure of Liberty: Justice and the Rule of Law* (Oxford: Oxford University Press, 1998), chap. 14; David Friedman, *The Machinery of Freedom: Guide to Radical Capitalism*, 2nd ed. (La Salle, IL: Open Court, 1989); John Hasnas, "The Obviousness of Anarchy," in *Anarchism/Minarchism: Is a Government Part of a Free Country?*, ed. Roderick T. Long and Tibor R. Machan (Burlington, VT: Ashgate, 2008), 111–132; John Hasnas, "The Depoliticization of Law," *Theoretical Inquiries in Law* 9, no. 2 (2007): 529–52; John Hasnas, "Reflections on the Minimal State," *Politics, Philosophy and Economics* 2, no. 1 (2003): 115–28, https://doi.org/10.1177/1470594X03002001426; Roderick T. Long, "Market Anarchism as Constitutionalism," in *Anarchism/Minarchism: Is Government Part of a Free Country?*, ed. Roderick T. Long and Tibor R. Machan (Burlington, VT: Ashgate, 2008), 133–54; Roderick T. Long, "Rule-Following, Praxeology, and Anarchy," *New Perspectives on Political Economy* 2, no. 1 (2006): 36–46; Gary Chartier, *Anarchy and Legal Order: Law and Politics for a Stateless Society* (New York: Cambridge University Press, 2013); and Aeon Skoble, *Deleting the State: An Argument about Government* (Chicago: Open Court, 2008).

36. The quote is from Friedrich A. Hayek, *The Road to Serfdom: The Definitive Edition*, ed. Bruce Caldwell, vol. 2, Collected Works of F. A. Hayek (Chicago: University of Chicago Press, 2007), 148. For his support of the state provision of public goods and public education, see Hayek, *The Constitution of Liberty*, ed. Ronald Hamowy, Collected Works of F. A. Hayek (Chicago: University of Chicago Press, 2011), 223 and chap. 24, respectively. On classical liberalism more generally, see Loren E. Lomasky, *Persons, Rights, and the Moral Community* (Oxford: Oxford University Press, 1987); Gerald F. Gaus, *The Order of Public Reason: A Theory of Freedom and Morality in a*

Diverse and Bounded World (New York: Cambridge University Press, 2011); Epstein, *Principles for a Free Society*; and Milton Friedman, *Capitalism and Freedom* (Chicago: University of Chicago Press, 1962).

37. For a helpful overview of different libertarian foundations, see Eric Mack, *Libertarianism* (New York: John Wiley & Sons, 2018), chap. 3. See also David Boaz, *The Libertarian Mind: A Manifesto for Freedom* (New York: Simon & Schuster, 2015).

38. Thus, Mises writes that "liberalism is a doctrine directed entirely toward the conduct of men in this world. In the last analysis, it has nothing else in view than the advancement of their outward, material welfare." See Ludwig von Mises, *Liberalism: In the Classical Tradition* (San Francisco: Cobden Press, 1985), 4. See also Friedman, *The Machinery of Freedom*, especially part 3; Milton Friedman, *Capitalism and Freedom*, 40th anniversary ed. (Chicago: University of Chicago Press, 2002); and Epstein, *Principles for a Free Society*.

39. See Jan Narveson, *The Libertarian Idea* (Philadelphia: Temple University Press, 1988); and James M. Buchanan, *The Limits of Liberty: Between Anarchy and Leviathan* (Chicago: University of Chicago Press, 1975).

40. The common label of "natural rights" actually masks a great deal of diversity within this group. Nozick's theory of rights as side-constraints, for instance, is best understood as grounded in the Kantian idea that individuals are ends in themselves and not mere means. Barnett, on the other hand, conceives of rights as hypothetical imperatives that allow individuals to live peaceful and prosperous lives. And Rothbard grounds his view of rights in a quasi-Thomistic account of natural law. See Barnett, *The Structure of Liberty*; Lysander Spooner, "Natural Law, or, The Science of Justice: A Treatise on Natural Law, Natural Justice, Natural Rights, Natural Liberty, and Natural Society; Showing That All Legislation Whatsoever Is an Absurdity, a Usurpation, and a Crime. Part First," in *The Collected Works of Lysander Spooner* (Indianapolis: Liberty Fund, 1882), 5:134–51; Lysander Spooner, "A Letter to Grover Cleveland, on His False Inaugural Address, the Usurpations and Crimes of Lawmakers and Judges, and the Consequent Poverty, Ignorance, and Servitude of the People," in *The Collected Works of Lysander Spooner* (Indianapolis: Liberty Fund, 1886), 5:184–305; Nozick, *Anarchy, State, and Utopia*; and Rothbard, *The Ethics of Liberty*.

41. See Douglas B. Rasmussen and Douglas J. Den Uyl, *Norms of Liberty: A Perfectionist Basis for Non-Perfectionist Politics* (University Park: Penn State University Press, 2005).

42. See Tibor R. Machan, *Individuals and Their Rights* (LaSalle, IL: Open Court, 1989); Tucker, *Instead of a Book*; and Ayn Rand, "The Objectivist Ethics," in *The Virtue of Selfishness* (New York: Signet, 1964). Even within this category, there are significant differences between the egoism of Rand and that of Tucker. See chapter 2.

43. This is true also of the twentieth century's most important anti-libertarian liberal philosopher, John Rawls. See John Rawls, *A Theory of Justice*, 1st ed. (Cambridge, MA: Belknap Press, 1971), 61.

44. See, for example, James Stacy Taylor, *Stakes and Kidneys: Why Markets in Human Body Parts Are Morally Imperative* (New York: Ashgate, 2005); Walter E. Block, "Free Market Transportation: Denationalizing the Roads," *Journal of*

Libertarian Studies 3, no. 2 (1979): 209–38; and Terry L. Anderson and Donald R. Leal, *Free Market Environmentalism* (Boulder, CO: Westview Press, 1991).

45. See, e.g., Auberon Herbert, "A Voluntaryist Appeal," *The Humanitarian: A Monthly Review of Sociological Science* (May 1898): 317; and Rothbard, *For a New Liberty*, 47.

46. See, e.g., Richard A. Epstein, *Takings: Private Property and the Power of Eminent Domain* (Cambridge, MA: Harvard University Press, 1985).

47. See, for example, Jan Narveson, who equates liberty with property and writes that it is therefore "plausible to construe all rights as property rights" (*The Libertarian Idea*, 66).

48. The classic statement of this argument is in chapter 5 of John Locke's *Second Treatise*. More recent, and more distinctively libertarian, versions can be found in Auberon Herbert, *The Right and Wrong of Compulsion by the State and Other Essays* (Indianapolis: Liberty Fund, 1978); and Rothbard, *The Ethics of Liberty*. Nozick's libertarian theory is often interpreted as resting on the premise of self-ownership, but see chapter 3 of this book for some doubts about that interpretation.

49. For the former, see Narveson, *The Libertarian Idea*. For the latter, see Horacio Spector, *Autonomy and Rights* (Oxford: Oxford University Press, 1992).

50. See David Schmidtz, "The Institution of Property," *Social Philosophy and Policy* 11, no. 2 (1994): 42–62.

51. See, for example, Gerald Gaus's survey of the empirical evidence in "Coercion, Ownership, and the Redistributive State: Justificatory Liberalism's Classical Tilt," *Social Philosophy and Policy* 27, no. 1 (2010): 233, https://doi.org/10.1017/S0265052509990100.

52. That fact that justice and utility both point in the same direction in so many libertarian arguments surely calls out for explanation. One possible explanation is the skeptical one. The reason justice and utility line up for libertarians, this line of reasoning goes, is because libertarians frame their arguments to fit their conclusions rather than the other way around. See, for a somewhat sympathetic expression of this skepticism, Jeffrey Friedman, "What's Wrong with Libertarianism?" *Critical Review* 11, no. 3 (1997): 407–67. However, there are other, less skeptical explanations available as well. For instance, perhaps justice and utility do not come into conflict because the content of justice is partly a function of utilitarian considerations. See, for a discussion of many such possible explanations, and an endorsement of one, Roderick T. Long, "Why Does Justice Have Good Consequences?" (paper presented at the Alabama Philosophical Society, Auburn University, October 26, 2002), http://praxeology.net/whyjust.htm. See also chapter 3 of this book.

53. See, for instance, Tucker, "State Socialism and Anarchism"; and Thomas Hodgskin, *Labour Defended against the Claims of Capital, or, The Unproductiveness of Capital Proved with Reference to the Present Combinations amongst Journeymen*, 1825.

54. See J. H. Levy, ed., *A Symposium on the Land Question* (London: T. Fisher Unwin, 1890); and J. H. Levy and Roland K. Wilson, *Individualism and the Land Question: A Discussion* (London: Personal Rights Association, 1912).

55. See, for instance, Friedrich A. Hayek, "The Use of Knowledge in Society," *American Economic Review* 35, no. 4 (1945): 519–30; and Friedrich A. Hayek, "The Pretense of Knowledge," in *New Studies in Politics, Economics and the History of Ideas* (London: Routledge, 1978), 25–34.

56. See, for instance, James Buchanan and Gordon Tullock, *The Calculus of Consent* (Ann Arbor: University of Michigan Press, 1962); and Gordon Tullock, R. D. Tollison, and C. K. Rowley, *The Political Economy of Rent Seeking* (Boston: Kluwer, 1988).

57. On this point, many libertarians follow Locke, who defined tyranny as "the exercise of power beyond right." *Second Treatise*, chap. 18, § 199.

58. See Jason Brennan, "Moral Parity between State and Non-state Actors," in *The Routledge Handbook of Anarchy and Anarchist Thought*, ed. Gary Chartier and Chad Van Schoelandt (New York: Routledge, 2021), 236. Brennan describes the moral parity thesis as holding that "government agents and private civilians are fundamentally morally equal."

59. Individuals can, of course, differ in their *nonderivative* rights and duties. A lifeguard has a duty to rescue drowning swimmers that others lack. A homeowners' association has a right to regulate the external appearance of your home and collect dues in ways that ordinary neighbors cannot. In these sorts of cases, however, the special rights and duties are derived from more basic rights that all persons have: the right to *create* new rights and duties through voluntary contract. The moral parity thesis does not rule out the possibility of government agents coming to have special rights in this ordinary way. It does rule out their having special rights simply by virtue of their status as agents of the state, and it rules out the possibility of their acquiring special rights in special ways—i.e., ways that are not open to ordinary citizens.

60. Locke, *Second Treatise*, § 176.

61. Bastiat: "The law is the organization of the natural right of lawful defense. It is the substitution of a common force for individual forces. And this common force is to do only what the individual forces have a natural and lawful right to do: to protect persons, liberties, and properties; to maintain the right of each, and to cause *justice* to reign over us all." Frédéric Bastiat, "The Law," in *"The Law," "The State," and Other Political Writings: 1843–1850*, ed. Jacques de Guenin (Indianapolis: Liberty Fund, 2012). Spooner: "It is self-evident that no number of men, by conspiring, and calling themselves a government, can acquire any rights whatever over other men, or other men's property, which they had not before, as individuals. And whenever any number of men, calling themselves a government, do anything to another man, or to his property, which they had no right to do as individuals, they thereby declare themselves trespassers, robbers, or murderers, according to the nature of their acts" ("A Letter to Grover Cleveland"). Herbert: "We hold that what one man cannot morally do, a million of men cannot morally do, and government, representing many millions of men, cannot do." Auberon Herbert, "The Principles of Voluntaryism and Free Life," in *The Right and Wrong of Compulsion by the State and Other Essays*, ed. Eric Mack (Indianapolis: Liberty Fund, 1978), 369–416. See also Rothbard, *For a New Liberty*, chap. 3; and Michael Huemer, *The Problem of Political Authority: An Examination of*

the Right to Coerce and the Duty to Obey (London: Palgrave Macmillan, 2012), chap. 1. For an overview, see Carl Watner, "The 'Criminal' Metaphor in the Libertarian Tradition," *Journal of Libertarian Studies* 5, no. 3 (1981): 313–25.

62. On the myth of the social contract, see Lysander Spooner, "No Treason, No. VI: The Constitution of No Authority," in *The Collected Works of Lysander Spooner* (Indianapolis: Liberty Fund, 1870), 4:171–229. For one representative libertarian account of the so-called "conquest theory" of the state, see Albert Jay Nock, *Our Enemy, the State* (San Francisco: Fox & Wilkes, 1994). Nock draws heavily on the work of the German sociologist Franz Oppenheimer, especially his *The State: Its History and Development Viewed Sociologically*, trans. John Gutterman (Indianapolis: Bobbs-Merrill, 1944).

63. For a highly sophisticated exposition of this position, see Huemer, *The Problem of Political Authority*.

64. For a contemporary overview of the debate, see Roderick T. Long and Tibor R. Machan, eds., *Anarchism/Minarchism: Is Government Part of a Free Society?* (Burlington, VT: Ashgate, 2008).

65. See Rothbard, *For a New Liberty*, 46–47.

66. On this point, see Julian Lincoln Simon, *The Ultimate Resource 2* (Princeton: Princeton University Press, 1998).

67. Auberon Herbert, for instance, condemns fraud as "the twin brother of force, wearing a mask over its features." Herbert, *The Right and Wrong of Compulsion by the State*, 329. For a dissenting view, see James Child, "Can Libertarianism Sustain a Fraud Standard?" *Ethics* 104, no. 4 (1994): 722–38.

68. This was Rothbard's view at the time that he wrote *For a New Liberty* in 1973. There, he wrote that "the vital fact about air pollution is that the polluter sends unwanted and unbidden pollutants—from smoke to nuclear radiation to sulfur oxides—through the air and into the lungs of innocent victims, as well as onto their material property. All such emanations which injure person or property constitute aggression against the private property of the victims. Air pollution, after all, is just as much aggression as committing arson against another's property or injuring him physically" (319). Over time, however, Rothbard's view on the subject took a distinctly conservative turn. For an overview, see Jeffrey Friedman, "Politics or Scholarship?" *Critical Review* 6, no. 2–3 (March 1992): 429–45, https://doi.org/10.1080 /08913819208443271; and Matt Zwolinski, "Libertarianism and Pollution," *Philosophy and Public Policy Quarterly* 32, no. 4 (2014): 9–21.

69. See, for instance, Hayek, "Use of Knowledge in Society"; and Leonard E. Read, "I, Pencil: My Family Tree as Told to Leonard E. Read" (Foundation for Economic Education, December 1958), https://oll.libertyfund.org/title/read-i-pencil-my-family -tree-as-told-to-leonard-e-read-dec-1958.

70. The example of feeding Paris is borrowed from Frédéric Bastiat, "There Are No Absolute Principles," in *Economic Sophisms* (Irvington-on-Hudson, NY: Foundation for Economic Education, 1964).

71. Adam Ferguson, *An Essay on the History of Civil Society* (T. Cadell, 1767), https://oll.libertyfund.org/title/ferguson-an-essay-on-the-history-of-civil-society,

part 3, section 2. See also Friedrich A. Hayek, "Kinds of Order in Society," *New Individualist Review* 3, no. 2 (1964): 3–12.

72. Charles W. Johnson, "Women and the Invisible Fist," November 2010, http://charleswjohnson.name/essays/women-and-the-invisible-fist/rpa-2010.

73. Adam Smith, *An Inquiry into the Nature and Causes of the Wealth of Nations*, ed. Edwin Cannan (London: Methuen, 1904), vol. 1, book IV, chap. 2.

74. See, for a discussion, John Hasnas, "Toward a Theory of Empirical Natural Rights," *Social Philosophy and Policy* 22, no. 1 (2005): 111–47.

75. See Robert C. Ellickson, *Order without Law: How Neighbors Settle Disputes* (Cambridge, MA: Harvard University Press, 1991); and Elinor Ostrom, *Governing the Commons: The Evolution of Institutions for Collective Action* (New York: Cambridge University Press, 1990).

76. See Elinor Ostrom, "Beyond Markets and States: Polycentric Governance of Complex Economic Systems," *American Economic Review* 100, no. 3 (2010): 641–72, https://doi.org/10.1257/aer.100.3.641.

77. Though James C. Scott does not use the terminology, his *Seeing Like a State: How Certain Schemes to Improve the Human Condition Have Failed* (New Haven: Yale University Press, 1998) serves as a useful study in the contrast between spontaneous and nonspontaneous orders, and his opening chapter on scientific forest management in Germany provides a poignant example of the unintended consequences that can arise from the attempt to impose a logical design on a complex ecosystem.

78. Some forms of radical libertarianism thus seem to embrace what the more conservative libertarian Thomas Sowell describes as the "unconstrained vision" of rationalist, Enlightenment progress. See, for discussion, Thomas Sowell, *A Conflict of Visions: Ideological Origins of Political Struggles*, rev. ed. (New York: Basic Books, 2007).

79. See chapter 2 for further discussion.

80. See Nozick, *Anarchy, State, and Utopia*, 32–33.

81. Nozick's account of libertarianism in *Anarchy, State, and Utopia* was famously criticized by Thomas Nagel for simply assuming the truth of libertarian rights and failing to provide them with any moral foundation. See our discussion of Nozick on "the separateness of persons" in chapter 3. See also Matt Zwolinski, "The Separateness of Persons and Liberal Theory," *Journal of Value Inquiry* 42, no. 2 (2008): 147–65, https://doi.org/10.1007/s10790-008-9107-y.

82. See Joel Feinberg, *Harmless Wrongdoing* (Oxford: Oxford University Press, 1990).

83. See Buchanan and Tullock, *The Calculus of Consent*.

84. See the discussion in the section "Skepticism of Authority."

85. The locus classicus of this distinction is Isaiah Berlin, "Two Concepts of Liberty," in *Four Essays on Liberty*, ed. Isaiah Berlin (Oxford: Oxford University Press, 1969), 118–72. It is worth noting that Berlin, too, uses the word "libertarian" in something like the broad sense that prevailed in the nineteenth century, referring to those intellectuals such as "Locke and Mill in England, and Constant and Tocqueville in France," who thought that "there ought to exist a certain minimum area of personal freedom which must on no account be violated" (124).

86. Mack and Gaus, "Classical Liberalism and Libertarianism," 116–17.

87. Spencer, *Social Statics*, 95. Interestingly, the decidedly nonlibertarian John Rawls would later adopt a strikingly similar idea as one of two fundamental principles of justice that he held ought to govern the basic structure of society. See Rawls, *A Theory of Justice*, 60. Rawls would later reject that principle in response to criticism from H.L.A. Hart. See Hart, "Rawls on Liberty and Its Priority," *University of Chicago Law Review* 40, no. 3 (1973): 534–55; and John Rawls, *Political Liberalism* (New York: Columbia University Press, 1993), lecture VIII.

88. See, e.g., Nozick, *Anarchy, State, and Utopia*, 32–33.

89. See Hillel Steiner, *An Essay on Rights* (New York: Blackwell, 1994).

90. Compare with John Locke, who wrote that the liberty we are concerned with is not "a liberty for every man to do what he lists" but rather "a liberty to dispose and order as he lists his person, actions, possessions, and his whole property, *within the allowance of those laws under which he is*, and therein not to be subject to the arbitrary will of another, but freely follow his own" (*Second Treatise*, § 57). George H. Smith contrasts this "social" conception of liberty with the "mechanistic" conception of Hobbes. See Smith, *The System of Liberty*, chap. 7.

Chapter 2. Three Eras of Libertarian Thought

1. Recall Sprading's claim that there was no incompatibility between socialism and libertarianism, so long as socialism is voluntary. See also Tucker, "State Socialism and Anarchism."

2. For a contemporary account of the relation between classical liberalism, progressive or "New" liberalism, and socialism, see A. V. Dicey, *Lectures on the Relation between Law and Public Opinion in England during the Nineteenth Century*, 1906, https://doi.org/10.2307/1273907.

3. Mill famously claimed that "unlike the laws of production, those of distribution are partly of human institution," and thus that "the things once there, mankind . . . can do with them as they like" (*Principles of Political Economy*, 21). Later libertarians have seized on this idea as a key moment in the transition from classical to progressive liberalism, and it is the reason many libertarians consider Mill as, at best, a "mixed figure" in the libertarian intellectual tradition and, at worst, a betrayer of it. Murray Rothbard's judgment is characteristically blunt: Mill was "a wooly minded man of mush" whose intellectual system was "a vast kitchen midden of diverse and contradictory positions." See Murray Rothbard, *An Austrian Perspective on the History of Economic Thought*, vol. 2, *Classical Economics* (Cheltenham: Edward Elgar, 1995), 277.

4. Pierre-Joseph Proudhon, *What Is Property?*, trans. Benjamin Tucker (Princeton, MA: Benj. R. Tucker, 1876); Robert L. Hale, "Coercion and Distribution in a Supposedly Non-Coercive State," *Political Science Quarterly* 38, no. 3 (1923): 470–94.

5. Auberon Herbert, "Mr. Spencer and the Great Machine," in *The Right and Wrong of Compulsion by the State and Other Essays by Auberon Herbert*, ed. Eric Mack (Indianapolis: Liberty Fund, 1978).

6. Dicey's *Lectures* (1905) provides a classic account of the rise and fall of individualist thought in nineteenth-century Britain, with special emphasis on the influence of Jeremy Bentham. Alberto Mingardi's *Herbert Spencer*, vol. 18 (New York: Continuum International Publishing Group, 2011) provides an excellent succinct overview of Spencer's political thought. Scholarship on the later and more clearly libertarian "Individualists" is more limited, but M. W. Taylor's *Men versus the State: Herbert Spencer and Late Victorian Individualism* (Oxford: Oxford University Press, 1992) is the best single source. More focused treatments can also be found in Edward Bristow, "The Liberty and Property Defense League and Individualism," *Historical Journal* 18, no. 4 (1975): 761–89; N. Soldon, "Laissez-Faire as Dogma: The Liberty and Property Defence League, 1882–1914," in *Essays in Anti-Labour History*, ed. Kenneth D. Brown (London: Palgrave Macmillan, 1974), 208–23, https://doi.org/10.1007/978-1-349-02039-3_9; John W. Mason, "Political Economy and the Response to Socialism in Britain, 1870–1914," *Historical Journal* 23, no. 3 (1980): 565–87, https://doi.org/10.1017/S0018246X00024894; Peter Ryley, *Making Another World Possible: Anarchism, Anti-Capitalism and Ecology in Late 19th and Early 20th Century Britain* (New York: Bloomsbury, 2013), chaps. 3–4; and Eric Mack, "Voluntaryism: The Political Thought of Auberon Herbert," *Journal of Libertarian Studies* 2, no. 4 (1978): 299–309.

7. Interestingly, Hodgskin's ideas appear to have had little direct influence on British libertarians of the late nineteenth century. This is perhaps because, in both substance and political "tone," his ideas were far more similar to those of nineteenth-century American libertarians than to libertarians of his own country. For a helpful overview, see Élie Halévy, *Thomas Hodgskin (1787–1869)* (Paris: Société nouvelle de librairie et d'édition, 1903).

8. Jeremy Bentham, *Defence of Usury* (Pall Mall: Payne and Foss, 1787).

9. Jeremy Bentham, *Not Paul, But Jesus, Volume III: Doctrine*, preliminary edition, ed. P. Schofield (London: Bentham Project, UCL, 2013), http://www.ucl.ac.uk/Bentham-Project/publications/npbj/npbj.html, "Offenses against the Self."

10. See Dicey, *Lectures*, lecture 6.

11. See Élie Halévy, *The Growth of Philosophical Radicalism*, trans. Mary Morris (New York: Macmillan, 1928).

12. See chapter 8 for a fuller account of this episode, and of the ideas of Richard Cobden.

13. Spencer, *Social Statics*, part 2, chap. 4, section 6.

14. Ibid., 51.

15. This interpretation was held both by certain contemporary classical liberals (see Dicey, *Lectures*, lecture 12) and by certain socialists and progressives (see Sidney Webb's essay in *Fabian Essays on Socialism* and Leonard Trelawny Hobhouse and L. T. Hobhouse, *Hobhouse: Liberalism and Other Writings* [New York: Cambridge University Press, 1994]). And it had a strong influence on many twentieth-century libertarians as well. Ludwig von Mises expresses a common libertarian objection to Mill in characteristically strong terms: "John Stuart Mill is an epigone of classical liberalism and, especially in his later years, under the influence of his wife, full of feeble

compromises. . . . Without a thorough study of Mill it is impossible to understand the events of the last two generations. For Mill is the great advocate of socialism. All the arguments that could be advanced in favour of socialism are elaborated by him with loving care. In comparison with Mill all other socialist writers—even Marx, Engels, and Lassalle—are scarcely of any importance" (*Liberalism*, 195). For a dissenting view, see Dale E. Miller, "Mill's 'Socialism,'" *Politics, Philosophy & Economics* 2, no. 2 (2003): 213–38, https://doi.org/10.1177/1470594X03002002004.

16. Dicey, *Lectures*, lecture 7.

17. See Mason, "Political Economy and the Response to Socialism," 567.

18. See, for example, the Ten Hours Act of 1847, the Employers' Liability Act of 1880, the Trade Boards Act of 1909, and the Coal Mines Act of 1912.

19. See John Lovell, "1889—Socialism and New Unionism," in *British Trade Unions: 1875–1933* (London: Palgrave Macmillan, 1977). Soldon identifies the London dock strike as a turning point. See Soldon, "Laissez-Faire as Dogma," 222.

20. Mason, "Political Economy and the Response to Socialism," 567.

21. Edward Dicey, "The Plea of a Malcontent Liberal," *Fortnightly* 37, no. 226 (1885): 467.

22. The title of two essays in Herbert Spencer, *The Man versus the State* (1884; Indianapolis: Liberty Fund, 1981).

23. We will discuss this shift in Spencer's thinking extensively in chapter 3.

24. Mark Francis writes, unsympathetically, that "Spencer's thought underwent another major change in the 1880s and he eventually did become an advocate of *laissez-faire*, though this was only in direct reaction to socialism and has little value as theory" ("Herbert Spencer and the Myth of Laissez-Faire," *Journal of the History of Ideas* 39, no. 2 [1978]: 327–28).

25. The term "individualist" (and the French equivalent *individualiste*) has a long and fascinating history in nineteenth-century political thought. Like many political labels, it appears to have originated as a term of opprobrium. See, for a history, Steven Lukes, *Individualism* (Colchester: ECPR Press, 1973). In the context of the LPDL, W. C. Crofts (the cousin of Wordsworth Donisthorpe and first secretary of the League) claimed responsibility for introducing the term into general usage in 1883. See Bristow, "The Liberty and Property Defense League and Individualism," 761.

26. Bristow cites Beatrice Webb, who described the LPDL as part of a "reaction against [the] empirical socialism" of the second Gladstone administration. See Bristow, "The Liberty and Property Defense League and Individualism," 761. For helpful overviews of the LPDL and its activities, see Soldon, "Laissez-Faire as Dogma."

27. Thomas Mackay, ed., *A Plea for Liberty: An Argument against Socialism and Socialistic Legislation* (1891; Indianapolis: Liberty Classics, 1981).

28. The quoted passage comes from the back matter of a pamphlet published and distributed by the League containing the text of a speech by Lord Bramwell, "Laissez-Faire" (London: Liberty and Property Defense League, 1884).

29. Ibid.

30. Ibid.

31. On the connection between the League and the alcohol industry, see Bristow, "The Liberty and Property Defense League and Individualism," 766. One battle in which the League involved itself was a bill that sought to make paying wages in public houses illegal. See ibid., 781. See also Lord Bramwell, "Drink," *Nineteenth Century* (May 1885): 878–82, a spirted celebration of the pleasures of alcoholic indulgence.

32. *Echo*, July 6, 1882, cited in Soldon, "Laissez-Faire as Dogma," 213.

33. The American libertarian Lysander Spooner had a different and much more · radical take on the Irish land situation. See Spooner, "Revolution: The Only Remedy for the Oppressed Classes of Ireland, England, and Other Parts of the British Empire. A Reply to 'Dunraven,'" in *The Collected Works of Lysander Spooner* (Indianapolis: Liberty Fund, 1880), 5:124–33. See also chapter 3 of this book.

34. Wordsworth Donisthorpe, "William Carr Crofts," *Personal Rights: A Monthly Journal of Freedom and Justice*, no. 150 (December 1894): 80.

35. Wordsworth Donisthorpe, "'Jus' and the League," *Jus: A Weekly Organ of Individualism* 2, no. 64 (March 23, 1888): 9.

36. Italics in original. This wording is taken from the back matter of one of the PRA's publications, *A Symposium on the Land Question*, edited by J. H. Levy and published in 1890 by T. Fisher Unwin.

37. See Mason, "Political Economy and the Response to Socialism," 571. See also Ryley, *Making Another World Possible*, chap. 3.

38. See A. Goff and J. H. Levy, *Politics and Disease* (London: P. S. King & Son, 1906). The PRA objected, of course, to the compulsory clause of the British Vaccination Act. But they also rejected the scientific validity of vaccination as a medical procedure. They therefore never truly grappled with the challenging question of whether mandatory vaccination might be justifiable if it really *were* effective at preventing the spread of deadly and contagious diseases.

39. J. H. Levy, *The Outcome of Individualism*, 3rd ed. (London: P. S. King & Son, 1892), 41.

40. See the collection of articles published by W. C. Crofts, *Municipal Socialism* (London: Liberty & Property Defence League, 1885).

41. See Orford Northcote, "Egoism: The Sole Basis of Ethics," *Free Review* (1897): 344–55; and A. S. Pringle-Pattison, "The Life and Philosophy of Herbert Spencer," *Quarterly Review* 200 (1904): 240–67. *The Eagle and the Serpent: A Journal of Egoistic Philosophy and Sociology* was the premier publication of this new individualism.

42. Helpful overviews of this tradition can be found in David M. Hart, "The Paris School of Liberal Political Economy," in *The Cambridge History of French Thought*, 1st ed., ed. Michael Moriarty and Jeremy Jennings (New York: Cambridge University Press, 2019), 301–12, https://doi.org/10.1017/9781316681572.036; and Leonard P. Liggio, "Bastiat and the French School of Laissez-Faire," *Journal des Economistes et des Etudes Humaines* 11, no. 2 (2001): 495–506, https://doi.org/10.2202/1145-6396 .1029. Robert Leroux and David Hart's *French Liberalism in the 19th Century: An Anthology* (New York: Routledge, 2012) provides a useful selection of primary source material from the era. More focused treatments of the work of Bastiat can be found in Robert Leroux, *Political Economy and Liberalism in France: The Contributions*

of Frédéric Bastiat (New York: Routledge, 2011); and Dean Russell, *Frederic Bastiat: Ideas and Influence* (Irvington-on-Hudson, NY: Foundation for Economic Education, 1969).

43. See Hart, "The Paris School," 301.

44. Jean-Baptiste Say, *A Treatise on Political Economy, or, The Production, Distribution, and Consumption of Wealth*, trans. C. R. Prinsep (New York: Augustus M. Kelley, 1964), book 1, chap. 1.

45. See Russell, *Frederic Bastiat: Ideas and Influence*; and George Charles Roche, *Frederic Bastiat: A Man Alone* (New Rochelle, NY: Arlington House, 1971) for biographical details.

46. Roche, *Frederic Bastiat: A Man Alone*, 51.

47. Frédéric Bastiat, "Petition by the Manufacturers of Candles, Etc.," in *Economic Sophisms and "What Is Seen and What Is Not Seen,"* ed. Jacques de Guenin (Indianapolis: Liberty Fund, 2017).

48. See chapter 8 for more on Cobden.

49. See, for discussion, Russell, *Frederic Bastiat: Ideas and Influence*, chap. 3.

50. Cited in Roche, *Frederic Bastiat: A Man Alone*, 58.

51. Cited in Russell, *Frederic Bastiat: Ideas and Influence*, 83.

52. Bastiat's output during the last year of his life is astonishing. In addition to "The Law" (written over the course of a few days in Mugron), Bastiat wrote his main positive treatise of economics, *Economic Harmonies*, and one of his most enduring essays, "What Is Seen and What Is Not Seen," in *Selected Essays on Political Economy*, ed. George B. de Huszar (Irvington-on-Hudson, NY: Foundation for Economic Education, 1995).

53. See our discussion of the "moral parity thesis" in chapter 1.

54. Bastiat, "The Law," 107.

55. Cited in Russell, *Frederic Bastiat: Ideas and Influence*, 116.

56. See Bastiat, "The Law," especially 115–19.

57. Frédéric Bastiat, "The State," in *"The Law," "The State," and Other Political Writings: 1843–1850*, ed. Jacques de Guenin (Indianapolis: Liberty Fund, 2012), 93.

58. See Frédéric Bastiat, "Individualism and Fraternity" (1848), in *"The Law," "The State," and Other Political Writings: 1843–1850*, ed. Jacques de Guenin (Indianapolis: Liberty Fund, 2012).

59. See Frédéric Bastiat, "Property and Law" (1850), in *"The Law," "The State," and Other Political Writings: 1843–1850*, ed. Jacques de Guenin (Indianapolis: Liberty Fund, 2012).

60. The 1849–50 debate between Bastiat and Proudhon on interest is available online at https://praxeology.net/FB-PJP-DOI.htm.

61. See Russell, *Frederic Bastiat: Ideas and Influence*, 108.

62. We will see Molinari's radicalism on full display when we turn to analysis of his most famous essay, "The Production of Security," in chapter 4. The contemporary description of Molinari can be found in John Rosén and Th[eodor] Westrin, "Molinari, Gustave de," encyclopedia entry in *Nordisk Familjebok: Konversationslexikon Och Realencyklopedi Innehållande Upplysningar Och Förklaringar Om Märkvärdiga*

Namn, Föremål Och Begrepp (Stockholm: Gernandts boktryckeri-aktiebolag, 1887), columns 208–9. See https://praxeology.net/Encyclopedia_entries_for_Gustave_de _Molinari.pdf.

63. "Property derives from a natural instinct with which the whole human species is endowed. This instinct reveals to man, prior to any reflection, that he is master of his own person and may use as he chooses all the potential attributes constituting his person, whether they remain part of him, or he has in fact separated himself from them" (Gustave de Molinari, *Les soirées de la rue Saint-Lazare (1849)* | *Online Library of Liberty* [Paris: Guillaumin, 1849], https://oll.libertyfund.org/title/molinari-les -soirees-de-la-rue-saint-lazare-1849, First Evening). Like Bastiat, and unlike many of the British libertarians of his day who tended to ground property on utilitarian concerns, Molinari's account of property is grounded in a quasi-Lockean theory of natural law and self-ownership. His account drew particular inspiration from the writings of Louis Leclerc, who develops a kind of labor-mixing account of property in considerably more detail than Locke. See Gustave de Molinari, "Some Simple Observations on the Rights of Property," *Journal des Économistes*, October 15, 1848.

64. Molinari, like Herbert Spencer, saw war and militarism as essentially vestiges of an earlier, more primitive form of society; they had been rendered largely irrelevant by the advent of industrial society and could perhaps be eliminated altogether if the freedom of the individual would continue to expand and the power of their governments to contract. See his *The Society of Tomorrow: A Forecast of Its Political and Economic Organization* (1899), trans. P. H. Lee Warner (New York: G. P. Putnam's Sons, 1904).

65. See David M. Hart, "Gustave de Molinari and the Future of Liberty: 'Fin de Siècle, Fin de la Liberté'?" (paper presented at the Australian Historical Association, University of Adelaide, July 2000), http://davidmhart.com/liberty/Papers/Molinari /FutureLiberty/GdM-FutureLiberty.html.

66. David M. Hart, "Gustave de Molinari (1819–1912): An Annotated Bibliography," Online Library of Liberty, n.d., https://oll.libertyfund.org/page/gustave-de -molinari-1819-1912-an-annotated-bibliography-by-david-hart.

67. The libertarian Cato Institute derives its name from *Cato's Letters*, not from the Roman statesman.

68. On the philosophical background to Jefferson's Declaration, see Smith, *The System of Liberty*, chap. 6.

69. See Wendy McElroy, *The Debates of Liberty: An Overview of Individualist Anarchism, 1881–1908* (New York: Lexington Books, 2003), 6. "For the most part, [the British Individualists] advocated limited government and, like their mentor, Auberon Herbert, they shied away from Anarchism. The labor theory of value, so integral to *Liberty*'s philosophy, was not widely accepted among the British Individualists. Nor was Stirnerite egoism."

70. For an overview, see Ryley, *Making Another World Possible*, chap. 4.

71. On the relationship between abolitionism and the libertarian and anarchist movements of late nineteenth-century America, see Lewis Perry, *Radical Abolitionism: Anarchy and the Government of God in Antislavery Thought* (Ithaca: Cornell

University Press, 1973); and Carl Watner, "The Radical Libertarian Tradition in Anti-slavery Thought," *Journal of Libertarian Studies* 3, no. 3 (1979): 299–329. See also James J. Martin, *Men against the State: The Expositors of Individualist Anarchism in America, 1827–1908* (DeKalb, IL: Adrian Allen Associates, 1953), especially chaps. 3–4; and William O. Reichert, *Partisans of Freedom: A Study in American Freedom* (Bowling Green, OH: Bowling Green University Popular Press, 1976), especially chap. 2.

72. Frank H. Brooks, *The Individualist Anarchists: An Anthology of Liberty (1881–1908)* (New Brunswick, NJ: Transaction Publishers, 1994) contains a selection of many of the most important essays from *Liberty*, organized topically; McElroy, *Debates* provides an extremely helpful overview of *Liberty*, its historical context, and many of the most important debates that raged within its pages. Discussions that place *Liberty* in the context of the broader American anarchist movement can be found in Reichert, *Partisans of Freedom*, and Martin, *Men against the State*.

73. McElroy, *Debates*, 3–4.

74. See Spooner, "Natural Law, or, The Science of Justice." See also chapter 4 of this book for further discussion.

75. The lines between the Spencerians and the natural rights theorists were blurry, as most of their energies were devoted to waging a united fight against egoism rather than to exploring the subtler differences between their respective creeds. Yarros himself embraced egoism for a time, before converting back to Spencerianism and, ultimately, to a political theory that rejected libertarianism altogether in favor of a form of social democracy. On the conversion from egoism to natural rights, see *Liberty* 8 (September 26, 1891). On the conversion to social democracy, see Victor S. Yarros, *Adventures in the Realm of Ideas: And Other Essays in the Fields of Philosophy, Science, Political Economy, Theology, Humanism, Semantics, Agnosticism, Immortality and Related Subjects* (Haldeman-Julius, 1947), chaps. 1 and 19.

76. See McElroy, *Debates*, 53. Rand's egoism, in contrast, took the form of a more familiar universal claim, holding that *each* individual's life constituted an objective standard of value for him or her. She strongly denied that "might makes right" and held that egoism was fully compatible with the recognition of universal natural rights. For a helpful brief overview, see David D'Amato, "Egoism in Rand and Stirner," *Libertarianism.org*, March 11, 2014, https://www.libertarianism.org/columns/egoism-rand-stirner.

77. One of the most persistent and provocative proponents of egoism in the pages of *Liberty* was James L. Walker, who wrote under the pseudonym Tak Kak. In one article titled "Killing Chinese," Walker argued against the proponent of natural rights Gertrude B. Kelly that Chinese workers who had been mistreated by American whites were "fitted by nature and heredity to remain a slave" and that Kelly's objection was based on the false idea that "all men are brothers." *Liberty* 3, no. 25 (March 6, 1886): 8.

78. Ibid.

79. See Benjamin Tucker, "Anarchism and the Children," *Liberty* 10, no. 26 (May 4, 1895): 5, 8, and "A Sound Criticism," *Liberty* 11, no. 4 (June 29, 1895): 3. For an overview of the debate on the rights of children, see McElroy, *Debates*, chap. 5. Tucker's

position on the rights of children contrasts sharply with the position set forth by Herbert Spencer in *Social Statics*. Spencer held that the rights of the child are completely "co-extensive with those of the adult" (*Social Statics*, 154).

80. Benjamin Tucker, "The Sin of Herbert Spencer," *Liberty* 2, no. 16 (May 17, 1884): 4–5.

81. These biographical details are taken from Burns, *Goddess of the Market*, 9, 21. Burns notes that "contrary to legend, Rand did not name herself after the Remington-Rand typewriter. . . . In a letter to a fan, she wrote, 'I must say that "Ayn" is both a real name and an invention,' and she identified that her first name was inspired by a Finnish writer (whom she declined to identify) and her last an abbreviation of Rosenbaum" (301). For another biography of Rand, see Anne C. Heller, *Ayn Rand and the World She Made* (New York: Doubleday, 2009).

82. Burns, *Goddess of the Market*, 32.

83. Cited in ibid., 59; full text at http://fare.tunes.org/liberty/library/taifc.html.

84. Burns, *Goddess of the Market*, 124–25.

85. Ibid., 34.

86. See Amity Shlaes, *The Forgotten Man: A New History of the Great Depression* (New York: Harper Collins, 2009), chap. 2. On Duranty, see Anne Applebaum, *Red Famine: Stalin's War on the Ukraine* (New York: Knopf Doubleday, 2017), chap. 14.

87. See Burns, *Goddess of the Market*, 67.

88. Ibid., 73.

89. Ibid., 78.

90. Lane was essentially a coauthor of the *Little House* books and "wove her libertarianism delicately throughout the nostalgic books, filling her fictional Fourth of July orations with musings on freedom and limited government and excising from her mother's past examples of state charity." Burns, *Goddess of the Market*, 119.

91. See Jennifer Burns, "The Three 'Furies' of Libertarianism: Rose Wilder Lane, Isabel Paterson, and Ayn Rand," *Journal of American History* 102, no. 3 (2015): 746–74, https://doi.org/10.1093/jahist/jav504. See also Doherty, *Radicals for Capitalism*, chap. 3.

92. See, for discussion, Doherty, *Radicals for Capitalism*, chap. 4.

93. Ibid., 1626. Hazlitt, an economic journalist, was one of the cofounders of FEE. His *Economics in One Lesson* was heavily indebted to Bastiat's essay "What Is Seen and What Is Not Seen."

94. For a relatively concise overview of Mises's economic thought, see Israel M. Kirzner, *Ludwig von Mises: The Man and His Economics* (Wilmington, DE: ISI Books, 2001).

95. Ludwig von Mises, *Bureaucracy* (Indianapolis: Liberty Fund, 2007), 10.

96. See Janek Wasserman's excellent history of the Austrian school, *Marginal Revolutionaries*, 128.

97. Bruce Caldwell, "*The Road to Serfdom* after 75 Years," *Journal of Economic Literature* 58, no. 3 (2020): 720–48, https://doi.org/10.1257/jel.20191542.

98. Hayek, *The Road to Serfdom*, 71.

99. Friedrich A. Hayek, *The Fatal Conceit: The Errors of Socialism*, ed. W. W. Bartley III (London: Routledge, 1988), 7.

100. For an overview of Hayek's life and ideas, see Bruce Caldwell, *Hayek's Challenge: An Intellectual Biography of F. A. Hayek* (Chicago: University of Chicago Press, 2004).

101. For helpful histories of the Mont Pelerin Society, see Ronald Max Hartwell, *A History of the Mont Pelerin Society* (Indianapolis: Liberty Fund, 1995); Burgin, *The Great Persuasion*; and Slobodian, *Globalists*.

102. Milton Friedman and Rose D. Friedman, *Two Lucky People: Memoirs* (Chicago: University of Chicago Press, 1998), 161.

103. Milton Friedman and George Stigler, "Roofs or Ceilings? The Current Housing Problem" (Irvington-on-Hudson, NY: Foundation for Economic Education, 1946).

104. Cited in Burns, *Goddess of the Market*, 117.

105. Ayn Rand, *Letters of Ayn Rand*, ed. Michael Berliner (New York: Penguin, 1995), 327.

106. Ibid., 320.

107. See Murray N. Rothbard, "What's Wrong with the Liberty Poll, or, How I Became a Libertarian," *Liberty* (July 1988): 55.

108. See Rothbard, *For a New Liberty*, 15–16.

109. Stan Lehr and Louis Rossetto Jr., "The New Right Credo—Libertarianism," *New York Times*, January 10, 1971.

110. See Doherty, *Radicals for Capitalism*, 251.

111. Ralph Raico, "How Nozick Became a Libertarian," *LewRockwell.com* (blog), February 5, 2002, https://www.lewrockwell.com/2002/02/ralph-raico/how-nozick-became-a-libertarian/.

112. Nozick, *Anarchy, State, and Utopia*, xv.

113. As George Will quipped in a memorial for George Stigler, "The Cold War is over, and the University of Chicago won it," https://www.washingtonpost.com/archive/opinions/1991/12/08/passing-of-a-prophet/c69252cc-2db9-486a-8bfc-f90a72ccfa93/.

114. Llewelyn Rockwell Jr., "The Case for Paleo-Libertarianism," *Liberty* 3, no. 3 (January 1990): 34–38.

115. Murray N. Rothbard, "Right-Wing Populism: A Strategy for the Paleo Movement," *Rothbard-Rockwell Report* (January 1992): 5–14.

116. See Lomasky, *Persons, Rights, and the Moral Community*; Loren E. Lomasky, "Libertarianism at Twin Harvard," *Social Philosophy and Policy* 22, no. 1 (2005): 178–99, https://doi.org/10.1017/S0265052505041075; David Schmidtz, *Elements of Justice* (Cambridge: Cambridge University Press, 2006); Gerald Gaus, "Liberal Neutrality: A Radical and Compelling Principle," in *Perfectionism and Neutrality*, ed. George Klosko and Steven Wall (Lanham, MD: Rowman and Littlefield, 2003), 137–65; Gerald Gaus, "On Justifying the Moral Rights of the Moderns: Old Wine in New Bottles," *Social Philosophy and Policy* 24, no. 1 (2007): 84–119; and Gaus, "Coercion, Ownership, and the Redistributive State."

117. Brink Lindsey, "Liberaltarians," *New Republic*, December 10, 2006, https://newrepublic.com/article/64443/liberaltarians.

118. Will Wilkinson, "Is Rawlsekianism the Future?" *Cato@Liberty* (blog), December 4, 2006, https://www.cato.org/blog/rawlsekianism-future.

119. Kenny Johnson and Lew Rockwell, "Do You Consider Yourself a Libertarian?" *LewRockwell.com* (blog), May 25, 2007, https://www.lewrockwell.com/2007/05/lew-rockwell/do-you-consider-yourself-a-libertarian.

Chapter 3. Land, Labor, and Ownership: The Right of Private Property

1. Aristotle, *Politics* 1254b20, quoted in Francisco de Vitoria, *Vitoria: Political Writings*, ed. Anthony Pagden and Jeremy Lawrance (Cambridge: Cambridge University Press, 1991), 239.

2. *Democrates Segundo o De Las Justas causas de la Guerra contra los Indios*, cited in Brian Tierney, *The Idea of Natural Rights*, Emory University Studies in Law and Religion (Grand Rapids, MI: Eerdmans, 1997), 273.

3. De Vitoria, *Vitoria: Political Writings*, 350.

4. Francisco de Vitoria, *The Rights and Obligations of Indians and Spaniards in the New World*, reconstructed by Luciano Pereña Vicente (Universidad Pontifica de Salamanca, 1991), 17.

5. De Vitoria, *Vitoria: Political Writings*, 251.

6. Ibid.

7. Ibid., 291.

8. See Tierney, *The Idea of Natural Rights*, 86.

9. It is because they regarded the right of self-ownership as a reflection of our essential nature as human beings that the Scholastics, and libertarians like Murray Rothbard who followed in their footsteps, regarded this right as *inalienable*. See more on this below. For discussion of this little-appreciated aspect of libertarian thought and some of its practical implications, see Williamson M. Evers, "Toward a Reformulation of the Law of Contracts," *Journal of Libertarian Studies* 1, no. 1 (1977): 3–13; Murray Rothbard, "Property Rights and the Theory of Contract," in *The Ethics of Liberty* (Atlantic Highlands, NJ: Humanities Press, 1982); and Randy E. Barnett, "Contract Remedies and Inalienable Rights*," *Social Philosophy and Policy* 4, no. 1 (1986): 179–202, https://doi.org/10.1017/S0265052500000479.

10. Vitoria himself, of course, was not a libertarian. Our claim, rather, is that he played an important role in articulating and developing the concept of self-ownership that would later play a central role in libertarian thought. Still, the concept of self-ownership was not the only libertarian (or proto-libertarian) element to be found in the writings of Vitoria and the other Spanish Scholastics. The Spanish Scholastics developed libertarian ideas not only in political philosophy but in economics as well. Juan de Medina, for instance, advanced the long-stagnant debate over usury by allowing that interest on loans could be legitimate if charged as compensation for risk of nonpayment,

and Martin de Azpilcueta Navarrus, a student of Vitoria's, opposed government price-fixing and defended a conception of the just price as the common market price. This view on the market price as just was bolstered by the "proto-Austrian" defense of a subjectivist theory of market value articulated and defended by Luis Saravía de la Calle, Diego de Covarrubias y Leiva, and Francisco García, among others. These libertarian elements of Spanish Scholasticism were famously and approvingly noted by Murray Rothbard in his *Economic Thought before Adam Smith*, and earlier in his "New Light on the Prehistory of the Austrian School," in *The Foundations of Modern Austrian Economics*, ed. Edwin Dolan (Kansas City, MO: Sheed and Ward, 1976), 52–74, both of which drew heavily on Marjorie Grice-Hutchinson's earlier work, *The School of Salamanca: Readings in Spanish Monetary Theory, 1544–1605* (Oxford: Clarendon Press, 1952). See also Jesús Huerta de Soto, "Juan de Mariana: The Influence of the Spanish Scholastics," in *15 Great Austrian Economists*, ed. Randall G. Holcombe (Auburn, AL: Ludwig von Mises Institute, 1999); Leonard P. Liggio, "The Heritage of the Spanish Scholastics," *Religion and Liberty* 10, no. 1 (2010), https://www.acton.org/pub/religion-liberty/volume-10-number-1/heritage-spanish-scholastics; and Carl Watner, "'All Mankind Is One': The Libertarian Tradition in Sixteenth Century Spain," *Journal of Libertarian Studies* 8, no. 2 (1987): 293–309.

11. Josiah Warren, *Equitable Commerce: A New Development of Principles* (New York: Fowlers and Wells, 1852), 26. Mill refers in his autobiography to "a remarkable American, Mr. Warren, [who] had framed a System of Society, on the foundation of 'the Sovereignty of the Individual,'" and acknowledges that his use of that phrase in his own *On Liberty* was borrowed from "the Warrenites" (John Stuart Mill, *Autobiography* [New York: Henry Holt and Company, 1874], 256).

12. Josiah Warren, *Practical Details in Equitable Commerce* (New York: Fowlers and Wells, 1852), 13.

13. Herbert, "The Principles of Voluntaryism and Free Life," 370–71.

14. Locke's famous invocation of self-ownership was preceded by several others in the English radical tradition, most notably in a letter written by the English Leveller Richard Overton, *An Arrow against All Tyrants* (Surrey: Canbury Press Limited, 2020). In Overton's words: "To every individual in nature is given an individual property by nature not to be invaded or usurped by any. For every one, as he is himself, so he has a self-propriety, else could he not *be* himself; and of this no second may presume to deprive any of without manifest violation and affront to the very principles of nature and of the rules of equity and justice between man and man. Mine and thine cannot be, except this be. No man has power over my rights and liberties, and I over no man's."

15. The role of self-ownership in Nozick's thought has been overstated by most political philosophers. It is often thought that self-ownership is the foundational concept of Nozick's argument for a libertarian minimal state. Yet the phrase "self-ownership" appears only *once* in his 367-page book. The section of the book where Nozick articulates the moral foundation of individual rights focuses not on self-ownership but on the *Kantian* principle of treating persons as ends in themselves, and never as a mere means. The real source of the supposed centrality of

self-ownership to Nozick's thought seems not to have been Nozick himself but his most famous *critic*—the Marxist philosopher G. A. Cohen. In *Self-Ownership, Freedom, and Equality* (Cambridge: Cambridge University Press, 1995), https://doi.org /10.1017/CBO9780511521270, Cohen presented one of the most influential attacks on libertarianism ever published. In contrast to Nozick, Cohen uses the phrase "self-ownership" over *six hundred times* in his book and makes almost no mention of Nozick's Kantian moral principles. For a helpful overview, see Eric Mack, "Robert Nozick's Political Philosophy," in *The Stanford Encyclopedia of Philosophy*, April 21, 2022, https://plato.stanford.edu/entries/nozick-political.

16. Auberon Herbert and J. H. Levy, *Taxation and Anarchism* (London: Personal Rights Association, 1912), essay VII. Rothbard would offer a similar argument for self-ownership in chapter 6 of *The Ethics of Liberty*. And Herbert's emphasis on "separate" minds and bodies is strikingly similar to the language used by Nozick in his argument for libertarian rights, more on which below.

17. Levy, *Taxation and Anarchism*, essay VIII. An even more thorough critique of Herbert's position was set forth by the British Individualist Wordsworth Donisthorpe. See his *Individualism: A System of Politics*, vol. 5 (London: Macmillan, 1889), chap. 5, https://doi.org/10.2307/2139176. Donisthorpe sets forth a series of seven cases in which one individual acquires a ruby from another by various means, and notes that "between any two of these roughly-graduated instances scores of delicate shades of unfairness could be drawn, concerning which it would be impossible for the subtlest casuist to generalize. If this is the case in so simple a matter as acquiring a ruby from its possessor, how can we expect to be able to deduce any general rules as to private morals or State functions from a single principle *a priori*? I regard the attempt as futile; and I hold that only by the experience of generations can any rough, practical working rules be arrived at—that is to say, by a process of careful induction and verification" (388).

18. Rothbard, *For a New Liberty*, 34. A later version of what is essentially the same argument appeared in Rothbard, *The Ethics of Liberty*, chap. 8.

19. See, for a critical discussion, Marian Eabrasu, "Rothbard's and Hoppe's Justifications of Libertarianism: A Critique," *Politics, Philosophy & Economics* 12, no. 3 (2012): 288–307, https://doi.org/10.1177/1470594x12460645.

20. This point traces back to Hohfeld, but Barbara H. Fried deploys it against libertarian theories in "Left-Libertarianism: A Review Essay," *Philosophy and Public Affairs* 32, no. 1 (2004): 66–93.

21. Nozick, *Anarchy, State, and Utopia*, 28–35. For a sophisticated and thorough reconstruction of Nozick's argument, see Mack, *Libertarianism*, 41–55.

22. On the contrast between Rawls's and Nozick's argument, see Matt Zwolinski, "The Separateness of Persons and Liberal Theory," *Journal of Value Inquiry* 42, no. 2 (2008): 147–65, https://doi.org/10.1007/s10790-008-9107-y.

23. Nozick, *Anarchy, State, and Utopia*, 32.

24. Ibid., 33.

25. Ibid., 57.

26. Ibid., 171.

27. Ibid., 331. See also Walter Block, "Toward a Libertarian Theory of Inalienability: A Critique of Rothbard, Barnett, Smith, Kinsella, Gordon, and Epstein," *Journal of Libertarian Studies* 17, no. 2 (2003): 39–85.

28. See Rothbard, *The Ethics of Liberty*, 40–41; Evers, "Toward a Reformulation of the Law of Contracts"; Barnett, "Contract Remedies and Inalienable Rights"; George H. Smith, "Inalienable Rights?" *Liberty* 10, no. 6 (July 1997); Richard Epstein, "A Theory of Strict Liability," *Journal of Legal Studies* 2, no. 1 (1973): 151–204; and N. Stephan Kinsella, "Inalienability and Punishment: A Reply to George Smith," *Journal of Libertarian Studies* 14, no. 1 (1999): 79–94.

29. For an early recognition of this problem, see Friedman, *The Machinery of Freedom*. For responses, see Nozick, *Anarchy, State, and Utopia*, 79–81; Murray N. Rothbard, "Law, Property Rights, and Air Pollution," *Cato Journal* 2, no. 1 (1982): 55–99. For discussion, see Zwolinski, "Libertarianism and Pollution."

30. The claim that socialist redistribution involves slavery is one that most advocates of socialism, of course, deny. But several prominent advocates of redistribution have agreed with libertarians that it requires the denial of full self-ownership. The most famous example is G. A. Cohen's *Self-Ownership, Freedom, and Equality*, especially chapters 9–10. See also Cécile Fabre, *Whose Body Is It Anyway?: Justice and the Integrity of the Person* (Oxford: Oxford University Press, 2006), which argues for the legitimacy of confiscating body parts and personal services for the sake of distributive justice. As we will see in the next section, however, not all theorists who favor redistribution of external property agree that it requires a denial of individual self-ownership.

31. Herbert Spencer, "The Coming Slavery," in *The Man versus the State*, ed. Herbert Spencer (Indianapolis: Liberty Fund, 1981), 56.

32. Nozick, *Anarchy, State, and Utopia*, 172.

33. For an overview of the influence of Locke on nineteenth-century radicals, both libertarian and socialist, see Daniel Layman, *Locke among the Radicals: Liberty and Property in the Nineteenth Century* (New York: Oxford University Press, 2020).

34. Locke, *Second Treatise*, § 27.

35. Nozick, *Anarchy, State, and Utopia*, 175.

36. Lysander Spooner, "Poverty: Its Illegal Causes and Legal Cure. Part First," in *The Collected Works of Lysander Spooner* (Indianapolis: Liberty Fund, 1846), 1:225.

37. See Rothbard, *For a New Liberty*, 41–45.

38. Locke, *Second Treatise*, § 31.

39. See Gopal Sreenivasan, *The Limits of Lockean Rights in Property* (Oxford: Oxford University Press, 1995); James Tully, *A Discourse on Property: John Locke and His Adversaries* (New York: Cambridge University Press, 1980); and C. B. Macpherson, *The Political Theory of Possessive Individualism: Hobbes to Locke* (Oxford: Oxford University Press, 1962). But for an influential dissenting interpretation, see Jeremy Waldron, *The Right to Private Property* (Oxford: Oxford University Press, 1988).

40. Indeed, Spooner explicitly rejects the idea of any proviso on original acquisition, writing that "there is no limit, fixed by the law of nature, to the amount of property one may acquire by simply taking possession of natural wealth, not already

possessed, except the limit fixed by his power," and later that "it cannot be said that the first corner is bound to leave something to supply the wants of the second. This argument would be just as good against the right of the second consumer, the third, the fourth, and so on indefinitely, as it is against the right of the first; for it might, with the same reason, be said of each of these, that he was bound to leave something for those who should come after him" ("The Law of Intellectual Property: An Essay on the Right of Authors and Inventors to a Perpetual Property in Their Ideas" [1855], in *The Collected Works of Lysander Spooner* [Indianapolis: Liberty Fund, 2010], 2:244, 246). For an extremely helpful discussion of Spooner's theory of property rights, see Layman, *Locke among the Radicals*, chap. 3. For Rothbard, see *For a New Liberty*, chap. 2. For another influential libertarian view that rejects the idea of a proviso, see Edward Feser, "There Is No Such Thing as an Unjust Initial Acquisition," *Social Philosophy and Policy* 22, no. 1 (2005): 56–80, https://doi.org/10.1017/S0265052505041038.

41. See, for instance, Eric Mack, "Self-Ownership, Marxism, and Egalitarianism: Part I: Challenges to Historical Entitlement," *Politics, Philosophy & Economics* 1, no. 1 (February 1, 2002): 75–108, https://doi.org/10.1177/1470594X02001001004; Eric Mack, "Self-Ownership, Marxism, and Egalitarianism: Part II: Challenges to the Self-Ownership Thesis," *Politics, Philosophy & Economics* 1, no. 2 (June 1, 2002): 237–76, https://doi.org/10.1177/1470594X02001002004; Jan Narveson, "Property Rights: Original Acquisition and Lockean Provisos," *Public Affairs Quarterly* 13, no. 3 (1999): 205–27; and B. van der Vossen, "What Counts as Original Appropriation?" *Politics, Philosophy & Economics* 8, no. 4 (October 30, 2009): 355–73, https://doi.org/10.1177/1470594X09343074.

42. Tucker, "State Socialism and Anarchism."

43. Nozick, *Anarchy, State, and Utopia*, 153.

44. Ibid., 151.

45. Spencer, *Social Statics*, 104.

46. "The important and yet perhaps trite fact to which I wish by these remarks to direct your attention is, that law and governments are intended, and always have been intended, to establish and protect a right of property, different from that which, in common with Mr. Locke, I say is ordained by nature. The right of property created and protected by the law, is the artificial or legal right of property, as contradistinguished from the natural right of property. It may be the theory that government ought to protect the natural right; in practice, government seems to exist only to violate it. Never has the law employed any means whatever to protect the property nature bestows on individuals; on the contrary, it is a great system of means devised to appropriate in a peculiar and unjust manner the gifts of nature." Thomas Hodgskin, "The Natural and Artificial Right of Property Contrasted" (London: B. Steil, 1832), 32. John Stuart Mill made a similar point in his *Principles of Political Economy*: "The principle of private property has never yet had a fair trial in any country; and less so, perhaps, in this country than in some others. The social arrangements of modern Europe commenced from a distribution of property which was the result, not of a just partition, or acquisition by industry, but of conquest and violence. . . . The

laws of property have never yet conformed to the principles on which the justification of private property rests. They have made property of things which never ought to be property, and absolute property where only a qualified property ought to exist" (book II, chap. 1).

47. Locke, *Second Treatise*, chap. 5, § 40.

48. We will return to this idea in our discussion of libertarian class theory in chapter 5.

49. Hodgskin, "Natural and Artificial," 51–52. For discussion of Hodgskin's theory of property and its relation to the labor theory of value, see Layman, *Locke among the Radicals*, chap. 2. See also David Stack, *Nature and Artifice: The Life and Thought of Thomas Hodgskin (1787–1869)* (Woodbridge: Boydell & Brewer, 1998); and Alberto Mingardi, *Classical Liberalism and the Industrial Working Class: The Economic Thought of Thomas Hodgskin* (New York: Routledge, 2020).

50. See Hodgskin, *Labour Defended against the Claims of Capital*.

51. See John Edward King, "Utopian or Scientific? A Reconsideration of the Ricardian Socialists," *History of Political Economy* 15, no. 3 (1983): 345–73.

52. See, for an overview, McElroy, *Debates*, chap. 8.

53. We will discuss libertarian views on intellectual property rights in the next section.

54. Lysander Spooner had a similar view of the relationship between the banking monopoly and wage labor. See his "Poverty." Not all of the writers for *Liberty* agreed with Tucker's economic analysis. See, in particular, McElroy's discussion of the debate between Benjamin Tucker and J. Greevz Fisher (*Debates*, 140–46). For a critical analysis by a twentieth-century libertarian, see Murray Rothbard, "The Spooner-Tucker Doctrine: An Economist's View," *Journal of Libertarian Studies* 20, no. 1 (2006): 5–15.

55. One notable exception is the left-libertarian Kevin Carson, who attempts to rehabilitate the labor theory of value in his *Studies in Mutualist Political Economy* (Kevin A. Carson, 2007).

56. Despite, or perhaps because of, his significant influence, George's ideas were widely and sharply criticized within the libertarian movement of his day. Benjamin Tucker, as we shall shortly see, disagreed with George about the basis of property, though the main source of his antagonism seems to have been George's refusal to use his prominence to call for clemency for those arrested during the Haymarket incident of May 4, 1886. See Benjamin Tucker, "Henry George, Traitor," *Liberty* 12, no. 9 (November 1896): 4. J. H. Levy, in contrast, held like George that because land is not the product of man's labor, "private property in land—apart from improvements—is essentially incompatible with individualism." Nevertheless, Levy sought to distance himself from George, primarily because Levy believed that innocent landowners would deserve compensation for the nationalization of their land, a position with which George persistently and vehemently disagreed. See Levy, *A Symposium on the Land Question*, 66, 77–78.

57. George Smith summarizes and assesses the debate between Spencer and George on this issue in a series of essays at his "Excursions" blog, beginning here:

https://www.libertarianism.org/publications/essays/excursions/herbert-spencer
-henry-george-land-question-part-1.

58. Henry George, *Progress and Poverty* (New York: D. Appleton, 1886), book VII, chap. 1, 306.

59. Ibid., book III, chap. 2.

60. George also defines rent as "the share of wealth given to landowners because they have an exclusive right to the use of those natural capabilities" (ibid.).

61. Thomas Spence, "The Real Rights of Man," in *The Origins of Left-Libertarianism: An Anthology of Historical Writings*, ed. Peter Vallentyne and Hillel Steiner (New York: Palgrave, 2000), 71–79.

62. Spencer, *Social Statics*, 108.

63. Ibid., 111, 116. For a contemporary and broadly Lockean libertarian critique of Spencer's argument, see the review by Thomas Hodgskin, Spencer's colleague at *The Economist* magazine: "Review of Herbert Spencer's *Social Statics*," *The Economist*, February 1851.

64. Also deleted were a famous chapter on "the right to ignore the state" and a prescient defense of women's suffrage. For more on the latter, see chapter 4 of this book.

65. Herbert Spencer, *The Principles of Ethics*, vol. 2 (Indianapolis: Liberty Fund, 1978), 101–9.

66. Ibid., 2:460.

67. Letter to James A. Skilton, January 6, 1893, reprinted in David Duncan and Herbert Spencer, *The Life and Letters of Herbert Spencer* (London: Methuen, 1908).

68. Spencer refused to join on the grounds that "it would be politic neither for the League nor myself that I should join it. Rightly or wrongly it has acquired the repute of a Tory organization" (ibid., 323). But the League certainly regarded Spencer as one of its intellectual guiding lights, reprinting and publishing his works in various venues such as its 1891 edited collection, *A Plea for Liberty*. And Spencer, while not a member of the League, supported it both "spiritually and financially." See Mackay, *A Plea for Liberty*, xvi.

69. Henry George, *A Perplexed Philosopher: Being an Examination of Mr. Herbert Spencer's Various Utterances on the Land Question, With Some Incidental Reference to His Synthetic Philosophy* (New York: Charles L. Webster & Company, 1892), chap. 8.

70. Ibid., 92.

71. See Albert Jay Nock, "Henry George: Unorthodox American," *The Freeman*, October 1938; and Steiner, *An Essay on Rights*. On geo-libertarianism, see Fred E. Foldvary, "Geo-Rent: A Plea to Public Economists," *Econ Journal Watch* 2, no. 1 (2005): 106–32.

72. On Tucker's rejection of natural rights, see McElroy, *Debates*, chap. 4, which covers the debate between advocates of Stirnerian egoism and advocates of natural rights in Tucker's periodical.

73. Benjamin Tucker, "The Land for the People," *Liberty* 1, no. 23 (June 24, 1882). See, for a sympathetic discussion, Carson, *Studies in Mutualist Political Economy*, chap. 5.

74. Spencer is explicit in claiming that intellectual property is a matter of justice, and not mere expediency or "trade policy." See *Social Statics*, 123.

75. Ibid., 122, emphasis in original. Spencer's main discussions of intellectual property can be found in chapter 11 of *Social Statics* ("The Right of Property in Ideas") and part IV, chapter 13 of *The Principles of Ethics*, vol. 2 ("The Right of Incorporeal Property").

76. Spencer, *The Principles of Ethics*, 2:126.

77. Ibid., 2:125–26. Spencer makes this argument with respect to the sort of creative works covered by copyright laws but notes that in the case of inventions covered by patents, the possibility arises that different individuals might make the same discovery independently. This, he thinks, justifies limiting patents to a temporary term. See Spencer, *Social Statics*, 127–28, and *The Principles of Ethics*, 2:129.

78. Spencer responds to this objection, rather unconvincingly, by saying that one person's use of an idea that another has discovered deprives the discoverer of the ability to *profit* from that idea. *The Principles of Ethics*, 2:122.

79. Spooner, "The Law of Intellectual Property," 249.

80. Ibid., 253.

81. Ibid., 348.

82. Victor Yarros defended intellectual property rights throughout the debate, adhering to a largely Spencerian understanding of their justification. See, for an overview of the debate, McElroy, *Debates*, chap. 6.

83. The line is from Tucker's memorial to Spooner, written after the latter's death on May 14, 1887. Benjamin Tucker, "Our Nestor Taken from Us," *Liberty* 4, no. 22 (May 28, 1887).

84. Tucker, "State Socialism and Anarchism," 3.

85. Benjamin Tucker, "More on Copyright," *Liberty* 7, no. 21 (February 7, 1891).

86. Benjamin Tucker, "The Attitude of Anarchism toward Industrial Combinations" (lecture delivered at the Conference on Trusts of the Chicago Civic Federation), September 14, 1899, https://praxeology.net/BT-AIC.htm.

87. Henry George, "Copyright Law," *The Standard*, June 23, 1888.

88. Benjamin Tucker, "Ergo and Presto!" *Liberty* 5, no. 24 (July 7, 1888).

89. See Ayn Rand, "Patents and Copyrights," in *Capitalism: The Unknown Ideal* (New York: New American Library, 1967), 141–45; Rothbard, *Man, Economy and State*, 652–60; Tom G. Palmer, "Are Patents and Copyrights Morally Justified: The Philosophy of Property Rights and Ideal Objects," *Harvard Journal of Law and Public Policy* 13 (1990): 817; N. Stephan Kinsella, *Against Intellectual Property* (Auburn, AL: Ludwig von Mises Institute, 2008); and Roderick T. Long, "The Libertarian Case against Intellectual Property Rights," in *Markets Not Capitalism: Individualist Anarchism against Bosses, Inequality, Corporate Power, and Structural Poverty*, ed. Gary Chartier and Charles Johnson (New York: Autonomedia, 2012), 187–98.

90. See Mises, *Human Action*; and Friedman, *Capitalism and Freedom*, 127–28. Hayek was somewhat more ambivalent, warning that "a slavish application of the concept of property as it has been developed for material things has done a great deal to foster the growth of monopoly and . . . here drastic reforms may be required

if competition is to be made to work." See Friedrich A. Hayek, *Individualism and Economic Order* (London: Routledge and Kegan Paul, 1949), 113–14.

91. See David Hume, *A Treatise of Human Nature*, ed. David Fate Norton and Mary Norton (New York: Oxford University Press, 2000), book III, part I, section II, "Of the Origin of Justice and Property." John Rawls would later famously describe these conditions as the "circumstances of justice" (*A Theory of Justice*, 126).

92. William Paley, *The Principles of Moral and Political Philosophy* (Indianapolis: Liberty Fund, 2002).

93. Garret Hardin, "The Tragedy of the Commons," *Science* 162, no. 3859 (1968): 1243–48. While the phrase was his, Hardin was not the first to identify the phenomenon. Indeed, Aristotle writes in book II of his *Politics*: "What is held in common by the largest number of people receives the least care. For people give most attention to their own property, less to what is communal, or only as much as falls to them to give. For apart from anything else, the thought that someone else is attending to it makes them neglect it the more." Aristotle, *Politics*, trans. C.D.C. Reeve (Indianapolis: Hackett, 1998), 28–29. Similarly, Aquinas writes that "man is more careful to procure what is for himself alone than that which is common to many or to all: since each one would shirk the labor and leave to another that which concerns the community, as happens where there is a great number of servants." Thomas Aquinas, *Summa Theologica* (London: R. T. Washbourne, 1918), 224. So too in Thomas Malthus's critique of Godwin, where Malthus writes that, without private property, "every man would be obliged to guard with force his little store. Selfishness would be triumphant. The subjects of contention would be perpetual. Every individual would be under a constant anxiety about corporal support, and not a single intellect would be left free to expatiate in the field of thought," and argues that in order to rectify this situation, individuals would call a kind of convention in which they would agree to "make a more complete division of land, and to secure every man's property against violation by the most powerful sanctions." Thomas Malthus, *An Essay on the Principle of Population*, 6th ed., vol. 2 (London: John Murray, 1826), 21, 30.

94. John Curl, *For All the People: Uncovering the Hidden History of Cooperation, Cooperative Movements, and Communalism in America* (Oakland, CA: PM Press, 2009), 20–21.

95. William Bradford, *Of Plymouth Plantation: 1620–1647*, ed. Samuel Eliot Morison (New Brunswick, NJ: Rutgers University Press, 1952), 121.

96. Ibid., 120.

97. Sometimes *communal* property can be a more appropriate solution. And sometimes communities can overcome the tragedy of the commons through informal systems of social norms. See Ostrom, *Governing the Commons*; and Schmidtz, "The Institution of Property."

98. Hume, *A Treatise of Human Nature*, 314.

99. Ibid., 315.

100. Hume gives all three of these examples himself. The latter two would go on to be invoked often in libertarian discussions of spontaneous order. Friedrich Hayek, for instance, would frequently refer to language in his discussions of the subject.

See Hayek, *Law, Legislation, and Liberty*, vol. 1, *Rules and Order*. And Carl Menger would, in 1871, provide an especially influential spontaneous-order account of the origins of money. See Carl Menger, *Principles of Economics* (New York: New York University Press, 1976), chap. 8.

101. Besides Hayek, one of the most prominent libertarians writing in this tradition is James Buchanan. For his Humean discussion of the origin of property, see Buchanan, *The Limits of Liberty*, 12–15.

102. Schmidtz, "The Institution of Property."

103. This latter point is often taken to be the most original contribution of Schmidtz's article, but Lysander Spooner appears to have made a strikingly similar point over one hundred years earlier. In responding to the Lockean idea that original appropriators should leave "enough and as good" for latecomers, Spooner retorts that "the history of the race proves that under [the rule of first possession], the last man's wants are better supplied than were those of the first, owing to the fact of the last man's having the skill and means of creating more wealth for himself, than the first one had. He has also the benefit of all the accumulations, which his predecessors have left him. The first man is a hungry, shivering savage, with all the wealth of nature around him. The last man revels in all the luxuries, which art, science, and nature, working in concert, can furnish him." Spooner, "The Law of Intellectual Property," section VI.

104. Harold Demsetz, "Toward a Theory of Property Rights," *American Economic Review* 57, no. 2 (1967): 347–59.

105. Robert C. Ellickson, "Property in Land," *Yale Law Journal* 102, no. 6 (1993): 1315–1400.

106. Ostrom, *Governing the Commons*.

107. Mack, *Libertarianism*, 5.

108. See Friedrich A. Hayek, "The Legal and Political Philosophy of David Hume," in *Studies in Philosophy, Politics, and Economics*, ed. Friedrich A. Hayek (Chicago: University of Chicago Press, 1967), 106–21.

109. On the idea of "several property," see Hayek, *The Constitution of Liberty*, 207n209. Hayek cites approvingly Henry Maine's use of the term in *Village Communities in the East and West: Six Lectures Delivered at Oxford to Which Are Added Other Lectures, Addresses, and Essays* (New York: Henry Holt, 1880), 230. For a discussion of the significance of this idea, see Barnett, *The Structure of Liberty*, 65.

110. On this point, see Hayek, "The Use of Knowledge in Society," especially section 2.

111. "The crucial point is that the prior development of several property is indispensable for the development of trading, and thereby for the formation of larger coherent and cooperating structures, and for the appearance of those signals we call prices" (Hayek, *The Fatal Conceit*, 31).

112. The importance of the division of labor in the generation of wealth is, of course, the central thesis of Smith, *The Wealth of Nations*. Matt Ridley helpfully develops and updates the idea in *The Rational Optimist: How Prosperity Evolves* (New York: Harper Perennial, 2010).

113. Friedrich A. Hayek, *Law, Legislation, and Liberty*, vol. 2, *The Mirage of Social Justice* (Chicago: University of Chicago Press, 1976), 108.

114. Ibid., 39.

115. Hayek, *The Constitution of Liberty*, 207.

116. Herbert Spencer, "Letter to the *Daily Chronicle*," August 29, 1894, in Herbert Spencer and Fre Verinder, *Mr. Herbert Spencer and the Land Restoration League* (London: Page and Pratt, 1895), 8–9. See also his discussion of this issue in "The Land Question," in *The Principles of Ethics*, appendix B.

117. Auberon Herbert, "Reply," in Levy, *A Symposium on the Land Question*, 70.

118. Spooner, "Revolution." Interestingly, Spooner's point here echoes one made by the early Herbert Spencer himself, who, in the original 1851 edition of his *Social Statics*, asked rhetorically, "How long does it take for what was originally a *wrong* to grow into a *right*? At what rate per annum do invalid claims become valid?" (105).

119. Murray N. Rothbard, "Confiscation and the Homestead Principle," *Libertarian Forum* 1, no. 6 (1969): 3–4. See also his brief discussion of the issue in *For a New Liberty* and the more extensive discussion in chapter 10 of *The Ethics of Liberty*, "The Problem of Land Theft." There, Rothbard asks us to "suppose that centuries ago, Smith was tilling the soil and therefore legitimately owning the land; and then that Jones came along and settled down near Smith, claiming by use of coercion the title to Smith's land, and extracting payment or 'rent' from Smith for the privilege of continuing to till the soil. Suppose that now, centuries later, Smith's descendants (or, for that matter, other unrelated families) are now tilling the soil, while Jones's descendants, or those who purchased their claims, still continue to exact tribute from the modern tillers. Where is the true property right in such a case? It should be clear that here, just as in the case of slavery, we have a case of *continuing* aggression against the true owners—the true possessors—of the land, the tillers, or peasants, by the illegitimate owner, the man whose original *and continuing* claim to the land and its fruits has come from coercion and violence. Just as the original Jones was a continuing aggressor against the original Smith, so the modern peasants are being aggressed against by the modern holder of the Jones-derived land title. In this case of what we might call 'feudalism' or 'land monopoly,' the feudal or monopolist landlords have no legitimate claim to the property. The current 'tenants,' or peasants, should be the absolute owners of their property, and, as in the case of slavery, the land titles should be transferred to the peasants, without compensation to the monopoly landlords" (66).

120. Wordsworth Donisthorpe makes this point in his own discussion of the problem of historical injustice, dismissing it as the product of "certain metaphysical notions of right and justice." See his *Individualism: A System of Politics*, chap. 4.

121. "Twere better, no doubt, that every one were possess'd of what is most suitable to him, and proper for his use: But besides, that this relation of fitness may be common to several at once, 'tis liable to so many controversies, and men are so partial and passionate in judging of these controversies, that such a loose and uncertain rule wou'd be absolutely incompatible with the peace of human society." Hume, *A Treatise of Human Nature*, 322.

122. Ibid.

123. Ibid.

124. Schmidtz, *Elements of Justice*, 212.

125. Hume, *A Treatise of Human Nature*, 324–26.

126. Rothbard, *For a New Liberty*, 31. A similar thesis is defended, much more rigorously, by George Smith in *The System of Liberty*, chap. 1.

127. Locke, *Second Treatise*, chap. 5, para. 33.

128. Ibid., para. 27.

129. Ibid., chap. 2, para. 37.

130. Nozick, *Anarchy, State, and Utopia*, 178.

131. Ibid., 182.

132. Ibid., 177.

133. Ibid., 180.

134. Ibid.

135. The ambiguity here is a reflection of Nozick's own uncertainty regarding how to define the appropriate baseline against which appropriations and uses of property ought to be compared for purposes of the Lockean proviso (ibid., 177).

136. See, for instance, Eric Mack, "The Self-Ownership Proviso: A New and Improved Lockean Proviso," *Social Philosophy and Policy* 12, no. 1 (1995): 186–218. On no-proviso libertarianism, see Feser, "There Is No Such Thing as an Unjust Initial Acquisition"; Rothbard, *The Ethics of Liberty*, 244; and Spooner, "The Law of Intellectual Property," chap. 1.

137. Hume, *A Treatise of Human Nature*, 319.

138. Frédéric Bastiat, "What Is Seen and What Is Not Seen," in *Selected Essays on Political Economy*, ed. George B. de Huszar (Irvington-on-Hudson, NY: Foundation for Economic Education, 1995).

139. Friedrich A. Hayek, "Principles or Expediency?" in *Toward Liberty: Essays in Honor of Ludwig von Mises*, ed. Friedrich A. Hayek et al., vol. 1 (Menlo Park, CA: Institute for Humane Studies, 1971), 30–31.

140. The influence of David Hume on Hayek in this respect is profound. For Hayek's own reflections on that influence, see Hayek, "The Legal and Political Philosophy of David Hume."

141. See Spencer, "Introduction," *Social Statics* (1851). "The expediency-philosophy, however, ignores this world full of facts. Though men have so constantly been balked in their attempts to secure, by legislation, any desired constituent of that complex whole, 'greatest happiness,' it nevertheless continues to place confidence in the unaided judgment of the statesman. . . . It thinks that man's intellect is competent, first, to observe accurately the facts exhibited by associated human nature; to form just estimates of general and individual character, of the effects of religions, customs, superstitions, prejudices, of the mental tendencies of the age, of the probabilities of future events, &c., &c.; and then, grasping at once the multiplied phenomena of this ever-agitated, ever-changing sea of life, to derive from them that knowledge of their governing principles which shall enable him to say whether such and such measures will conduce to 'the greatest happiness of the greatest number.' . . . Considering that men as yet so imperfectly understand *man*—the instrument by which, and the

material on which, laws are to act—and that a complete knowledge of the unit—*man*, is but a first step to the comprehension of the mass—*society*, it seems obvious enough that to educe from the infinitely-ramified complications of universal humanity, a true philosophy of national life, and to found thereon a code of rules for the obtainment of 'greatest happiness' is a task far beyond the ability of any finite mind" (12–13).

142. Hume, *A Treatise of Human Nature*, 337.

143. Smith, *The Wealth of Nations*, 687, emphasis added.

144. Barnett, *The Structure of Liberty*, 4–5.

145. Hasnas, "Toward a Theory of Empirical Natural Rights." Here Hasnas follows Hayek, who wrote in this context about the "false dichotomy" between the "natural" and the "artificial." See Hayek, *Law, Legislation, and Liberty*, vol. 1, *Rules and Order*, 20–22.

146. Taylor, *Stakes and Kidneys*.

147. Nozick, *Anarchy, State, and Utopia*, ix.

148. Spooner, "A Letter to Grover Cleveland," emphasis added.

Chapter 4. Demystifying the State: Libertarian Anarchism

1. U.S. Postal Service, "Rates for Domestic Letters, 1792–1863," USPS.com, August 2008, http://about.usps.com/who-we-are/postal-history/domestic-letter-rates -1792-1863.pdf.

2. Lucille J. Goodyear, "Spooner vs. U.S. Postal System," *American Legion Magazine*, January 1981, http://www.lysanderspooner.org/STAMP3.htm. Dissatisfaction with the government delivery of mail found expression on the other side of the ocean as well. For an account by one of the British Individualists, see Frederick Millar, "The Evils of State Trading as Illustrated by the Post Office," in *A Plea for Liberty: An Argument against Socialism and Socialistic Legislation*, ed. Thomas Mackay (Indianapolis: Liberty Classics, 1981).

3. "An Act to Establish the Post-Office and Post-Roads within the United States," February 20, 1792, 2nd Cong., 1st Sess., Ch. 7. I Stat. L., 232.

4. Charles Shively, "Biography," in *The Collected Works of Lysander Spooner* (Weston, MA: M & S Press, 1971), 1:29.

5. Lysander Spooner, "To the Members of the Legislature of Massachusetts," in *The Collected Works of Lysander Spooner* (Indianapolis: Liberty Fund, 1835), 1:15–17.

6. See the discussion of Moses Harman and Angela and Ezra Heywood later in this chapter.

7. Lysander Spooner to Charles Wickliffe, January 11, 1844, Spooner Papers, New York Historical Society, cited in Shively, "Biography," 30.

8. Cited in Goodyear, "Spooner vs. U.S. Postal System."

9. Lysander Spooner, "The Unconstitutionality of the Laws of Congress, Prohibiting Private Mails," in *The Collected Works of Lysander Spooner* (Indianapolis: Liberty Fund, 1844), 1:195–218.

10. Ibid., 1:199.

11. Ibid., 1:201. Spooner would expand upon this argument in his later and more famous work, "The Unconstitutionality of Slavery," in *The Collected Works of Lysander Spooner* (Indianapolis: Liberty Fund, 1860), 3:57–188, where he would argue that the social contract that underlies the Constitution "cannot lawfully authorize government to destroy or take from men their natural rights: for natural rights are inalienable, and can no more be surrendered to government—which is but an association of individuals—than to a single individual." Any contract that violates "the natural rights of any person or persons whatsoever" is thus "unlawful and void" and has "no moral sanction" (3:64–65). On Spooner's theory of legal interpretation, see Randy E. Barnett, "Was Slavery Unconstitutional before the Thirteenth Amendment? Lysander Spooner's Theory of Interpretation," *Pacific Law Journal* 28 (1997): 977.

12. Spooner, "The Unconstitutionality of the Laws of Congress," 218.

13. Lysander Spooner, "Who Caused the Reduction in Postage? Ought He to Be Paid?" in *The Collected Works of Lysander Spooner* (Indianapolis: Liberty Fund, 1850), 1:332.

14. Ibid., 1:346.

15. Shively, "Biography," 31.

16. As both a trained lawyer and an uncompromising believer in natural rights, Spooner was capable of putting forth both moderate "internal" critiques of social institutions and more radical "external" arguments. See chapter 7 for a fuller account of Spooner's radical abolitionism. For a helpful overview of Spooner's thought on natural law and freedom, see Eric Mack, "Lysander Spooner: Nineteenth-Century America's Last Natural Rights Theorist," *Social Philosophy and Policy* 29, no. 2 (July 17, 2012): 139–76, https://doi.org/10.1017/S0265052511000264.

17. United States Declaration of Independence. More precisely, Spooner thought that the only way that governments could have any just powers was *if* they obtained the consent of the governed. Even then, government power would be severely limited since not even consent is sufficient to divest an individual of his *inalienable* rights. But, for all practical purposes, this is a moot point. Since no government actually *has* obtained the consent of the governed, and since such consent is a necessary condition for legitimate political authority, political authority is a myth and government is little more than "mere usurpation." Spooner develops this argument in detail in his "No Treason, No. VI." As he argues there, "The Constitution has no inherent authority or obligation. It has no authority or obligation at all, unless as a contract between man and man. And it does not so much as even purport to be a contract between persons now existing. It purports, at most, to be only a contract between persons living eighty years ago. . . . Those persons, if any, who did give their consent formally, are all dead now. *And the Constitution, so far as it was their contract, died with them*" (173).

18. See Lysander Spooner, "An Essay on the Trial by Jury," in *The Collected Works of Lysander Spooner* (Indianapolis: Liberty Fund, 1852), 2:130, 132, 175, 212.

19. Max Weber, "Politics as a Vocation," in *From Max Weber: Essays in Sociology*, ed. H. H. Gerth and C. Wright Mills (Oxford: Oxford University Press, 1946).

20. Proudhon, *What Is Property?* Proudhon's book was published in France in 1840, but it was not until 1876 that it received its first English translation by Benjamin

Tucker. Google's N-gram viewer makes clear the influence of Proudhon, via Tucker, on the English language. Prior to 1875, the chart is essentially a long flat line at the zero point. Between 1875 and 1900, the frequency of the word "anarchist" in English-language books increased by a factor of *40*.

21. Smith, *The System of Liberty*, chap. 5.

22. Ibid., 97.

23. Robert Filmer, *Patriarcha and Other Writings*, ed. Johann P. Sommerville (Cambridge: Cambridge University Press, 1991), 3.

24. Ibid., 141.

25. *Modus ponens* is an argumentative form that begins by asserting that *p* implies *q*, and then asserting that since *p* is true, *q* must therefore be true also. *Modus tollens* likewise begins by asserting that *p* implies *q*, but then asserts that because *q* is false, *p* must therefore be false as well. What one concludes from the fact that *p* implies *q*, therefore, depends on whether one takes the truth of *p*, or the falsity of *q*, as a given.

26. Spencer, *Social Statics* (1995), 185.

27. As we noted in chapter 2, this chapter, along with several others, was omitted from the 1892 revised edition of his *Social Statics*.

28. As we will see in the concluding section of this chapter, Spencer's closest and most well-known follower, Auberon Herbert, consistently refused to employ the label of "anarchism" to his view, in spite of the fact that he seemed to deny authority to all monopolistic and coercive governments. Indeed, as Wendy McElroy has noted, most Spencerians identified themselves as nonanarchist "individualists" rather than anarchists. The most prominent exception to this generalization is Victor Yarros, whose libertarianism is somewhat idiosyncratic and interesting in many other respects as well. See Wendy McElroy, "Benjamin Tucker, Individualism, & Liberty: Not the Daughter, but the Mother of Order," *Literature of Liberty* 4, no. 3 (Autumn 1981): 7–39.

29. The closing paragraphs of the original chapter emphasize that the principles set out in it are applicable only to a "perfect state" of society and that "there are many changes yet to be passed through before it can begin to exercise much influence" (Spencer, *Social Statics*, 193–94). Later Spencerians and even non-Spencerian Individualists would similarly qualify their anarchism. For instance, Wordsworth Donisthorpe claimed that "no one with the smallest claim to attention has been known to affirm that this or any other nation is yet ripe for the abolition of the State. . . . And if it must be admitted that we are not yet ripe for that unconditioned individual liberty which may be the type of the society of the future, it follows that *for the present* we must recognise some form of State-interference as necessary and beneficent." Wordsworth Donisthorpe, "The Limits of Liberty," in *A Plea for Liberty: An Argument against Socialism and Socialistic Legislation*, ed. Thomas Mackay (Indianapolis: Liberty Classics, 1981). Similarly, Victor Yarros, who *did* identify himself as an anarchist, conceded that "the abolition of the external State must be preceded by the decay of the notions which breathe life and vigour into that clumsy monster: in other words, it is only when the people learn to value liberty, and to understand the truths of the anarchistic philosophy, that the question of practically abolishing the State looms up and acquires significance" (84).

30. Edmund Burke, *A Vindication of Natural Society, or, a View of the Miseries and Evils Arising to Mankind from Every Species of Artificial Society. In a Letter to Lord ** by a Late Noble Writer*, ed. Frank N. Pagano (Indianapolis: Liberty Fund, 1982), https://oll.libertyfund.org/title/burke-a-vindication-of-natural-society.

31. Ibid.

32. William Godwin, *An Enquiry Concerning Political Justice and Its Influence on General Virtue and Happiness*, ed. Isaac Krammick, 2 vols. (Harmondsworth: Penguin Classics, 1976), book 1, chap. 2.

33. Edmund Burke, *The Inherent Evil of All State Governments Demonstrated; Being a Reprint of Edmund Burke's Celebrated Essay, Entitled "A Vindication of Natural Society"* (London: Holyoake and Company, 1858), v. Max Nettlau speculates that the publisher of the reprint, and author of the extensive appendix and notes, was one Ambrose Cuddon, an anarchist who had spent some time living in Josiah Warren's Modern Times community, more on which anon. See Max Nettlau, "Anarchism in England Fifty Years Ago," *Liberty* 15, no. 3 (February 1906): 2747.

34. Murray N. Rothbard, "A Note on Burke's *Vindication of Natural Society*," *Journal of the History of Ideas* 19, no. 1 (1958): 114, 116.

35. Ibid., 114.

36. See, for a convincing presentation of the evidence, John C. Weston, "The Ironic Purpose of Burke's Vindication Vindicated," *Journal of the History of Ideas* 19, no. 3 (1958): 435–41.

37. William Lloyd Garrison, "Declaration of Sentiments of the American Anti-Slavery Convention," in *Selections from the Writings and Speeches of William Lloyd Garrison* (Boston: R. F. Wallcut, 1852), 66–71.

38. Wright Journal (HCL) XXXII, 189–215, November 1836, cited in Perry, *Radical Abolitionism*, 52.

39. See, for a fascinating overview, Perry, *Radical Abolitionism*. This logic of seeing slavery as just an instance of a more general problem led some radical abolitionists to eventually place a lesser weight on the abolition of slavery. The *real* problem, some came to believe, was establishing the proper relation of authority between God and man, or between men and civil governments. Slavery was merely a symptom of a larger problem, and no long-term good could come of addressing the symptom by itself. Thus, when asked whether he would, if given the opportunity, cast the decisive vote to abolish slavery, and thereby participate to some extent in the government to which he objected, Henry Wright answered that he would not. For even in such a situation, to vote would merely be to "ensure the prolongation of man's bondage to man" (89).

40. J. H. Hammond, "Slavery in the Light of Political Science," in *Cotton Is King and Proslavery Arguments*, ed. E. N. Elliott (Augusta, GA, 1860), 677–78, cited in Perry, *Radical Abolitionism*, 28.

41. George Fitzhugh, *Cannibals All!, or, Slaves without Masters* (A. Morris, 1857).

42. See Reichert, *Partisans of Freedom*, 293–98.

43. Wendy McElroy, "The Life of a Grand Old Liberal," *Independent Institute* (blog), February 1, 1999, https://www.independent.org/news/article.asp?id=17.

44. *State v. Walker*, 13 (Kan. 1887).

45. Ibid.

46. Reichert, *Partisans of Freedom*, 309.

47. Ibid.

48. Angela and Ezra Heywood faced similar persecution for their role in publishing an anarchist newsletter called *The Word*, which routinely printed criticisms of organized religion and the institution of legal marriage, as well as frank discussions of sexual matters. See Reichert, *Partisans of Freedom*, 289–98. For further discussion, and reprints of some of Angela Heywood's more important writings from *The Word*, see Wendy McElroy, *Individualist Feminism of the Nineteenth Century: Collected Writings and Biographical Profiles* (Jefferson, NC: McFarland, 2001), chap. 1.

49. See McElroy, *Debates*, chap. 1.

50. Moses Harman, like Ezra Heywood and many other individualist anarchists in late nineteenth-century America, saw themselves as working on the side of labor against capital in the social struggle of the time. But, as we saw in chapter 2, this has less to do with their rejection of libertarian ideas than it does with their application of those ideas to a particular economic and social context. Harman and Heywood were not socialists in any contemporary sense of that term. On the free love movement in nineteenth-century America, see Hal D. Sears, *The Sex Radicals: Free Love in High Victorian America* (Lawrence: Regents Press of Kansas, 1977). On the connections between the anarchist, free thought, free love, and labor reform movements more generally, see Reichert, *Partisans of Freedom*.

51. Moses Harman, "Anarchism Again," *Lucifer the Light-Bearer* (March 19, 1886): 2.

52. Huemer, *The Problem of Political Authority*, 3. Lysander Spooner puts forward a similar hypothetical in "A Letter to Grover Cleveland," 5:197.

53. For an excellent overview of Tucker's writings and those of his associates at *Liberty*, see McElroy, *Debates*.

54. Victor S. Yarros, "Anarchism," in *The Encyclopedia of Social Reforms*, ed. William D. P. Bliss (New York: Funk & Wagnalls, 1897), 56. A similar argument can be found in the writings of John Locke, from whom many nineteenth-century libertarians drew their inspiration. "Should a robber break into my house, and with a dagger at my throat make me seal deeds to convey my estate to him, would this give him any title? Just such a title, by his sword, has an unjust conqueror, who forces me into submission. The injury and the crime is equal, whether committed by the wearer of a crown, or some petty villain. The title of the offender, and the number of his followers, make no difference in the offence, unless it be to aggravate it" (*Second Treatise*, chap. 16, § 176).

55. Yarros, "Anarchism," 56.

56. This quotation is from one of Spooner's last and most forceful writings, his famous "Letter to Grover Cleveland" (5:189–90), the full title of which gives some sense of the intensity of Spooner's dislike for that president: "A Letter to Grover Cleveland, on His False Inaugural Address, the Usurpations and Crimes of Lawmakers and Judges, and the Consequent Poverty, Ignorance, and Servitude of the People."

Actually, this title is rather tempered in its tone compared to the original July 1886 title, "A Letter to Grover Cleveland, on his False, Absurd, Self-Contradictory, and Ridiculous Inaugural Address." This is perhaps the only extant example of Spooner growing more moderate with the passage of time.

57. Rothbard, *For a New Liberty*, 29.

58. Ibid.

59. Ibid., 57.

60. See, for a fascinating discussion of the psychology of authority, Huemer, *The Problem of Political Authority*, chap. 7.

61. The first of those phrases comes from John Beverly Robinson, the second from Benjamin Tucker. Both cited in Reichert, *Partisans of Freedom*, 186, 155.

62. Ibid., 14.

63. Étienne de la Boétie, *The Discourse on Voluntary Servitude* (Indianapolis: Liberty Fund, 1942).

64. John Stuart Mill, *On Liberty* (London: John Parker and Sons, 1859), 12.

65. Tucker, *Instead of a Book*, 22.

66. Nozick's formulation of the example is presented in *Anarchy, State, and Utopia*, 290–92, Spencer's in "The Coming Slavery," 55–57. Spencer's formulation is presented as a philosophical argument, rather than a rhetorical thought experiment, and thus is in many ways more substantively interesting and well-developed than Nozick's more famous presentation.

67. This debate took place between November and December 1896 in the pages of Tucker's *Liberty* and is summarized in McElroy, *Debates*, 23–25. The original articles are anthologized in Brooks, *The Individualist Anarchists*, 299–305.

68. The first of these essays is actually titled "No Treason, No. VI." Despite the title, however, there were only three parts actually written to his No Treason series: parts 1, 2, and 6.

69. Spooner, "No Treason, No. VI." Emphasis in original.

70. Nozick, *Anarchy, State, and Utopia*, 287. Spooner's "No Treason" works through the arguments that individuals tacitly consent to government by either voting or paying taxes, rejecting each in turn. For a contemporary libertarian critique of consent-based arguments for political authority, see Huemer, *The Problem of Political Authority*, chaps. 2–3.

71. See Bryan Caplan, *The Myth of the Rational Voter* (Princeton: Princeton University Press, 2007); and Jason Brennan, *Against Democracy* (Princeton: Princeton University Press, 2016). Despite their critique of democracy, both of these authors nevertheless support some sort of broadly (though restrictive) democratic system. One peculiar strand of contemporary libertarianism, however, argues that monarchy would be a superior form of government. See Hans-Hermann Hoppe, *Democracy— The God That Failed: The Economics and Politics of Monarchy, Democracy, and Natural Order* (New Brunswick, NJ: Transaction Publishers, 2011). A similar penchant for monarchy can be found among certain intellectuals of the "alt right," many followers of which have been drawn to the anti-democratic and racist elements in Hoppe's writings.

72. One sees this strand most clearly in the line of libertarian thought that draws inspiration from the ideas of Friedrich Nietzsche, e.g., Albert Jay Nock, H. L. Mencken, and Ayn Rand. Nock's dismissal is typical of this line of thought: "I could see how 'democracy' might do very well in a society of saints and sages led by an Alfred or an Antoninus Pius. Short of that, I was unable to see how it could come to anything but an ochlocracy of mass-men led by a sagacious knave. The collective capacity for bringing forth any other outcome seemed simply not there." Albert Jay Nock, *Memoirs of a Superfluous Man* (New York: Harper & Brothers, 1943), 131. But even non-Nietzschean libertarians, indeed even libertarians who are strongly in favor of democracy on net, sometimes express similar views. Ludwig von Mises, for instance, notes that "most people do not have the intellectual endowments required to think through the—after all very complicated—problems of social cooperation, and they certainly do not have the will power necessary to make those provisional sacrifices that all social action demands" (*Liberalism*, 157–58).

73. See Jason Brennan, *Libertarianism: What Everyone Needs to Know* (Oxford: Oxford University Press, 2012), 69–71.

74. Herbert Spencer to John Stuart Mill, August 9, 1867, in Duncan and Spencer, *The Life and Letters of Herbert Spencer*, 2:138.

75. Victor S. Yarros, "Woman-Suffrage and Anarchism," *Liberty* 10, no. 7 (August 11, 1894): 2–4. Yarros's view was opposed later that month in John Beverly Robinson, "Woman-Suffrage and Liberty," *Liberty* 10, no. 8 (August 28, 1894): 2.

76. Lysander Spooner, "Against Woman Suffrage," *Liberty* 1, no. 22 (June 10, 1882): 4.

77. Yarros, in "Woman-Suffrage and Anarchism," reasons similarly: "The Anarchists and individualists oppose woman's suffrage simply and solely because they are convinced that woman's political activity would be directed toward tyranny and would arrest the political emancipation of all of us."

78. Spencer to Mill, August 9, 1867. Spencer went on to argue that women lack the "political foresight" necessary to accept the short-term pains necessary to the realization of long-term freedom and that their minds are deficient in "those most complex faculties, intellectual and moral, which have political action as their sphere."

79. For the historical details and analyses of these visits, see Andrew Farrant, Edward McPhail, and Sebastian Berger, "Preventing the 'Abuses' of Democracy: Hayek, the 'Military Usurper' and Transitional Dictatorship in Chile?" *American Journal of Economics and Sociology* 71, no. 3 (July 2012), https://doi.org/10.1111/j .1536-7150.2012.00824.x; and Bruce Caldwell and Leonidas Montes, "Friedrich Hayek and His Visits to Chile," *Review of Austrian Economics* 28, no. 3 (2015): 261–309, https://doi.org/10.1007/s11138-014-0290-8.

80. Report of the Commission of Truth and Reconciliation (Rettig Commission), 1991, cited in Caldwell and Montes, "Friedrich Hayek and His Visits to Chile," 270.

81. F. A. Hayek, in *El Mercurio*, November 18, 1977, cited in Caldwell and Montes, "Friedrich Hayek and His Visits to Chile," 279–80.

82. Hayek in *El Mercurio*, April 12, 1981, cited in Caldwell and Montes, "Friedrich Hayek and His Visits to Chile," 298.

83. Hayek, *The Road to Serfdom*, 110.

84. Mises, *Liberalism*, 41–42. The quasi-Hobbesian anarchist Wordsworth Donisthorpe was also relatively enthusiastic toward democracy, by libertarian standards. See his 1889 book, *Individualism: A System of Politics*.

85. Godwin, *An Enquiry Concerning Political Justice and Its Influence on General Virtue and Happiness*, 408, 554.

86. It is precisely these kinds of considerations that led Ludwig von Mises to condemn anarchism in his 1927 book, *Liberalism*, where he wrote that anarchism "is mistaken in assuming that everyone, without exception, will be willing to observe [society's rules of conduct] *voluntarily*" (36–37, emphasis in original). In making this critique, Mises appears not to have had in mind the anarcho-capitalism of Molinari, Tucker, and Rothbard, since those views do not assume that cooperation with social rules will be voluntary, nor that coercion could be dispensed with in an anarchist society. These views will be discussed later in this chapter.

87. David Hart, "Gustave de Molinari and the Anti-Statist Liberal Tradition, Part I," *Journal of Libertarian Studies* 5, no. 3 (1981): 266.

88. Godwin, *An Enquiry Concerning Political Justice and Its Influence on General Virtue and Happiness*, 533.

89. Locke, *Second Treatise*, chap. 1, § 13.

90. Reichert, *Partisans of Freedom*, 100, 105.

91. Spencer, *Social Statics*, 58–59, 409.

92. William Bailie, *Josiah Warren, the First American Anarchist* (Boston: Small, Maynard & Company, 1906).

93. See, for a brief overview of the New Harmony experiment with emphasis on Warren's reaction, Martin, *Men against the State*, chap. 1.

94. Quoted in ibid., 10.

95. Warren, *Equitable Commerce*, 26.

96. By and large, this principle dropped out of twentieth-century libertarian thought altogether, mainly due to the fall of the underlying labor theory of value and the rise of marginalism and subjectivism in economics. Among libertarians, the influence of Austrian economists such as Carl Menger and Ludwig von Mises was particularly important in these respects.

97. Cited in Martin, *Men against the State*, 18.

98. Warren, quoted in Reichert, *Partisans of Freedom*, 74.

99. Ibid., 75.

100. Spencer, *Social Statics*, 185.

101. Gustave de Molinari, "Dé la production de la sécurité," *Journal des Économistes* 21, no. 1 (1849). Molinari's proposal was so radical that the editor of the journal apparently felt the need to publicly defend his decision to publish the article, noting that while its conclusions appeared "utopian," it nevertheless represented an important effort to "formulate strictly the boundaries outside of which the intervention of authority becomes anarchical and tyrannical rather than protective and profitable." Joseph Garnier, cited in Murray N. Rothbard, *An Austrian Perspective on the History of Economic Thought*, vol. 2, *Classical Economics* (Cheltenham: Edward Elgar, 1995), 455.

102. Molinari, "Dé la production de la sécurité."

103. Ibid.

104. Gustave de Molinari, *Ireland* (1880), cited in Yves Guyot, "M. G. de Molinari," *Journal des Économistes* 33 (February 1912): 177–92.

105. Gustave de Molinari, "L'utopie de la liberté: Lettres aux socialistes," *Journal des Économistes* 20, no. 82 (June 15, 1848): 328–32.

106. Gustave de Molinari, "Le droit électoral," *Courrier Français*, July 23, 1846, reprinted in Gustave de Molinari, *Questions d'économie politique et de droit public* (Brussels: Lacroix, 1861), 2:273.

107. A discussion of this meeting, from which the quotations that follow were drawn, was published by an unknown author, possibly Joseph Garnier, the editor of the journal, in "Questions of the Limits of State Action and Individual Action Discussed at the Society of Political Economy," *Journal des Économistes* 24, no. 103 (1849): 314–16.

108. Charles Coquelin, "Review of Gustave de Molinari's *Soirées*," *Journal des Économistes* 24, no. 104 (1849): 364–72. Coquelin also had a more strategic kind of worry about Molinari's view. Along with Frédéric Bastiat, Coquelin worried that Molinari's "eccentric opinions" would be used by the socialists to undermine all *economists*, including more moderate ones like himself.

109. Molinari, *The Society of Tomorrow*.

110. Herbert, *The Right and Wrong of Compulsion by the State*, 185, 186.

111. Herbert, "The Principles of Voluntaryism and Free Life," 390.

112. Paul Émile de Puydt, "Panarchy," *Revue Trimestruelle* (1860): 222–45.

113. David M. Hart, "Gustave de Molinari and the Anti-Statist Liberal Tradition: Part III," *Journal of Libertarian Studies* 5, no. 3 (1982): 86.

114. The term "anarcho-capitalist" is now widely used to distinguish libertarian anarchists such as Molinari and Rothbard, who advocated for a stateless society combined with strong rights of private property and a free market economic system, from other anarchists such as Emma Goldman and P. J. Proudhon, who likewise favored the abolition of the state but envisioned its replacement by a socialist community, and from "philosophical anarchists" who reject the notion of state authority but advance no positive vision of a stateless society. The term appears to have been first publicly used in a 1969 *Playboy* article by libertarian essayist Karl Hess titled "The Death of Politics."

115. S. R., "An Economist on the Future of Society," *Liberty* 14, no. 23 (September 1904): 1. "S. R." is possibly S. H. Randall. See Morgan Edwards, "Neither Bombs Nor Ballots: *Liberty* and the Strategy of Anarchism," in *Benjamin R. Tucker and the Champions of Liberty: A Centenary Anthology*, ed. Michael E. Coughlin, Charles H. Hamilton, and Mark A. Sullivan (St. Paul, MN: Michael E. Coughlin, 1987), 65–91, 90n.

116. Benjamin Tucker, "Contract or Organism, What's That to Us?" *Liberty* 4, no. 26 (July 30, 1887): 4.

117. Rothbard, *For a New Liberty*, 57.

118. Rothbard, *The Ethics of Liberty*, 236–37.

119. The distinction between law and legislation was made central to libertarian legal theory in Hayek, *Law, Legislation, and Liberty*, vol. 1, *Rules and Order*, chap. 4.

120. See Harold J. Berman, *Law and Revolution: The Formation of the Western Legal Tradition* (Cambridge, MA: Harvard University Press, 1983).

121. See Friedman, *The Machinery of Freedom*, part 3.

122. Rand, "The Nature of Government," 112.

123. See Roy A. Childs, "Objectivism and the State: An Open Letter to Ayn Rand," in *Liberty against Power: Essays by Roy A. Childs, Jr.*, ed. Joan Kennedy Taylor (San Francisco: Fox & Wilkes, 1994). Childs sent a copy of his letter to Rand in the mail. He received, in response, a notification that his subscription to her newsletter, "The Objectivist," had been canceled. Later in life, Childs would come to reject anarchism. Unfortunately, he never explained the reason why. See Roy A. Childs, "Anarchist Illusions," in *Liberty against Power: Essays by Roy A. Childs, Jr.*, ed. Joan Kennedy Taylor (San Francisco: Fox & Wilkes, 1994), 179–83.

124. Nozick, *Anarchy, State, and Utopia*, xv.

125. Ibid., xi.

126. Ibid., 16–17.

127. Ibid., 101–8.

128. Eric Mack, "Nozickian Arguments for the More-than-Minimal State," in *The Cambridge Companion to Nozick's Anarchy, State, and Utopia*, ed. Ralf M. Bader and John Meadowcroft (New York: Cambridge University Press, 2011), 95–99.

129. See Randy Barnett, "Whither Anarchy? Has Robert Nozick Justified the State?" *Journal of Libertarian Studies* 1, no. 1 (1977): 15–21. Also see Mack, "Nozickian Arguments for the More-than-Minimal State."

130. See Roy Childs, "The Invisible Hand Strikes Back," *Journal of Libertarian Studies* 1, no. 1 (1977): 23–33; and Murray N. Rothbard, "Robert Nozick and the Immaculate Conception of the State," *Journal of Libertarian Studies* 1, no. 1 (1977): 45–57.

131. Robert Nozick, "The Zigzag of Politics," in *The Examined Life: Philosophical Meditations*, ed. Robert Nozick (New York: Simon & Schuster, 1987), 286–96.

132. Robert Nozick, *Invariances: The Structure of the Objective World* (Cambridge, MA: Harvard University Press, 2001), chap. 5.

133. Julian Sanchez, "An Interview with Robert Nozick," July 26, 2001, http://www.juliansanchez.com/an-interview-with-robert-nozick-july-26-2001.

134. Molinari referred to himself simply as an "economist." Herbert coined the term "Voluntaryism" for his own position.

135. On the distinction between state and government, see Gustave de Molinari, "Nations," in the *Dictionnaire de l'économie politique . . .*, ed. Charles Coquelin et Gilbert-Urbain Guillaumin (Paris: Guillaumin, 1853), 2:259–62.

136. Herbert, "Mr. Spencer and the Great Machine," 313, 312. See also his debate with the more moderate individualist J. H. Levy, in which Herbert explicitly denies that he is an anarchist and endorses the idea that "compulsory taxation for purposes of defense" is a "legitimate State function." Auberon Herbert and J. H. Levy, *Taxation and Anarchism* (London: Personal Rights Association, 1912), 40–42.

137. See, for example, the discussion of anarcho-capitalism at "The Anarchist FAQ": http://anarchism.pageabode.com/afaq/secF1.html.

Chapter 5. Big Business and Free Markets

1. Ayn Rand, "America's Persecuted Minority, Big Business," in *Capitalism: The Unknown Ideal* (New York: New American Library, 1967), 44.

2. Murray Rothbard would later call this one of Ayn Rand's "more ludicrous pronouncements." One wonders whether to take this more or less seriously coming from someone whose own preferred candidate for America's most persecuted minority was tobacco smokers. http://www.lewrockwell.com/rothbard/rothbard138.html.

3. Probably the most influential entry in this genre was a memorandum written by future Supreme Court Justice Lewis Powell in 1971 titled "Attack on American Free Enterprise System," https://scholarlycommons.law.wlu.edu/powellmemo/. For a discussion, see Kimberly Phillips-Fein, *Invisible Hands: The Businessmen's Crusade against the New Deal* (New York: W. W. Norton, 2010), chap. 7. A fascinating antecedent to Rand's celebration of the heroic entrepreneur can be found in the work of W. H. Mallock, whose voluminous writings, according to the historian John Mason, were devoted to rebutting socialism and defending the idea that "economic progress and social justice depend on the talents and energy of a few men of 'ability.'" Mason, "Political Economy and the Response to Socialism," 582. See William Hurrell Mallock, *Social Equality: A Short Study in a Missing Science* (New York: G. P. Putnam's Sons, 1882), and *A Critical Examination of Socialism* (New York: Harper & Brothers, 1907).

4. Murray Rothbard to Ayn Rand, cited in Justin Raimondo, *An Enemy of the State: The Life of Murray N. Rothbard* (New York: Prometheus Books, 2000), 117–18.

5. Murray Rothbard to Richard Cornuelle, cited in Raimondo, *Enemy of the State*, 117.

6. In many ways, but not all. As the split between them deepened, Rothbard found much to criticize in Rand's ideas as well, writing in a letter to Richard Cornuelle that "the good stuff in Ayn's system is not Ayn's original contribution at all" and criticizing her ignorance of the tradition of thinking about ideas such as natural rights that she claimed to have invented on her own. See, for discussion, Burns, *Goddess of the Market*, 152–53.

7. Ayn Rand, *Atlas Shrugged* (New York: New American Library, 1957), part 2, chap. 2.

8. Murray N. Rothbard, "Left and Right: The Prospects for Liberty," *Left and Right: A Journal of Libertarian Thought* 1, no. 1 (Spring 1965): 12.

9. Ibid.

10. Gabriel Kolko, *The Triumph of Conservatism: A Reinterpretation of American History, 1900–1916* (New York: Free Press, 1963).

11. Ibid., 26.

12. Ibid., 262.

13. Rothbard, "Left and Right," 5.

14. Ibid., 6.

15. Ibid., 7. Rothbard recognizes that there is a significant strand of socialism, exemplified in the work of individuals like Bakunin and even Marx, that is closer

to libertarianism in its nature. But it was not this strand but rather the relatively authoritarian Saint-Simonian strand that would come to dominate, politically if not intellectually.

16. "Libertarianism is a people's movement and a liberation movement. . . . Libertarians can and should propose specific revolutionary tactics and goals which would have specific meaning to poor people and to all people. . . . What, for instance, might or should happen to General Motors in a liberated society?" Karl Hess, "What Are the Specifics?" *Libertarian Forum* 1, no. 6 (June 15, 1969).

17. Charles Woolsey Cole, *French Mercantilism: 1683–1700* (New York: Octagon Books, 1965), 176.

18. Eli Filip Heckscher, *Mercantilism* (London: George Allen & Unwin, 1955), 173.

19. Paul Samuelson and William Nordhaus, *Economics*, 16th ed. (Boston: Irwin McGraw-Hill, 1998), 703; Roy Ruffin and Paul R. Gregory, *Principles of Microeconomics* (Glenview, IL: Scott, Foresman, 1990), 450.

20. Rothbard, *Economic Thought before Adam Smith*, 213.

21. Jacob Viner, *Studies in the Theory of International Trade* (New York: Harper and Brothers, 1937), 59.

22. Ibid., 58–59.

23. Charles Woolsey Cole, *Colbert and a Century of French Mercantilism* (North Haven, CT: Archon Books, 1964), 135.

24. Ibid.

25. Rothbard, *Economic Thought before Adam Smith*, 220.

26. As Adam Smith wrote in his critique of mercantilism, "It is the industry which is carried on for the benefit of the rich and the powerful that is principally encouraged. . . . That which is carried on for the benefit of the poor and the indigent is too often either neglected or oppressed" (*Wealth of Nations*, book IV, chap. 8, ¶ 4; 644).

27. Indeed, it was in direct connection with Colbert that the phrase "laissez-faire"—a phrase that perhaps more than any other has come to symbolize the libertarian creed—was allegedly first used. As the story goes, around 1680 Colbert was visiting a group of French merchants led by M. Le Gendre. When Colbert asked the group what the French state could do to promote commerce and aid the merchants, Le Gendre is said to have responded simply: "laissez-nous faire"—leave us alone. The slogan would later be popularized by Vincent de Gournay, French intendant of commerce in the 1750s and proponent of trade liberalization. Gournay's own expanded version of the slogan—"laissez-faire et laissez-passer, le monde va de lui même" (Leave things alone and let them pass; the world runs by itself)—gained widespread popularity through its adoption by the Physiocratic school of economics, of which he was a head. See Rothbard, *Economic Thought before Adam Smith*, 260–61.

28. The contrast here could be read to support a common misunderstanding of Smith, viz., that his analysis of political economy was a purely consequentialist one, rather than one rooted in concepts of justice or moral rights. This is at best an overstatement and at worst a gross distortion. Even in *The Wealth of Nations*, book IV concludes with an endorsement of what Smith describes as "the obvious and simple system of natural liberty" (IV.ix). And his discussion here should be read in light of

his more lengthy treatments of justice in *The Theory of Moral Sentiments* and his *Lectures on Jurisprudence*.

29. John Maynard Keynes, *The General Theory of Employment, Interest, and Money* (New York: Prometheus Books, 1997), chap. 2.

30. Consumption can be productive when the potential of a resource to satisfy human wants is depleted in the course of producing other producers' or consumers' goods, as in the case of the depletion of capital equipment through productive use.

31. Jean-Baptiste Say, *Catechism of Political Economy, or, Familiar Conversations on the Manner in Which Wealth Is Produced, Distributed, and Consumed in Society* (London: Sherwood, Neely, and Jones, 1816), 12.

32. Cases of trade that involve one party providing the other with unaltered natural resources, including land, might seem to present a counterexample insofar as such resources can entice a trade without seeming to require any productive activity on their owner's part. It should be remembered, however, that Say defines productivity simply as taking "a product in one state and putting it into another in which it has more utility and value," and that productive activity in this sense is only contingently related to productivity in the sense of physical or mental effort exerted in the transformation of physical objects. To bring fruit that one has found in the forest to the market is to put that fruit into a state in which it has more value in virtue of its being in a location where it requires less effort to consume, even if the physical characteristics of the fruit itself remain unchanged.

33. Charles Comte, "De l'organisation sociale considérée dans ses rapports avec les moyens de subsistence des peuples," *Le censeur européen* 1 (1817): 22.

34. Say, *A Treatise on Political Economy*, 146–47.

35. Bastiat, "The Law," 5. Charles Comte presented a similar analysis as part of his class theory, though for Comte there were *three* ways that men could meet their needs: they can take advantage of the spontaneous offerings of nature, they can produce wealth, or they can plunder the wealth that others have produced. See Charles Comte, "Considerations sur l'état moral de la nation française, et sur les causes de l'instabilité de ses institutions," *Le censeur européen* 1 (March 1817): 1–2, 9.

36. Thomas Hodgskin's *Labour Defended against the Claims of Capital* is unremitting in its critique of capitalism and capitalists. Yet even Hodgskin recognized that capitalists could be economically productive. The mere act of *owning* capital was not in itself productive, of course. But capitalists also often bring to the table the "knowledge and skill of the master manufacturer, and of the man who plans and arranges a productive operation, who must know the state of the markets and the qualities of different materials, and who has some tact in buying and selling." This sort of skill is just as essential to economic production as "the operations of the hands" (26).

37. Karl Marx and Friedrich Engels, *Selected Correspondence* (Moscow: Progress, 1965), 69. See also Marx's letter to Engels of July 27, 1854, at p. 87.

38. Karl Marx and Friedrich Engels, *Selected Works* (Moscow: Progress, 1968), 170–71.

39. Ibid., 261.

40. Oppenheimer, *The State*, 15.

41. Ibid., 14.

42. Nock, *Our Enemy, the State*, 26.

43. "Some writers have so confounded society with government, as to leave little or no distinction between them; whereas they are not only different, but have different origins. Society is produced by our wants, and government by our wickedness. . . . Society in every state is a blessing, but Government, even in its best state, is but a necessary evil; in its worst state an intolerable one." Thomas Paine, *Common Sense*, in *Paine: Political Writings* (New York: Cambridge University Press, 2000), 3.

44. Nock, *Our Enemy, the State*, 24. Note again the similarity between the libertarian theory of exploitation and the better-known Marxist version.

45. Ibid.

46. Ibid.

47. Nock borrowed this phrase from Jeremy Bentham, who coined it to describe terms applied "chiefly to the defense of things which under their proper name are manifestly indefensible; for example, persecutors have no such word as *persecution*, but *zeal*. It substitutes an object of approbation for an object of censure." See Albert Jay Nock, "Imposter Terms," in *Free Speech and Plain Language* (New York: W. Morrow, 1937).

48. Ibid.

49. Rothbard, *Power and Market*, 37.

50. Joseph Stromberg, "The Political Economy of Liberal Corporatism" (pamphlet for the Center for Libertarian Studies, 1977), http://archive.ph/YlaE.

51. See Carson, *Studies in Mutualist Political Economy*, 142; and Roderick T. Long, "Corporations versus the Market, or Whip Conflation Now," in *Markets Not Capitalism: Individualist Anarchism against Bosses, Inequality, Corporate Power, and Structural Poverty*, ed. Gary Chartier and Charles Johnson (New York: Autonomedia, 2012).

52. See Philip Mattera and Anna Purinton, *Shopping for Subsidies: How Wal-Mart Uses Taxpayer Money to Finance Its Never-Ending Growth* (Washington, DC: Good Jobs First, 2004), http://www.goodjobsfirst.org/pdf/wmtstudy.pdf. For an analysis of how the Wagner Act limited the effectiveness of certain forms of organized labor, see Kevin A. Carson, "Labor Struggle: A Free Market Model," Center for a Stateless Society Paper No. 10 (2010), https://c4ss.org/wp-content/uploads/2010/09/C4SS-Labor.pdf.

53. Roy Childs, "Big Business," in *Liberty against Power: Essays by Roy A. Childs, Jr.*, ed. Joan Kennedy Taylor (San Francisco: Fox & Wilkes, 1994), 25.

54. Stromberg, "The Political Economy of Liberal Corporatism."

55. Buchanan and Tullock, *The Calculus of Consent*, 20.

56. James M. Buchanan, "Politics without Romance," in *The Logical Foundations of Constitutional Liberty* (Indianapolis: Liberty Fund, 1999).

57. See Mancur Olson, *The Logic of Collective Action: Public Goods and the Theory of Groups* (Cambridge, MA: Harvard University Press, 1971).

58. Russell Hardin and Garrett Cullity, "The Free Rider-Problem," in *Stanford Encyclopedia of Philosophy*, ed. Edward Zalta (Winter 2020), https://plato.stanford.edu/archives/win2020/entries/free-rider/.

59. See William Mitchell and Randy T. Simmons, *Beyond Politics: Markets, Welfare, and the Failure of Bureaucracy* (Boulder, CO: Westview Press, 1994), 68–70.

60. Compare this with the more widely recognized problem of negative externalities on the market. See C. Wolf, *Markets or Governments: Choosing between Imperfect Alternatives* (Cambridge, MA: MIT Press, 1993), 20–21. We expect individuals to pollute because, by and large, the benefits of pollution are internalized to the polluter whereas the costs of pollution are externalized onto third parties. On the public choice analysis above, political activities such as legislation and voting can often usefully be thought of as a kind of pollution. See, for a discussion, Caplan, *The Myth of the Rational Voter*.

61. Friedman, *The Machinery of Freedom*, 107.

62. This definition is derived from the pioneering work of Gordon Tullock on this subject. See James Buchanan, R. D. Tollison, and Gordon Tullock, *Toward a Theory of the Rent-Seeking Society* (College Station: Texas A&M University Press, 1980); Gordon Tullock, "Rent Seeking," in *Lexeconics: The Interaction of Law and Economics* (Boston: Martinus Nijhoff, 1981); and Tullock, Tollison, and Rowley, *The Political Economy of Rent Seeking*. See also James M. Buchanan, "From Private Preferences to Public Philosophy: The Development of Public Choice," in *The Economics of Politics* (London: Institute of Economic Affairs, 1978), 15–25.

63. George J. Stigler, "The Theory of Economic Regulation," *Bell Journal of Economics and Management Science* 2, no. 1 (1971): 3–21.

64. Brink Lindsey and Steven Michael Teles, *The Captured Economy: How the Powerful Enrich Themselves, Slow Down Growth, and Increase Inequality* (New York: Oxford University Press, 2017), 92. Most occupational licensing in the United States is done at the state rather than the federal level, and states differ markedly in terms of which occupations they subject to or exempt from licensing.

65. As Lindsey and Teles note, empirical studies discover little or no connection between occupational licensing and the quality of service provided to consumers. Training requirements, they further point out, appear to be largely arbitrary and unrelated to the significance of the safety concerns involved in the field. Thus, while cosmetologists must complete an average of 372 days of training in order to receive their license, emergency medical technicians (EMTs) must complete an average of only 33 days (*The Captured Economy*, 94).

66. Jane Mayer, *Dark Money: The Hidden History of the Billionaires behind the Radical Right* (New York: Knopf Doubleday, 2016), 135.

67. See Jim Powell, *The Triumph of Liberty: A 2,000-Year History, Told through the Lives of Freedom's Greatest Champions* (New York: Free Press, 2000), 359.

68. See Phillips-Fein, *Invisible Hands*, chap. 2.

69. On the first point, see ibid. On the second two, see Doherty, *Radicals for Capitalism*, 185–86. For the role of business in the creation of the discipline of law and

economics, see Steven M. Teles, *The Rise of the Conservative Legal Movement: The Battle for the Control of the Law* (Princeton: Princeton University Press, 2008).

70. The Liberty and Property Defense League was founded in 1882 by Lord Elcho, later the Earl of Wemyss. For more on its history and beliefs, see Edward Bristow, "The Liberty and Property Defense League and Individualism," *Historical Journal* 18, no. 4 (1975): 761–89; and Taylor, *Men versus the State*, introduction.

71. See Herbert, *The Right and Wrong of Compulsion by the State*; Wordsworth Donisthorpe, *Individualism: A System of Politics*, vol. 5 (London: Macmillan, 1889), https://doi.org/10.2307/2139176; and Bruce Smith, *Liberty and Liberalism: A Protest against the Growing Tendency toward Undue Interference by the State, with Individual Liberty, Private Enterprise, and the Rights of Property* (London: Longmans, Green, 1887).

72. On Cobden and the League, see chapter 8.

73. Doherty, *Radicals for Capitalism*, 612.

74. Kimberly Phillips-Fein notes that Mises was extremely popular among libertarian-leaning businessmen, much more so than Hayek, whom they tended to view as too "soft" and willing to compromise with the left. See *Invisible Hands*, chap. 2.

75. See Joseph T. Salerno and Matthew McCaffrey, eds., "A Conversation with Murray N. Rothbard," in *The Rothbard Reader* (Auburn, AL: Ludwig von Mises Institute, 2016).

76. Murray N. Rothbard, "The Clark Campaign: Never Again," *Libertarian Forum* 13, no. 5–6 (December 1980): 1–10.

77. For an account of the dispute between Rothbard and the "Kochtopus," see Doherty, *Radicals for Capitalism*, 413–18.

78. See Slobodian, *Globalists*. Tyler Cowen, for example, has argued for the overriding importance of economic growth as a moral consideration in *Stubborn Attachments: A Vision for a Society of Free, Prosperous, and Responsible Individuals* (San Francisco: Stripe Press, 2018). His favorable attitude toward big business is captured in the title of his 2019 book, *Big Business: A Love Letter to an American Anti-Hero* (New York: St. Martin's, 2019).

79. See McElroy, *Debates*, especially chap. 8.

80. Molinari, *Soirées*, 105–9.

81. See Donisthorpe, *Individualism*, chap. 7. For a succinct overview, see Ryley, *Making Another World Possible*, 67–69.

82. Auberon Herbert, "The True Line of Deliverance," in *A Plea for Liberty: An Argument against Socialism and Socialistic Legislation*, ed. Thomas Mackay (Indianapolis: Liberty Classics, 1981), 477. See also Herbert Spencer's discussion of trade unionism in volume 3 of his *Principles of Sociology* (New York: D. Appleton, 1900), especially 545–46: "the trade-union policy carried out to the full, has the effect that every kind of wage-earner is taxed for the benefit of every other kind of wage-earner."

83. Herbert Spencer, "From Freedom to Bondage," in *A Plea for Liberty: An Argument against Socialism and Socialistic Legislation*, ed. Thomas Mackay (Indianapolis: Liberty Classics, 1981).

84. George Howell, "Liberty for Labour," in *A Plea for Liberty: An Argument against Socialism and Socialistic Legislation*, ed. Thomas Mackay (Indianapolis: Liberty Classics, 1981).

85. A business that requires all workers to pay union dues is known as an "agency shop." The rationale behind such arrangements is to avoid free-riding by workers who benefit from union services without paying dues. The 1947 Taft-Hartley Act gives states the option to prohibit agency shops. Contrary to a popular misconception, Right to Work laws do not prevent workers from being forced to *join* a union. That freedom is already protected by federal legislation prohibiting "closed shops."

86. Friedman, *Capitalism and Freedom*, 115–16.

87. Hayek, *The Constitution of Liberty*, 290.

88. See, especially, Carson, "Labor Struggle: A Free Market Model."

89. Smith, *The Wealth of Nations*, I.2.2.

90. Charles G. Koch, *Good Profit: How Creating Value for Others Built One of the World's Most Successful Companies* (New York: Crown, 2015).

91. See Israel M. Kirzner, *Competition and Entrepreneurship* (Chicago: University of Chicago Press, 1993), http://www.vlebooks.com/vleweb/product/openreader?id =none&isbn=9780226375489.

92. Joseph Alois Schumpeter, *Capitalism, Socialism, and Democracy* (New York: Routledge, 2003).

93. "Go into the Exchange in London, that place more venerable than many a court, and you will see representatives of all the nations assembled there for the profit of mankind. There the Jew, the Mahometan, and the Christian deal with one another as if they were of the same religion, and reserve the name of infidel for those who go bankrupt." Voltaire, *The Works of Voltaire*, vol. 6 (Philosophical Dictionary Part 4) (E. R. Dumont, 1764).

94. Montesquieu, *The Complete Works of M. de Montesquieu*, vol. 2, *The Spirit of the Laws*, book XX, chap. 1, p. 1.

Chapter 6. Poverty and Spontaneous Order

1. Phillips Thompson, "The Political Economist and the Tramp," *Labor Standard* (New York), December 14, 1878.

2. In April 2012, President Obama delivered a rousing address before the National Press Club. Touting his own plan to expand welfare coverage, Obama pointed out that his Republican opponents were proposing a deficit-reduction plan which, though hardly libertarian, called for cutting back some welfare programs while lowering taxes. About the Republican proposal, Obama declared: "Disguised as a deficit reduction plan, it's really an attempt to impose a radical vision on our country. It is nothing but thinly-veiled Social Darwinism." "Remarks by the President at the Associated Press Luncheon," April 3, 2012, http://www.whitehouse.gov/the-press-office/2012/04 /03/remarks-president-associated-press-luncheon.

3. Donald Bellomy presents a masterful history of the concept in "'Social Darwinism' Revisited," *Perspectives in American History*, n.s., 1 (1984): 1–129. See also

Geoffrey M. Hodgson, "Social Darwinism in Anglophone Academic Journals: A Contribution to the History of the Term," *Journal of Historical Sociology* 17, no. 4 (2004): 436.

4. Bellomy's article surveys the various and conflicting (but always pejorative) meanings that have been attached to the phrase. For the particularly troubling confusion between Social Darwinism as support for eugenics and Social Darwinism as support for laissez-faire, see Thomas C. Leonard, "Mistaking Eugenics for Social Darwinism: Why Eugenics Is Missing from the History of American Economics," *History of Political Economy* 37 (2005): 200–233; and Thomas C. Leonard, "Origins of the Myth of Social Darwinism: The Ambiguous Legacy of Richard Hofstadter's *Social Darwinism in American Thought*," *Journal of Economic Behavior & Organization* 71, no. 1 (2009): 37–51, https://doi.org/10.1016/j.jebo.2007.11.004.

5. Thompson's poem about Social Darwinism, which attacked Spencer by name, was sarcastically "dedicated" to Sumner.

6. Richard Hofstadter, "William Graham Sumner, Social Darwinist," *New England Quarterly* 14, no. 3 (1941): 457–77; Hofstadter, *Social Darwinism in American Thought* (Boston: Beacon Press, 1992). Geoffrey Hodgson's bibliometric analysis, which traces the use of "Social Darwinism" before and after the 1940s, reveals an explosion in the term's popularity following Hofstadter's work. See Hodgson, "Social Darwinism in Anglophone Academic Journals," especially 445–48.

7. Hofstadter, *Social Darwinism in American Thought*, xi.

8. Hofstadter, "William Graham Sumner, Social Darwinist," 457.

9. Spencer, *Social Statics* (1995), 337, 38–40, emphasis added. Quoted by Hofstadter in *Social Darwinism in American Thought*, 41. Elsewhere in *Social Statics*, Spencer writes: "the poverty of the incapable, the distresses that come upon the imprudent, the starvation of the idle, and those shoulderings aside of the weak by the strong, which leave so many 'in shallows and miseries' are the decrees of a large, far-seeing benevolence" (289), and the interference in this process by "well-meaning" men "stops the purifying process" (289–90).

10. William Graham Sumner, *The Challenge of Facts and Other Essays* (New Haven: Yale University Press, 1914), 423, emphasis added.

11. See, for instance, George H. Smith, "Will the Real Herbert Spencer Please Stand Up?" in *Atheism, Ayn Rand, and Other Heresies* (New York: Prometheus Books, 1991), 239–50; and H. A. Scott Trask, "William Graham Sumner: Against Democracy, Plutocracy, and Imperialism," *Journal of Libertarian Studies* 18, no. 4 (2004): 1–27.

12. See Robert C. Bannister, "William Graham Sumner's Social Darwinism: A Reconsideration," *History of Political Economy* 5, no. 1 (1973): 89–109; Robert C. Bannister, *Social Darwinism: Science and Myth in Anglo-American Social Thought* (Philadelphia: Temple University Press, 1979); Bellomy, "'Social Darwinism' Revisited"; Leonard, "Origins of the Myth of Social Darwinism"; and Matt Zwolinski, "Social Darwinism and Social Justice: Herbert Spencer on Our Duties to the Poor," in *Distributive Justice Debates in Social and Political Thought: Perspectives on Finding a Fair Share*, ed. Camilla Boisen and Matthew Murray (New York: Routledge, 2016). Even the *Stanford Encyclopedia of Philosophy*, the leading reference guide written by

and for academic philosophers, now opens by noting that Spencer is "typically, *though quite wrongly*, considered a coarse social Darwinist" (emphasis added). David Weinstein, "Herbert Spencer," in *The Stanford Encyclopedia of Philosophy*, ed. Edward Zalta (Fall 2012), http://plato.stanford.edu/archives/fall2012/entries/spencer/.

13. Herbert Spencer, "Mr. Martineau on Evolution," *Contemporary Review* 20 (June–November 1872): 147.

14. Mingardi, *Herbert Spencer*, 56–63; Spencer, *Principles of Sociology*, chaps. 17–18.

15. Spencer, *Social Statics* (1995), 102.

16. Sumner frequently decried the growing influence of wealth on politics as "plutocracy" and eventually came to see it as an even greater threat than socialism to the average American working class. For Sumner, there was a world of difference between businessmen who earned their wealth on the free market and those who earned it by political means: "A great capitalist is no more necessarily a plutocrat than a great general is a tyrant. A plutocrat is a man who, having the possession of capital, and having the power of it at his disposal, uses it, not industrially, but politically; instead of employing laborers, he enlists lobbyists. Instead of applying capital to land, he operates upon the market by legislation, by artificial monopoly, by legislative privileges; he creates jobs, and erects combinations, which are half political and half industrial; he practices upon the industrial vices, makes an engine of venality, expends his ingenuity, not on processes of production, but on 'knowledge of men,' and on the tactics of the lobby. The modern industrial system gives him a magnificent field, one far more profitable, very often, than that of legitimate industry." William Graham Sumner, "Democracy and Plutocracy," in *Earth-Hunger and Other Essays*, ed. William Graham Sumner and Albert Galloway Keller (New Haven: Yale University Press, 1913), 298.

17. On the connection between eugenics and Progressive Era economic reform, see David Bernstein and Thomas C. Leonard, "Excluding Unfit Workers: Social Control versus Social Justice in the Age of Economic Reform," *Law and Contemporary Problems* 72, no. 3 (2009): 177–204; Leonard, "Mistaking Eugenics for Social Darwinism"; Thomas C. Leonard, "American Economic Reform in the Progressive Era: Its Foundational Beliefs and Their Relation to Eugenics," *History of Political Economy* 41, no. 1 (2009): 109–41, https://doi.org/10.1215/00182702-2008-040; Thomas C. Leonard, "Eugenics and Economics in the Progressive Era," *Journal of Economic Perspectives* 19, no. 4 (2005): 109–41.

18. See Spencer, *Principles of Sociology*, part 8, chaps. 20–21; and William Graham Sumner, *What Social Classes Owe to Each Other* (Auburn, AL: Ludwig von Mises Institute, 2007), chap. 6.

19. See Spencer, *Social Statics*, chap. 16. Interestingly, Spencer did not stop at advocating the *formal* equality of women before the law and condemned not only "despotism in the state" but also "despotism in the family." "There is a fatal incongruity between the matrimonial servitude which our law recognises, and the relationship that ought to exist between husband and wife" (147).

20. Samuel Fleischacker, *A Short History of Distributive Justice* (Cambridge, MA: Harvard University Press, 2004), 166n37. Spencer was dogged by such accusations

throughout his life. When even his friend Thomas Henry Huxley wrote that Spencer's system required that the poor be left to starve, Spencer replied that "for nearly fifty years I have contended that the pains attendant on the struggle for existence may be fitly qualified by the aid which private sympathy prompts." Bitter at the unjust misrepresentation of his views by a friend, Spencer broke off his relationship with Huxley. It took years, and the interventions of many friends, to repair it. See Duncan and Spencer, *The Life and Letters of Herbert Spencer*, 335–36.

21. Gertrude Himmelfarb, *The De-moralization of Society: From Victorian Virtues to Modern Values* (New York: Vintage Books, 1996).

22. William Graham Sumner, "The Forgotten Man," in *The Forgotten Man and Other Essays*, ed. Albert Galloway Keller (New Haven: Yale University Press, 1918). The idea that the poor have a claim of justice when poverty is the result of bad luck but not when it is due to bad choices is defended by many contemporary egalitarian philosophers. For example, Richard J. Arneson, "Egalitarianism and the Undeserving Poor," *Journal of Political Philosophy* 5, no. 3 (1997): 1–34.

23. Spencer, *Social Statics*, 195.

24. Almost all the examples Spencer chose to illustrate this point involve the use of state power to benefit the rich and powerful, at the expense of the poor and marginalized: the way in which the English Inclosure Acts ran roughshod over "the claims of the poor cottagers," the privileging of landed interests in electoral politics and tax law, the disparate legal treatment of "gentleman sinecurists" and simple workmen, and so on. See ibid., 195–96.

25. In his later work, *The Principles of Ethics*, Spencer would express regret regarding the "very erroneous impression" produced in some readers by *Social Statics*: "In its full scope, the moral system to be set forth unites sternness with kindness; but thus far attention has been drawn almost wholly to the sternness. Extreme misapprehensions and gross misstatements have hence resulted" (30). For Spencer's discussion of the moral duty to relieve poverty, see *Social Statics* (1995), 203–5, 291–92, and Spencer, *The Principles of Ethics*, parts V and VI. For a summary, see Zwolinski, "Social Darwinism and Social Justice." On Sumner, see the concluding section of his *What Social Classes Owe to Each Other*, titled, "Wherefore We Should Love One Another": "It is the common frailty in the midst of a common peril which gives us a kind of solidarity of interest to rescue the one for whom the chances of life have turned out badly just now. Probably the victim is to blame. He almost always is so. A lecture to that effect in the crisis of his peril would be out of place, because it would not fit the need of the moment; but it would be very much in place at another time, when the need was to avert the repetition of such an accident to somebody else. Men, therefore, owe to men, in the chances and perils of this life, aid and sympathy, on account of the common participation in human frailty and folly" (137).

26. Sumner, "Democracy and Plutocracy," 283–84.

27. Sumner, *What Social Classes Owe to Each Other*, 101.

28. Sumner, "Democracy and Plutocracy," 283.

29. Herbert Spencer, *The Study of Sociology* (London: Henry S. King, 1873), 270–71.

30. Ibid., 271–73.

31. Herbert Spencer, "Over-Legislation," in *The Man versus the State*, ed. Herbert Spencer (Indianapolis: Liberty Fund, 1981), 278–79.

32. Herbert Spencer, "State-Tamperings with Money and Banks," in *Essays: Scientific, Political, and Speculative*, ed. Herbert Spencer (New York: D. Appleton, 1864), 2:320.

33. John Maynard Keynes, "Economic Possibilities for Our Grandchildren," in *Essays in Persuasion* (New York: Palgrave Macmillan), 321–32.

34. For example, Tom G. Palmer, "Poverty, Morality, and Liberty," in *After the Welfare State*, ed. Tom Palmer (Ottawa, IL: Jameson Books, 2012), 109–33.

35. See the discussion in Friedrich A. Hayek, "Dr. Bernard Mandeville," *Proceedings of the British Academy* 52 (1967): 125–41.

36. Bernard de Mandeville, *The Fable of the Bees, or, Private Vices, Publick Benefits* (Indianapolis: Liberty Fund, 1988), 1:356–57. Locke offers a similar argument in his discussion of the vast range of labor embodied in the "bread we eat" (*Second Treatise*, § 43).

37. Hayek would later suggest that Mandeville and David Hume might be called "Darwinists" before Darwin. Hayek writes: "in many respects Darwin is the culmination of a development which Mandeville more than any other single man had started" ("Dr. Bernard Mandeville," 93). Hayek says elsewhere: "Hume may be called the precursor to Darwin in the field of ethics" ("The Legal and Political Philosophy of David Hume," 111).

38. Mandeville, *Fable of the Bees*, 358.

39. The term "division of labor" may have been inspired by Mandeville. In a second edition of *Fable of the Bees* published in 1732 he writes: "When once Men come to be govern'd by written Laws, all the rest comes on a-pace. Now Property, and Safety of Life and Limb, may be secured: This naturally will forward the Love of Peace, and make it spread. No number of Men, when once they enjoy Quiet, and no Man needs to fear his Neighbour, will be long without learning to divide and subdivide their Labour."

40. "The Grumbling Hive," in *Fable of the Bees*, 37.

41. Vernon L. Smith, "Human Nature: An Economic Perspective," *Daedalus* 133, no. 4 (2004): 67.

42. Smith, *The Wealth of Nations*, IV.viii.4, 644.

43. On the system of natural liberty, see ibid., IV.9. The final quotation is from a lecture in 1755, quoted in Dugald Stewart, *Account of the Life and Writings of Adam Smith LL.D*, section IV, 25, https://delong.typepad.com/files/stewart.pdf.

44. Jacob Viner, "Adam Smith and Laissez Faire," *Journal of Political Economy* 35, no. 2 (1927): 198–232. See also Fleischacker, *A Short History of Distributive Justice*, 63; and Dennis Rasmussen, *The Problems and Promise of Commercial Society: Adam Smith's Response to Rousseau* (University Park: Penn State University Press, 2015), 106.

45. Mises, *Liberalism* (1927), 14.

46. Mises, *Human Action*, 830.

47. Ibid., 164–65.

48. Ayn Rand, "The Monument Builders," in *The Virtue of Selfishness* (New York: Signet, 1964), 100–107.

49. Nathaniel Branden, "The Divine Right of Stagnation," in *The Virtue of Selfishness* (New York: Signet, 1964), 141–46.

50. Friedman, *Capitalism and Freedom*, 190.

51. Ibid., 191.

52. Friedrich A. Hayek, *Law, Legislation and Liberty*, vol. 3, *The Political Order of a Free People* (London: Routledge and Kegan Paul, 1979), 55.

53. Friedman, *Capitalism and Freedom*, 191–92.

54. Charles A. Murray, *In Our Hands: A Plan to Replace the Welfare State* (Washington, DC: AEI Press, 2006).

55. See Michael D. Tanner, "The American Welfare State: How We Spend Nearly $1 Trillion a Year Fighting Poverty—and Fail," *Cato Policy Analysis* (Washington, DC: Cato Institute, April 11, 2012).

56. The $10,000 figure is Murray's. Checks would be issued to all adults over the age of twenty-one, regardless of income or willingness to work. Those earning incomes over $25,000, however, would pay back a portion of the grant in taxes. For further discussion of how a basic income might work, see Miranda Fleischer and Daniel Hemel, "The Architecture of a Basic Income," *University of Chicago Law Review* 87, no. 3 (2020): 625–881.

57. David Green, *Reinventing Civil Society: The Rediscovery of Welfare without Politics* (London: Civitas, 1993).

58. David Beito, *From Mutual Aid to the Welfare State: Fraternal Societies and Social Services, 1890–1967* (Chapel Hill: University of North Carolina Press, 1999).

59. P.H.J.H. Gosden, *Self-Help: Voluntary Associations in Nineteenth-Century Britain* (New York: Harper & Row, 1974).

60. Simon Cordery, *British Friendly Societies, 1750–1914* (Houndmills: Palgrave Macmillan, 2003).

61. David Beito, "Mutual Aid for Social Welfare: The Case of American Fraternal Societies," in *After the Welfare State*, ed. Tom G. Palmer (Ottawa, IL: Jameson Books, 2012), 67. See also Beito, *From Mutual Aid to the Welfare State*.

62. Quoted in Beito, *From Mutual Aid to the Welfare State*, 71.

63. Ibid., 75.

64. Ryley, *Making Another World Possible*, 53.

65. This sentence, and the previous two, borrow from Beito, *From Mutual Aid to the Welfare State*, 77.

66. J. W. Mason, "Thomas Mackay: The Anti-Socialist Philosophy of the Charity Organisation Society," in *Essays in Anti-Labour History*, ed. Kenneth D. Brown (London: Palgrave Macmillan, 1974), 291, https://doi.org/10.1007/978-1-349-02039-3_12.

67. Quoted in ibid., 299.

68. Quoted in ibid., 292.

69. See Hart, "The Paris School of Liberal Political Economy."

70. Spooner, "Poverty," 225.

71. Ibid., 223.

72. As discussed in chapter 5, Donisthorpe believed that wage labor was exploitative and impoverishing and should be replaced by a system of "labor capitalization," or workers cooperatives.

73. Spooner, "Poverty," 228.

74. Ibid., 229. Director's Law, named after the Chicago economist Aaron Director and popularized by George Stigler, states that the bulk of public programs are designed primarily to benefit the middle class but financed by the upper and lower classes. See George J. Stigler, "Director's Law of Public Income Redistribution," *Journal of Law and Economics* 13, no. 1 (April 1970): 1–10, https://doi.org/10.1525/sp.2007.54.1.23.

75. Spooner, "Poverty," 278.

76. Spooner, "A Letter to Grover Cleveland," 5:200.

77. Spooner, "Poverty," 258–59.

78. Brooks, *The Individualist Anarchists*, 110.

79. Benjamin Tucker, *Liberty* 1, no. 1 (August 6, 1881): 112, 113–14.

80. Ibid., 114.

81. Simon Cordery writes: "These collective-self-help organizations.... constituted the largest set of voluntary associations in Britain, reaching about six million members—equivalent to one-half of all adult males—by 1904." Quoted with citation information in Tom G. Palmer, "Bismarck's Legacy," in *After the Welfare State*, ed. Tom G. Palmer (Ottawa, IL: Jameson Books, 2012), 49. See also Green, *Reinventing Civil Society*, 61–62.

82. Nozick, *Anarchy, State, and Utopia*, 151.

83. Nozick flirted with the idea that "patterned principles of justice" might be justified as rough approximations of what full compensation to the victims of past injustice would require. Indeed, for rectification of historical injustice, Nozick considers a principle strikingly similar to Rawls's difference principle. *Anarchy, State, and Utopia*, 231.

84. Friedman, *Capitalism and Freedom*, 195.

85. Quoted by Roderick T. Long, "Rothbard's 'Left and Right': Forty Years Later," *Mises Daily*, April 8, 2006.

86. Lindsey, "Liberaltarians."

87. Wilkinson, "Is Rawlsekianism the Future?"

88. David Weigel, "A Purge at the Cato Institute?" *Slate* (blog), August 23, 2010, https://slate.com/news-and-politics/2010/08/a-purge-at-the-cato-institute.html.

89. About Rawls, Buchanan continues: "Gordon Tullock and I discovered him, or he discovered us, I forget which . . . and we have since gotten to know him personally." Also, on June 8, 1970, Baldy Harper of the Institute for Humane Studies (IHS) sent a form letter to leading libertarians in the network, requesting recommendations of scholars who were "deeply perceptive of the fundamentals of law in a libertarian society." Hayek returned his form with three names handwritten at the bottom: the first was "John Rawls" (letter shared with us by Phillip Magness, IHS).

90. On the distinction between scholarly and popular usages, see Hayek, *Law, Legislation, and Liberty*, vol. 2, *The Mirage of Social Justice*, 63, esp. at n. 3.

91. Ibid., xiii.

92. Ibid., 100.

93. Geoffrey Brennan and James Buchanan, *The Reason of Rules: Constitutional Political Economy*, Collected Works of James M. Buchanan, vol. 10 (Indianapolis: Liberty Fund, 2000), 36–37.

94. James Buchanan and Gordon Tullock, *The Calculus of Consent* (Ann Arbor: University of Michigan Press, 1962), 77–81, and explicitly at 356. On the history of the phrase "veil of uncertainty," see also James M. Buchanan, *Better than Plowing, and Other Personal Essays* (Chicago: University of Chicago Press, 1992), 22–24. Buchanan credits the idea to John C. Harsanyi, "Cardinal Welfare, Individualistic Ethics, and Interpersonal Comparisons of Utility," *Journal of Political Economy* 63, no. 4 (1955): 309–21. Rawls likewise credits Harsanyi (*A Theory of Justice*, 137).

95. Buchanan and Tullock, *The Calculus of Consent*, 78.

96. Brennan and Buchanan, *Reason of Rules*, 35.

97. Ibid. Intriguingly, Buchanan's contractarian reasoning led him to adopt something like a basic income scheme as a requirement of fairness. See James M. Buchanan, "Can Democracy Promote the General Welfare?" *Social Philosophy and Policy* 14, no. 2 (1997): 165–79.

98. Which society might be chosen on the basis of that informational constraint? Hayek writes: "The Good Society is one in which the chances of anyone selected at random are likely to be as great [that is, as favorable] as possible" (*Mirage of Social Justice*, 132). Hayek eventually chose to send his children to the United States. But, in an indication of how deeply committed he was to this fairness-tracking approach, Hayek states that he chose the United States in part because of a defect (or peek-hole) in his fairness-detecting apparatus: he could predict that his children "would be placed there with a white and not with a coloured family" (189). America would not have passed the test of fairness, especially when one focused on the possibility that one could turn out to be what Rawls would later call "a representative member of the worst off class"—which in the case of 1940s America might well have meant to be Black.

99. Here is Rawls's depiction of the relationship between his approach and that of Buchanan and Tullock: "Both arguments are similar in that in each case an attempt is made to formulate a general principle to apply to the choice and design of a constitution, and the decision on a constitution is to be made first in the absence of certain kinds of information and is to regulate subsequent decisions and actions. The approaches differ in that Buchanan and Tullock use as the principle of choice Pareto's criterion as adjusted to apply to institutions, and they are mainly concerned with that part of the constitution having to do with legislative procedure, for example, with the advisability of majority rule; they take the fundamental constitutional liberties as more or less given" (John Rawls, "Constitutional Liberty and the Concept of Justice," *NOMOS: American Society for Political and Legal Philosophy* 6 [1963]: 100n1). As Buchanan would later reflect: "The coincidence both in the timing of our

initial work and in the basic similarity in analytic constructions has made me share an affinity with Rawls that has seemed mysterious to critics of both of us" (*Better than Plowing*, 24).

100. "Bleeding Heart Libertarianism," *Bleeding Heart Libertarians*, March 3, 2011, http://bleedingheartlibertarians.com/2011/03/bleeding-heart-libertarianism/.

101. For example, Jessica Flanigan, "BHL's and UBI's," *Bleeding Heart Libertarians* (blog), April 30, 2012, https://bleedingheartlibertarians.com/2012/04/bhls-ubis/; Christopher Freiman, "A Moral Case for a Basic Income," *Bleeding Heart Libertarians* (blog), April 16, 2016, https://bleedingheartlibertarians.com/2016/04/a-moral-case-for-a-basic-income/.

102. Steve Horwitz and Sara Skwire, "Is There a Libertarian Position on Pornography?" *Bleeding Heart Libertarians* (blog), March 6, 2014, https://bleedingheartlibertarians.com/2014/03/7452/; Andrew J. Cohen, "Psychological Harm and Free Speech on Campus," *Bleeding Heart Libertarians* (blog), July 5, 2017, https://bleedingheartlibertarians.com/2017/07/psychological-harm-free-speech-campus/.

103. Kevin Vallier, "The Libertarian Position on Religion in Public Life," *Bleeding Heart Libertarians* (blog), March 6, 2016, https://bleedingheartlibertarians.com/2016/03/the-libertarian-position-on-religion-in-public-life/; Kevin Vallier, "In Defense of Hobby Lobby," *Bleeding Heart Libertarians* (blog), November 29, 2013, https://bleedingheartlibertarians.com/2013/11/in-defense-of-hobby-lobby/.

104. Jason Brennan, "A Simple Libertarian Argument for Environmental Regulation," *Bleeding Heart Libertarians* (blog), September 26, 2011, https://bleedingheartlibertarians.com/2011/09/a-simple-libertarian-argument-for-environmental-regulation/; Matt Zwolinski, "Objections to the Simple Libertarian Argument for Environmental Regulation," *Bleeding Heart Libertarians* (blog), October 1, 2011, https://bleedingheartlibertarians.com/2011/10/objections-to-the-simple-libertarian-argument-for-environmental-regulation/; Matt Zwolinski, "A New Essay on Libertarianism and Pollution," *Bleeding Heart Libertarians* (blog), May 30, 2014, http://bleedingheartlibertarians.com/2014/05/a-new-essay-on-libertarianism-and-pollution/.

105. Tom G. Palmer, "Oddballs vs. Scholars, For Negative Liberty, Against the Welfare State," *Cato Unbound* (blog), March 25, 2007, https://www.cato-unbound.org/2007/03/25/tom-g-palmer/oddballs-vs-scholars-negative-liberty-against-welfare-state/. But see Jason Brennan, "On Positive Liberty," *Bleeding Heart Libertarians* (blog), February 7, 2013, http://bleedingheartlibertarians.com/2013/02/on-positive-liberty/.

106. Kevin Carson, "An Introduction to Left Libertarianism?" *Center for a Stateless Society* (blog), June 15, 2014, https://c4ss.org/content/28216.

107. Roderick T. Long, "Whence I Advene," *Bleeding Heart Libertarians* (blog), March 9, 2011, https://bleedingheartlibertarians.com/2011/03/whence-i-advene/.

108. Gary Chartier, "Embracing Markets, Opposing 'Capitalism,'" *Bleeding Heart Libertarians* (blog), March 22, 2011, https://bleedingheartlibertarians.com/2011/03/embracing-markets-opposing-capitalism/.

109. Charles Johnson, "Libertarian Anticapitalism," *Bleeding Heart Libertarians* (blog), August 18, 2011, https://bleedingheartlibertarians.com/2011/08/libertarian-anticapitalism/.

110. See Kevin Carson, *Studies in Mutualist Political Economy* (Kevin A. Carson, 2007).

111. Roderick T. Long, "Libertarianism Means Worker Empowerment," *Bleeding Heart Libertarians* (blog), July 10, 2012, https://bleedingheartlibertarians.com/2012/07/libertarianism-means-worker-empowerment/; Roderick T. Long, "Why Libertarians Should Oppose Sweatshops," *Bleeding Heart Libertarians* (blog), June 9, 2012, https://bleedingheartlibertarians.com/2012/06/why-libertarians-should-oppose-sweatshops.

112. Kevin A. Carson, "Reparations: Cui Bono?"*Mutualist.org* (blog), 2008, http://www.mutualist.org/id9.html.

113. Tyler Cowen, "What Libertarianism Has Become and Will Become—State Capacity Libertarianism," *Marginal Revolution* (blog), January 1, 2020, https://marginalrevolution.com/marginalrevolution/2020/01/what-libertarianism-has-become-and-will-become-state-capacity-libertarianism.html.

114. Tyler Cowen, "The Paradox of Libertarianism," *Cato Unbound* (blog), March 11, 2007, https://www.cato-unbound.org/2007/03/11/tyler-cowen/paradox-libertarianism/. For a critique of state capacity libertarianism, see Samuel Hammond, "Three Motivations for State Capacity Libertarianism," *Niskanen Center* (blog), January 24, 2020, https://www.niskanencenter.org/three-motivations-for-state-capacity-libertarianism/; Ilya Somin, "Tyler Cowen on 'State Capacity Libertarianism' I: Is It the Wave of the 'Smart' Libertarian Future?" *The Volokh Conspiracy* (blog), January 16, 2020, https://reason.com/volokh/2020/01/16/tyler-cowen-on-state-capacity-libertarianism-i-is-it-the-wave-of-the-smart-libertarian-future/; Ilya Somin, "Tyler Cowen on 'State Capacity Libertarianism' II: Is It the Right Path for Libertarians to Follow?" *The Volokh Conspiracy* (blog), January 19, 2020, https://reason.com/volokh/2020/01/19/tyler-cowen-on-state-capacity-libertarianism-ii-is-it-the-right-path-for-libertarians-to-follow/; Ryan Murphy and Colin O'Reilly, "Assessing State Capacity Libertarianism," *Cato Journal*, Fall 2020, https://www.cato.org/cato-journal/fall-2020/assessing-state-capacity-libertarianism; David Henderson, "The Meaning of Libertarianism," *Defining Ideas* (blog), January 9, 2020, https://www.hoover.org/research/meaning-libertarianism.

Chapter 7. Racial Justice and Individualism

1. Jonathan Blanks, "Looking Back to Look Forward: Blacks, Liberty, and the State," *Libertarianism.org* (blog), June 27, 2014, https://www.libertarianism.org/columns/looking-back-look-forward-blacks-liberty-state.

2. Thomas Carlyle, "Occasional Discourse on the Negro Question," *Fraser's Magazine for Town and Country* 40 (December 1840): 670–79.

3. Ibid., 675.

4. Hayek refers to Carlyle as "an arch-reactionary" ("The Legal and Political Philosophy of David Hume," in *Studies in Philosophy, Politics, and Economics*, ed. Friedrich A. Hayek [Chicago: University of Chicago Press, 1967], 110).

5. Thomas Carlyle, "The Present Time," in *Latter-Day Pamphlets* (London: Chapman and Hall, 1850), 58.

6. Ibid., 59.

7. Ibid., 67.

8. John Stuart Mill, "The Negro Question," *Fraser's Magazine* 41 (January 1850): 25–310, in John Stuart Mill, *The Collected Works of John Stuart Mill, Volume XXI—Essays on Equality, Law, and Education*, ed. John M. Robson (Toronto: University of Toronto Press, 1984) [downloaded from the Online Library of Liberty].

9. John Stuart Mill, "The Negro Question," *Fraser's Magazine for Town and Country*, reprinted in *Littell's Living Age* 24 (1850): 465–69.

10. Adam Smith. *An Inquiry into the Nature and Causes of the Wealth of Nations* (Glasgow ed., 1776), 28.

11. Jim Powell, *Greatest Emancipations: How the West Abolished Slavery* (New York: St. Martin's, 2008), 88.

12. Parliament passed the Slavery Abolition Act in 1833.

13. Perry, *Radical Abolitionism*, 95.

14. Quoted in Carl Watner, "Those 'Impossible Citizens': Civil Resistants in 19th Century New England," *Journal of Libertarian Studies* 3, no. 2 (1980): 182.

15. Garrison, "Declaration of Sentiments," 68.

16. Perry, *Radical Abolitionism*, 48–49.

17. Garrison, "Declaration of Sentiments," 69.

18. Perry, *Radical Abolitionism*, 58.

19. Quoted in George H. Smith, "Abolitionism: Wendell Phillips on Voting and Political Action," *Libertarianism.org* (blog), January 20, 2017, p. 3, https://www.libertarianism.org/columns/abolitionism-wendell-phillips-voting-political-action.

20. Henry Clarke Wright to *The Liberator* (c. March 1844), in William Lloyd Garrison, *Documents of Upheaval: Selections from William Lloyd Garrison's "The Liberator," 1831–1865*, ed. Truman Nelson (New York: Hill and Wang, 1966), 196.

21. Henry C. Wright, "The New National Organization," *The Liberator*, no. 490 (May 22, 1840): 83.

22. Henry C. Wright, *No Rights, No Duties, or, Slaveholders, as Such, Have No Rights; Slaves, as Such, Owe No Duties* (Boston: Henry C. Wright, 1860), 15.

23. Henry C. Wright, *Human Life: Illustrated in My Individual Experience as a Child, a Youth, and a Man* (Boston: Bela Marsh, 1849), 369.

24. Wendell Phillips Garrison and Francis Jackson Garrison, *William Lloyd Garrison, 1805–1879: The Story of His Life Told by His Children* (New York: Century Company, 1885), 159.

25. Perry, *Radical Abolitionism*, 234.

26. Ibid., 236.

27. Spooner, "Poverty," 58–59.

28. Lysander Spooner, *The Unconstitutionality of Slavery* (Boston: Bela Marsh, 1845), 20.

29. Lysander Spooner, "A Plan for the Abolition of Slavery, and to the Non-Slaveholders of the South" (1858), in *The Collected Works of Lysander Spooner* (Indianapolis: Liberty Fund, 1860), 3:1.

30. Spooner, "The Unconstitutionality of Slavery," 3:98.

31. Spooner, "A Plan for the Abolition of Slavery," 3:1. It is merely habits of complacency that led other reformers of Spooner's day, including other so-called abolitionists, to accept the slow and uncertain path of legal abolition (for example, as followed in the case of England). People have positive duties, grounded in natural law, to assist such slave rebellions whenever possible: "This duty being naturally inherent in human relations and necessities, governments and laws have no authority in opposition to it. If they interpose themselves, they must be trampled under foot without ceremony, as we would trample underfoot laws that forbid us to rescue men from wild beasts, or from burning buildings" (Spooner, "A Plan for the Abolition of Slavery," 2).

32. See generally Watner, "The Radical Libertarian Tradition in Antislavery Thought."

33. Quoted in George H. Smith, "Gerrit Smith, Lysander Spooner, and Dio Lewis on Prohibition," *Libertarianism.org* (blog), April 21, 2017, https://www.libertarianism.org/columns/gerrit-smith-lysander-spooner-dio-lewis-prohibition.

34. Frederick Douglass, *Narrative of the Life of Frederick Douglass* (New York: Dover, 1995), 111.

35. Ibid., 113. Douglass repeatedly emphasized the centrality of economic liberty to freedom and its absence as a central defining feature of the wrongness of slavery. In his essay "The Nature of Slavery," Douglass writes: "A master is one—to speak the vocabulary of the southern states—who claims and exercises a right of property in the person of a fellow man." Regarding the slave, by contrast: "He can own nothing, possess nothing, acquire nothing, but what must belong to another. To eat the fruit of his own toil, to clothe his person with the work of his own hands, is considered stealing. He toils that another may reap the fruit; he is industrious that another may live in idleness." From *Libertarianism.org*, Libertarian Library, "You Are a Man and So Am I," 2, https://www.libertarianism.org/publications/essays/you-are-man-so-am-i.

36. Quoted in Nicholas Buccola, *The Political Thought of Frederick Douglass: In Pursuit of American Liberty* (New York: New York University Press, 2013), 47.

37. Ibid.

38. Ibid., 52.

39. Ibid.

40. Ibid., 118.

41. See especially Frederick Douglass, "Who and What Is Woman? An Address Delivered in Boston, Massachusetts, on 24 May 1886," originally published in *Boston Women's Journal*, June 5, 1886, reprinted in *The Frederick Douglass Papers*, ser. 1: Speeches, Debates, and Interviews, vol. 5: 1881–95, ed. John Blassingame and John McKivigan (New Haven: Yale University Press, 1985).

42. For a discussion on Douglass's positions with respect to Chinese immigrants and Mormons, see Buccola, *The Political Thought of Frederick Douglass*, chap. 3.

43. Douglass's conversations with Gerrit Smith also eventually led him away from Garrison's view that the Constitution is pro-slavery, as well as the Garrisonian corollary that slavery could only be ended by dissolving the Union.

44. David W. Blight, *Frederick Douglass: Prophet of Freedom* (New York: Simon & Schuster, 2018), 296. This paragraph and the next draw freely on Blight's account.

45. Ibid., 305.

46. Ibid., 260.

47. "Self-Made Men" [1859], in John Blassingame and John McKivigan, eds., *The Frederick Douglass Papers*, ser. 1, vol. 4 (New Haven: Yale University Press, 1992), 545–75.

48. "Rand Paul on the Civil Rights Act," *The Rachel Maddow Show*, May 19, 2010, MSNBC.

49. Ibid.

50. Congressman Ron Paul, Rand Paul's father, also faced criticism for objecting to the Civil Rights Act. For example, see Jonathan Chait, "How Ron Paul's Libertarian Principles Support Racism," *New York Magazine*, January 2, 2012. A fundraising newsletter, sent out in Ron Paul's name, states: "Boy, it sure burns me to have a national holiday for Martin Luther King. I voted against this outrage time and again as a Congressman. What an infamy that Ronald Reagan approved it! We can thank him for our annual Hate Whitey Day." Quoted from "The Coming Race War," in *Ron Paul Newsletter*, February 1990. Paul faced ferocious criticism: for example, James Kirchick, "Angry White Man," *New Republic* (blog), January 7, 2008, https:// newrepublic.com/article/61771/angry-white-man; and Ta-Nehisi Coates, "MLK Day Fact Check," *The Atlantic* (blog), January 7, 2012, https://www.theatlantic.com /politics/archive/2012/01/mlk-day-fact-check/251037/.

51. *The Situation Room*, hosted by Wolf Blitzer, May 20, 2010, CNN.

52. Walter Williams, "The Right to Discriminate," *Creators Syndicate*, June 1, 2010, https://www.creators.com/read/walter-williams/06/10/the-right-to-discriminate.

53. *Fox News America Live*, hosted by Megyn Kelly, May 20, 2010, Fox News Channel.

54. Ayn Rand, "Racism" (1963), in *The Virtue of Selfishness* (New York: Signet, 1964), 120.

55. Ibid.

56. In 1963, Rand wrote about the proposed civil rights legislation, "if that 'civil rights' bill is passed it will be the worst breach of property rights in the sorry record of American history in respect to that subject" (ibid., 127).

57. Ibid., 122.

58. Mises critiques what he calls "racial polylogism," which "ascribes to each race a peculiar logical structure of mind." Ludwig von Mises, *Human Action* (1949; Auburn, AL: Ludwig von Mises Institute, 1999), 75.

59. Friedman is following Gary S. Becker, *The Economics of Discrimination* (Chicago: University of Chicago Press, 1971).

60. Friedman, *Capitalism and Freedom*, 110.

61. Ibid., 109.

62. Ibid., 110.

63. Rothbard makes a similar argument: "in the free market any such discrimination is costly, and will have to be paid for by the property owner concerned" (*For a New Liberty*, 255).

64. Rand, "Racism," 125.

65. Note that libertarians have expressed ambivalence about states' rights, sometimes seeing them as possible bulwarks against socialism. See Murray Rothbard, "Letter to State's Rights Democrats Headquarters" (date unknown but presumably 1948), https://www.lewrockwell.com/1970/01/murray-n-rothbard/rothbard-writes-the-dixiecrats/.

66. Friedman, *Capitalism and Freedom*, 111.

67. Ibid., 113.

68. Ibid., 114.

69. Ibid. See also "Friedman Cautions against Rights Bill," *Harvard Crimson*, May 5, 1964, https://www.thecrimson.com/article/1964/5/5/friedman-cautions-against-rights-bill-pmilton/.

70. For example, public schooling, which was intended in part to increase integration, in fact has deepened segregation. See Milton Friedman, "Whose Intolerance?" *Newsweek*, October 6, 1975, p. 73, https://miltonfriedman.hoover.org/internal/media/dispatcher/214153/full.

71. Robert Nozick quoted in Albert Zlabinger, "An Interview with Robert Nozick," *Libertarian Review* (December 1977), https://www.libertarianism.org/publications/essays/interview-robert-nozick.

72. Barry Goldwater, "Speech on Rights," *New York Times*, June 19, 1964, https://www.nytimes.com/1964/06/19/archives/text-of-goldwater-speech-on-rights.html.

73. Thomas Sowell, "Affirmative Action Reconsidered: Was It Necessary in Academia? Evaluation Studies 27," American Enterprise Institute, December 1975, https://files.eric.ed.gov/fulltext/ED130570.pdf.

74. "A Poignant Anniversary," *National Review*, August 27, 2013, https://www.nationalreview.com/2013/08/poignant-anniversary-thomas-sowell/#pq=PKnYWG.

75. Sowell, "Affirmative Action Reconsidered," 9.

76. Ibid. See also Thomas Sowell, "The Day Cornell Died," *Weekly Standard*, no. 4 (May 3, 1999), https://www.hoover.org/research/day-cornell-died; Jason L. Riley, *Maverick: A Biography of Thomas Sowell* (New York: Basic Books, 2021); and especially, Thomas Sowell, *A Personal Odyssey* (New York: Free Press, 2000).

77. Walter Williams, "Affirmative Action or Racism," *WND* (blog), January 29, 2003, https://www.wnd.com/2003/01/16984/. See also Walter Williams, "Discrimination and Liberty," *Foundation for Economic Education* (blog), April 1, 1998, https://fee.org/articles/discrimination-and-liberty/; and Williams, "The Right to Discriminate."

78. Williams, "Discrimination and Liberty."

79. Anthony Machi, *"Good Intentions" with Walter E. Williams*, https://www.youtube.com/watch?v=L5TS8QUJWXo.

80. Ibid.

81. Rand, "Racism"; Milton Friedman, "The Negro in America," *Newsweek*, December 11, 1967, 89; Murray N. Rothbard, "The Black Revolution," *Left and Right* 3, no. 3 (Spring/Autumn 1967): 8; Murray N. Rothbard, "The Negro Revolution," *New Individualist Review* 3, no. 1 (Summer 1963): 429–37, from Ralph Raico, *New Individualist Review*, intro. Milton Friedman (Indianapolis: Liberty Fund, 1981).

82. Rockwell, "The Case for Paleo-Libertarianism."

83. Ibid., 34.

84. Ibid., 34–35.

85. Ibid., 34.

86. Ibid., 35.

87. Ibid.

88. Ibid., 37.

89. Ibid.

90. Ibid.

91. Ibid., 38.

92. Llewellyn Rockwell Jr., "It's Safe Streets versus Urban Terror: In the '50's, Rampant Crime Didn't Exist Because Offenders Feared What the Police Would Do," *Los Angeles Times*, March 10, 1991, https://www.latimes.com/archives/la-xpm-1991 -03-10-op-178-story.html.

93. Rothbard, "Right-Wing Populism," 8–9.

94. Murray N. Rothbard, "Marshall, Civil Rights, and the Court" (1991), in *The Irrepressible Rothbard: The Rothbard-Rockwell Report Essays of Murray Rothbard*, ed. Llewellyn Rockwell (Burlingame, CA: Center for Libertarian Studies, 2000), 374.

95. Rothbard credits this three-part categorization to Emil Franzi (ibid., 12).

96. Rothbard, "The Black Revolution," 8.

97. Ibid., 12.

98. Ibid., 13.

99. Ibid.

100. Blanks, "Looking Back to Look Forward," 1.

101. There were significant differences between the acts. The 1875 law prohibited discrimination in "public accommodations"; the 1964 law also forbade discrimination in employment. The later act, but not the earlier one, authorized federal action to combat school segregation.

102. During this period, state-imposed laws required segregation, and the state systematically failed to protect the persons and the property of minorities. So we might well debate the fairness of this test of the "libertarian program." Nonetheless, even commentators sympathetic to libertarianism have questioned the record of libertarian principles during this period. See Bruce Bartlett, "Rand Paul Is No Barry Goldwater on Civil Rights," *Capital Gains and Games* (blog), May 20, 2010, http:// capitalgainsandgames.com/blog/bruce-bartlett/1734/rand-paul-no-barry-goldwater -civil-rights.

103. As Lyndon Johnson put the point in a 1965 commencement address to Howard University, "You do not take a person who, for years, has been hobbled by chains

and liberate him, bring him up to the starting line of a race and then say, 'you are free to compete with all the others,' and still justly believe that you have been completely fair."

104. David Bernstein, "Context Matters: A Better Libertarian Approach to Anti-discrimination Law," *Cato Unbound* (blog), June 16, 2010, https://www.cato-unbound .org/2010/06/16/david-e-bernstein/context-matters-better-libertarian-approach -antidiscrimination-law/.

105. Ibid.

106. Ibid.

107. Ibid.

108. Sheldon Richman, "Context-Keeping and Community Organizing," *Cato Unbound* (blog), June 18, 2010, https://www.cato-unbound.org/2010/06/18/sheldon -richman/context-keeping-community-organizing/.

109. David T. Beito and Linda Royster Beito, *Black Maverick: T.R.M. Howard's Fight for Civil Rights and Economic Power* (Champaign: University of Illinois Press, 2009).

110. Richman, "Context-Keeping and Community Organizing."

111. Ibid.

112. Ibid.

113. Emily Ekins, "Libertarians Are More Racially Diverse than Some May Realize," *Cato@Liberty* (blog), June 13, 2016, https://www.cato.org/blog/libertarians-are -more-racially-diverse-people-realize.

114. Jonathan Blanks, "Why Aren't There More Black Libertarians," *Libertarianism.org*, May 23, 2014, https://www.libertarianism.org/columns/why-are-there-so -few-Black-libertarians. Note: the phrase "white liberty" is our own.

115. David Boaz, "Up from Slavery," *Reason.com* (blog), April 6, 2010, https:// reason.com/2010/04/06/up-from-slavery/.

116. Blanks, "Why Aren't There More Black Libertarians."

117. Jacob Levy, "Black Liberty Matters," *Niskanen Center*, September 20, 2017, https://www.niskanencenter.org/Black-liberty-matters/.

118. Ibid.

119. Fabio Rojas, "Race and the Contamination of Freedom," *Bleeding Heart Libertarianism* (blog), January 2, 2019, https://bleedingheartlibertarians.com/2012/06 /why-libertarians-should-oppose-sweatshops/; see also Fabio Rojas, "Race and Libertarianism," in *The Routledge Companion to Libertarianism*, ed. Matt Zwolinski and Benjamin Ferguson (New York: Routledge, 2022).

120. This is merely a stipulative definition. Whether "racism" is the proper term to describe institutional forms of this type is an interesting question that we do not pursue here.

121. Jacob Levy, "Of Groups, Intersections, and the People Who Inhabit Them," *Cato Unbound*, May 18, 2020, https://www.cato-unbound.org/2020/05/18/jacob-t -levy/groups-intersections-people-who-inhabit-them/.

122. Will Wilkinson, "Grand Racist Party," *The Economist*, August 22, 2012, https://www.economist.com/democracy-in-america/2012/08/22/grand-racist-party.

123. Charles G. Koch and Mark V. Holden, "The Overcriminalization of America," *Politico*, January 7, 2015, https://www.politico.com/magazine/story/2015/01/overcriminalization-of-america-113991.

124. Matthew Feeney, "Why 1619 Matters in 2019," *Cato@Liberty* (blog), August 19, 2019, https://www.cato.org/blog/why-1619-matters-2019; Jonathan Blanks, "The 1619 Project: Confronting the Legacies of American Slavery," *Cato@Liberty* (blog), August 19, 2019, https://www.cato.org/blog/1619-project-confronting-legacies-american-slavery.

125. Michael F. Cannon, "John Lewis, Hero of Liberty," *Cato Institute* (blog), January 17, 2020, https://www.cato.org/publications/commentary/john-lewis-libertarian-hero.

126. Levy, "Of Groups, Intersections, and the People Who Inhabit Them"; Phillip W. Magness, "Does Classical Liberalism Need Intersectionality Theory?" *Cato Unbound*, May 26, 2020, https://www.cato-unbound.org/2020/05/26/phillip-w-magness/does-classical-liberalism-need-intersectionality-theory/; Fabio Rojas, "Intersectionality: Friend or Foe of Classical Liberalism?" *Cato Unbound*, May 28, 2020, https://www.cato-unbound.org/2020/05/28/fabio-rojas/intersectionality-friend-or-foe-classical-liberalism/; Kimberlé Crenshaw, "Demarginalizing the Intersection of Race and Sex: A Black Feminist Critique of Antidiscrimination Doctrine, Feminist Theory and Antiracist Politics," *University of Chicago Legal Forum*, no. 1 (1989): 139–67.

Chapter 8. Global Justice and Nonintervention

1. Free Trade Union, *A Message from the Forties: A Free Trade Masque* (London: Free Trade Union, 1909). See also Frank Trentmann, *Free Trade Nation: Commerce, Consumption, and Civil Society in Modern Britain* (Oxford: Oxford University Press, 2008).

2. Other thinkers in the libertarian tradition, however, have formulated their own ideas about global justice in terms of orthodox principles of international relations theory—including a libertarian just war theory, and even a distinctively libertarian peace hypothesis.

3. Loren E. Lomasky and Fernando R. Tesón, *Justice at a Distance: Extending Freedom Globally* (New York: Cambridge University Press, 2015), 1.

4. In one of its first issues, *The Economist* published an excerpt from the "Anti-Bread-Tax Circular" that gives a sense of the organizational energy and efficiency of the League in promoting its lectures: "From a fortnight to three weeks' notice has been given throughout the county, by advertisements in the local papers, by placards posted in all the towns and villages within twenty miles of the place of meeting and handbills distributed to the farmers visiting the principal markets. . . . With a view to giving the widest and most correct publicity to the proceedings, able reporters have invariably accompanied the deputation from London, who have taken down the speeches verbatim, which have been printed and systematically distributed by agents

of the League throughout every parish in the county." "Movements of the Anti-Corn-Law League," *The Economist*, September 2, 1843, https://www.economist.com/node/1857278/print. In London itself, the League rented Covent Garden and Drury Lane theater for weeks at a time.

5. See chapter 5.

6. This paragraph and the one proceeding borrow from William Dyer Grampp, *The Manchester School of Economics* (Stanford: Stanford University Press, 1960), 85 (Online Library of Liberty ed., at p. 45/83).

7. See John Atkinson Hobson, *Richard Cobden: The International Man* (New York: Henry Holt, 1919), 391–95; and Grampp, *The Manchester School of Economics*, 46/83–49/83.

8. Quoted in Hobson, *Richard Cobden*, 393–94.

9. See, generally, Grampp, *The Manchester School of Economics*, 10/83–19/83; and Razeen Sally, *Classical Liberalism and International Economic Order: Studies in Theory and Intellectual History* (New York: Routledge, 2002), 39.

10. Smith, *The Wealth of Nations*.

11. David Ricardo wrote two important essays on the Corn Laws: *An Essay on the Influence of a Low Price of Corn on the Profits of Stock . . .* (1815) and *On Protection to Agriculture* (John Murray, Albemarle-Streer, 1822).

12. Quoted in Grampp, *The Manchester School of Economics*, 12/83, who cites: "On Protection to Agriculture," *The Works and Correspondence of David Ricardo*, ed. Piero Sraffa (Cambridge: Cambridge University Press, 1951), 4:244.

13. Ricardo's famous theory of wages was set out formally in *On the Principles of Political Economy and Taxation* (John Murray, 1817).

14. See, for example, David Hume, "Of the Jealousy of Trade" (1742), in *Essays: Moral, Political, and Literary* (Indianapolis: Liberty Fund, 1985); and Smith, *The Wealth of Nations*, book IV, "Systems of Political Economy."

15. Quoted in Edwin van de Haar, *Classical Liberalism and International Relations Theory: Hume, Smith, Mises, and Hayek* (New York: Palgrave Macmillan, 2009), 43.

16. *The Theory of Moral Sentiments; or, An Essay towards an Analysis of the Principles by which Men naturally judge concerning the Conduct and Character, first of their Neighbours, and afterwards of themselves. To which is added, A Dissertation on the Origins of Languages. New Edition. With a biographical and critical Memoir of the Author, by Dugald Stewart* (London: Henry G. Bohn, 1853), part 3, chap. 3.

17. Hume writes: "And as nature has implanted in every one a superior affection to his own country, we never expect any regard to distant nations, where competition arises." Improvements to the lives and liberties of distant others are best achieved by keeping the nation central. So Hume continues: "Not to mention, that, while every man consults the good of his own community, we are sensible, that the general interest of mankind is better promoted, than by any loose indeterminate views to the good of the species, whence no beneficial action could ever result, for want of a duly limited object, on which they could exert themselves." Quoted in Sally, *Classical Liberalism and International Economic Order*, 57.

18. Ibid.

19. Quoted in van de Haar, *Classical Liberalism and International Relations Theory*, 54.

20. Sally, *Classical Liberalism and International Economic Order*, 58.

21. Liberty Fund, "Did Bastiat Say 'When Goods Don't Cross Borders, Soldiers Will'?" Online Library of Liberty, https://oll.libertyfund.org/pages/did-bastiat-say-when-goods-don-t-cross-borders-soldiers-will.

22. Frédéric Bastiat, "Metaphors," in *Economic Sophisms and "What Is Seen and What Is Not Seen,"* ed. Jacques de Guenin (Indianapolis: Liberty Fund, 2017), 1st ser., chap. 22.

23. Frédéric Bastiat, "Our Products Are Burdened by Taxes," in *Economic Sophisms and "What Is Seen and What Is Not Seen,"* ed. Jacques de Guenin (Indianapolis: Liberty Fund, 2017), 1st ser., chap. 5.

24. Molinari, *The Society of Tomorrow*.

25. Gustave de Molinari, "Protection," in *Cyclopedia of Political Science, Political Economy, and the Political History of the United States*, ed. John Joseph Lalor (Chicago: Melbert B. Cary & Company, 1881), 3:413–23.

26. Gustave de Molinari, "The Production of Security," trans. J. Huston McCulloch, Occasional Papers Series #2, ed. Richard Ebeling (New York: Center for Libertarian Studies, May 1977), https://mises.org/library/production-security-0.

27. Trentmann, *Free Trade Nation*.

28. Quoted in Hobson, *Richard Cobden*, 2.

29. Similarly, the libertarian U.S. politician Ron Paul would find himself attacked by many on the right after blaming the terrorist attacks of 9/11 on interventionist U.S. foreign policy. We discuss this incident later in the chapter.

30. Quoted in Hobson, *Richard Cobden*, 106.

31. As one commentator astutely observes: "Pacifism was Cobden's ruling purpose, and that is the most informative thing that can be said about him." Grampp, *The Manchester School of Economics*, 52/83.

32. Ibid., 53/83.

33. Ibid., 52/83.

34. Hobson, *Richard Cobden*, 37–38.

35. Ibid., 389.

36. Ibid., 112.

37. Ibid., 64–65.

38. Ibid., 140.

39. Ibid., 192–93. Cobden's public career was not completely spent. Between 1859 and 1860, he was sent to France, where he negotiated a treaty with Napoleon III to lower the trade barriers between those two countries (the Cobden-Chevalier Treaty).

40. See Herbert Spencer, "The Proper Sphere of Government," in *The Man versus the State* (Indianapolis: Liberty Fund, 1981), 220–21; Spencer, *Social Statics* (1995), chap. 27.

41. Herbert Spencer, "Patriotism," in *Facts and Comments* (New York: D. Appleton, 1902).

42. William Graham Sumner, "The Conquest of the United States by Spain," in *War and Other Essays*, ed. Albert Galloway Keller (New Haven: Yale University Press, 1911), 309.

43. Robert L. Beisner, *Twelve against Empire: The Anti-Imperialists, 1898–1900* (New York: McGraw-Hill, 1968).

44. See chapters 3 and 7 for more on the connection between libertarianism and radical abolitionism in general, and Lysander Spooner's connection to John Brown in particular.

45. Harold Francis Williamson, *Edward Atkinson: The Biography of an American Liberal, 1827–1905* (Boston: Old Corner Book Store, 1934).

46. See Duncan and Spencer, *The Life and Letters of Herbert Spencer*, 135.

47. See Robert C. Bannister, "William Graham Sumner's Social Darwinism: A Reconsideration," *History of Political Economy* 5, no. 1 (1973): 102–5.

48. Wendy McElroy, "Benjamin Tucker, Liberty, and Individualist Anarchism," *Independent Review* 2, no. 3 (1998): 431.

49. See David Hart, "Gustave de Molinari and the Future of Liberty: 'Fin de Siècle, Fin de La Liberté'?" (presented at the Australian Historical Association, University of Adelaide, July 2000), http://davidmhart.com/liberty/Papers/Molinari/FutureLiberty/GdM-FutureLiberty.html.

50. Lane's *The Discovery of Freedom* was published in 1943—the same year as Paterson's *The God of the Machine* and Ayn Rand's *The Fountainhead*. For more on the relationship between these three women and the larger libertarian movement, see Doherty, *Radicals for Capitalism*, chap. 3, and Burns, "The Three 'Furies' of Libertarianism."

51. See especially Garet Garrett's novel *The Blue Wound* (New York: G. P. Putnam's Sons, 1921).

52. Ibid., 90–91.

53. Ibid., 72–73.

54. On Nock, see *Memoirs of a Superfluous Man*. Nietzsche seems to have played a role in the inegalitarian views of some libertarians, especially H. L. Mencken and Ayn Rand. On his influence on Rand, see Burns, *Goddess of the Market*. For an argument that Nietzsche influenced Hayek in this respect as well, see Corey Robin, "Nietzsche's Marginal Children: On Friedrich Hayek," *The Nation*, May 7, 2013, https://www.thenation.com/article/archive/nietzsches-marginal-children-friedrich-hayek/.

55. Richard M. Ebeling, "Friedrich A. Hayek: A Centenary Appreciation," *The Freeman*, May 1, 1999, https://fee.org/articles/friedrich-a-hayek-a-centenary-appreciation/.

56. Hayek, *Road to Serfdom*, 224.

57. Ibid.

58. Ibid., 235.

59. Molinari, *The Society of Tomorrow*.

60. Friedrich A. Hayek, "The Economic Conditions of Interstate Federalism" (1939), from Hayek, *Individualism and Economic Order*, 255.

61. Hayek, *Road to Serfdom*, 233.

62. Hayek, "The Economic Conditions of Interstate Federalism," 255.

63. Ibid., 269.

64. Ludwig von Mises, *Liberalism: The Classical Tradition*, trans. Ralph Raico, Liberty Fund Library of the Works of Ludwig von Mises, 2005 (originally published 1927), 105.

65. Ibid., 106.

66. Ibid., 113.

67. Ibid., 111–12. See also Mises, *Human Action*, 824–27.

68. Mises, *Liberalism*, 119.

69. Ibid., 121.

70. Ibid., 125.

71. Ibid.

72. Ibid., 109.

73. Ibid., 137. Elsewhere, Mises argues that open immigration also would remove a major cause of war: *Human Action*, 820.

74. Mises, *Liberalism*, 142.

75. Ibid., 149–50.

76. Ibid., 147–48.

77. Ibid., 147–51. See also Mises, *Human Action*, 820–28.

78. That file is now publicly available online at https://discovery.nationalarchives .gov.uk/details/r/C11602890. For an autobiographical account of Meyer's experiences with communism, see Frank S. Meyer, *The Moulding of Communists: The Training of the Communist Cadre*, vol. 120 (New York: Harcourt, Brace, 1961).

79. Meyer defended fusionism in a series of essays published in *National Review* and elsewhere. Many of these are collected in Frank S. Meyer, *In Defense of Freedom* (Indianapolis: Liberty Fund, 1996). It is important to note that while Meyer is often described as seeking to create a fusion between libertarianism and conservatism, he explicitly repudiated this aim and stressed that his actual intent was to create a fusion between libertarianism and the idea of *virtue*. See Frank S. Meyer, "Why Freedom," *National Review*, September 25, 1962, at 223, reprinted in Meyer, *In Defense of Freedom*.

80. As Jennifer Burns notes, the desire for an underlying system of moral values to give shape and meaning to the libertarian commitment to freedom was common not only among conservatives but among followers of Ayn Rand as well. As one Objectivist put it, "After freedom . . . what?" See Burns, *Goddess of the Market*, 260.

81. Frank Chodorov, "Reds Are Natives," in *Fugitive Essays: Selected Writings of Frank Chodorov*, ed. Charles H. Hamilton (Indianapolis: Liberty Fund, 1980), 325–26.

82. Frank Chodorov, "The Return of 1940?" *The Freeman* (September 1954). See also: Ratchet effect. "All wars come to an end, at least temporarily. But the authority acquired by the state hangs on; political power never abdicates. Note how the 'emergency' taxes of World War II have hardened into permanent fiscal policy. While a few of the more irritating war agencies were dropped, others were enlarged, under various pretexts, and the sum total is more intervention and more interveners than

we suffered before 1939." Frank Chodorov, "A Jeremiad," in *Fugitive Essays: Selected Writings of Frank Chodorov*, ed. Charles H. Hamilton (Indianapolis: Liberty Fund, 1980), 361–64. And: "The state never relinquishes entirely the prerogatives it acquires during an emergency, and so, after a series of wars and depressions direct taxation became a fixture of our fiscal policy, and those upon whom it falls must content themselves to whittling down the levies or trying to transfer them from shoulder to shoulder." Frank Chodorov, *Human Rights Pamphlet No. 15, Taxation Is Robbery* (Chicago: Human Events Associates, 1947), 8.

83. Murray Rothbard, "For a New Isolationism," *LewRockwell.com* (blog), 1959, https://www.lewrockwell.com/1970/01/murray-n-rothbard/for-a-new-isolationism/.

84. Frank S. Meyer, "The Twisted Tree of Liberty," *National Review*, January 16, 1962.

85. Murray Rothbard, "Listen, YAF," *Libertarian Forum* 1, no. 9 (August 15, 1969): 2.

86. For a detailed account of the convention, see Doherty, *Radicals for Capitalism*, chap. 6.

87. Rothbard, *The Ethics of Liberty*, 189.

88. Rothbard, *For a New Liberty*, 332.

89. Ibid., 330.

90. Ibid., 332.

91. Murray N. Rothbard, "War, Peace, and the State," *The Standard* (April 1963): 2–5, quoting Randolph Silliman Bourne, "Unfinished Fragment on the State," in *Untimely Papers* (New York: B. W. Huebsch, 1919).

92. Rothbard, *For a New Liberty*, 336. See also Murray N. Rothbard, "America's Two Just Wars: 1775 and 1861," in *The Costs of War: America's Pyrrhic Victories*, ed. John Denson (New York: Routledge, 2017), 119–34.

93. Rothbard, *For a New Liberty*, 336.

94. Rothbard, "America's Two Just Wars," 119, emphasis added.

95. Ibid., 126.

96. Ibid.

97. See Lysander Spooner, "No Treason, No. 1," in *The Collected Works of Lysander Spooner* (Indianapolis: Liberty Fund, 1860), 3:124–37.

98. Rothbard, "America's Two Just Wars," 122–29.

99. Rothbard, *For a New Liberty*, 338.

100. Ibid., 339.

101. Ibid., 342.

102. Ibid., 365.

103. Ibid., 367.

104. Ibid., 368.

105. Ayn Rand, "The Roots of War" (1966), in *Capitalism: The Unknown Ideal* (New York: New American Library, 1967), 31.

106. Ibid., 39.

107. Ibid., 35.

108. Ibid., 34.

109. Ibid.

110. Daniel Dordon, "Milton Friedman and Israel," *Jerusalem Post*, December 13, 2016, https://www.jpost.com/opinion/op-ed-contributors/milton-friedman-and -israel.

111. Milton Friedman, "Israel's Other War," *Newsweek*, August 22, 1977, 57. See also Milton Friedman, "Opening Address," in *Transcript of the Symposium on American-Israeli Economic Relations* (presented at the Symposium on American-Israeli Economic Relations, New York, June 5, 1988), 8–18.

112. Ayn Rand, "Censorship: Local and Express" (Ford Hall Forum Lecture, October 21, 1973), from *Ayn Rand's Answers: The Best of Her Q & A*, by Robert Mayhew (New York: Penguin, 2005).

113. Murray Rothbard, "Ayn Rand's Monstrous Views on the Middle East," *Libertarian Forum* (December 1971).

114. Murray N. Rothbard, "War Guilt in the Middle East," *Left and Right* 3, no. 3 (Spring–Autumn 1967): 23.

115. Ibid., 28.

116. Rothbard says Israel has only two options: "Either to continue on her present course, and, after years of mutual hostility and conflict be overthrown by an Arab people's guerrilla war. Or—to change direction drastically, to cut herself loose completely from Western imperial ties, and simply become Jewish citizens of the Middle East. If she did that, then peace and harmony and justice would at last reign in that tortured region" (ibid., 30).

117. Mises, *Liberalism*.

118. Frederick Douglass, "Our Composite Nationality," in *The Speeches of Frederick Douglass: A Critical Edition* (New Haven: Yale University Press, 2018).

119. William Leggett, "Foreign 'Paupers,'" in *Democratick Editorials: Essays in Jacksonian Political Economy* (Indianapolis: Liberty Press, 1984), 271–74. Much of Leggett's essay is devoted to rebutting the claim that immigrants will be an economic burden on American society. His arguments—that immigrants will actually be a boon because of the useful labor they provide—echo John Locke's discussion of a similar argument in his 1693 essay, "For a General Naturalisation," in *Locke: Political Essays*, ed. Mark Goldie (New York: Cambridge University Press, 1997), 392–96.

120. Milton Friedman, "What Is America?" (lecture, University of Chicago, October 3, 1977), https://miltonfriedman.hoover.org/objects/57282/what-is-america.

121. Classically Liberal, "What Milton Friedman Really Said about Immigration," February 5, 2008, http://freestudents.blogspot.com/2008/02/what-milton-friedman -really-said.html.

122. See, for examples of this sort of argument, Murray N. Rothbard, "Nations by Consent: Decomposing the Nation State," *Journal of Libertarian Studies* 11, no. 1 (1994): 1–10; and Hans-Hermann Hoppe, "The Case for Free Trade and Restricted Immigration," *Journal of Libertarian Studies* 2 (Summer 1998): 221–33. Such arguments never make entirely clear why public places should be regarded as private property rather than as a kind of unowned commons; nor do they make clear why majorities ought to have the power to restrict immigration even over the objections of

dissenting minorities within the communities. Slobodian, *Globalists*, documents the nationalist and racist elements in Hoppe's work and attempts to trace those back to certain strands in the work of Mises. For a persuasive response, see Phillip W. Magness, "Racial Determinism and Immigration in the Works of Ludwig von Mises: A Critique of Slobodian's Alt-Right Thesis," December 8, 2019, https://papers.ssrn.com /sol3/papers.cfm?abstract_id=3490778.

123. See Hoppe, *Democracy—The God That Failed*, 218.

124. Christopher Cantwell, "Why I Consider Myself Alt-Right," *Racial Agenda* (blog), August 17, 2017, https://web.archive.org/web/20170818131202 /https://christophercantwell.com/2017/08/17/consider-alt-right/.

125. Llewelyn Rockwell Jr., "Open Borders Are an Assault on Private Property" (paper presented at the Mises Circle, Phoenix, AZ, November 7, 2015), https://mises .org/library/open-borders-are-assault-private-property.

126. See Michael Huemer, "Is There a Right to Immigrate?" *Social Theory and Practice* 36, no. 3 (2010): 429–61; Chandran Kukathas, *Immigration and Freedom* (Princeton: Princeton University Press, 2021).

127. See Bryan Caplan and Zach Weinersmith, *Open Borders: The Science and Ethics of Immigration* (New York: First Second, 2019).

128. See Alex Nowrasteh and Benjamin Powell, *Wretched Refuse? The Political Economy of Immigration and Institutions*, 1st ed., Cambridge Studies in Economics, Choice, and Society (New York: Cambridge University Press, 2020).

Conclusion

1. See, for one account, Zach Weissmueller, Nick Gillespie, and Danielle Thompson, "Inside the Mises Caucus Takeover of the Libertarian Party," *Reason.com* (blog), June 15, 2022, https://reason.com/video/2022/06/15/inside-the-mises-caucus -takeover-of-the-libertarian-party/.

2. Many Mises Caucus members were especially upset when Jo Jorgensen tweeted, in response to the killing of George Floyd and the nationwide protests that followed, that "it is not enough to be passively not racist, we must be actively antiracist. #BlackLivesMatter #VoteGold." https://twitter.com/joforliberty/status /1281638042315489284?s=21.

3. See, for discussion, the report published by the Southern Poverty Law Center: Creede Newton, "Mises Caucus: Could It Sway the Libertarian Party to the Hard Right?" May 25, 2022, https://www.splcenter.org/hatewatch/2022/05/25/mises -caucus-could-it-sway-libertarian-party-hard-right.

Acton, John Emerich Edward Dalberg. "Inaugural Lecture on the Study of History." In *Lectures on Modern History*. London: Macmillan, 1906.

Anderson, Terry L., and Donald R. Leal. *Free Market Environmentalism*. Boulder, CO: Westview Press, 1991.

Applebaum, Anne. *Red Famine: Stalin's War on the Ukraine*. New York: Knopf Doubleday, 2017.

Aquinas, Thomas. *Summa Theologica*. London: R. T. Washbourne, 1918.

Aristotle. *Politics*. Trans. C.D.C. Reeve. Indianapolis: Hackett, 1998.

Arneson, Richard J. "Egalitarianism and the Undeserving Poor." *Journal of Political Philosophy* 5, no. 3 (1997): 1–34.

Bailie, William. *Josiah Warren, the First American Anarchist*. Boston: Small, Maynard & Company, 1906.

Bannister, Robert C. *Social Darwinism: Science and Myth in Anglo-American Social Thought*. Philadelphia: Temple University Press, 1979.

———. "William Graham Sumner's Social Darwinism: A Reconsideration." *History of Political Economy* 5, no. 1 (1973): 89–109.

Barnett, Randy E. "Contract Remedies and Inalienable Rights*." *Social Philosophy and Policy* 4, no. 1 (1986): 179–202. https://doi.org/10.1017/S0265052500000479.

———. *The Structure of Liberty: Justice and the Rule of Law*. Oxford: Oxford University Press, 1998.

———. "Was Slavery Unconstitutional before the Thirteenth Amendment? Lysander Spooner's Theory of Interpretation." *Pacific Law Journal* 28 (1997): 977–1014.

———. "Whither Anarchy? Has Robert Nozick Justified the State?" *Journal of Libertarian Studies* 1, no. 1 (1977): 15–21.

Barry, Norman P. *On Classical Liberalism and Libertarianism*. London: Macmillan, 1986.

Bartlett, Bruce. "Rand Paul Is No Barry Goldwater on Civil Rights." *Capital Gains and Games* (blog), May 20, 2010. http://capitalgainsandgames.com/blog/bruce-bartlett/1734/rand-paul-no-barry-goldwater-civil-rights.

Bastiat, Frédéric. "Individualism and Fraternity." In *"The Law," "The State," and Other Political Writings: 1843–1850*, ed. Jacques de Guenin. Indianapolis: Liberty Fund, 2012.

———. "The Law." In *"The Law," "The State," and Other Political Writings: 1843–1850*, ed. Jacques de Guenin. Indianapolis: Liberty Fund, 2012.

———. "Metaphors." In *Economic Sophisms and "What Is Seen and What Is Not Seen,"* ed. Jacques de Guenin. Indianapolis: Liberty Fund, 2017.

———. "Our Products Are Burdened by Taxes." In *Economic Sophisms and "What Is Seen and What Is Not Seen,"* ed. Jacques de Guenin. Indianapolis: Liberty Fund, 2017.

Bastiat, Frédéric. "Petition by the Manufacturers of Candles, Etc." In *Economic Sophisms and "What Is Seen and What Is Not Seen,"* ed. Jacques de Guenin. Indianapolis: Liberty Fund, 2017.

———. "Property and Law." In *"The Law," "The State," and Other Political Writings: 1843–1850*, ed. Jacques de Guenin. Indianapolis: Liberty Fund, 2012.

———. "The State." In *"The Law," "The State," and Other Political Writings: 1843–1850*, ed. Jacques de Guenin, 93–104. Indianapolis: Liberty Fund, 2012.

———. "There Are No Absolute Principles." In *Economic Sophisms*. Irvington-on-Hudson, NY: Foundation for Economic Education, 1964.

———. "What Is Seen and What Is Not Seen." In *Selected Essays on Political Economy*, ed. George B. de Huszar. Irvington-on-Hudson, NY: Foundation for Economic Education, 1995.

Becker, Gary S. *The Economics of Discrimination*. Chicago: University of Chicago Press, 1971.

Beisner, Robert L. *Twelve against Empire: The Anti-Imperialists, 1898–1900*. New York: McGraw-Hill, 1968.

Beito, David. *From Mutual Aid to the Welfare State: Fraternal Societies and Social Services, 1890–1967*. Chapel Hill: University of North Carolina Press, 1999.

———. "Mutual Aid for Social Welfare: The Case of American Fraternal Societies." In *After the Welfare State*, ed. Tom G. Palmer. Ottawa, IL: Jameson Books, 2012.

Beito, David T., and Linda Royster Beito. *Black Maverick: T.R.M. Howard's Fight for Civil Rights and Economic Power*. Champaign: University of Illinois Press, 2009.

Bellomy, Donald C. "'Social Darwinism' Revisited." *Perspectives in American History*, n.s., 1 (1984): 1–129.

Bentham, Jeremy. *Defence of Usury*. Pall Mall: Payne and Foss, 1787.

———. *Not Paul, But Jesus, Volume III. Doctrine*. Preliminary edition, ed. P. Schofield. London: Bentham Project, UCL, 2013. http://www.ucl.ac.uk/Bentham-Project/publications/npbj/npbj.html.

Berlin, Isaiah. "Two Concepts of Liberty." In *Four Essays on Liberty*, ed. Isaiah Berlin, 118–72. Oxford: Oxford University Press, 1969.

Berman, Harold J. *Law and Revolution: The Formation of the Western Legal Tradition*. Cambridge, MA: Harvard University Press, 1983.

Bernstein, David. "Context Matters: A Better Libertarian Approach to Antidiscrimination Law." *Cato Unbound* (blog), June 16, 2010. https://www.cato-unbound.org/2010/06/16/david-e-bernstein/context-matters-better-libertarian-approach-antidiscrimination-law/.

Bernstein, David, and Thomas C. Leonard. "Excluding Unfit Workers: Social Control versus Social Justice in the Age of Economic Reform." *Law and Contemporary Problems* 72, no. 3 (2009): 177–204.

Blanks, Jonathan. "Looking Back to Look Forward: Blacks, Liberty, and the State." *Libertarianism.org* (blog), July 27, 2014. https://www.libertarianism.org/columns/looking-back-look-forward-blacks-liberty-state.

———. "The 1619 Project: Confronting the Legacies of American Slavery." *Cato@Liberty* (blog), August 19, 2019. https://www.cato.org/blog/1619-project-confronting-legacies-american-slavery.

———. "Why Aren't There More Black Libertarians?" *Libertarianism.org* (blog), May 23, 2014. https://www.libertarianism.org/columns/why-are-there-so-few -black-libertarians.

Blight, David W. *Frederick Douglass: Prophet of Freedom.* New York: Simon & Schuster, 2018.

Block, Walter E. "Free Market Transportation: Denationalizing the Roads." *Journal of Libertarian Studies* 3, no. 2 (1979): 209–38.

———. "Toward a Libertarian Theory of Inalienability: A Critique of Rothbard, Barnett, Smith, Kinsella, Gordon, and Epstein." *Journal of Libertarian Studies* 17, no. 2 (2003): 39–85.

Boaz, David. *The Libertarian Mind: A Manifesto for Freedom.* New York: Simon & Schuster, 2015.

———. "Up from Slavery." *Reason.com* (blog), April 6, 2010. https://reason.com/2010 /04/06/up-from-slavery/.

Boétie, Étienne de la. *The Discourse on Voluntary Servitude.* Indianapolis: Liberty Fund, 1942.

Boettke, Peter J. "Libertarianism and the Austrian School of Economics." In *The Routledge Companion to Libertarianism*, ed. Matt Zwolinski and Benjamin Ferguson. New York: Routledge, 2022.

Bourne, Randolph Silliman. "Unfinished Fragment on the State." In *Untimely Papers.* New York: B. W. Huebsch, 1919.

Bradford, William. *Of Plymouth Plantation: 1620–1647.* Ed. Samuel Eliot Morison. New Brunswick, NJ: Rutgers University Press, 1952.

Bramwell, Lord. "Drink." *The Nineteenth Century* (May 1885): 878–82.

———. "Laissez Faire." London: Liberty and Property Defense League, 1884.

Branden, Nathaniel. "The Divine Right of Stagnation." In *The Virtue of Selfishness*, 141–46. New York: Signet, 1964.

Brennan, Geoffrey, and James Buchanan. *The Reason of Rules: Constitutional Political Economy.* The Collected Works of James M. Buchanan 10. Indianapolis: Liberty Fund, 2000.

Brennan, Jason. *Against Democracy.* Princeton: Princeton University Press, 2016.

———. *Libertarianism: What Everyone Needs to Know.* Oxford: Oxford University Press, 2012.

———. "Moral Parity between State and Non-State Actors." In *The Routledge Handbook of Anarchy and Anarchist Thought*, ed. Gary Chartier and Chad Van Schoelandt. New York: Routledge, 2021.

———. "On Positive Liberty." *Bleeding Heart Libertarians* (blog), February 7, 2013. http://bleedingheartlibertarians.com/2013/02/on-positive-liberty/.

———. "A Simple Libertarian Argument for Environmental Regulation." *Bleeding Heart Libertarians* (blog), September 26, 2011. https://bleedingheartliber tarians.com/2011/09/a-simple-libertarian-argument-for-environmental -regulation/.

Brennan, Jason, and John Tomasi. "Classical Liberalism." In *The Oxford Handbook of Political Philosophy*, ed. David Estlund, 115–32. Oxford: Oxford University Press, 2012.

Bristow, Edward. "The Liberty and Property Defense League and Individualism." *Historical Journal* 18, no. 4 (1975): 761–89.

Brooks, Frank. *The Individualist Anarchists: An Anthology of Liberty (1881–1908)*. New Brunswick, NJ: Transaction Publishers, 1994.

Buccola, Nicholas. *The Political Thought of Frederick Douglass: In Pursuit of American Liberty*. New York: New York University Press, 2013.

Buchanan, James M. *Better than Plowing, and Other Personal Essays*. Chicago: University of Chicago Press, 1992.

———. "Can Democracy Promote the General Welfare?" *Social Philosophy and Policy* 14, no. 2 (1997): 165–79.

———. "From Private Preferences to Public Philosophy: The Development of Public Choice." In *The Economics of Politics*, 15–25. London: Institute of Economic Affairs, 1978.

———. *The Limits of Liberty: Between Anarchy and Leviathan*. Chicago: University of Chicago Press, 1975.

———. "Politics without Romance." In *The Logical Foundations of Constitutional Liberty*. Indianapolis: Liberty Fund, 1999.

Buchanan, James, R. D. Tollison, and Gordon Tullock. *Toward a Theory of the Rent-Seeking Society*. College Station: Texas A&M University Press, 1980.

Buchanan, James, and Gordon Tullock. *The Calculus of Consent*. Ann Arbor: University of Michigan Press, 1962.

Burgin, Angus. *The Great Persuasion: Reinventing Free Markets since the Depression*. Cambridge, MA: Harvard University Press, 2012.

Burke, Edmund. *The Inherent Evil of All State Governments Demonstrated; Being a Reprint of Edmund Burke's Celebrated Essay, Entitled "A Vindication of Natural Society."* London: Holyoake and Company, 1858.

———. *A Vindication of Natural Society, or, A View of the Miseries and Evils Arising to Mankind from Every Species of Artificial Society. In a Letter to Lord ** by a Late Noble Writer*. Ed. Frank N. Pagano. Indianapolis: Liberty Fund, 1982. https://oll.libertyfund.org/title/burke-a-vindication-of-natural-society.

Burns, Jennifer. *Goddess of the Market: Ayn Rand and the American Right*. New York: Oxford University Press, 2009.

———. "The Three 'Furies' of Libertarianism: Rose Wilder Lane, Isabel Paterson, and Ayn Rand." *Journal of American History* 102, no. 3 (2015): 746–74. https://doi.org/10.1093/jahist/jav504.

Caldwell, Bruce. *Hayek's Challenge: An Intellectual Biography of F. A. Hayek*. Chicago: University of Chicago Press, 2004.

———. "*The Road to Serfdom* after 75 Years." *Journal of Economic Literature* 58, no. 3 (2020): 720–48. https://doi.org/10.1257/jel.20191542.

Caldwell, Bruce, and Leonidas Montes. "Friedrich Hayek and His Visits to Chile." *Review of Austrian Economics* 28, no. 3 (2015): 261–309. https://doi.org/10.1007/s11138-014-0290-8.

Cannon, Michael F. "John Lewis, Hero of Liberty." *Cato Institute* (blog), January 17, 2020. https://www.cato.org/commentary/john-lewis-hero-liberty.

Cantwell, Christopher. "Why I Consider Myself Alt-Right." *Racial Agenda* (blog), August 17, 2017. https://web.archive.org/web/20170818131202/https://christopher cantwell.com/2017/08/17/consider-alt-right/.

Caplan, Bryan. *The Myth of the Rational Voter.* Princeton: Princeton University Press, 2007.

Caplan, Bryan, and Zach Weinersmith. *Open Borders: The Science and Ethics of Immigration.* New York: First Second, 2019.

Carlyle, Thomas. *Latter-Day Pamphlets.* London: Chapman and Hall, 1850.

——. "Occasional Discourse on the Negro Question." *Fraser's Magazine for Town and Country* 40 (December 1840): 670–79.

Carson, Kevin A. "An Introduction to Left-Libertarianism." *Center for a Stateless Society* (blog), June 15, 2014. https://c4ss.org/content/28216.

——. "Labor Struggle: A Free Market Model." Center for a Stateless Society Paper No. 10 (2010). https://c4ss.org/wp-content/uploads/2010/09/C4SS-Labor.pdf.

——. "Reparations: Cui Bono?" *Mutualist.org* (blog), 2008. http://www.mutualist .org/id9.html.

——. *Studies in Mutualist Political Economy.* Kevin A. Carson, 2007. https://kevin carson.org/publication/mpe/.

Chait, Jonathan. "How Ron Paul's Libertarian Principles Support Racism." *New York Magazine*, January 2, 2012.

Chartier, Gary. *Anarchy and Legal Order: Law and Politics for a Stateless Society.* New York: Cambridge University Press, 2013.

——. "Embracing Markets, Opposing 'Capitalism.'" *Bleeding Heart Libertarians* (blog), March 22, 2011. https://bleedingheartlibertarians.com/2011/03/embracing -markets-opposing-capitalism/.

Child, James. "Can Libertarianism Sustain a Fraud Standard?" *Ethics* 104, no. 4 (1994): 722–38.

Childs, Roy A. "Anarchist Illusions." In *Liberty against Power: Essays by Roy A. Childs, Jr.*, ed. Joan Kennedy Taylor, 179–83. San Francisco: Fox & Wilkes, 1994.

——. "Big Business." In *Liberty against Power: Essays by Roy A. Childs, Jr.*, ed. Joan Kennedy Taylor. San Francisco: Fox & Wilkes, 1994.

——. "The Invisible Hand Strikes Back." *Journal of Libertarian Studies* 1, no. 1 (1977): 23–33.

——. "Objectivism and the State: An Open Letter to Ayn Rand." In *Liberty against Power: Essays by Roy A. Childs, Jr.*, ed. Joan Kennedy Taylor. San Francisco: Fox & Wilkes, 1994.

Childs, Roy A., Joseph R. Stromberg, and Roger Alexander. "The Political Economy of Liberal Corporativism: Essays." Center for Libertarian Studies, 1978.

Chodorov, Frank. *Human Rights Pamphlet No. 15, Taxation Is Robbery.* Chicago: Human Events Associates, 1947.

——. "A Jeremiad." In *Fugitive Essays: Selected Writings of Frank Chodorov*, ed. Charles H. Hamilton, 361–64. Indianapolis: Liberty Fund, 1980.

——. "Reds Are Natives." In *Fugitive Essays: Selected Writings of Frank Chodorov*, ed. Charles H. Hamilton, 325–26. Indianapolis: Liberty Fund, 1980.

——. "The Return of 1940?" *The Freeman* (September 1954).

Classically Liberal. "What Milton Friedman Really Said about Immigration." February 5, 2008. http://freestudents.blogspot.com/2008/02/what-milton-friedman-really-said.html.

Coates, Ta-Nehisi. "MLK Day Fact Check." *The Atlantic* (blog), January 7, 2012. https://www.theatlantic.com/politics/archive/2012/01/mlk-day-fact-check/251037/.

Cohen, Andrew J. "Psychological Harm and Free Speech on Campus." *Bleeding Heart Libertarians* (blog), July 5, 2017. https://bleedingheartlibertarians.com/2017/07/psychological-harm-free-speech-campus/.

Cohen, G. A. *Self-Ownership, Freedom, and Equality*. Cambridge: Cambridge University Press, 1995. https://doi.org/10.1017/CBO9780511521270.

Cole, Charles Woolsey. *Colbert and a Century of French Mercantilism*. North Haven, CT: Archon Books, 1964.

———. *French Mercantilism: 1683–1700*. New York: Octagon Books, 1965.

Comte, Charles. "Considerations sur l'état moral de la nation française, et sur les causes de l'instabilité de ses institutions." *Le censeur européen* 1 (March 1817): 1–2, 9.

———. "De l'organisation sociale considérée dans ses rapports avec les moyens de subsistence des peuples." *Le censeur européen* 2 (1817): 1–66.

Coquelin, Charles. "Review of Gustave de Molinari's *Soirées*." *Journal des Économistes* 24, no. 104 (1849): 364–72.

Cordery, Simon. *British Friendly Societies, 1750–1914*. Houndmills: Palgrave Macmillan, 2003.

Coughlin, Michael E., Charles H. Hamilton, and Mark A. Sullivan, eds. *Benjamin R. Tucker and the Champions of Liberty: A Centenary Anthology*. St. Paul, MN: Michael E. Coughlin, 1987.

Cowen, Tyler. *Big Business: A Love Letter to an American Anti-Hero*. New York: St. Martin's, 2019.

———. "The Paradox of Libertarianism." *Cato Unbound* (blog), March 11, 2007. https://www.cato-unbound.org/2007/03/11/tyler-cowen/paradox-libertarianism/.

———. *Stubborn Attachments: A Vision for a Society of Free, Prosperous, and Responsible Individuals*. San Francisco: Stripe Press, 2018.

———. "What Libertarianism Has Become and Will Become—State Capacity Libertarianism." *Marginal Revolution* (blog), January 1, 2020. https://marginalrevolution.com/marginalrevolution/2020/01/what-libertarianism-has-become-and-will-become-state-capacity-libertarianism.html.

Crenshaw, Kimberlé. "Demarginalizing the Intersection of Race and Sex: A Black Feminist Critique of Antidiscrimination Doctrine, Feminist Theory, and Antiracist Politics." *University of Chicago Legal Forum*, no. 1 (1989): 139–67.

Crofts, W. C. *Municipal Socialism*. London: Liberty & Property Defence League, 1885.

Curl, John. *For All the People: Uncovering the Hidden History of Cooperation, Cooperative Movements, and Communalism in America*. Oakland, CA: PM Press, 2009.

D'Amato, David. "Egoism in Rand and Stirner." *Libertarianism.org*, March 11, 2014. https://www.libertarianism.org/columns/egoism-rand-stirner.

De Vitoria, Francisco. *Vitoria: Political Writings*. Ed. Anthony Pagden and Jeremy Lawrance. Cambridge: Cambridge University Press, 1991.

Déjacque, Joseph. "De l'être-humain mâle et femelle." May 1857. http://joseph.dejacque .free.fr/ecrits/lettreapjp.htm.

Demsetz, Harold. "Toward a Theory of Property Rights." *American Economic Review* 57, no. 2 (1967): 347–59.

Dicey, A. V. *Lectures on the Relation between Law and Public Opinion in England during the Nineteenth Century.* 1905. https://doi.org/10.2307/1273907.

Dicey, Edward. "The Plea of a Malcontent Liberal." *Fortnightly* 37, no. 226 (1885): 463–77.

Doherty, Brian. *Radicals for Capitalism: A Freewheeling History of the Modern American Libertarian Movement.* New York: Public Affairs, 2007.

Donisthorpe, Wordsworth. *Individualism: A System of Politics.* Vol. 5. London: Macmillan, 1889. https://doi.org/10.2307/2139176.

———. "'Jus' and the League." *Jus: A Weekly Organ of Individualism* 2, no. 64 (March 23, 1888): 8–9.

———. "The Limits of Liberty." In *A Plea for Liberty: An Argument against Socialism and Socialistic Legislation*, ed. Thomas Mackay. Indianapolis: Liberty Classics, 1981.

———. "William Carr Crofts." *Personal Rights: A Monthly Journal of Freedom and Justice*, no. 150 (December 1894): 79–80.

Dordon, Daniel. "Milton Friedman and Israel." *Jerusalem Post*, December 13, 2016. https://www.jpost.com/opinion/op-ed-contributors/milton-friedman-and-israel.

Douglass, Frederick. "Our Composite Nationality." In *The Speeches of Frederick Douglass: A Critical Edition.* New Haven: Yale University Press, 2018.

———. "Who and What Is Woman? An Address Delivered in Boston, Massachusetts, on 24 May 1886." *Boston Women's Journal*, June 5, 1886.

Duncan, David, and Herbert Spencer. *The Life and Letters of Herbert Spencer.* 2 vols. London: Methuen, 1908.

Eabrasu, Marian. "Rothbard's and Hoppe's Justifications of Libertarianism: A Critique." *Politics, Philosophy & Economics* 12, no. 3 (2012): 288–307. https://doi.org /10.1177/1470594x12460645.

Ebeling, Richard M. "Friedrich A. Hayek: A Centenary Appreciation." *The Freeman*, May 1, 1999. https://fee.org/articles/friedrich-a-hayek-a-centenary-appreciation/.

Ekins, Emily. "Libertarians Are More Racially Diverse than Some May Realize." *Cato@ Liberty* (blog), June 13, 2016. https://www.cato.org/blog/libertarians-are-more -racially-diverse-people-realize.

Ellickson, Robert C. *Order without Law: How Neighbors Settle Disputes.* Cambridge, MA: Harvard University Press, 1991.

———. "Property in Land." *Yale Law Journal* 102, no. 6 (1993): 1315–1400.

Emmett, Ross B. *The Elgar Companion to the Chicago School of Economics.* Cheltenham: Edward Elgar, 2010.

———. "Libertarianism and the Chicago School of Economics." In *The Routledge Companion to Libertarianism*, ed. Matt Zwolinski and Ben Ferguson. New York: Routledge, 2022.

Epstein, Richard A. *Principles for a Free Society: Reconciling Individual Liberty with the Common Good.* New York: Basic Books, 1998.

Epstein, Richard A. *Takings: Private Property and the Power of Eminent Domain.* Cambridge, MA: Harvard University Press, 1985.

———. "A Theory of Strict Liability." *Journal of Legal Studies* 2, no. 1 (1973): 151–204.

Evers, Williamson M. "Toward a Reformulation of the Law of Contracts." *Journal of Libertarian Studies* 1, no. 1 (1977): 3–13.

Fabre, Cécile. *Whose Body Is It Anyway?: Justice and the Integrity of the Person.* Oxford: Oxford University Press, 2006.

Farrant, Andrew, Edward McPhail, and Sebastian Berger. "Preventing the 'Abuses' of Democracy: Hayek, the 'Military Usurper' and Transitional Dictatorship in Chile?" *American Journal of Economics and Sociology* 71, no. 3 (July 2012). https://doi.org /10.1111/j.1536-7150.2012.00824.x.

Feeney, Matthew. "Why 1619 Matters in 2019." *Cato@Liberty* (blog), August 19, 2019. https://www.cato.org/blog/why-1619-matters-2019.

Feinberg, Joel. *Harmless Wrongdoing.* Oxford: Oxford University Press, 1990.

Ferguson, Adam. *An Essay on the History of Civil Society.* T. Cadell, 1767. https://oll .libertyfund.org/title/ferguson-an-essay-on-the-history-of-civil-society.

Feser, Edward. "There Is No Such Thing as an Unjust Initial Acquisition." *Social Philosophy and Policy* 22, no. 1 (2005): 56–80. https://doi.org/10.1017 /S0265052505041038.

Filmer, Robert. *Patriarcha and Other Writings.* Ed. Johann P. Sommerville. Cambridge: Cambridge University Press, 1991.

Fitzhugh, George. *Cannibals All!, or, Slaves without Masters.* A. Morris, 1857.

Flanigan, Jessica. "BHL's and UBI's." *Bleeding Heart Libertarians* (blog), April 30, 2012. https://bleedingheartlibertarians.com/2012/04/bhls-ubis/.

Fleischacker, Samuel. *A Short History of Distributive Justice.* Cambridge, MA: Harvard University Press, 2004.

Foldvary, Fred E. "Geo-Rent: A Plea to Public Economists." *Econ Journal Watch* 2, no. 1 (2005): 106–32.

Francis, Mark. "Herbert Spencer and the Myth of Laissez-Faire." *Journal of the History of Ideas* 39, no. 2 (1978): 317–28.

Free Trade Union. *A Message from the Forties: A Free Trade Masque.* London: Free Trade Union, 1909.

Freiman, Christopher. "A Moral Case for a Basic Income." *Bleeding Heart Libertarians* (blog), April 29, 2016. https://bleedingheartlibertarians.com/2016/04/a-moral -case-for-a-basic-income/.

Fried, Barbara H. "Left-Libertarianism: A Review Essay." *Philosophy and Public Affairs* 32, no. 1 (2004): 66–93.

"Friedman Cautions against Rights Bill." *Harvard Crimson,* May 5, 1964. https:// www.thecrimson.com/article/1964/5/5/friedman-cautions-against-rights-bill -pmilton/.

Friedman, David. *The Machinery of Freedom: Guide to Radical Capitalism.* 2nd ed. La Salle, IL: Open Court, 1989.

Friedman, Jeffrey. "Politics or Scholarship?" *Critical Review* 6, no. 2–3 (March 1992): 429–45. https://doi.org/10.1080/08913819208443271.

——. "What's Wrong with Libertarianism?" *Critical Review* 11, no. 3 (1997): 407–67.

Friedman, Milton. *Capitalism and Freedom*. Chicago: University of Chicago Press, 1962.

——. "Israel's Other War." *Newsweek*, August 22, 1977.

——. "The Negro in America." *Newsweek*, December 11, 1967.

——. "Opening Address." Presented at the Symposium on American-Israeli Economic Relations, New York, June 5, 1988.

——. "What Is America?" University of Chicago, October 3, 1977. https://miltonfriedman.hoover.org/objects/57282/what-is-america.

——. "Whose Intolerance?" *Newsweek*, October 6, 1975. https://miltonfriedman.hoover.org/internal/media/dispatcher/214153/full.

Friedman, Milton, and Rose D. Friedman. *Free to Choose: A Personal Statement*. Boston: Houghton Mifflin Harcourt, 1990.

——. *Two Lucky People: Memoirs*. Chicago: University of Chicago Press, 1998.

Friedman, Milton, and George Stigler. "Roofs or Ceilings? The Current Housing Problem." Irvington-on-Hudson, NY: Foundation for Economic Education, 1946.

Garrett, Garet. *The Blue Wound*. New York: G. P. Putnam's Sons, 1921.

Garrison, Wendell Phillips, and Francis Jackson Garrison. *William Lloyd Garrison, 1805–1879: The Story of His Life Told by His Children*. New York: Century Company, 1885.

Garrison, William Lloyd. "Declaration of Sentiments of the American Anti-Slavery Convention." In *Selections from the Writings and Speeches of William Lloyd Garrison*, 66–71. Boston: R. F. Wallcut, 1852.

——. *Documents of Upheaval: Selections from William Lloyd Garrison's "The Liberator," 1831–1865*. Ed. Truman Nelson. New York: Hill and Wang, 1966.

Gaus, Gerald F. "Coercion, Ownership, and the Redistributive State: Justificatory Liberalism's Classical Tilt." *Social Philosophy and Policy* 27, no. 1 (2010): 233. https://doi.org/10.1017/S0265052509990100.

——. "Liberal Neutrality: A Radical and Compelling Principle." In *Perfectionism and Neutrality*, ed. George Klosko and Steven Wall, 137–65. Lanham, MD: Rowman and Littlefield, 2003.

——. "On Justifying the Moral Rights of the Moderns: Old Wine in New Bottles." *Social Philosophy and Policy* 24, no. 1 (2007): 84–119.

——. *The Order of Public Reason: A Theory of Freedom and Morality in a Diverse and Bounded World*. New York: Cambridge University Press, 2011.

George, Henry. "Copyright Law." *The Standard*, June 23, 1888.

——. *A Perplexed Philosopher: Being an Examination of Mr. Herbert Spencer's Various Utterances on the Land Question, With Some Incidental Reference to His Synthetic Philosophy*. New York: Charles L. Webster & Company, 1892.

——. *Progress and Poverty*. New York: D. Appleton, 1886.

Godwin, William. *An Enquiry Concerning Political Justice and Its Influence on General Virtue and Happiness*. Ed. Isaac Krammick. 2 vols. Harmondsworth: Penguin Classics, 1976.

Goff, A., and J. H. Levy. *Politics and Disease*. London: P. S. King & Son, 1906.

Goldwater, Barry. "Speech on Rights." *New York Times*, June 19, 1964. https://www .nytimes.com/1964/06/19/archives/text-of-goldwater-speech-on-rights.html.

"Good Intentions" with Walter E. Williams. 1985. https://www.youtube.com/watch?v =L5TS8QUJWXo.

Goodyear, Lucille J. "Spooner vs. U.S. Postal System." *American Legion Magazine*, January 1981. http://www.lysanderspooner.org/STAMP3.htm.

Gosden, P.H.J.H. *Self-Help: Voluntary Associations in Nineteenth-Century Britain*. New York: Harper & Row, 1974.

Grampp, William. *The Manchester School of Economics*. Stanford: Stanford University Press, 1960. https://oll.libertyfund.org/title/grampp-the-manchester-school -of-economics.

Green, David. *Reinventing Civil Society: The Rediscovery of Welfare without Politics*. London: Civitas, 1993.

Grice-Hutchinson, Marjorie. *The School of Salamanca, Readings in Spanish Monetary Theory, 1544–1605*. Oxford: Clarendon Press, 1952.

Guyot, Yves. "M. G. de Molinari." *Journal des Économistes* 53 (February 1912): 177–92.

Haar, Edwin van de. *Classical Liberalism and International Relations Theory: Hume, Smith, Mises, and Hayek*. New York: Palgrave Macmillan, 2009.

Hale, Robert L. "Coercion and Distribution in a Supposedly Non-Coercive State." *Political Science Quarterly* 38, no. 3 (1923): 470–94.

Halévy, Élie. *The Growth of Philosophical Radicalism*. Trans. Mary Morris. New York: Macmillan, 1928.

———. *Thomas Hodgskin (1787–1869)*. Paris: Société nouvelle de librairie et d'édition, 1903.

Hammond, J. H. "Slavery in the Light of Political Science." In *Cotton Is King and Proslavery Arguments*, ed. E. N. Elliott, 629–88. Augusta, GA, 1860.

Hammond, Samuel. "Three Motivations for State Capacity Libertarianism." *Niskanen Center* (blog), January 24, 2020. https://www.niskanencenter.org/three -motivations-for-state-capacity-libertarianism/.

Hardin, Garret. "The Tragedy of the Commons." *Science* 162, no. 3859 (1968): 1243–48.

Hardin, Russell, and Garrett Cullity. "The Free Rider Problem." In *The Stanford Encyclopedia of Philosophy*, ed. Edward Zalta (Winter 2020). https://plato.stanford.edu /archives/win2020/entries/free-rider/.

Harman, Moses. "Anarchism Again." *Lucifer the Light-Bearer*, March 19, 1886, p. 2.

Harsanyi, John C. "Cardinal Welfare, Individualistic Ethics, and Interpersonal Comparisons of Utility." *Journal of Political Economy* 63, no. 4 (1955): 309–21.

Hart, David M. "Gustave de Molinari (1819–1912): An Annotated Bibliography." Online Library of Liberty, n.d. https://oll.libertyfund.org/page/gustave-de-molinari-1819 -1912-an-annotated-bibliography-by-david-hart.

———. "Gustave de Molinari and the Anti-Statist Liberal Tradition, Part I." *Journal of Libertarian Studies* 5, no. 3 (1981): 263–90.

———. "Gustave de Molinari and the Anti-Statist Liberal Tradition: Part III." *Journal of Libertarian Studies* 5, no. 3 (1982): 83–104.

———. "Gustave de Molinari and the Future of Liberty: 'Fin de Siècle, Fin de La Liberté'?" Paper presented at the Australian Historical Association, University of Adelaide, July 2000. http://davidmhart.com/liberty/Papers/Molinari/FutureLiberty/GdM-FutureLiberty.html.

———. "The Paris School of Liberal Political Economy." In *The Cambridge History of French Thought*, 1st ed., ed. Michael Moriarty and Jeremy Jennings, 301–12. New York: Cambridge University Press, 2019. https://doi.org/10.1017/9781316681572.036.

Hart, H.L.A. "Rawls on Liberty and Its Priority." *University of Chicago Law Review* 40, no. 3 (1973): 534–55.

Hartwell, Ronald Max. *A History of the Mont Pelerin Society*. Indianapolis: Liberty Fund, 1995.

Hasnas, John. "The Depoliticization of Law." *Theoretical Inquiries in Law* 9, no. 2 (2007): 529–52.

———. "The Obviousness of Anarchy." In *Anarchism/Minarchism: Is a Government Part of a Free Country?*, ed. Roderick T. Long and Tibor R. Machan, 111–32. Burlington, VT: Ashgate, 2008.

———. "Reflections on the Minimal State." *Politics, Philosophy and Economics* 2, no. 1 (2003): 115–28. https://doi.org/10.1177/1470594X03002001426.

———. "Toward a Theory of Empirical Natural Rights." *Social Philosophy and Policy* 22, no. 1 (2005): 111–47.

Hayek, Friedrich A. *The Constitution of Liberty*. Ed. Ronald Hamowy. The Collected Works of F. A. Hayek, 17. Chicago: University of Chicago Press, 2011.

———. "Dr. Bernard Mandeville." *Proceedings of the British Academy* 52 (1967): 125–41.

———. "The Economic Conditions of Interstate Federalism." In *Individualism and Economic Order*, 255–72. London: Routledge and Kegan Paul, 1949.

———. *The Fatal Conceit: The Errors of Socialism*. Ed. W. W. Bartley III. London: Routledge, 1988.

———. *Individualism and Economic Order*. London: Routledge and Kegan Paul, 1949.

———. "Kinds of Order in Society." *New Individualist Review* 3, no. 2 (1964): 3–12.

———. *Law, Legislation, and Liberty*. Vol. 1, *Rules and Order*. London: Routledge, 1973.

———. *Law, Legislation, and Liberty*. Vol. 2, *The Mirage of Social Justice*. Chicago: University of Chicago Press, 1976.

———. *Law, Legislation, and Liberty*. Vol. 3, *The Political Order of a Free People*. London: Routledge and Kegan Paul, 1979.

———. "The Legal and Political Philosophy of David Hume." In *Studies in Philosophy, Politics, and Economics*, ed. Friedrich A. Hayek, 106–21. Chicago: University of Chicago Press, 1967.

———. "The Pretense of Knowledge." In *New Studies in Politics, Economics and the History of Ideas*, 25–34. London: Routledge, 1978.

———. "Principles or Expediency?" In *Toward Liberty: Essays in Honor of Ludwig von Mises*, ed. Friedrich A. Hayek, Henry Hazlitt, Leonard E. Read, Gustavo Velasco, and Floyd Arthur Harper, 1:29–45. Menlo Park, CA: Institute for Humane Studies, 1971.

Hayek, Friedrich A. *The Road to Serfdom: The Definitive Edition*. Ed. Bruce Caldwell. Vol. 2. The Collected Works of F. A. Hayek. Chicago: University of Chicago Press, 2007.

———. "The Use of Knowledge in Society." *American Economic Review* 35, no. 4 (1945): 519–30.

Heckscher, Eli Filip. *Mercantilism*. London: George Allen & Unwin, 1955.

Heller, Anne C. *Ayn Rand and the World She Made*. New York: Doubleday, 2009.

Henderson, David. "The Meaning of Libertarianism." *Defining Ideas* (blog), January 9, 2020. https://www.hoover.org/research/meaning-libertarianism.

Herbert, Auberon. "Mr. Spencer and the Great Machine." In *The Right and Wrong of Compulsion by the State and Other Essays by Auberon Herbert*, ed. Eric Mack. Indianapolis: Liberty Fund, 1978.

———. "The Principles of Voluntaryism and Free Life." In *The Right and Wrong of Compulsion by the State and Other Essays by Auberon Herbert*, ed. Eric Mack, 369–416. Indianapolis: Liberty Fund, 1978.

———. *The Right and Wrong of Compulsion by the State and Other Essays by Auberon Herbert*. Ed. Eric Mack. Indianapolis: Liberty Fund, 1978.

———. "A Voluntaryist Appeal." *The Humanitarian: A Monthly Review of Sociological Science* (May 1898): 313–29.

Herbert, Auberon, and J. H. Levy. *Taxation and Anarchism*. London: Personal Rights Association, 1912.

Hess, Karl. "The Death of Politics." *Playboy*, June 1969.

———. "What Are the Specifics?" *Libertarian Forum* 1, no. 6 (June 15, 1969).

Himmelfarb, Gertrude. *The De-Moralization of Society: From Victorian Virtues to Modern Values*. New York: Vintage Books, 1996.

Hobhouse, Leonard Trelawny, and L. T. Hobhouse. *Hobhouse: Liberalism and Other Writings*. New York: Cambridge University Press, 1994.

Hobson, John Atkinson. *Richard Cobden: The International Man*. New York: Henry Holt, 1919.

Hodgskin, Thomas. *Labour Defended against the Claims of Capital, or, The Unproductiveness of Capital Proved with Reference to the Present Combinations amongst Journeymen*. 1825.

———. "The Natural and Artificial Right of Property Contrasted." London: B. Steil, 1832.

———. "Review of Herbert Spencer's *Social Statics*." *The Economist*, February 1851.

Hodgson, Geoffrey M. "Social Darwinism in Anglophone Academic Journals: A Contribution to the History of the Term." *Journal of Historical Sociology* 17, no. 4 (2004): 428–63. https://doi.org/10.1111/j.1467-6443.2004.00239.x.

Hofstadter, Richard. *Social Darwinism in American Thought*. Boston: Beacon Press, 1992.

———. "William Graham Sumner, Social Darwinist." *New England Quarterly* 14, no. 3 (1941): 457–77.

Holcombe, Randall G., ed. *The Great Austrian Economists*. Auburn, AL: Ludwig von Mises Institute, 2009.

Hoppe, Hans-Hermann. "The Case for Free Trade and Restricted Immigration." *Journal of Libertarian Studies* 2 (Summer 1998): 221–33.

——. *Democracy—The God That Failed: The Economics and Politics of Monarchy, Democracy, and Natural Order.* New Brunswick, NJ: Transaction Publishers, 2011.

Horn, Rob Van, and Philip Mirowski. "4. The Rise of the Chicago School of Economics and the Birth of Neoliberalism." In *The Road from Mont Pèlerin*, 139–78. Cambridge, MA: Harvard University Press, 2015. https://doi.org/10.4159/9780674054264-005.

Horwitz, Steve, and Sarah Skwire. "Is There a Libertarian Position on Pornography?" *Bleeding Heart Libertarians* (blog), March 6, 2014. https://bleedingheartlibertarians.com/2014/03/7452/.

Howell, George. "Liberty for Labour." In *A Plea for Liberty: An Argument against Socialism and Socialistic Legislation*, ed. Thomas Mackay. Indianapolis: Liberty Classics, 1981.

Huemer, Michael. "Is There a Right to Immigrate?" *Social Theory and Practice* 36, no. 3 (2010): 429–61.

——. *The Problem of Political Authority: An Examination of the Right to Coerce and the Duty to Obey.* London: Palgrave Macmillan, 2012.

Huerta de Soto, Jesús. "Juan de Mariana: The Influence of the Spanish Scholastics." In *15 Great Austrian Economists*, ed. Randall G. Holcombe. Auburn, AL: Ludwig von Mises Institute, 1999.

Hume, David. "Of the Jealousy of Trade." In *Essays: Moral, Political, and Literary.* Indianapolis: Liberty Fund, 1985.

——. *A Treatise of Human Nature.* Ed. David Fate Norton and Mary Norton. New York: Oxford University Press, 2000.

Johnson, Charles W. "Libertarian Anticapitalism." *Bleeding Heart Libertarians* (blog), August 18, 2011. https://bleedingheartlibertarians.com/2011/08/libertarian-anticapitalism/.

——. "Women and the Invisible Fist." November 2010. http://charleswjohnson.name/essays/women-and-the-invisible-fist/rpa-2010.

Johnson, Kenny, and Lew Rockwell. "Do You Consider Yourself a Libertarian?" *LewRockwell.com* (blog), May 25, 2007. https://www.lewrockwell.com/2007/05/lew-rockwell/do-you-consider-yourself-a-libertarian/.

Keynes, John Maynard. "Economic Possibilities for Our Grandchildren." In *Essays in Persuasion*, 321–32. New York: Palgrave Macmillan, 2010.

——. *The General Theory of Employment, Interest, and Money.* New York: Prometheus Books, 1997.

King, John Edward. "Utopian or Scientific? A Reconsideration of the Ricardian Socialists." *History of Political Economy* 15, no. 3 (1983): 345–73.

Kinsella, N. Stephan. *Against Intellectual Property.* Auburn, AL: Ludwig von Mises Institute, 2008.

——. "Inalienability and Punishment: A Reply to George Smith." *Journal of Libertarian Studies* 14, no. 1 (1999): 79–94.

Kinsella, N. Stephan. "The Origin of 'Libertarianism.'" *Mises Wire* (blog), September 10, 2011. https://mises.org/wire/origin-libertarianism.

Kirchick, James. "Angry White Man." *New Republic* (blog), January 7, 2008. https://newrepublic.com/article/61771/angry-white-man.

Kirzner, Israel M. *Competition and Entrepreneurship.* Chicago: University of Chicago Press, 1993. http://www.vlebooks.com/vleweb/product/openreader?id=none&isbn=9780226375489.

———. *Ludwig Von Mises: The Man and His Economics.* Wilmington, DE: ISI Books, 2001.

Koch, Charles G. *Good Profit: How Creating Value for Others Built One of the World's Most Successful Companies.* New York: Crown, 2015.

Koch, Charles G., and Mark V. Holden. "The Overcriminalization of America." *Politico,* January 7, 2015. https://www.politico.com/magazine/story/2015/01/overcriminalization-of-america-113991/.

Kolko, Gabriel. *The Triumph of Conservatism: A Reinterpretation of American History, 1900–1916.* New York: Free Press, 1963.

Kukathas, Chandran. *Immigration and Freedom.* Princeton: Princeton University Press, 2021.

Layman, Daniel. *Locke among the Radicals: Liberty and Property in the Nineteenth Century.* New York: Oxford University Press, 2020.

Leggett, William. "Foreign 'Paupers.'" In *Democratick Editorials: Essays in Jacksonian Political Economy,* 271–74. Indianapolis: Liberty Press, 1984.

Lehr, Stan, and Louis Rossetto Jr. "The New Right Credo—Libertarianism." *New York Times,* January 10, 1971.

Leonard, Thomas C. "American Economic Reform in the Progressive Era: Its Foundational Beliefs and Their Relation to Eugenics." *History of Political Economy* 41, no. 1 (2009): 109–41. https://doi.org/10.1215/00182702-2008-040.

———. "Eugenics and Economics in the Progressive Era." *Journal of Economic Perspectives* 19, no. 4 (2005): 207–24.

———. "Mistaking Eugenics for Social Darwinism: Why Eugenics Is Missing from the History of American Economics." *History of Political Economy* 37 (2005): 200–233.

———. "Origins of the Myth of Social Darwinism: The Ambiguous Legacy of Richard Hofstadter's *Social Darwinism in American Thought." Journal of Economic Behavior & Organization* 71, no. 1 (2009): 37–51. https://doi.org/10.1016/j.jebo.2007.11.004.

Leroux, Robert. *Political Economy and Liberalism in France: The Contributions of Frédéric Bastiat.* New York: Routledge, 2011. https://doi.org/10.4324/9780203826584.

Leroux, Robert, and David M. Hart, eds. *French Liberalism in the 19th Century: An Anthology.* New York: Routledge, 2012.

Levy, J. H. *The Outcome of Individualism.* London: P. S. King and Son, 1892.

———, ed. *A Symposium on the Land Question.* London: T. Fisher Unwin, 1890.

Levy, J. H., and Roland K. Wilson. *Individualism and the Land Question: A Discussion.* London: Personal Rights Association, 1912.

Levy, Jacob. "Black Liberty Matters." *Niskanen Center* (blog), September 20, 2017. https://www.niskanencenter.org/black-liberty-matters/.

———. "Of Groups, Intersections, and the People Who Inhabit Them." *Cato Unbound*, May 18, 2020. https://www.cato-unbound.org/2020/05/18/jacob-t-levy/groups -intersections-people-who-inhabit-them/.

Liberty Fund. "Did Bastiat Say 'When Goods Don't Cross Borders, Soldiers Will'?" Online Library of Liberty. https://oll.libertyfund.org/pages/did-bastiat-say-when -goods-don-t-cross-borders-soldiers-will.

Liggio, Leonard P. "Bastiat and the French School of Laissez-Faire." *Journal des Economistes et des Etudes Humaines* 11, no. 2 (2001): 495–506. https://doi.org/10.2202 /1145-6396.1029.

———. "The Heritage of the Spanish Scholastics." *Religion and Liberty* 10, no. 1 (2010). https://www.acton.org/pub/religion-liberty/volume-10-number-1/heritage -spanish-scholastics.

Lindsey, Brink. "Liberaltarians." *New Republic*, December 10, 2006. https://newrepublic .com/article/64443/liberaltarians.

Lindsey, Brink, and Steven Michael Teles. *The Captured Economy: How the Powerful Enrich Themselves, Slow Down Growth, and Increase Inequality.* New York: Oxford University Press, 2017.

Locke, John. "For a General Naturalisation." In *Locke: Political Essays*, ed. Mark Goldie, 392–96. New York: Cambridge University Press, 1997.

Lomasky, Loren E. "Libertarianism at Twin Harvard." *Social Philosophy and Policy* 22, no. 1 (January 2005): 178–99. https://doi.org/10.1017/S0265052505041075.

———. *Persons, Rights, and the Moral Community.* Oxford: Oxford University Press, 1987.

Lomasky, Loren E., and Fernando R. Tesón. *Justice at a Distance: Extending Freedom Globally.* New York: Cambridge University Press, 2015.

Long, Roderick T. "Corporations versus the Market, or, Whip Conflation Now." In *Markets Not Capitalism: Individualist Anarchism against Bosses, Inequality, Corporate Power, and Structural Poverty*, ed. Gary Chartier and Charles W. Johnson. New York: Autonomedia, 2012.

———. "The Libertarian Case against Intellectual Property Rights." In *Markets Not Capitalism: Individualist Anarchism against Bosses, Inequality, Corporate Power, and Structural Poverty*, ed. Gary Chartier and Charles Johnson, 187–98. New York: Autonomedia, 2012.

———. "Libertarianism Means Worker Empowerment." *Bleeding Heart Libertarians* (blog), July 10, 2012. https://bleedingheartlibertarians.com/2012/07 /libertarianism-means-worker-empowerment/.

———. "Market Anarchism as Constitutionalism." In *Anarchism/Minarchism: Is Government Part of a Free Country?*, ed. Roderick T. Long and Tibor R. Machan, 133–54. Burlington, VT: Ashgate, 2008.

———. "Rothbard's 'Left and Right': Forty Years Later." *Mises Daily*, April 8, 2006.

———. "Rule-Following, Praxeology, and Anarchy." *New Perspectives on Political Economy* 2, no. 1 (2006): 36–46.

Long, Roderick T. "Whence I Advene." *Bleeding Heart Libertarians* (blog), March 9, 2011. https://bleedingheartlibertarians.com/2011/03/whence-i-advene/.

———. "Why Does Justice Have Good Consequences?" Paper presented at the Alabama Philosophical Society, Auburn University, October 26, 2002. https://praxeology .net/whyjust.htm.

———. "Why Libertarians Should Oppose Sweatshops." *Bleeding Heart Libertarians* (blog), June 9, 2012. https://bleedingheartlibertarians.com/2012/06/why -libertarians-should-oppose-sweatshops/.

Long, Roderick T., and Tibor R. Machan, eds. *Anarchism/Minarchism: Is Government Part of a Free Society?* Burlington, VT: Ashgate, 2008.

Lovell, John. "1889—Socialism and New Unionism." In *British Trade Unions: 1875– 1933*. London: Palgrave Macmillan, 1977.

Lukes, Steven. *Individualism*. Colchester: ECPR Press, 1973.

Machan, Tibor R. "Educating for Freedom: An Interview with Leonard Read." *Reason*, April 1975. https://reason.com/1975/04/01/educating-for-freedom/.

———. *Individuals and Their Rights*. LaSalle, IL: Open Court, 1989.

Mack, Eric. *Libertarianism*. New York: John Wiley & Sons, 2018.

———. "Lysander Spooner: Nineteenth-Century America's Last Natural Rights Theorist." *Social Philosophy and Policy* 29, no. 2 (July 17, 2012): 139–76. https://doi.org /10.1017/S0265052511000264.

———. "Nozickian Arguments for the More-than-Minimal State." In *The Cambridge Companion to Nozick's Anarchy, State, and Utopia*, ed. Ralf M. Bader and John Meadowcroft, 89–115. New York: Cambridge University Press, 2011.

———. "Robert Nozick's Political Philosophy." In *The Stanford Encyclopedia of Philosophy*, April 21, 2022. https://plato.stanford.edu/entries/nozick-political/.

———. "Self-Ownership, Marxism, and Egalitarianism: Part I: Challenges to Historical Entitlement." *Politics, Philosophy & Economics* 1, no. 1 (February 1, 2002): 75–108. https://doi.org/10.1177/1470594X02001001004.

———. "Self-Ownership, Marxism, and Egalitarianism: Part II: Challenges to the Self-Ownership Thesis." *Politics, Philosophy & Economics* 1, no. 2 (June 1, 2002): 237–76. https://doi.org/10.1177/1470594X02001002004.

———. "The Self-Ownership Proviso: A New and Improved Lockean Proviso." *Social Philosophy and Policy* 12, no. 1 (1995): 186–218.

———. "Voluntaryism: The Political Thought of Auberon Herbert." *Journal of Libertarian Studies* 2, no. 4 (1978): 299–309.

Mack, Eric, and Gerald Gaus. "Classical Liberalism and Libertarianism: The Liberty Tradition." In *Handbook of Political Theory*, ed. Gerald Gaus and Chandran Kukathas, 115–30. London: Sage, 2004.

Mackay, Thomas, ed. *A Plea for Liberty: An Argument against Socialism and Socialistic Legislation*. Indianapolis: Liberty Classics, 1981.

Macpherson, C. B. *The Political Theory of Possessive Individualism: Hobbes to Locke*. Oxford: Oxford University Press, 1962.

Magness, Phillip W. "Does Classical Liberalism Need Intersectionality Theory?" *Cato Unbound*, May 26, 2020. https://www.cato-unbound.org/2020/05/26/phillip-w -magness/does-classical-liberalism-need-intersectionality-theory/.

——. "Racial Determinism and Immigration in the Works of Ludwig von Mises: A Critique of Slobodian's Alt-Right Thesis." December 8, 2019. https://papers.ssrn .com/sol3/papers.cfm?abstract_id=3490778.

Maine, Henry. *Village Communities in the East and West: Six Lectures Delivered at Oxford to Which Are Added Other Lectures, Addresses, and Essays.* New York: Henry Holt, 1880.

Maitland, Frederick William. "William Stubbs, Bishop of Oxford." *English Historical Review* 16, no. 63 (July 1901): 417–26.

Mallock, William Hurrell. *A Critical Examination of Socialism.* New York: Harper & Brothers, 1907.

——. *Social Equality: A Short Study in a Missing Science.* New York: G. P. Putnam's Sons, 1882.

Malthus, Thomas. *An Essay on the Principle of Population.* 6th ed. Vol. 2. London: John Murray, 1826.

Mandeville, Bernard de. *The Fable of the Bees, or, Private Vices, Publick Benefits.* Indianapolis: Liberty Fund, 1988.

Martin, James J. *Men against the State: The Expositors of Individualist Anarchism in America, 1827–1908.* DeKalb, IL: Adrian Allen Associates, 1953.

Marx, Karl, and Friedrich Engels. *Selected Correspondence.* Moscow: Progress, 1965.

——. *Selected Works.* Moscow: Progress, 1968.

Mason, John W. "Political Economy and the Response to Socialism in Britain, 1870–1914." *Historical Journal* 23, no. 3 (1980): 565–87. https://doi.org/10.1017 /S0018246X00024894.

——. "Thomas Mackay: The Anti-Socialist Philosophy of the Charity Organisation Society." In *Essays in Anti-Labour History,* ed. Kenneth D. Brown, 290–316. London: Palgrave Macmillan, 1974. https://doi.org/10.1007/978-1-349-02039-3_12.

Mattera, Philip, and Anna Purinton. *Shopping for Subsidies: How Wal-Mart Uses Taxpayer Money to Finance Its Never-Ending Growth.* Washington, DC: Good Jobs First, 2004. https://www.goodjobsfirst.org/sites/default/files/docs/pdf /wmtstudy.pdf.

Mayer, Jane. *Dark Money: The Hidden History of the Billionaires behind the Rise of the Radical Right.* New York: Knopf Doubleday, 2016.

Mayhew, Robert. *Ayn Rand Answers: The Best of Her Q & A.* New York: Penguin, 2005.

McElroy, Wendy. "Benjamin Tucker, Individualism, & Liberty: Not the Daughter, but the Mother of Order." *Literature of Liberty* 4, no. 3 (Autumn 1981): 7–39.

——. "Benjamin Tucker, Liberty, and Individualist Anarchism." *Independent Review* 2, no. 3 (1998): 421–34.

——. *The Debates of Liberty: An Overview of Individualist Anarchism, 1881–1908.* New York: Lexington Books, 2003.

——. *Individualist Feminism of the Nineteenth Century: Collected Writings and Biographical Profiles.* Jefferson, NC: McFarland, 2001.

——. "The Life of a Grand Old Liberal." *Independent Institute* (blog), February 1, 1999. https://www.independent.org/news/article.asp?id=17.

Mencken, H. L. *Letters of H. L. Mencken.* Ed. Guy Forge. New York: Knopf, 1961.

Menger, Carl. *Principles of Economics.* New York: New York University Press, 1976.

Meyer, Frank S. *In Defense of Freedom*. Indianapolis: Liberty Fund, 1996.

———. *The Moulding of Communists: The Training of the Communist Cadre*. Vol. 120. New York: Harcourt, Brace, 1961.

———. "The Twisted Tree of Liberty." *National Review*, January 16, 1962.

Mill, John Stuart. *Autobiography*. New York: Henry Holt and Company, 1874.

———. "The Negro Question." In *Essays on Equality, Law, and Education*, ed. John M. Robson, 21:130–37. The Collected Works of John Stuart Mill. London: Routledge & Kegan Paul, 1984.

———. *On Liberty*. London: John Parker and Sons, 1859.

———. *Principles of Political Economy (Ashley ed.)*. 8 vols. London: Longmans, Green, 1848.

Miller, Dale E. "Mill's 'Socialism.'" *Politics, Philosophy & Economics* 2, no. 2 (2003): 213–38. https://doi.org/10.1177/1470594X03002002004.

Mingardi, Alberto. *Classical Liberalism and the Industrial Working Class: The Economic Thought of Thomas Hodgskin*. New York: Routledge, 2020.

———. *Herbert Spencer*. Vol. 18. New York: Continuum International Publishing Group, 2011.

Mises, Ludwig von. *Bureaucracy*. Indianapolis: Liberty Fund, 2007.

———. *Human Action: A Treatise on Economics*. 4th rev. ed. Indianapolis: Liberty Fund, 1996.

———. *Liberalism: In the Classical Tradition*. San Francisco: Cobden Press, 1985.

Mitchell, William, and Randy T. Simmons. *Beyond Politics: Markets, Welfare, and the Failure of Bureaucracy*. Boulder, CO: Westview Press, 1994.

Molinari, Gustave de. "Dé la production de la sécurité." *Journal des Économistes* 21, no. 1 (1849).

———. "Le droit électoral." *Courrier Français*, July 23, 1846.

———. "Nations." In *Dictionnaire de l'économie politique, contenant l'exposition des principes de la science, l'opinion des écrivains qui ont le plus contribué à sa fondation et à ses progrès, la bibliographie générale de l'économie politique par noms d'auteurs et par ordre de matières, avec des notices biographiques, et une appréciation raisonnée des principaux ouvrages*, ed. Charles Coquelin and Gilbert-Urbain Guillaumin, 2:259–62. Paris: Guillaumin, 1853.

———. "Protection." In *Cyclopedia of Political Science, Political Economy, and the Political History of the United States*, ed. John Joseph Lalor, 3:413–23. Chicago: Melbert B. Cary & Company, 1881.

———. *Questions d'économie politique et de droit public*. 2 vols. Brussels: Lacroix, 1861.

———. *The Society of Tomorrow: A Forecast of Its Political and Economic Organization*. 1899. Trans. P. H. Lee Warner. New York: G. P. Putnam's Sons, 1904.

———. *Les soirées de la rue Saint-Lazare (1849) | Online Library of Liberty*. Paris: Guillaumin, 1849. https://oll.libertyfund.org/title/molinari-les-soirees-de-la-rue -saint-lazare-1849.

———. "Some Simple Observations on the Rights of Property." *Journal des Économistes*, October 15, 1848.

———. "L'utopie de la liberté: Lettres aux socialistes." *Journal des Économistes* 20, no. 82 (June 15, 1848): 328–32.

Montesquieu. *The Spirit of the Laws*. Vol. 1. Trans. Thomas Nugent. London: Colonial Press, 1900.

"Movements of the Anti-Corn-Law League." *The Economist*, September 2, 1843. https://www.economist.com/node/1857278/print.

Murphy, Ryan, and Colin O'Reilly. "Assessing State Capacity Libertarianism." *Cato Journal*, Fall 2020. https://www.cato.org/cato-journal/fall-2020/assessing-state -capacity-libertarianism.

Murray, Charles A. *In Our Hands: A Plan to Replace the Welfare State*. Washington, DC: AEI Press, 2006.

Narveson, Jan. *The Libertarian Idea*. Philadelphia: Temple University Press, 1988.

———. "Property Rights: Original Acquisition and Lockean Provisos." *Public Affairs Quarterly* 13, no. 3 (1999): 205–27.

Nettlau, Max. "Anarchism in England Fifty Years Ago." *Liberty* 15, no. 3 (February 1906): 2740–47.

Nock, Albert Jay. "Henry George: Unorthodox American." *The Freeman*, October 1938.

———. "Imposter-Terms." In *Free Speech and Plain Language*. New York: W. Morrow, 1937.

———. *Letters from Albert Jay Nock, 1924–1945 to Edmund C. Evans, Mrs. Edmund C. Evans and Ellen Winsor*. Ed. Frank Garrison. Caldwell, ID: Caxton Printers, 1949.

———. *Memoirs of a Superfluous Man*. New York: Harper & Brothers, 1943.

———. *Our Enemy, the State*. San Francisco: Fox & Wilkes, 1994.

Northcote, Orford. "Egoism: The Sole Basis of Ethics." *Free Review* (1897): 344–55.

Nowrasteh, Alex, and Benjamin Powell. *Wretched Refuse? The Political Economy of Immigration and Institutions*. 1st ed. Cambridge Studies in Economics, Choice, and Society. New York: Cambridge University Press, 2020.

Nozick, Robert. *Anarchy, State, and Utopia*. New York: Basic Books, 1974.

———. *Invariances: The Structure of the Objective World*. Cambridge, MA: Harvard University Press, 2001.

———. "The Zigzag of Politics." In *The Examined Life: Philosophical Meditations*, ed. Robert Nozick, 286–96. New York: Simon & Schuster, 1987.

Obama, Barack. "Remarks by the President at Associated Press Luncheon." Marriott Waldman Park, April 3, 2012. https://obamawhitehouse.archives.gov/the-press -office/2012/04/03/remarks-president-associated-press-luncheon.

Olson, Mancur. *The Logic of Collective Action: Public Goods and the Theory of Groups*. Cambridge, MA: Harvard University Press, 1971.

Oppenheimer, Franz. *The State: Its History and Development Viewed Sociologically*. Trans. John Gutterman. Indianapolis: Bobbs-Merrill, 1944.

Ostrom, Elinor. "Beyond Markets and States: Polycentric Governance of Complex Economic Systems." *American Economic Review* 100, no. 3 (2010): 641–72. https://doi.org/10.1257/aer.100.3.641.

———. *Governing the Commons: The Evolution of Institutions for Collective Action*. New York: Cambridge University Press, 1990.

Overton, Richard. *An Arrow against All Tyrants*. Surrey: Canbury Press Limited, 2020.

Overtveldt, Johan Van. *The Chicago School: How the University of Chicago Assembled the Thinkers Who Revolutionized Economics and Business*. Evanston, IL: Agate Publishing, 2009.

Paine, Thomas. *Paine: Political Writings*. New York: Cambridge University Press, 2000.

Paley, William. *The Principles of Moral and Political Philosophy*. Indianapolis: Liberty Fund, 2002.

Palmer, Tom G. "Are Patents and Copyrights Morally Justified: The Philosophy of Property Rights and Ideal Objects." *Harvard Journal of Law and Public Policy* 13 (1990): 817–65.

———. "Bismarck's Legacy." In *After the Welfare State*, ed. Tom G. Palmer, 33–54. Ottawa, IL: Jameson Books, 2012.

———. "Oddballs vs. Scholars, For Negative Liberty, Against the Welfare State." *Cato Unbound* (blog), March 25, 2007. https://www.cato-unbound.org/2007/03/25 /tom-g-palmer/oddballs-vs-scholars-negative-liberty-against-welfare-state/.

———. "Poverty, Morality, and Liberty." In *After the Welfare State*, ed. Tom G. Palmer, 109–33. Ottawa, IL: Jameson Books, 2012.

Perry, Lewis. *Radical Abolitionism: Anarchy and the Government of God in Antislavery Thought*. Ithaca: Cornell University Press, 1973.

Phillips-Fein, Kimberly. *Invisible Hands: The Businessmen's Crusade against the New Deal*. New York: W. W. Norton, 2010.

Powell, Jim. *Greatest Emancipations: How the West Abolished Slavery*. New York: St. Martin's, 2008.

———. *The Triumph of Liberty: A 2,000-Year History, Told through the Lives of Freedom's Greatest Champions*. New York: Free Press, 2000.

Powell, Lewis F., Jr. "Attack on American Free Enterprise System." 1971. https:// scholarlycommons.law.wlu.edu/powellmemo/.

Pringle-Pattison, A. S. "The Life and Philosophy of Herbert Spencer." *Quarterly Review* 200 (1904): 240–67.

Proudhon, Pierre-Joseph. *What Is Property?* Trans. Benjamin Tucker. Princeton, MA: Benj. R. Tucker, 1876.

Puydt, Paul Émile de. "Panarchy." *Revue Trimestruelle* (1860): 222–45.

"Questions of the Limits of State Action and Individual Action Discussed at the Society of Political Economy." *Journal des Économistes* 24, no. 103 (1849): 314–16.

Radosh, Ronald, and Murray Rothbard, eds. *A New History of Leviathan: Essays on the Rise of the American Corporate State*. New York: E. P. Dutton, 1972.

Raico, Ralph. "How Nozick Became a Libertarian." *LewRockwell.com* (blog), February 5, 2002. https://www.lewrockwell.com/2002/02/ralph-raico/how-nozick -became-a-libertarian/.

Raimondo, Justin. *An Enemy of the State: The Life of Murray N. Rothbard*. New York: Prometheus Books, 2000.

Rand, Ayn. "America's Persecuted Minority, Big Business." In *Capitalism: The Unknown Ideal*. New York: New American Library, 1967.

———. *Atlas Shrugged*. New York: New American Library, 1957.

———. "Brief Summary." *The Objectivist* 10, no. 9 (September 1971): 1–4.

———. *The Fountainhead*. Indianapolis: Bobbs-Merrill Company, 1943.

———. *Letters of Ayn Rand*. Ed. Michael Berliner. New York: Penguin, 1995.

———. "The Monument Builders." In *The Virtue of Selfishness*, 100–107. New York: Signet, 1964.

———. "The Nature of Government." In *The Virtue of Selfishness*, 125–34. New York: Signet, 1964.

———. "The Objectivist Ethics." In *The Virtue of Selfishness*. New York: Signet, 1964.

———. "Patents and Copyrights." In *Capitalism: The Unknown Ideal*, 141–45. New York: New American Library, 1967.

———. "Racism." In *The Virtue of Selfishness*, 147–57. New York: Signet, 1964.

———. "The Roots of War." In *Capitalism: The Unknown Ideal*, 30–39. New York: New American Library, 1967.

Rasmussen, Dennis C. *The Problems and Promise of Commercial Society: Adam Smith's Response to Rousseau*. University Park: Penn State University Press, 2015.

Rasmussen, Douglas B., and Douglas J. Den Uyl. *Norms of Liberty: A Perfectionist Basis for Non-Perfectionist Politics*. University Park: Penn State University Press, 2005.

Rawls, John. "Constitutional Liberty and the Concept of Justice." *NOMOS: American Society for Political and Legal Philosophy* 6 (1963): 98–125.

———. *Political Liberalism*. New York: Columbia University Press, 1993.

———. *A Theory of Justice*. 1st ed. Cambridge, MA: Harvard University Press, 1971.

Read, Leonard E. "I, Pencil: My Family Tree as Told to Leonard E. Read." Foundation for Economic Education, December 1958. https://oll.libertyfund.org/title/read-i-pencil-my-family-tree-as-told-to-leonard-e-read-dec-1958.

———. *Talking to Myself*. Irvington-on-Hudson, NY: Foundation for Economic Education, 1970.

Reichert, William O. *Partisans of Freedom: A Study in American Freedom*. Bowling Green, OH: Bowling Green University Popular Press, 1976.

Ricardo, David. *An Essay on the Influence of a Low Price of Corn on the Profits of Stock, with Remarks on Mr. Malthus' Two Last Publications*, 1815.

———. *On Protection to Agriculture*. John Murray, Albemarle-Streer, 1822.

———. *On the Principles of Political Economy and Taxation*. John Murray, 1817.

———. *The Works and Correspondence of David Ricardo*. Ed. Piero Sraffa. Vol. 4. Cambridge: Cambridge University Press, 1951.

Richman, Sheldon. "Context-Keeping and Community Organizing." *Cato Unbound* (blog), June 18, 2010. https://www.cato-unbound.org/2010/06/18/sheldon-richman/context-keeping-community-organizing/.

Ridley, Matt. *The Rational Optimist: How Prosperity Evolves*. New York: Harper Perennial, 2010.

Riley, Jason L. *Maverick: A Biography of Thomas Sowell*. New York: Basic Books, 2021.

Robin, Corey. "Nietzsche's Marginal Children: On Friedrich Hayek." *The Nation*, May 7, 2013. https://www.thenation.com/article/archive/nietzsches-marginal-children-friedrich-hayek/.

Robinson, John Beverly. "Woman-Suffrage and Liberty." *Liberty* 10, no. 8 (August 28, 1894): 2.

Roche, George Charles. *Frederic Bastiat: A Man Alone*. New Rochelle, NY: Arlington House, 1971.

Rockwell, Llewelyn, Jr. "The Case for Paleo-Libertarianism." *Liberty* 3, no. 3 (January 1990): 34–38.

———. "It's Safe Streets versus Urban Terror: In the '50's, Rampant Crime Didn't Exist Because Offenders Feared What the Police Would Do." *Los Angeles Times*, March 10, 1991. https://www.latimes.com/archives/la-xpm-1991-03-10-op-178-story.html.

———. "Open Borders Are an Assault on Private Property." Paper presented at the Mises Circle, Phoenix, AZ, November 7, 2015. https://mises.org/library/open-borders-are -assault-private-property.

Rojas, Fabio. "Intersectionality: Friend or Foe of Classical Liberalism?" *Cato Unbound*, May 28, 2020. https://www.cato-unbound.org/2020/05/28/fabio-rojas /intersectionality-friend-or-foe-classical-liberalism/.

———. "Race and Libertarianism." In *The Routledge Companion to Libertarianism*, ed. Matt Zwolinski and Ben Ferguson. New York: Routledge, 2022.

———. "Race and the Contamination of Freedom." *Bleeding Heart Libertarians* (blog), January 2, 2019. https://bleedingheartlibertarians.com/2012/06/why-libertarians -should-oppose-sweatshops/.

Rosén, John, and [J.] Th[eodor] Westrin. "Molinari, Gustave de." In *Nordisk Familje- bok: Konversationslexikon Och Realencyklopedi Innehållande Upplysningar Och Förklaringar Om Märkvärdiga Namn, Föremål Och Begrepp*, columns 208–9. Stockholm: Gernandts boktryckeri-aktiebolag, 1887. https://praxeology.net /Encyclopedia_entries_for_Gustave_de_Molinari.pdf.

Rothbard, Murray N. *America's Great Depression*. Princeton: D. Van Nostrand, 1963.

———. "America's Two Just Wars: 1775 and 1861." In *The Costs of War: America's Pyrrhic Victories*, ed. John Denson, 119–34. New York: Routledge, 2017.

———. *An Austrian Perspective on the History of Economic Thought*. Vol. 1, *Economic Thought before Adam Smith*. Cheltenham: Edward Elgar, 1995.

———. *An Austrian Perspective on the History of Economic Thought*. Vol. 2, *Classical Economics*. Cheltenham: Edward Elgar, 1995.

———. "Ayn Rand's Monstrous Views on the Middle East." *Libertarian Forum* (December 1971).

———. "The Black Revolution." *Left and Right* 3, no. 3 (Spring/Autumn 1967): 7–17.

———. "The Clark Campaign: Never Again." *Libertarian Forum* 13, no. 5–6 (December 1980): 1–10.

———. "Confiscation and the Homestead Principle." *Libertarian Forum* 1, no. 6 (1969): 3–4.

———. *The Ethics of Liberty*. Atlantic Highlands, NJ: Humanities Press, 1982.

———. "For a New Isolationism." *LewRockwell.com* (blog), 1959. https://www .lewrockwell.com/1970/01/murray-n-rothbard/for-a-new-isolationism/.

———. *For a New Liberty*. New York: Collier, 1973.

———. "Law, Property Rights, and Air Pollution." *Cato Journal* 2, no. 1 (1982): 55–99.

———. "Left and Right: The Prospects for Liberty." *Left and Right: A Journal of Libertarian Thought* 1, no. 1 (Spring 1965): 4–22.

———. "Listen, YAF." *Libertarian Forum* 1, no. 9 (August 15, 1969): 2.

———. *Man, Economy and State.* 1962. Los Angeles: Nash, 1970.

———. "Marshall, Civil Rights, and the Court." In *The Irrepressible Rothbard: The Rothbard-Rockwell Report Essays of Murray Rothbard*, ed. Llewellyn Rockwell, 370–77. Burlingame, CA: Center for Libertarian Studies, 2000.

———. "Nations by Consent: Decomposing the Nation-State." *Journal of Libertarian Studies* 11, no. 1 (1994): 1–10.

———. "The Negro Revolution." *New Individualist Review* 3, no. 1 (Summer 1963): 429–37.

———. "New Light on the Prehistory of the Austrian School." In *The Foundations of Modern Austrian Economics*, ed. Edwin Dolan, 52–74. Kansas City, MO: Sheed and Ward, 1976.

———. "A Note on Burke's *Vindication of Natural Society*." *Journal of the History of Ideas* 19, no. 1 (1958): 114–18.

———. *Power and Market.* Kansas City, MO: Sheed Andrews & McMeel, 1970.

———. "Property Rights and the Theory of Contract." In *The Ethics of Liberty*. Atlantic Highlands, NJ: Humanities Press, 1982.

———. "Rand on the Middle East." *Libertarian Forum* 5, no. 12 (December 1973): 7.

———. "Right-Wing Populism: A Strategy for the Paleo Movement." *Rothbard-Rockwell Report* (January 1992): 5–13.

———. "Robert Nozick and the Immaculate Conception of the State." *Journal of Libertarian Studies* 1, no. 1 (1977): 45–57.

———. "Rothbard Writes the Dixiecrats." https://www.lewrockwell.com/1970/01/murray-n-rothbard/rothbard-writes-the-dixiecrats/.

———. *The Sociology of the Ayn Rand Cult.* Burlingame, CA: Center for Libertarian Studies, 1972.

———. "The Spooner-Tucker Doctrine: An Economist's View." *Journal of Libertarian Studies* 20, no. 1 (2006): 5–15.

———. "War Guilt in the Middle East." *Left and Right* 3, no. 3 (Spring/Autumn 1967): 20–30.

———. "War, Peace, and the State." *The Standard* (April 1963): 2–5.

———. "What's Wrong with the Liberty Poll, or, How I Became a Libertarian." *Liberty* (July 1988): 52–53, 55.

Ruffin, Roy, and Paul R. Gregory. *Principles of Microeconomics.* Glenview, IL: Scott, Foresman, 1990.

Russell, Dean. *Frederic Bastiat: Ideas and Influence.* Irvington-on-Hudson, NY: Foundation for Economic Education, 1969.

———. "Who Is a Libertarian?" *The Freeman*, May 1, 1950. http://www.fee.org/the_freeman/detail/who-is-a-libertarian#axzz2d1BZd095.

Ryley, Peter. *Making Another World Possible: Anarchism, Anti-Capitalism and Ecology in Late 19th and Early 20th Century Britain.* New York: Bloomsbury, 2013.

S. R. "An Economist on the Future of Society." *Liberty* 14, no. 23 (September 1904): 1.

Salerno, Joseph T., and Matthew McCaffrey, eds. "A Conversation with Murray Rothbard." In *The Rothbard Reader*. Auburn, AL: Ludwig von Mises Institute, 2016.

Sally, Razeen. *Classical Liberalism and International Economic Order: Studies in Theory and Intellectual History*. New York: Routledge, 2002.

Salmieri, Gregory. "Objectivism." In *The Routledge Companion to Libertarianism*, ed. Matt Zwolinski and Ben Ferguson. New York: Routledge, 2022.

Samuelson, Paul, and William Nordhaus. *Economics*. 16th ed. Boston: Irwin McGraw-Hill, 1998.

Sanchez, Julian. "An Interview with Robert Nozick." July 26, 2001. http://www.juliansanchez.com/an-interview-with-robert-nozick-july-26-2001/.

Say, Jean-Baptiste. *Catechism of Political Economy, or, Familiar Conversations on the Manner in Which Wealth Is Produced, Distributed, and Consumed in Society*. London: Sherwood, Neely, and Jones, 1816.

——. *A Treatise on Political Economy, or, The Production, Distribution, and Consumption of Wealth*. Trans. C. R. Prinsep. New York: Augustus M. Kelley, 1964.

Schmidtz, David. *Elements of Justice*. Cambridge: Cambridge University Press, 2006.

——. "The Institution of Property." *Social Philosophy and Policy* 11, no. 2 (1994): 42–62.

Schumpeter, Joseph Alois. *Capitalism, Socialism, and Democracy*. New York: Routledge, 2003.

Scott, James C. *Seeing Like a State: How Certain Schemes to Improve the Human Condition Have Failed*. New Haven: Yale University Press, 1998.

Sears, Hal D. *The Sex Radicals: Free Love in High Victorian America*. Lawrence: Regents Press of Kansas, 1977.

Seeley, John Robert. *The Life and Times of Stein, or, Germany and Prussia in the Napoleonic Age*. Vol. 3. Cambridge: Cambridge University Press, 1878.

Shaw, Bernard. *Fabian Essays in Socialism*. Boston: Ball Publishing Company, 1908.

Shively, Charles. "Biography." In *The Collected Works of Lysander Spooner*, 1:15–62. Weston, MA: M & S Press, 1971.

Shlaes, Amity. *The Forgotten Man: A New History of the Great Depression*. New York: HarperCollins, 2009.

Simon, Julian Lincoln. *The Ultimate Resource 2*. Princeton: Princeton University Press, 1998.

Skoble, Aeon. *Deleting the State: An Argument about Government*. Chicago: Open Court, 2008.

Slobodian, Quinn. *Globalists: The End of Empire and the Birth of Neoliberalism*. Cambridge, MA: Harvard University Press, 2018.

Smith, Adam. *The Theory of Moral Sentiments*. Indianapolis: Liberty Fund, 2009.

——. *The Wealth of Nations*. Indianapolis: Liberty Fund, 1982.

Smith, Bruce. *Liberty and Liberalism: A Protest against the Growing Tendency toward Undue Interference by the State, with Individual Liberty, Private Enterprise, and the Rights of Property*. London: Longmans, Green, 1887.

Smith, George H. "Abolitionism: Wendell Phillips on Voting and Political Action." *Libertarianism.org* (blog), January 20, 2017. https://www.libertarianism.org/columns/abolitionism-wendell-phillips-voting-political-action.

———. "Gerrit Smith, Lysander Spooner, and Dio Lewis on Prohibition." *Libertarianism.org* (blog), April 21, 2017. https://www.libertarianism.org/columns/gerrit-smith-lysander-spooner-dio-lewis-prohibition.

———. "Inalienable Rights?" *Liberty* 10, no. 6 (July 1997).

———. *The System of Liberty: Themes in the History of Classical Liberalism.* New York: Cambridge University Press, 2013.

———. "Will the Real Herbert Spencer Please Stand Up?" In *Atheism, Ayn Rand, and Other Heresies*, 239–50. New York: Prometheus Books, 1991.

Smith, Vernon L. "Human Nature: An Economic Perspective." *Daedalus* 133, no. 4 (2004): 67–76.

Soldon, N. "Laissez-Faire as Dogma: The Liberty and Property Defence League, 1882–1914." In *Essays in Anti-Labour History*, ed. Kenneth D. Brown, 208–33. London: Palgrave Macmillan, 1974. https://doi.org/10.1007/978-1-349-02039-3_9.

Somin, Ilya. "Tyler Cowen on 'State Capacity Libertarianism' I: Is It the Wave of the 'Smart' Libertarian Future?" *The Volokh Conspiracy* (blog), January 16, 2020. https://reason.com/volokh/2020/01/16/tyler-cowen-on-state-capacity-libertarianism-i-is-it-the-wave-of-the-smart-libertarian-future/.

———. "Tyler Cowen on 'State Capacity Libertarianism' II: Is It the Right Path for Libertarians to Follow?" *The Volokh Conspiracy* (blog), January 19, 2020. https://reason.com/volokh/2020/01/19/tyler-cowen-on-state-capacity-libertarianism-ii-is-it-the-right-path-for-libertarians-to-follow/.

Sowell, Thomas. "Affirmative Action Reconsidered: Was It Necessary in Academia? Evaluation Studies 27." American Enterprise Institute, December 1975. https://files.eric.ed.gov/fulltext/ED130570.pdf.

———. *A Conflict of Visions: Ideological Origins of Political Struggles.* Rev. ed. New York: Basic Books, 2007.

———. "The Day Cornell Died." *Weekly Standard*, no. 4 (May 3, 1999). https://www.hoover.org/research/day-cornell-died.

———. *A Personal Odyssey.* New York: Free Press, 2000.

———. "A Poignant Anniversary." *National Review*, August 27, 2013. https://www.nationalreview.com/2013/08/poignant-anniversary-thomas-sowell/.

Spector, Horacio. *Autonomy and Rights.* Oxford: Oxford University Press, 1992.

Spence, Thomas. "The Real Rights of Man." In *The Origins of Left-Libertarianism: An Anthology of Historical Writings*, ed. Peter Vallentyne and Hillel Steiner, 71–79. New York: Palgrave, 2000.

Spencer, Herbert. "The Coming Slavery." In *The Man versus the State*, ed. Herbert Spencer, 31–70. Indianapolis: Liberty Fund, 1981.

———. "From Freedom to Bondage." In *A Plea for Liberty: An Argument against Socialism and Socialistic Legislation*, ed. Thomas Mackay. Indianapolis: Liberty Classics, 1981.

Spencer, Herbert, ed. *The Man versus the State*. Indianapolis: Liberty Classics, 1884.

———. "Mr. Martineau on Evolution." *Contemporary Review* 20 (June–November 1872): 147.

———. "Over-Legislation." In *The Man versus the State*, ed. Herbert Spencer. Indianapolis: Liberty Classics, 1981.

———. "Patriotism." In *Facts and Comments*. New York: D. Appleton, 1902.

———. *The Principles of Ethics*. Vol. 2. Indianapolis: Liberty Fund, 1978.

———. *The Principles of Sociology*. Vol. 3. New York: D. Appleton, 1900.

———. "The Proper Sphere of Government." In *The Man versus the State*, ed. Herbert Spencer. Indianapolis: Liberty Fund, 1981.

———. *Social Statics*. 1851. New York: Robert Schalkenbach Foundation, 1995.

———. "State-Tamperings with Money and Banks." In *Essays: Scientific, Political, and Speculative*, ed. Herbert Spencer, 2:293–323. New York: D. Appleton, 1864.

———. *The Study of Sociology*. London: Henry S. King, 1873.

Spencer, Herbert, and Fre Verinder. *Mr. Herbert Spencer and the Land Restoration League*. London: Page and Pratt, 1895.

Spooner, Lysander. "Against Woman Suffrage." *Liberty* 1, no. 22 (June 10, 1882): 4.

———. "An Essay on the Trial by Jury." In *The Collected Works of Lysander Spooner*, 2:1–224. Indianapolis: Liberty Fund, 1852.

———. "The Law of Intellectual Property: An Essay on the Right of Authors and Inventors to a Perpetual Property in Their Ideas." 1855. In *The Collected Works of Lysander Spooner*, 2:225–463. Indianapolis: Liberty Fund, 2010.

———. "A Letter to Grover Cleveland, on His False Inaugural Address, the Usurpations and Crimes of Lawmakers and Judges, and the Consequent Poverty, Ignorance, and Servitude of the People." In *The Collected Works of Lysander Spooner*, 5:184–305. Indianapolis: Liberty Fund, 1886.

———. "Natural Law, or, The Science of Justice: A Treatise on Natural Law, Natural Justice, Natural Rights, Natural Liberty, and Natural Society; Showing That All Legislation Whatsoever Is an Absurdity, a Usurpation, and a Crime. Part First." In *The Collected Works of Lysander Spooner*, 5:134–51. Indianapolis: Liberty Fund, 1882.

———. "No Treason, No. 1." In *The Collected Works of Lysander Spooner*, 3:124–37. Indianapolis: Liberty Fund, 1860.

———. "No Treason, No. VI: The Constitution of No Authority." In *The Collected Works of Lysander Spooner*, 4:171–229. Indianapolis: Liberty Fund, 1870.

———. "Poverty: Its Illegal Causes and Legal Cure. Part First." In *The Collected Works of Lysander Spooner*, 1:219–326. Indianapolis: Liberty Fund, 1846.

———. "Revolution: The Only Remedy for the Oppressed Classes of Ireland, England, and Other Parts of the British Empire. A Reply to 'Dunraven.'" In *The Collected Works of Lysander Spooner*, 5:124–33. Indianapolis: Liberty Fund, 1880.

———. "To the Members of the Legislature of Massachusetts." In *The Collected Works of Lysander Spooner*, 1:15–17. Indianapolis: Liberty Fund, 1835.

———. "The Unconstitutionality of Slavery." In *The Collected Works of Lysander Spooner*, 3:57–188. Indianapolis: Liberty Fund, 1860.

——. "The Unconstitutionality of the Laws of Congress, Prohibiting Private Mails." In *The Collected Works of Lysander Spooner*, 1:195–218. Indianapolis: Liberty Fund, 1844.

——. "Who Caused the Reduction in Postage? Ought He to Be Paid?" In *The Collected Works of Lysander Spooner*, 1:327–77. Indianapolis: Liberty Fund, 1850.

Sprading, Charles T. *Liberty and the Great Libertarians*. Los Angeles: Golden Press, 1913.

Sreenivasan, Gopal. *The Limits of Lockean Rights in Property*. Oxford: Oxford University Press, 1995.

Stack, David. *Nature and Artifice: The Life and Thought of Thomas Hodgskin (1787–1869)*. Woodbridge: Boydell & Brewer, 1998.

Steiner, Hillel. *An Essay on Rights*. New York: Blackwell, 1994.

Stigler, George J. "Director's Law of Public Income Redistribution." *Journal of Law and Economics* 13, no. 1 (1970): 1–10. https://doi.org/10.1525/sp.2007.54.1.23.

——. "The Theory of Economic Regulation." *Bell Journal of Economics and Management Science* 2, no. 1 (1971): 3–21.

Sumner, William Graham. *The Challenge of Facts and Other Essays*. New Haven: Yale University Press, 1914.

——. "The Conquest of the United States by Spain." In *War and Other Essays*, ed. Albert Galloway Keller. New Haven: Yale University Press, 1911.

——. "Democracy and Plutocracy." In *Earth-Hunger and Other Essays*, ed. William Graham Sumner and Albert Galloway Keller. New Haven: Yale University Press, 1913.

——. "The Forgotten Man." In *The Forgotten Man and Other Essays*, ed. Albert Galloway Keller. New Haven: Yale University Press, 1918.

——. *What Social Classes Owe to Each Other*. Auburn, AL: Ludwig von Mises Institute, 2007.

Tak Kak. "Killing Chinese." *Liberty* 3, no. 25 (March 6, 1886): 8.

Tanner, Michael D. "The American Welfare State: How We Spend Nearly $1 Trillion a Year Fighting Poverty—and Fail." *Cato Policy Analysis*. Washington, DC: Cato Institute, April 11, 2012.

Taylor, James Stacy. *Stakes and Kidneys: Why Markets in Human Body Parts Are Morally Imperative*. New York: Ashgate, 2005.

Taylor, M. W. *Men versus the State: Herbert Spencer and Late Victorian Individualism*. Oxford: Oxford University Press, 1992.

Teles, Steven Michael. *The Rise of the Conservative Legal Movement: The Battle for Control of the Law*. Princeton Studies in American Politics: Historical, International, and Comparative Perspectives. Princeton: Princeton University Press, 2008.

Thompson, Phillips. "The Political Economist and the Tramp." *Labor Standard (New York)*, December 14, 1878.

Tierney, Brian. *The Idea of Natural Rights*. Emory University Studies in Law and Religion. Grand Rapids, MI: Eerdmans, 1997.

Tomasi, John. *Free Market Fairness*. Princeton: Princeton University Press, 2012.

Trask, H. A. Scott. "William Graham Sumner: Against Democracy, Plutocracy, and Imperialism." *Journal of Libertarian Studies* 18, no. 4 (2004): 1–27.

Trentmann, Frank. *Free Trade Nation: Commerce, Consumption, and Civil Society in Modern Britain*. Oxford: Oxford University Press, 2008.

Tucker, Benjamin. "Anarchism and the Children." *Liberty* 10, no. 26 (May 4, 1895): 5, 8.

———. "The Attitude of Anarchism toward Industrial Combinations." Lecture delivered at the Conference on Trusts of the Chicago Civic Federation, September 14, 1899. https://praxeology.net/BT-AIC.htm.

———. "Contract or Organism, What's That to Us?" *Liberty* 4, no. 26 (July 30, 1887): 4.

———. "Ergo and Presto!" *Liberty* 5, no. 24 (July 7, 1888).

———. "Henry George, Traitor." *Liberty* 12, no. 9 (November 1896): 3–5.

———. *Instead of a Book: By a Man Too Busy to Write One*. New York: Elibron Classics, 2005.

———. "The Land for the People." *Liberty* 1, no. 23 (June 24, 1882).

———. "More on Copyright." *Liberty* 7, no. 21 (February 7, 1891).

———. "Our Nestor Taken from Us." *Liberty* 4, no. 22 (May 28, 1887).

———. "The Sin of Herbert Spencer." *Liberty* 2, no. 16 (May 17, 1884): 4–5.

———. "A Sound Criticism." *Liberty* 11, no. 4 (June 29, 1895).

———. "State Socialism and Anarchism: How Far They Agree, and Wherein They Differ." *Liberty* 5, no. 16 (March 10, 1888): 2–3, 6.

Tullock, Gordon. "Rent Seeking." In *Lexeconics: The Interaction of Law and Economics*. Boston: Martinus Nijhoff, 1981.

Tullock, Gordon, R. D. Tollison, and C. K. Rowley. *The Political Economy of Rent Seeking*. Boston: Kluwer, 1988.

Tully, James. *A Discourse on Property: John Locke and His Adversaries*. New York: Cambridge University Press, 1980.

U.S. Postal Service. "Rates for Domestic Letters, 1792–1863." USPS.com, August 2008. https://about.usps.com/who-we-are/postal-history/domestic-letter-rates-1792-1863.pdf.

Vallier, Kevin. "In Defense of Hobby Lobby." *Bleeding Heart Libertarians* (blog), November 29, 2013. https://bleedingheartlibertarians.com/2013/11/in-defense-of-hobby-lobby/.

———. "The Libertarian Position on Religion in Public Life." *Bleeding Heart Libertarians* (blog), March 6, 2016. https://bleedingheartlibertarians.com/2016/03/the-libertarian-position-on-religion-in-public-life/.

———. "Neoliberalism." *The Stanford Encyclopedia of Philosophy*, June 9, 2021. https://plato.stanford.edu/entries/neoliberalism/.

Vaughn, Karen Iversen. *Austrian Economics in America: The Migration of a Tradition*. Historical Perspectives on Modern Economics. New York: Cambridge University Press, 1994.

Viner, Jacob. "Adam Smith and Laissez Faire." *Journal of Political Economy* 35, no. 2 (1927): 198–232.

———. *Studies in the Theory of International Trade*. New York: Harper & Brothers, 1937.

Vossen, B. van der. "What Counts as Original Appropriation?" *Politics, Philosophy & Economics* 8, no. 4 (October 30, 2009): 355–73. https://doi.org/10.1177/1470594X09343074.

Waldron, Jeremy. *The Right to Private Property*. Oxford: Oxford University Press, 1988.

Warren, Josiah. *Equitable Commerce: A New Development of Principles*. New York: Fowlers and Wells, 1852.

———. *Practical Details in Equitable Commerce*. New York: Fowlers and Wells, 1852.

Wasserman, Janek. *The Marginal Revolutionaries*. New Haven: Yale University Press, 2019.

Watner, Carl. "'All Mankind Is One': The Libertarian Tradition in Sixteenth Century Spain." *Journal of Libertarian Studies* 8, no. 2 (1987): 293–309.

———. "The 'Criminal' Metaphor in the Libertarian Tradition." *Journal of Libertarian Studies* 5, no. 3 (1981): 313–25.

———. "The Radical Libertarian Tradition in Antislavery Thought." *Journal of Libertarian Studies* 3, no. 3 (1979): 299–329.

———. "Those 'Impossible Citizens': Civil Resistants in 19th Century New England." *Journal of Libertarian Studies* 3, no. 2 (1980): 170–93.

Weber, Max. "Politics as a Vocation." In *From Max Weber: Essays in Sociology*, ed. H. H. Gerth and C. Wright Mills. Oxford: Oxford University Press, 1946.

Weigel, David. "A Purge at the Cato Institute?" *Slate* (blog), August 23, 2010. https://slate.com/news-and-politics/2010/08/a-purge-at-the-cato-institute.html.

Weinstein, David. *Equal Freedom and Utility: Herbert Spencer's Liberal Utilitarianism*. New York: Cambridge University Press, 1998.

———. "Herbert Spencer." In *The Stanford Encyclopedia of Philosophy*, ed. Edward Zalta (Fall 2012). http://plato.stanford.edu/archives/fall2012/entries/spencer/.

Weston, John C. "The Ironic Purpose of Burke's Vindication Vindicated." *Journal of the History of Ideas* 19, no. 3 (1958): 435–41.

Wilkinson, Will. "Grand Racist Party?" *The Economist*, August 22, 2012. https://www.economist.com/democracy-in-america/2012/08/22/grand-racist-party.

———. "Is Rawlsekianism the Future?" *Cato@Liberty* (blog), December 4, 2006. https://www.cato.org/blog/rawlsekianism-future.

Will, George. "Passing of a Prophet." *Washington Post*, December 8, 1991. https://www.washingtonpost.com/archive/opinions/1991/12/08/passing-of-a-prophet/c69252cc-2db9-486a-8bfc-f90a72ccfa93/.

Williams, Walter. "Affirmative Action or Racism?" *WND* (blog), January 29, 2003. https://www.wnd.com/2003/01/16984/.

———. "Discrimination and Liberty." *Foundation for Economic Education* (blog), April 1, 1998. https://fee.org/articles/discrimination-and-liberty/.

———. "The Right to Discriminate." *Creators Syndicate*, June 1, 2010. https://www.creators.com/read/walter-williams/06/10/the-right-to-discriminate.

Williamson, Harold Francis. *Edward Atkinson: The Biography of an American Liberal, 1827–1905*. Boston: Old Corner Book Store, 1934.

Wolf, C. *Markets or Governments: Choosing between Imperfect Alternatives*. Cambridge, MA: MIT Press, 1993.

Woodcock, George. *Anarchism: A History of Libertarian Ideas and Movements*. Toronto: University of Toronto Press, 2009.

Wright, Henry C. *Human Life: Illustrated in My Individual Experience as a Child, a Youth, and a Man*. Boston: Bela Marsh, 1849.

———. "The New National Organization." *The Liberator*, no. 490 (May 22, 1840): 83.

Wright, Henry C. *No Rights, No Duties, or, Slaveholders, as Such, Have No Rights; Slaves, as Such, Owe No Duties*. Boston: Henry C. Wright, 1860.

Yarros, Victor S. *Adventures in the Realm of Ideas: And Other Essays in the Fields of Philosophy, Science, Political Economy, Theology, Humanism, Semantics, Agnosticism, Immortality and Related Subjects*. Haldeman-Julius, 1947.

———. "Anarchism." In *The Encyclopedia of Social Reforms*, ed. William D. P. Bliss, 54–66. New York: Funk & Wagnalls, 1897.

———. "Woman-Suffrage and Anarchism." *Liberty* 10, no. 7 (August 11, 1894): 2–4.

Zlabinger, Albert. "An Interview with Robert Nozick." *Libertarian Review*, December 1977. https://www.libertarianism.org/publications/essays/interview-robert-nozick.

Zwolinski, Matt. "Libertarianism and Pollution." *Philosophy and Public Policy Quarterly* 32, no. 4 (2014): 9–21.

———. "A New Essay on Libertarianism and Pollution." *Bleeding Heart Libertarians* (blog), May 30, 2014. http://bleedingheartlibertarians.com/2014/05/a-new-essay-on-libertarianism-and-pollution/.

———. "Objections to the Simple Libertarian Argument for Environmental Regulation." *Bleeding Heart Libertarians* (blog), October 1, 2011. https://bleedingheartlibertarians.com/2011/10/objections-to-the-simple-libertarian-argument-for-environmental-regulation/.

———. "The Separateness of Persons and Liberal Theory." *Journal of Value Inquiry* 42, no. 2 (2008): 147–65. https://doi.org/10.1007/s10790-008-9107-y.

———. "Social Darwinism and Social Justice: Herbert Spencer on Our Duties to the Poor." In *Distributive Justice Debates in Political and Social Thought: Perspectives on Finding a Fair Share*, ed. Camilla Boisen and Matthew Murray, 56–76. New York: Routledge, 2016. https://doi.org/10.4324/9781315737607.

Zwolinski, Matt, and Ben Ferguson, eds. *The Routledge Companion to Libertarianism*. New York: Routledge, 2022

A NOTE ON THE TYPE

THIS BOOK has been composed in Miller, a Scotch Roman typeface designed by Matthew Carter and first released by Font Bureau in 1997. It resembles Monticello, the typeface developed for The Papers of Thomas Jefferson in the 1940s by C. H. Griffith and P. J. Conkwright and reinterpreted in digital form by Carter in 2003.

Pleasant Jefferson ("P. J.") Conkwright (1905–1986) was Typographer at Princeton University Press from 1939 to 1970. He was an acclaimed book designer and AIGA Medalist.

The ornament used in this book was designed by Pierre Simon Fournier (1712–1768) and was a favorite of Conkwright's, used in his design of the *Princeton University Library Chronicle*.